DISC
S0-AEQ-285

AFRICAN DISCOVERY

MARGERY PERHAM
and
J. SIMMONS

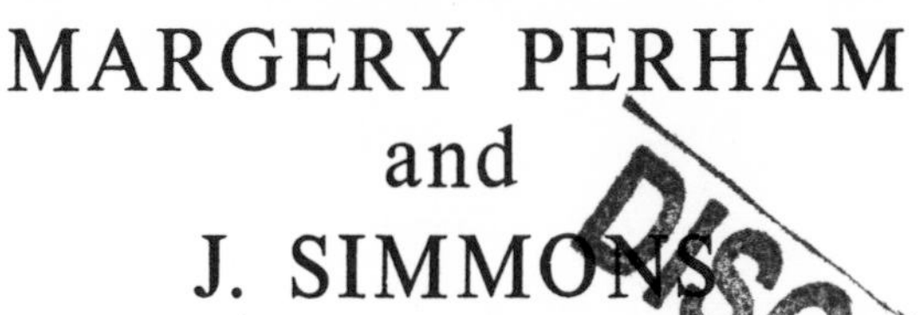

AFRICAN DISCOVERY

an anthology of exploration

NORTHWESTERN UNIVERSITY PRESS

ISBN 0-8101-0193-9

Published in U.S.A. 1963
by Northwestern University Press

Printed in the United States of America

Reprinted, 1971

CONTENTS

CONTENTS

ILLUSTRATIONS

NOTE

The rectangles on this map indicate the areas covered by the sectional maps in the text.

1. Bruce, 1769–72
2. Park, 1795–7 and 1805–6
3. Clapperton, 1822–7
4. Lander, 1825–34
5. Livingstone, 1841–64
6. Baikie (3rd Niger Expedition), 1854
7. Burton, 1854–5
8. Burton and Speke, 1857–9
9. Speke and Baker, 1860–5
10. Livingstone and Stanley, 1858–73

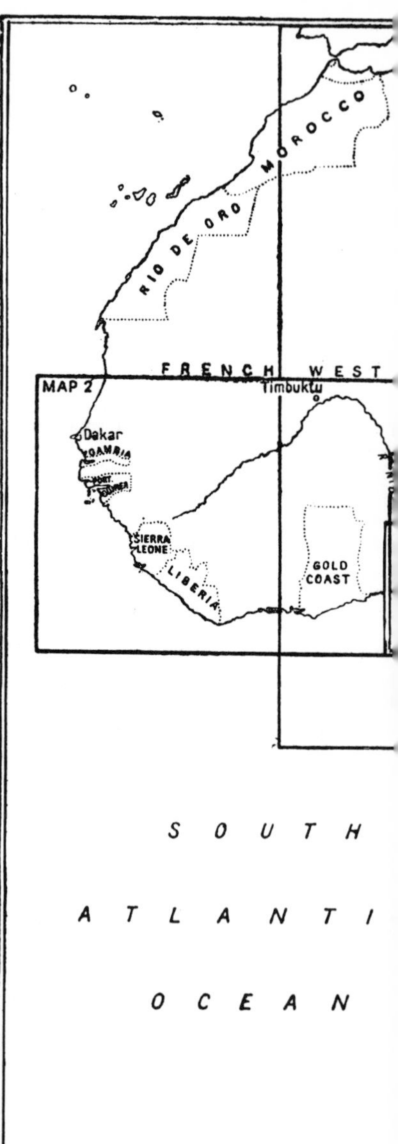

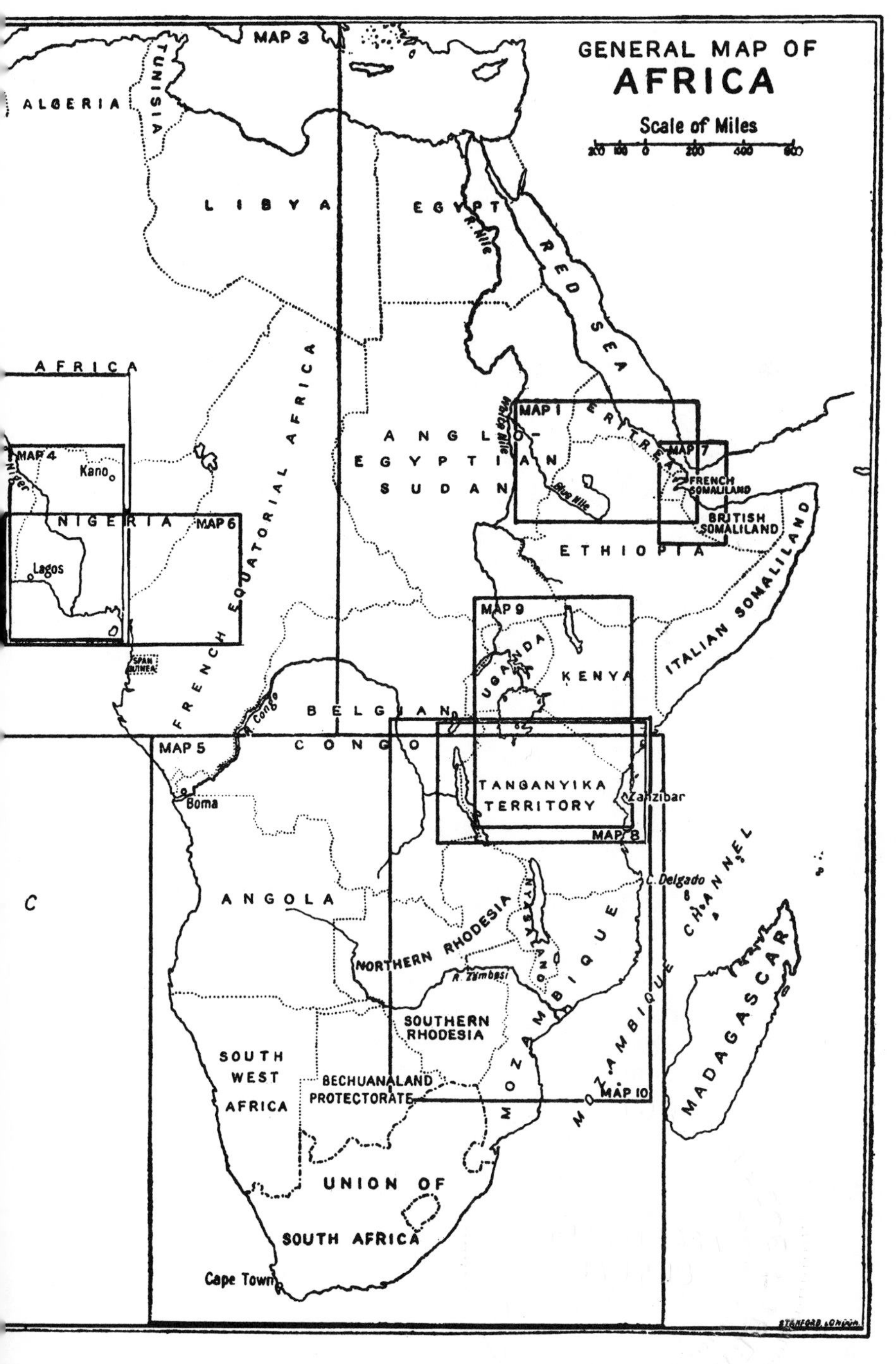
GENERAL MAP OF
AFRICA
Scale of Miles
200 100 0 200 400 600
MAP 3
TUNISIA
ALGERIA
LIBYA
EGYPT
R. Nile
RED SEA
FRENCH EQUATORIAL AFRICA
AFRICA
MAP 4
Kano
Niger
NIGERIA
MAP 6
Lagos
SPAN GUINEA
ANGLO-EGYPTIAN SUDAN
White Nile
Blue Nile
MAP 1
ERITREA
MAP 7
FRENCH SOMALILAND
BRITISH SOMALILAND
ETHIOPIA
ITALIAN SOMALILAND
MAP 9
UGANDA
KENYA
BELGIAN CONGO
Congo
MAP 5
Boma
TANGANYIKA TERRITORY
Zanzibar
MAP 8
C. Delgado
ANGOLA
NORTHERN RHODESIA
NYASA
R. Zambesi
MOZAMBIQUE
SOUTHERN RHODESIA
MOZAMBIQUE CHANNEL
MADAGASCAR
SOUTH WEST AFRICA
BECHUANALAND PROTECTORATE
MAP 10
UNION OF SOUTH AFRICA
Cape Town
STANFORD, LONDON

MAPS

PREFACE

This is an anthology from the works of the British explorers of Africa, covering the period from 1769 to 1873. Its scope and purpose are more fully outlined in the Introduction; but a brief preface is necessary in order to explain its plan.

Our extracts have been taken from the books of eleven travellers: they are arranged in the order in which the writers first arrived in Africa. The career of Livingstone extends over such a long period that we have found it necessary to divide our extracts from his books into two parts: Section IV relates to his first journey, Section IX (in which he is bracketed with Stanley) to his last. The short introductions which precede the extracts and are printed in italics contain brief details of the travellers' careers and are designed to fit the chosen passages into the perspective of their lives and work.

We have closely followed the spelling and punctuation of the originals, altering them only when it seemed essential to do so for the sake of clearness. We have reproduced the travellers' own spelling of proper names (except in the matter of accents, which have been omitted throughout): where the modern version is so different as to be unrecognizable, we have added it in square brackets; in our commentary and on the maps we have generally used the modern forms. Omissions of short passages have been denoted by dots in the text, of several pages by a line of dots: a blank space indicates that there is a space in the original. All but a few of the travellers' footnotes have been left out: the unsigned notes are our own.

The purpose of the maps in the text is to indicate the main outline of the travellers' journeys and the position of the principal places mentioned. They must be regarded merely as sketch-maps, since in order to make them clear certain minor journeys and deviations have been omitted, and it is impossible in some cases to determine the exact position of places which no longer exist to-day. The general map at the end of the book is designed to bring the smaller maps into relation with each other and with the continent of Africa as a whole, and to illustrate the Introduction.

PREFACE

For permission to include the illustrations from Livingstone's *Last Journals* and our extracts from Stanley's *How I Found Livingstone* we are indebted to Messrs. John Murray and Messrs. Sampson Low, Marston & Co. Ltd., respectively.

In this new edition we have taken the opportunity of correcting a number of small errors and misprints.

M.P.
J.S.

Oxford
11th March 1957

INTRODUCTION

I. PURPOSE AND CHARACTER OF THE ANTHOLOGY

by Margery Perham

The motives which move people to produce anthologies seem, in the main, to be creditable. If I may judge by myself, and if I judge myself rightly, these motives are intellectual altruism or, at the least, literary gregariousness, while the writer who turns editor must impose some temporary restraint upon his egotism. For many years my work has led me to study the records of African travel and often I have almost exclaimed aloud at the interest or dramatic character of certain passages, and have wished to go out of my study, book in hand, to find someone with whom to share my appreciation. As such action was not always convenient nor certain of immediate success, the alternative plan of making an anthology of African travel began to take shape. It changed from shape into substance only when I met Mr. Simmons, and found in him not merely a fellow enthusiast but a colleague in African studies, ready to share with me equally in the labour and in the love—not to speak of the laughter—which were bound up with the task.

The first question the would-be reader of an anthology must ask of the compilers is 'Upon what thread have you strung your jewels?' We used only one criterion for these selections, and it is perhaps too bare and subjective to satisfy our more serious questioners, that of 'readability'. We have simply picked out some of the passages which struck us most, and it still remains, therefore, for our readers and ourselves to put the further very justifiable 'Why?'

To this second question many answers can be given and those of our readers may be as good as, or better than, our own. Sometimes the reason for choice seems to have been sheer literary merit; sometimes the intrinsic interest of the subject; sometimes the dramatic character of the episode; sometimes the revelation of human character. The wares we wish to advertise, the writings of the great travellers, are so rich both in abundance and variety that no one kind of sample would have done them justice. There is material for all tastes and types of readers, from those sensationalists whom the purveyors of the mysterious drums and sorceries of 'Darkest Africa' have so long exploited to those whose perceptions are trained to distil the subtlest flavours of irony, comedy or pathos even from these forthright records. For those who like a good story, a tour, recorded day by day, makes a natural plot, and the 'on and on-ness' which gives its flavour to the most sober walking or motoring tour in England, reaches its supreme expression in journeys launched into savage and utterly unknown lands. As for the naturalists—but here I will quote from our first explorer, Bruce, to whose advice we have attended in this matter: 'With regard to the Natural History, however numerous and respectable they may be who have dedicated themselves to this study, they bear but a very small proportion to those who for amusement or instruction, seek the miscellaneous and general occurrences of life that ordinarily compose a series of travels.' It is 'unpleasant to have a very rapid, well-told narrative . . . interrupted by the appearance of a nettle or a daffodil'. Thus, although the Natural History of Africa, in its impressive, pervasive, and frequently dynamic character, is fully treated in the explorers' records, it is not proportionately represented in these selections. Adventures with dangerous animals, which make up the bulk of these accounts, seem to raise the legitimate self-dramatization of the traveller to a distasteful point, as our extract from Baker on this theme—in significant contrast to the other from Livingstone—may illustrate. I hope our readers will agree that for our generation the killing or wounding of large animals satiates as quickly in the relation as I know that it can in actuality.

While there are subjects for all tastes, there is one idea which must dominate, directly or indirectly, a collection of this kind. It is that contained in our title, that which goaded the travellers from the waxing domestic and material comforts of nineteenth-century England into the wilderness—the hunger for discovery.

These discoverers seem to be almost like a separate species of man, or men set apart by some strange mental condition. They illustrate human purposefulness in such extreme and naked fashion as to take on a symbolic meaning. This reaches, perhaps, its highest expression in Mungo Park and David Livingstone, and in the latter it is welded with a spiritual passion that has set him among the very great. It induced also at times a ruthlessness and intolerance directed not only towards the explorers' own suffering bodies but—notably in Livingstone, upon his Zambesi expedition, and in Park upon his second journey—towards their European companions. The physical and mental miseries that Africa at her worst can inflict upon the civilized stranger are illustrated in this volume sufficiently to make marvels of the decision of these men to endure such things a second and a third time, and to endow with something sacramental the refusal of Livingstone to accept the escape which Stanley came to offer him. It is no accident that of the ten explorers represented in this book, half failed to reach the age of forty and half died in Africa.

These men may have been self-selected for their task by reason of their own discipline and energy, but their achievements must be seen also as a response to the ideas of their time. In the section immediately following Mr. Simmons has placed their work in the sequence, and upon the map, of African discovery, and it is only in this setting that they can be fully understood. At this period there was great honour for geographical discovery, and it was to this spur that their spirits answered, though for most, honour was certainly not synonymous with honours. Livingstone, above all, gave the word his own special meaning. These men were necessarily of strongly marked character and behind the record of travel lies another story of personal sacrifice, generosities, and, unfortunately, of jealousies, which in the case of Speke and Burton may have reached—for the truth is not wholly clear—to the height of tragedy.

The explorers were put to two hard tests of human nature, that of facing danger, loneliness and barbarism and that of recording—generally without possibility of challenge—their own conduct in this ordeal. These journals will reveal more than any of the writers intended: different facets of character will strike the reader according to his own angle of vision and, according to his own standards, he will judge how well or how badly these men represented their century, their nation, and their religion. It is an interesting exercise to see how far these first intruders from a capitalist world into an innocent continent can be made to fit into their proper place in modern pictures of imperialism, whether these are painted in tones of gold or red.

So much of the men. What of the background, physical and human, against which they could so justifiably dramatize themselves? In their journals the continent plays such an active and, indeed, violent part as to fill something like a distinct role in the drama, certainly that of the villain. Africa is allowed at times her beauties, but the general impression given by the explorers is one of caprice, of treachery, of violent extremes, and of hostility to men, which, combined with the allure which held them, has suggested the ready analogy of the dark slave, ravished, beautiful but untameable. She was still at the height of her power against these first intruders, and the passages in this book are sufficient to show how strongly she guarded to the last the secret of the great waters in her rivers and lakes, which had been hidden from the civilized world for the thousands of years of its history.

The contemporaries for whom the explorers wrote were probably more interested in the character of the continent than of its peoples. That order is reversed to-day and to many the most interesting subject upon which their evidence can be sought is that of the state of African society when untouched by direct contact with the civilized world. These extracts have not been made with any considered reference to this large question, and it would be unwise to draw general conclusions from this selection in a sphere where further reading would give the richest results. Yet even these extracts raise some problems and provoke some interpretation.

I found, myself, that the first and most important effect of the travellers' books was one of revaluation. At school and subsequently, I had absorbed the idea that pre-European Africa was a place of complete and anarchic savagery. I do not know how this impression was received, but it was probably an accumulation from many sources. Now, as a student of these matters, I have come across many opinions expressed by administrators, missionaries and colonists in Africa, both living and dead, which repeat this view. 'South Africa,' wrote a Colonial Secretary of the last century, 'beyond the reach of the White man is one scene of violence and rapine.' This view still lingers, in spite of the revelations of the anthropologists, and it has important results. It helps to fix an uncritical and generalized attitude of superiority towards Africans and it acts not only as a justification of European annexation and government, for which a less gloomy view of the old Africa might suffice, but as an excuse for the less defensible activities of imperialism. How often have I heard it said in answer to some criticism of European policy or conduct, 'Well, after all, think what Africa was before the white man came!' Well, what *was* Africa? How far do our travellers help us here? It would take a volume analysing the evidence of their many volumes to give the full answer this question deserves. But even in the following pages we get some indications.

We should distinguish two spheres of Africa into which our travellers penetrated. To the north lay countries reached by the tide of world civilization, if only in a shallow and half stagnant fringe, or from which it had long ago ebbed to leave isolated pools. In the Western Sudan Islam was professed, and the Saharan caravan routes linked this region, however weakly, to the great Moslem world and drew at second hand upon the products of Europe. This semi-civilization had radiated its influences to some of the hostile pagan peoples to the south. From the sea Africa had been injected with such economic and cultural forces from Europe as slave-ships could carry. To the east, Somaliland and Harar, for all their savagery and stagnation, were part of Islam, that comity of peoples in which Burton had qualified himself to masquerade and which was so much more widely fraternal than anything Christendom achieved. Cut off by these marcher-lands of the Prophet, on her fortress of mountains, stood Abyssinia, the outpost of another great world religion, where Europe and Asia had fused with Africa. Here Bruce found churches, courts and kings, literacy and fire-arms, a sense of nationalism, and an ancient Christian history.

Further south, and down to the missionary outposts of the Cape, was the great central block of Africa shut off, for geographical reasons to be given in the next section, from the civilized world. Here, in lands sealed at once from the culture and the fanaticism of the two world-religions, the travellers had to deal with scores of separate tribes with all their variety of customs, languages, and organization. They were, or had been until a few years before, as utterly cut off from contact with the outside world as was possible for people who had, after all, lived for thousands of years on the same continent as the ancient Egyptians, and had received wave upon wave of migration from the north-east. The penetration of Arab slave-traders inland from the coast only just preceded the explorations of the Europeans and these it at once stimulated and, in parts, facilitated. Sometimes, indeed, as with Livingstone in Manyuema, and with Baker in Unyoro, the arrival was simultaneous.

This distinction between the two spheres of Africa must be given, but it must not be carried too far. Savagery still survived in the semi-civilized parts while elements of civilization, as these pages will bear witness, were not unknown in the more isolated regions. And almost everywhere, even though most of these travellers were too much part of their self-confident day and generation to emphasize this, there was, upon its own primitive level, a fully functioning society which met all the main needs of man.

This point deserves a moment's thought. The peoples the explorers found were narrow in their tribal boundaries; they were desperately poor in their equipment for living and therefore helpless in their dependence upon a very cruel and moody nature. But nowhere did savagery spell anarchy. The element of 'degree' lauded by Shakespeare's Ulysses, without which 'each thing meets in mere oppugnancy' was almost everywhere visible in:

> 'The primogenity and due of birth,
> Prerogative of age, crowns, sceptres, laurels . . .'

Everywhere, kings, chiefs, or headmen were found even if it was only to obstruct these astonishing strangers. Everywhere markets were in operation from the famous caravan-hub of Kano, to the emporium of the kingless Manyuema, guarded by the rigid sanctuary of the 'market-peace' which it took the intruding Arabs to shatter. Trade was indeed almost everywhere encountered, with tracks, tolls, ferries, simple manufactures and, often, close and admirable cultivation. These peoples—again on the level of their poverty—shared nearly all the joys of the civilized: singing and dancing and drinking; the display of dress and martial splendour; the indulgence of oratory and, to a much lesser extent, the self-expression of the manual arts.

That the explorers seldom drew these conclusions from what they observed may be due to two reasons. The first is that the original pattern of African society they saw was, over large areas, broken or marred by the Asiatic or internal African slave-trade. From Bruce to Livingstone, from Senegal to Zanzibar, we see how this other—and older—trade reproduced the coastal traffic of the Europeans in the heart of Africa and prolonged the evil to our own day. Full allowance for this must be made in trying to form any view of pre-European Africa, especially as it was the character of the trade to corrupt the stronger tribes as well as to destroy the weaker and to radiate like a quick infection far away from the narrow routes trodden by the merchants themselves. It is thus at times a society almost in dissolution, or at least deeply wounded by its first contact with an outer world more cruel than itself, that we are being shown.

The word 'cruelty' calls to mind the need for another caution, and one that is not easy to phrase without causing misunderstanding. It is probable that Anglo-Saxon—and with it perhaps, Scandinavian—society in the last century and a half has, in spite of certain inconsistencies, reached the highest standards of humanity towards human beings and animals that the world has known. As man successively exalts each virtue to priority, so its opposite vice sinks into a proportionate depth of opprobrium. The emotions to some extent react automatically to the current moral habit, and when they are called into action, a sense of historical perspective is rarely summoned to regulate them. Acts of cruelty therefore powerfully command both the feelings and the attentions of our travellers as they do of their readers; the result is in all probability a distorted picture of African society. Thus Speke's Uganda will probably be best remembered for the sudden and apparently meaningless murders by its king—it was the shocking fantasy of the Queen of Hearts' 'Off with her head!' in grim fact—and the state of his kingdom will be only half seen. Yet that kingdom, with its high degree of organization, its graded ranks of officers, its roads and large buildings, was an astonishing phenomenon in the heart of equatorial Africa. The price paid for this order was the divine right to do wrong of the representative of the ancient dynasty which had been its centre and symbol, and his victims themselves seemed prepared to pay the price. It was only with the increase of European influences and the coming of rival missionaries that the Uganda polity collapsed, and the first British Commissioner, Sir Harry Johnston, charged to restore artificially through foreign power the native order that had been lost, himself declared that the Baganda might well look back on their life under Mtesa and his predecessors as one of ideal happiness.

This question of cruelty is raised again in a most interesting form by Bruce who makes us believe at once in the charm, sensibility and —by English standards—utter inhumanity of the King of Abyssinia, his friend. Yet this throne, held to-day by the Emperor Hailé Selassie, was, for all its eclipse in Bruce's day, the nucleus round which a relatively civilized kingdom had been built up and maintained in a region of backward and divided tribes.

We must ask where this argument is taking us. It is not to the conclusion that we should dilute our hatred of cruelty or cease to rejoice that Speke and Bruce and, above all, Livingstone, found its crude African expression intolerable. It need not even lead us to the vain regret that African society came under European control. But if we can remember that cruelty may not be the deepest defect of men and nations, and that in its grossest embodiment it went hand in hand with the civilization of our Elizabethans and was strong even in some of the greatest of them, we may take a more favourable view of the past of Africans, and therefore—which is even more important—of their future. It is also worth remembering that the inhumanity witnessed by the travellers was committed by men to whom, in the given situation, no other behaviour could ever have been suggested by any external agency to their minds. Yet—and this is surely the real mystery—there could be collected from these writers almost as much evidence of the natural goodness as of the natural sinfulness of man.

This brings us to consider the treatment dealt out by Africans to these first white intruders into their tropical sanctuary. Looking at the matter from the point of view of the large number of small separate societies in a state of hostility, or, at best, of armed neutrality towards their neighbours, and with no civic obligations outside their own small group, it seems at first sight almost culpable negligence on their part that only two of these ten Europeans were killed. The strangers often came to a tribe straight from the headquarters of its bitterest enemies. They were generally unable to give any intelligible reason for their presence. (It was characteristic common sense on the part of the later Mary Kingsley to travel as a merchant, a profession some of our explorers proudly renounced.) Their behaviour was generally unaccountable and often menacing and improper. They made sinister attempts to reach places that were profitless or forbidden. They were possessed of novel and exciting possessions which were a standing temptation to robbery, and, finally, they had powers and weapons that made them a mystery and a danger. Yet these men, utterly dependent and sometimes destitute, were allowed to pass chief after chief and tribe after tribe at the cost here of some restraint upon their impatient purposes and there of a persecution for presents nearly always stopping short of the violence which was well within the power of these chiefs. They were, on the contrary, not infrequently assisted at the cost of their hosts.

There is sadness in the reflection that Africans were allowed at this first moment of their contact with Europeans to show qualities that have since been crushed with the establishment of our absolute domination. The equal friendship in sport and arms formed by Bruce with the young bloods of the Abyssinian court; the hospitality of Rumanika; the discreet generosity of Mansong—what counterparts could they have to-day, as between Africans and Europeans? The Galla wept for Burton, and, in perhaps one of the most poignant biographical passages in our literature, the derelict and utterly insignificant Park was cherished by an unknown African woman. Finally, there was that great act of unconstrained courage and devotion by which the bones of the one explorer who may be said to have lived and died for Africans rather than for Africa, were carried for a thousand miles through every danger by his negro servants. But to-day Africans are subjected to our beneficence as well as to our power. How long will it be before they, who are now asked only to serve and to accept, will be able to turn to us again that side of their nature which gives?

There remain some few excuses and explanations to be made.

We must first defend ourselves from the charge of insularity. This is not difficult. Among the great foreign explorers not many were in action in this period between the last great days of the Portuguese and the first efforts of the most famous Germans and Frenchmen. The discovery of the source of the Nile, and the opening up of the vast regions of Central Africa were mainly the work of British travellers. Even had it not been so, it would have been small justice to a foreign explorer, in an anthology in which the style, and sometimes the literary merit, of the writer are inseparable from his other qualifications, to present him in the medium of translation.

We must also point out that we had to choose between, on the one side, a book so loaded with editorial matter that many of the readers we wished to reach would have flinched away from its very appearance, and, on the other, one offering the bare minimum of explanation required to make our extracts intelligible. It was difficult to fix upon any half-way point between these courses. We chose the second and the brevity of the introductions often obliged us to deal summarily with geographical or personal questions that are still open to dispute, and to make omissions and unqualified generalizations. Again, there is hardly a page which could not have carried notes explaining the exact meaning of native or other terms used, 'placing' some minor character, or putting some event into relation with earlier incidents. Where the lack of this information did not seem to destroy the general sense of the narrative, we assumed our readers would prefer not to have their attention distracted by annotation. The manner in which we have interspersed our commentary with the extracts has been governed by our desire to present them as a continuous story, in which the incidents can be seen against the background of the explorers' lives and travels.

We can only justify this treatment by our main object in making this anthology. This brings me back to the point from which I began this introduction. Our hope, of course, is that having taken this ground-bait you will be lured into following up the explorers into their own volumes. These are the precious calf-bound productions of the eighteenth and early nineteenth century with their characteristic lettering and magnificent wood-engravings, and the Victorian books, which, less elegant in their workmanship and cruder in the appeal of their illustrations to our sense of adventure, are yet racy of their period. The enjoyment of these books does not depend upon any previous knowledge of Africa and its geography. In the course of my work I have myself followed these explorers west to Kano; east to Berbera; south to the Victoria Falls, and along the Nile from its birth in the great Lakes to its Egyptian delta; yet I do not think this has added much to my appreciation of their writings. My own impressions may, indeed, have slightly blurred their pictures. Their continent has changed so quickly, if not in appearance—though bridges span the Ripon and Victoria Falls and carry railways over the Niger and the junction of the Niles—at least in its whole atmosphere. The peace of Europe, the huge framework of her state systems, embrace those little warring, lusty communities in a wide, firm grip. Yet, in the books from which we have made this anthology, the old Africa, with its open challenge to the science, courage and compassion of the nineteenth century, comes to life again.

II. THE CONTINENT AND THE EXPLORERS

by J. Simmons

Any survey of the exploration of Africa must begin by discussing the physical features of the continent; for all penetration from the outside has been governed, or at least conditioned, by them.

The coast of Africa is extremely uninviting. Vast stretches of it hardly afford even a sheltering roadstead, and, except on the north, good natural harbours are very rare. Nearly half of it is backed by desert or semi-desert; much of the rest by thick forest, difficult or impossible to penetrate. Few of the rivers are navigable: either their course is impeded by cataracts, or their mouths are blocked by bars, or they run out into the sea through a maze of creeks, bordered by jungle. Access to the interior by water is therefore difficult. By land, until the coming of mechanical transport, it was little easier; for the presence of the tsetse-fly made it impossible to use horses or cattle of any kind over large areas of Africa: the interior could only be reached on foot, using human porterage. The climate of the continent, except at its northern and southern extremities, has always been unpleasant to Europeans, and until the modern treatment of tropical diseases had been evolved it was often fatal to them.

In the face of these obstacles, it is not surprising that the 'opening-up' of Africa has only been achieved in recent times. Yet it has been attempted, sometimes with an astonishing measure of success, for at least three thousand years—for much more, if we include here the racial migrations into the continent from the north-east.

The story of the exploration of Africa by Europeans divides itself naturally into five phases.[1] The first of these includes the dis-

[1] It must be remembered that Africa was not explored only by Europeans. During the Middle Ages the continent was far better known to the Arabs, who maintained caravan routes across the Sahara from the north coast to Timbuktu: Ibn Battuta, the most famous of Arab travellers, wrote a full account of this area in the fourteenth century. But, like all the other information about Africa acquired by the Arabs, it remained unknown outside the Moslem world and had little influence on the course of later exploration.

coveries made by Egyptian, Greek and Roman pioneers along three main routes, the east and west coasts and the valley of the Nile. Their knowledge of the shores of Africa extended down to Cape Delgado and Sierra Leone; while they knew something of the White Nile as far up as the *sudd* and the great swamp which begins in about latitude 9° N. The mystery of its source fascinated geographers in ancient, as it has in modern, times. This is not surprising: it was the longest river known to Europeans before the discovery of the New World; it had nourished the ancient civilization of Egypt; it flowed in great volume through a thousand miles of desert without receiving a single tributary; the way to its source was barred by tropical swamp and fabulous peoples. In the second period, stretching from the fifteenth century to the seventeenth, explorers from Western Europe, led by the Portuguese, completed the outline of the coasts of Africa; and some information was gained about the interior, notably by the Jesuit missionaries in Abyssinia and Angola. The third period, the 'classical age' of African discovery, starts with Bruce's journey in 1769 and ends with the death of Livingstone 104 years later. The fourth may be called the period of political exploration: it comprises roughly the last quarter of the nineteenth century, beginning with Stanley's journey down the Congo in 1874 and ending with the Partition of Africa between the European Powers. The fifth phase is that of detailed scientific exploration, a necessary prelude to the full political and economic development of the country. We are still in this stage to-day.

It is with the third of these periods that this book is concerned. When it opened, very little of the interior of the continent had been visited by Europeans and less still had been at all carefully described: nor was the coast fully known—it was not adequately charted until the great survey of Captain Owen in 1821–5. The journey of JAMES BRUCE,[1] which may be said to begin the new phase, was no great event in the history of geography: he did not visit any place of importance which had not been reached by earlier travellers. The significance of his work lies rather in the purpose for which he undertook it and in the manner of its presentation. The very title of his book, *Travels to discover the source of the Nile*, indicates his modern attitude of mind. Bruce was the first great scientific explorer of Africa, the first to go out there neither for

[1] The names of explorers represented in this book are printed in capital letters.

trade, nor for war, nor to hoist a flag, nor for the glory of God, but from curiosity—to find out *the truth* about the source of the Nile. That he did not discover the whole truth, that what he did find (the source of the Blue Nile) had been found 150 years earlier by one of those Portuguese Jesuits he wrongly despised—none of this mattered: he collected a great deal of valuable detail about the country he visited, which he published in a sober, yet delightfully readable form, and he stimulated the interest of the civilized world in Africa, just as Cook had aroused it in the Pacific.

That interest had previously been confined almost entirely to the West India proprietors, who looked to Africa for the slave labour on which their plantations depended. While Bruce was still in Abyssinia, the attack on the slave trade had opened in England. The subject had been forced into notice by Lord Mansfield's judgment in the Somerset case in 1772: this was the match that eventually set ablaze the whole train laid with such care by the Abolitionists—Granville Sharp, Zachary Macaulay, Clarkson, above all Wilberforce. Inevitably, the stir this case aroused had the effect of increasing public interest in Africa; and there were other causes, too, which helped to bring it into prominence in these years—the strategic importance of the West Coast in the naval war of 1778–83, the capture of Goree from the French and its subsequent return to them at the peace.[1]

Such were some of the reasons for the growth of interest in Africa in the late eighteenth century. A symptom of it was the founding in 1788 of the African Association, a dining-club presided over by Sir Joseph Banks, the most famous English scientist of his day. The Association's attention was directed not to the Nile but to another major geographical problem, the problem of the Niger. This was even more perplexing than the ancient riddle of the source of the Nile: for the Niger was not yet known as a river, it was only a name; no one knew where it rose, or where it ended—whether in the sea or in some great lake; no one even knew in what direction it flowed. Was it perhaps the Upper Nile? Or were the Senegal and the Gambia (on which French and British traders had long been established) its mouths? The African Association set itself to solve these questions.

[1] Goree is an island at the entrance to the bay on which stands the modern port of Dakar. Its importance in eighteenth-century naval strategy was somewhat similar to that of Dakar to-day: it should not be forgotten that they are virtually one and the same.

Its first attempts were unfortunate. Four travellers—Ledyard, Lucas, Hornemann, Houghton—were sent out one after another under its auspices, but all of them were unsuccessful and three died in Africa. The Association's fifth choice was MUNGO PARK, who did reach the Niger, established the fact that it flowed eastward, and brought home the natives' account of its geography. It still remained to find where the river rose, to trace its course, and to discover its mouth. Many lives were lost in attempting to settle these questions. Park himself made a second journey, this time at the expense of Government: he sailed down the Niger for more than half its length, but was killed near Bussa early in 1806. Expeditions were planned to start from Egypt, from the Bight of Benin, from Morocco; Tuckey was sent up the Congo in 1816, on the chance that it and the Niger might prove to be one. All these attempts miscarried: but they were not fruitless, for each failure bred a new effort, and—more important than the solution of any mere geographical conundrum—intelligent people began to take a deeper interest in Africa than they ever had before.

In 1822 came another step forward, when Laing succeeded in determining the position of the Niger sources: the lower course of the river had yet to be traced, and its mouth to be found. Next year another expedition set forth on this quest: it was better organized and in its results more valuable than any which had been sent out since the death of Park. Its three white members were Dixon Denham, HUGH CLAPPERTON, and Walter Oudney. Starting from Tripoli, they crossed the Sahara and discovered Lake Chad: Clapperton visited Kano and Sokoto, Denham found the River Shari. Timbuktu, that fabulous city, was reached by Laing in 1825 and by the astonishing young Frenchman René Caillié, who spent some time there and described it fully, two years later. The *réclame* of these feats penetrated even the torpor of an English university of that day. The subject set for the Chancellor's Gold Medal for English verse at Cambridge in 1829 was 'Timbuctoo': the prize was won by an undergraduate of Trinity, Alfred Tennyson.

If these last journeys contributed little to solving the Niger problem, they added much useful information about the Southern Sahara and revealed its highly organized Moslem civilization. They had another result, too, which commended them to a great body of Englishmen who were not particularly interested in geography, but who did care about Africa warmly and for the most part sincerely—the evangelical anti-slavery party. To them, and to the British Government, which on this question thought with them, the opening-up of the interior seemed to offer a new line of attack on the slave trade, a possibility of cutting off its supply at the source. As always, the intelligent Abolitionists urged, quite rightly, that it was useless to try and destroy it unless 'legitimate commerce' took its place: and it was to open up trade relations with Sultan Bello of Sokoto (who was the dominant power in the Western Sudan) that Clapperton was sent out by Government on his second journey. With him went his servant RICHARD LANDER. He reached his objective, this time by way of the Bight of Benin, but found that Bello, who on his previous visit had welcomed him kindly, was not interested in the treaty, and he died without managing to conclude it. His papers were brought back to England by Lander, who was under that old, recognizable spell which African travellers have so often felt, the imperative urge to return there. At once he agreed to go out and resume the search for the mouth of the Niger—again under the orders, and at the expense, of the British Government. He took his brother with him: they started inland from Badagri, reached the Niger at Bussa, and thence, with comparative ease though not without some excitements, sailed down to the sea. They came out in November 1830 by way of those 'Oil Rivers' which had long been known to Europeans as a market for palm-oil and slaves.

With the publication of the Landers' account of their travels in 1832 the last great question as to the course of the Niger was settled, and the geographers were for the moment satisfied. But not the Abolitionists or the traders: for them this was the beginning, not the end, of the story. The book came out at an opportune moment (perhaps that was why John Murray was willing to pay 1,000 guineas for it), for Africa was in the news: the great attack on slavery was brewing. In the next year, just after Wilberforce's death, the Emancipation Act was passed, which declared slavery illegal in the British colonies. This did something to right a crying and ancient wrong; but the more far-seeing of the Abolitionists—and notably their leader Thomas Fowell Buxton—realized that it did not fulfil all their objects (just as the more intelligent Reformers had understood that the Act of 1832 did not of itself end all Parliamentary injustices and abuses). Buxton and his friends at once proclaimed that the attack, so successfully carried through in England, must be pursued relentlessly against the Powers which countenanced slavery and the slave trade; and that at the same time another attempt must be made to stop up the sources of supply in the heart of Africa. Here they joined hands with the merchants, who hoped to recoup the losses they had suffered through the abolition of slavery in the West Indies, and the consequent decline in the sugar production of the islands, by finding new crops to exploit and new markets for their goods, and who turned naturally enough to Africa.

Soon after Lander returned to England he was approached by Macgregor Laird, a Liverpool shipowner, with an invitation to accompany a new expedition to the Niger for the purpose of promoting trade. He accepted, and the party set off in July 1832. Their equipment was elaborate, including two steamships; but the venture proved unlucky. Lander himself was killed in a skirmish with some natives in the delta, and of the other 47 Europeans who went out, 38 died (mostly from disease) before the expedition returned in 1834. Seven years later another expedition was dispatched, this time by Government, strongly supported by the Abolitionists, Exeter Hall, and the Prince Consort: it was on a much larger scale, and it was similarly disastrous. The official account of it, published in 1848, was scornfully reviewed by Dickens, who exposed the follies—he almost called them crimes—committed by the ill-informed philanthropists who backed it. He returned to the charge in a lighter vein when he created the immortal Mrs. Jellyby, with her settlement of Borrioboola-Gha on the Niger, in *Bleak House*.

Such criticisms did not deflect the British Government from its purpose of opening up the interior of Africa by whatever means and whatever route might prove practicable. Success was close at hand: the 'fifties were to prove the most fruitful decade in the history of the European penetration of the continent.

In 1849 another expedition was sent out to explore the Southern Sahara and to make contact with its Moslem states. James Richardson was chosen to lead it: with him went two Germans, Heinrich Barth and Adolf Overweg. They crossed the desert from Tripoli. Richardson died in 1851, Overweg in 1852, but Barth went on: in his wanderings, which lasted five and a half years, he discovered the Upper Benue, visited Katsina, Sokoto and Timbuktu, and eventually returned over the Sahara, reaching England in September 1855. Barth's journey is one of the greatest feats in the history of African travel, and the huge book in which he described it one of the masterpieces of the subject. For the moment, however, his discoveries were not followed up.

But they had already had one indirect result of great significance. When Barth was lost in the interior a search-party was sent to look for him, not across the Sahara but up the Niger. It was to have been commanded by John Beecroft, British Consul for the Bights of Benin and Biafra;[1] but he died before starting, and his place was taken by W. B. BAIKIE. The search for Barth was unsuccessful, but in other respects the expedition was a triumph. It showed that steamships could be taken up the Niger, and a considerable distance up the Benue. More important still, it proved that by the constant use of quinine Europeans could avoid that fever which had decimated the previous expeditions: not one man died of disease on the whole trip.

Meanwhile, a journey of a very different character from any of those we have previously considered was in progress further south. In 1841, the year of that disastrous Niger expedition which had aroused the sarcasm of Dickens, DAVID LIVINGSTONE arrived in South Africa. For eight years he worked as a missionary in Bechuanaland. Then, in 1849, actuated not so much by geographical curiosity as by the desire to see what fields for missionary enterprise lay further north, he crossed the Kalahari and discovered Lake Ngami. Here he heard that the country which lay beyond was populous and watered by many rivers—very different from the barren land he had been living in and the desert he had just crossed. Into this region, which held out such wonderful promises, he determined to advance as quickly as he could; and in 1852 he began the great journey which was to take him first to the Atlantic and then across the continent to the Indian Ocean. This is not the place to describe that journey or the two which followed it: an outline of them will be found in the sections dealing with Livingstone below. Here we are only concerned with their results.

In the first place they drew attention to what may be called East Central Africa—the valley of the Zambesi and the country northwards up to Lake Tanganyika: this huge area had previously been quite unknown, except in a very limited degree to the Portuguese. Livingstone showed that much of it was thickly populated and fertile, that it had great economic potentialities—but that it was devastated by the slave trade.

This was not the West Coast trade, which was now nearing its

[1] The establishment of this post in 1849 is evidence of the increasing interest which was now being taken in this region by the British Government, urged on by the Liverpool merchants.

end (it received its death-blows in the early 'sixties), but another, of which little had been heard before, having its centre at Zanzibar and supplying the slave markets of Arabia and the Persian Gulf. It was carried on by Arabs and the mixed Arab-African Swahili, who were financed in many cases by Indian merchants living at Zanzibar and on the coast opposite. The slave-traders were at this time making their way ever further and further into the interior in search of their victims. But not all the slaves they acquired were seized by themselves: they bought many of them from native chiefs who, greedy for the goods the traders offered them (especially the guns and cloth), raided their neighbours; and the consequence was those wars which were ravaging the country when Livingstone and Stanley saw it. There was nothing new in this: in West Africa slave-raiding had gone on, unchecked, for centuries. But that was at last being ended, on the initiative of Britain: and Livingstone now demanded that the East Coast trade should be stopped too. The means he proposed for suppressing it were similar to those which had been advocated by Buxton and his party in the 'forties: a naval squadron for seizing the slave-ships, combined with the opening-up of the interior by means of Christianity and commerce (a union which offers an obvious target for cynics, but which was in fact neither hypocritical nor ineffective). The Zambesi expedition of 1858, which Livingstone took out to put these principles into practice, bears some resemblance to the Niger expedition of 1841. But though they were alike in their lack of complete success, Livingstone's gained a great deal of valuable information and, in spite of all its shortcomings, justified the money spent on it, where the Niger expedition had been a complete disaster. Nor was this surprising: for he had practical knowledge of the country he was to operate in and of the conditions of work there, while the organizers of the earlier expedition had little but zeal, excellent intentions, and the accounts given by previous travellers, to go upon.

Livingstone was not the only explorer to direct attention to East Africa at this time. While he was still on his great journey across the continent, RICHARD BURTON made his *début* as an African traveller much further north, with a dangerous expedition across Somaliland to the unknown city of Harar. He set off again on a more momentous journey two months before Livingstone reached England. Accompanied by J. H. SPEKE, he travelled inland from the coast opposite Zanzibar: after a march of seven and a half months they reached Lake Tanganyika. This was the first of the three great Central African lakes to be discovered: six months afterwards, on 30th July 1858, Speke caught his first glimpse of Victoria Nyanza, the greatest of them; a little over a year later Livingstone found the third, Nyasa.

Speke at once made up his mind, by intuition well founded on probability and the reports of Arab traders, that the Victoria Nyanza was much more than a mere lake: that it was the source of the Nile; that he had solved the question which, as he himself wrote, had been 'the first geographical desideratum of many thousand years to ascertain, and the ambition of the first monarchs of the world to unravel'.

Inevitably, his claims were doubted; and as soon as he came home he began to make arrangements for another expedition to prove them. This he succeeded in doing by his great journey, with J. A. Grant, from Zanzibar to Gondokoro on the Nile. It is true that, even after the publication of his splendid account of it, his achievement was still questioned (notably by his former companion Burton, who was now his bitter enemy), on the grounds that he had not himself traced the whole of the upper course of the river; but this omission was soon repaired by SAMUEL BAKER and H. M. STANLEY, and all but a few irreconcilable critics were satisfied.

The 'fifties, then, saw an immense development in the knowledge of Africa, through the labours of Barth, Baikie, Livingstone, Burton and Speke. They also saw a new political interest in the continent on the part of the European Powers. It was at this time that Britain took the first small step that led eventually to the establishment of Nigeria: in 1851 she declared a virtual protectorate over Lagos (made absolute ten years later), solely in order to facilitate the suppression of the slave trade. The foundations of the huge French West African empire were also laid in these years by Faidherbe, who became Governor of Senegal in 1854.

The 'scramble' for East Africa began later and went on more slowly. The first sign of it was, paradoxically, the Anglo-French Declaration of 1862, binding both Powers to respect the Sultan of Zanzibar's independence. The Declaration was followed by a steady growth of British influence at Zanzibar, which eventually, in 1890, developed into a full protectorate. This influence made itself decisively felt in 1873, when the Sultan agreed to prohibit his subjects from exporting slaves overseas. That meant in effect the end of the Arab slave trade from Africa: it was a complete victory for Livingstone.

But he was not alive to see it. In March 1866 he had started out from Zanzibar on his third and last journey. For nearly six years the outside world had no certain news of him. Then, in the spring of 1872, H. M. Stanley arrived in England and announced that he had 'found' Livingstone. He had gone on his quest as a journalist, sent by his paper the *New York Herald.* (How many other explorers besides Livingstone have had a 'news value' which could have made this worth while?) With great efficiency, backed—as on all his African journeys—by ample funds, Stanley performed his mission, reached Livingstone at Ujiji, supplied his wants, and sent up porters from the coast to aid him. Thus reinforced (when Stanley found him his condition was poor indeed), Livingstone determined to finish off his work, the examination of the country south of Lake Tanganyika, and to return home as quickly as possible. But, weakened by disease, even his constitution was unequal to this final demand upon it, and near Lake Bangweolo he died—five weeks before the treaty which virtually ended the East African slave trade was concluded.

Stanley was a man of very different type from Livingstone. But he came back deeply impressed—there can be no doubt of it—by 'the Doctor's' character; and when he heard the news of his death, in February 1874, he determined that he would himself carry on what he conceived to be Livingstone's work. This he did, in his own way, by his second journey in 1874–7, which solved most of the problems that preoccupied Livingstone in his last years: he secured final confirmation of Speke's theory of the source of the Nile and he proved that the Lualaba was one with the Congo, which he followed down to the sea at Boma. The last of the four great African rivers had at length been traced.

But this immense journey had a much wider importance too. It led directly to the Partition of Africa. Stanley was alive to the political significance of the work he had done, and he pressed Britain to take control of the Congo basin and to open it up by a road and railway from the sea to the point at which the river becomes navigable (now known as Stanley Pool). Here he failed; but he was successful in another quarter: King Leopold II of the Belgians entered readily enough into his plans, which linked up with the founding of the International African Association (its name is, surely unconsciously, reminiscent of Banks's club of 1788). This led in its turn to the establishment of the Congo Free State and the 'scramble' for tropical Africa which began in 1884.

Stanley's second journey was in fact, in its results if not its original intention, the first of the new political expeditions ('imperialist', if you will). In its execution, too, it offers a strong contrast to most of those which are described in this book. Its brutal attitude to hostile or puzzled African chiefs, its lavish equipment, its huge array of porters, the ruthless discipline under which they were kept, would have amazed, and often horrified, Lander or Livingstone or Speke. Yet in a sense they were only the logical conclusion of the work of the earlier travellers: it was inevitable that when once the physical obstacles to the exploration of Africa were overcome and a need for her products developed, Europe should intervene in full strength to exploit the country those travellers had revealed.

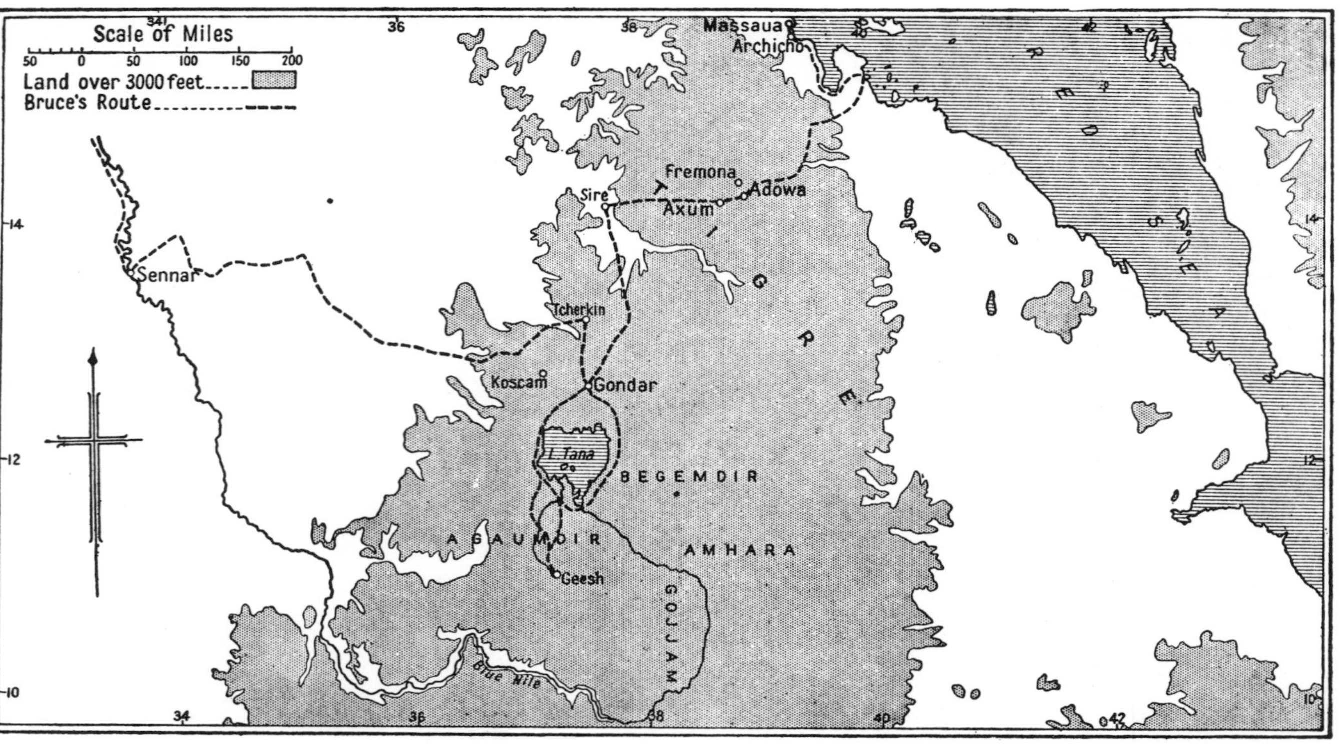

1. The Travels of Bruce in Abyssinia, 1769–72

I

JAMES BRUCE

1730–1794

Bruce was a Scotchman of good position and education, and of striking appearance, being six foot four, with dark red hair, and a commanding presence. He went to school at Harrow and afterwards studied law. During a residence in Spain he took up Arabic, and having learned something of Ethiopia and the Amharic language, he conceived a great longing to discover the source of the Nile. During the 'sixties he lived and travelled in Mediterranean countries. He distinguished himself as Consul at Algiers at a dangerous time and went on to travel, study and draw antiquities in Italy, Barbary, Libya, Syria and Crete. In 1768 he was in Egypt where, by acting as a doctor to some of the ruling personalities, he gained from them valuable letters of recommendation to Moslem authorities on the Red Sea, with others from the Patriarch of Alexandria to the Christian Smyrna Greeks in Ethiopia.

Thus provided, he made an arduous and dangerous journey at his own expense, travelling, equipped with heavy scientific instruments, by Aswan, Cosseir and Jiddah to Massaua. After a dangerous interlude at Massaua, he scaled the escarpment up to the heights of Tigre—the language of which country he had already learned—and with many adventures, which make exciting reading in his journal, reached Gondar, the then capital of Ethiopia, in 1770. Europeans had before this visited the country only at rare intervals and Bruce was one of only two or three Europeans known to have entered during the eighteenth century.

He found that Ethiopia was the scene of civil wars and that the real ruler of the country was the aged, cruel, but very able Ras Michael of Tigre who dominates his story. He had already made away with two kings and with many of his rivals. The existing king, the young Tecla Haimanot, was now in his power but he was by no means a puppet in character and he is described by Bruce as being of great physical beauty and charm. When Bruce arrived at Gondar both Ras and King were away fighting a leading Galla chieftain, Fasil. He was able, however, to win the favour of one of the leading nobles, Ayto Aylo, of the Queen Mother (the Iteghe) and of Ras Michael's young, spirited, and beautiful wife, Ozoro Esther, by curing the latter's son, Confu, and others of their household at Koscam, from smallpox, and stemming the plague by measures of hygiene. He at once provoked the jealousy and suspicion of some of the clergy, whose attempts at a miraculous cure had failed, and especially of Abba Salama, who as the Acab Saat, was the third head—the Abuna was the first—of the Ethiopian Church and religious guardian of the palace.

The first extract opens at the point where, upon the return of the King and the old Ras from their expedition, Bruce is ushered into the formidable presence of the latter.

1. RECEPTION AT GONDAR

We went in and saw the old man sitting upon a sofa; his white hair was dressed in many short curls. He appeared to be thoughtful, but not displeased; his face was lean, his eyes quick and vivid, but seemed to be a little sore from exposure to the weather. He seemed to be about six feet high, though his lameness made it difficult to guess with accuracy. His air was perfectly free from constraint, what the French call *dégagée*. In face and person he was liker my learned and worthy friend the Count de Buffon, than any two men I ever saw in the world. They must have been bad physiognomists that did not discern his capacity and understanding by his very countenance. Every look conveyed a sentiment with it: he seemed to have no occasion for other language, and indeed he spoke little. I offered, as usual, to kiss the ground before him; and of this he seemed to take little notice, stretching his hand and shaking mine upon rising.

I sat down with Aylo, three or four of the judges, Petros, Heikel the queen's chamberlain, and an Azage from the king's house, who whispered something in his ear, and went out; which interruption prevented me from speaking as I was prepared to do, or give him my present, which a man held behind me. He began gravely, 'Yagoube, I think that is your name, hear what I say to you, and mark what I recommend to you. You are a man, I am told, who make it your business to wander in the fields in search after trees and grass in solitary places, and to sit up all night alone looking at the stars of the heavens. Other countries are not like this, though this was never so bad as it is now. These wretches here are enemies to strangers; if they saw you alone in your own parlour, their first thought would be how to murder you; though they knew they were to get nothing by it, they would murder you for mere mischief.'—'The devil is strong in them,' says a voice from a corner of the room, which appeared to be that of a priest. 'Therefore,' says the Ras, 'after a long conversation with your friend Aylo, whose advice I hear you happily take, as indeed we all do, I have thought that situation best which leaves you at liberty to follow your own designs, at the same time that it puts your person in safety; that you will not be troubled with monks about their religious matters, or in danger from these rascals that may seek to murder you for money.'

'What are the monks?' says the same voice from the corner; 'the monks will never meddle with such a man as this.'—'Therefore the king,' continued the Ras, without taking any notice of the interruption, 'has appointed you Baalomaal,[1] and to command the Koccob horse, which I thought to have given to Francis, an old soldier of mine; but he is poor, and we will provide for him better, for these appointments have honour, but little profit.' 'Sir,' says Francis, who was in presence, but behind, 'it is in much more honourable hands than either mine or the Armenian's, or any other white man's, since the days of Hatze Menas, and so I told the king to-day.' 'Very well, Francis,' says the Ras; 'it becomes a soldier to speak the truth, whether it makes for or against himself. Go then to the king, and kiss the ground upon your appointment. I see you have already learned this ceremony of ours; Aylo and Heikel are very proper persons to go with you. The king expressed his surprise to me last night he had not seen you; and there too is Tecla Mariam, the king's secretary, who came with your appointment from the palace to-day.' The man in the corner, that I took for a priest, was this Tecla Mariam, a scribe. Out of the king's presence men of this order cover their heads, as do the priests, which was the reason of my mistake.

I then gave him a present, which he scarce looked at, as a number of people were pressing in at the door from curiosity or business. Among them I discerned Abba Salama. Everybody then went out but myself, and these people were rushing in behind me, and had divided me from my company. The Ras, however, seeing me standing alone, cried, 'Shut the door;' and asked me, in a low tone of voice, 'Have you anything private to say?' 'I see you are busy, Sir,' said I, 'but I will speak to Ozoro Esther.' His anxious countenance brightened up in a moment. 'That is true,' says he, 'Yagoube; it will require a long day to settle that account with you. Will the boy live?' 'The life of man is in the hand of God,' said I, 'but I should hope the worst is over;' upon which he called to one of his servants, 'Carry Yagoube to Ozoro Esther.'

[1] Literally 'keeper of the goods, or effects'. It is a post resembling that of our lords of the bed-chamber. The Koccob horse are the cavalry in the guards. (*Bruce's note.*)

It is needless for me to take up the reader's time with anything but what illustrates my travels; he may therefore guess the conversation that flowed from a grateful heart on that occasion. I ordered her child to be brought to her every forenoon, upon condition she returned him soon after mid-day. I then took a speedy leave of Ozoro Esther, the reason of which I told her when she was following me to the door. She said, 'When shall I lay my hands upon that idiot Aylo? The Ras would have done anything; he had appointed you Palambaras, but, upon conversing with Aylo he had changed his mind. He says it will create envy and take up your time. What signifies their envy? Do not they envy Ras Michael? And where can you pass your time better than at court, with a command under the king?' I said, 'all is for the best; Aylo did well; all is for the best.' I then left her unconvinced, and saying, 'I will not forgive this to Ayto Aylo these seven years.'

Aylo and Heikel had gone on to the palace, wondering, as did the whole company, what could be my private conference with Michael, which, after playing abundantly with theircuriosity, I explained to them next day.

I went afterwards to the king's palace, and met Aylo and Heikel at the door of the presence chamber. Tecla Mariam walked before us to the foot of the throne; after which I advanced and prostrated myself upon the ground. 'I have brought you a servant,' says he to the king, 'from so distant a country, that if you ever let him escape, we shall never be able to follow him, or know where to seek him.' This was said facetiously by an old familiar servant; but the king made no reply, as far as we could guess, for his mouth was covered, nor did he shew any alteration of countenance. Five people were standing on each side of the throne, all young men, three on his left, and two on his right. One of these, the son of Tecla Mariam, (afterwards my great friend) who stood uppermost on the left hand, came up, and taking hold of me by the hand, placed me immediately above him; when seeing I had no knife in my girdle, he pulled out his own and gave it to me. Upon being placed, I again kissed the ground.

The king was in an alcove; the rest went out of sight from where the throne was, and sat down. The usual questions now began about Jerusalem and the holy places—where my country was? which it was impossible to describe, as they knew the situation of no country but their own—why I came so far?—whether the moon and the stars, but especially the moon was the same in my country as in theirs?—and a great many such idle and tiresome questions. I had several times offered to take my present from the man who held it, that I might offer it to his Majesty and go away; but the king always made a sign to put it off, till, being tired to death with standing, I leaned against the wall. Aylo was fast asleep, and Ayto Heikel and the Greeks cursing their master in their heart for spoiling the good supper that Anthule his treasurer had prepared for us. This, as we afterwards found out, the king very well knew, and resolved to try our patience to the utmost. At last, Ayto Aylo stole away to bed, and everybody else after him, except those who had accompanied me, who were ready to die with thirst, and drop down with weariness. It was agreed by those that were out of sight, to send Tecla Mariam to whisper in the king's ear, that I had not been well, which he did, but no notice was taken of it. It was now past ten o'clock and he shewed no inclination to go to bed.

Hitherto, while there were strangers in the room, he had spoken to us by an officer called Kal Hatze, *the voice or word of the king*; but now, when there were nine or ten of us, his menial servants only, present, he uncovered his face and mouth, and spoke himself. Sometimes it was about Jerusalem, sometimes about horses, at other times about shooting; again about the Indies; how far I could look into the heavens with my telescopes: and all these were deliberately and circumstantially repeated, if they were not pointedly answered. I was absolutely in despair, and scarcely able to speak a word, inwardly mourning the hardness of my lot in this my first preferment, and sincerely praying it might be my last promotion in this court. At last all the Greeks began to be impatient and got out of the corner of the room behind the alcove and stood immediately before the throne. The king seemed to be astonished at seeing them and told them he thought they had all been at home long ago. They said, however, they would not go without me; which the king said could not be, for one of the duties of my employment was to be charged with the door of his bed-chamber that night.

I think I could almost have killed him in that instant. At last Ayto Heikel, taking courage, came forward to him, pretending a message from the queen, and whispered him something in the ear, probably that the Ras would take it ill. He then laughed, said he thought we had supped, and dismissed us.

We went all to Anthule's house to supper in violent rage, such anger as is usual with hungry men. We brought with us from the palace three of my brother Baalomaals, and one who had stood to make up the number, though he was not in office; his name was Guebra Mascal; he was a Sister's son of the Ras, and commanded one-third of the troops of Tigre, which carried fire-arms, that is about 2000 men. He was reputed the best officer of that kind that the Ras had, and was a man about 30 years of age, short, square, and well made, with a very unpromising countenance; flat nose, wide mouth, of a very yellow complexion, and much pitted with the smallpox; he had a most uncommon presumption upon the merit of past services, and had the greatest opinion of his own knowledge in the use of fire-arms, to which he did not scruple to say Ras Michael owed all his victories. Indeed it was to the good opinion that the Ras had of him as a soldier that he owed his being suffered to continue at Gondar; for he was suspected to have been familiar with one of his uncle's wives in Tigre, by whom it was thought he had a child; at least the Ras put away his wife, and never owned the child to be his.

This man supped with us that night, and thence began one of the most serious affairs I ever had in Abyssinia. Guebra Mascal, as usual, vaunted incessantly his skill in fire-arms, the wonderful gun that he had, and feats he had done with it. Petros said, laughing, to him, 'You have a genius for shooting, but you have had no opportunity to learn. Now Yagoube is come, he will teach you something worth talking of.' They had all drank abundantly, and Guebra Mascal had uttered words that I thought were in contempt of me. 'I believe,' replied I, peevishly enough, 'Guebra Mascal, I should suspect from your discourse, you neither knew men nor guns; every gun of mine in the hands of my servants shall kill twice as far as yours; for my own, it is not worth my while to put a ball in it. When I compare with you, the end of a tallow-candle in my gun shall do more execution than an iron ball in the best of yours, with all the skill and experience you pretend to.'

He said I was a Frank, and a liar, and, upon my immediately rising up, he gave me a kick with his foot. I was quite blind with passion, seized him by the throat and threw him on the ground, stout as he was. The Abyssinians know nothing either of wrestling or boxing. He drew his knife as he was falling, attempting to cut me in the face; but his arm not being at freedom, all he could do was to give me a very trifling stab, or wound, near the crown of the head, so that the blood trickled down over my face. I had tript him up, but till then had never struck him. I now wrested the knife from him with a full intention to kill him; but Providence directed better. Instead of the point, I struck so violently with the handle upon his face as to leave scars, which would be distinguished even among the deep marks of the small-pox. An adventure so new, and so unexpected, presently overcame the effects of wine. It was too late to disturb any body either in the palace or at the house of the Ras. A hundred opinions were immediately started; some were for sending us up to the king, as we were actually in the precincts of the palace, where lifting a hand is death. Ayto Heikel advised that I should go, late as it was to Koscam, and Petros, that I should repair immediately to the house of Ayto Aylo, while the Baalomaals were for taking me to sleep in the palace. Anthule, in whose house I was, and who was therefore most shocked at the outrage, wished me to stay in his house, where I was, from a supposition that I was seriously wounded, which all of them, seeing the blood fall over my eyes, seemed to think was the case; and he, in the morning, at the king's rising, was to state the matter as it happened. All these advices appeared good when they were proposed;

for my part, I thought they only tended to make bad worse, and bore the appearance of guilt, of which I was not conscious.

I now determined to go home, and to bed in my own house. With that intention, I washed my face and wound with vinegar, and found the blood to be already staunched. I then wrapt myself up in my cloak and returned home without accident, and went to bed. But this would neither satisfy Ayto Heikel nor Petros, who went to the house of Ayto Aylo, then past midnight, so that early in the morning when scarce light, I saw him come into my chamber. Guebra Mascal had fled to the house of Kefla Yasous his relation; and the first news we heard in the morning after Ayto Aylo arrived, were, that Guebra Mascal was in irons at the Ras's house.

Every person that came afterward brought up some new account; the whole people present had been examined and had given, without variation, the true particulars of my forbearance, and his insolent behaviour. Every body trembled for some violent resolution the Ras was to take on my first complaint. The town was full of Tigre soldiers, and nobody saw clearer than I did, however favourable a turn this had taken for me in the beginning, it might be my destruction in the end.

I asked Ayto Aylo his opinion. He seemed at a loss to give it to me; but said, in an uncertain tone of voice, he could wish that I would not complain of Guebra Mascal while I was angry, or while the Ras was so inveterate against him, till some of his friends had spoken, and appeased, at least, his first resentment. I answered, 'That I was of a contrary opinion, and that no time was to be lost: remember the letter of Mahomet Gibberti; remember his confidence yesterday of my being safe where he was; remember the influence of Ozoro Esther, and do not let us lose a moment.' 'What,' says Aylo to me in great surprise, 'are you mad? Would you have him cut to pieces in the midst of 20,000 of his countrymen? Would you be dimmenia, that is, guilty of the blood of all the province of Tigre, through which you must go in your way home?' 'Just the contrary,' said I; 'nobody has so great a right over the Ras's anger as I have, being the person injured; and, as you and I can get access to Ozoro Esther when we please, let us go immediately thither, and stop the progress of this affair while it is not yet generally known. People that talk of my being wounded expect to see me, I suppose, without a leg or an arm. When they see me so early riding in the street, all will pass for a story as it should do. Would you wish to pardon him entirely?'—'That goes against my heart, too,' says Aylo; 'he is a bad man.'—'My good friend,' said I, 'be in this guided by me; I know we both think the same thing. If he is a bad man, he was a bad man before I knew him. You know what you told me yourself of the Ras's jealousy of him. What if he was to revenge his own wrongs, under pretence of giving me satisfaction for mine? Come, lose no time, get upon your mule, go with me to Ozoro Esther, I will answer for the consequences.'

We arrived there; the Ras was not sitting in judgment; he had drank hard the night before, on occasion of Powussen's marriage, and was not in bed when the story of the fray reached him. We found Ozoro Esther in a violent anger and agitation, which was much alleviated by my laughing. On her asking me about my wound, which had been represented to her as dangerous, 'I am afraid,' said I 'poor Guebra Mascal is worse wounded than I.' 'Is he wounded too?' says she; 'I hope it is in his heart.' 'Indeed,' replied I, 'Madam, there are no wounds on either side. He was very drunk, and I gave him several blows upon the face as he deserved, and he has already got all the chastisement he ought to have; it was all a piece of folly.' 'Prodigious!' says she, 'is this so?' 'It is so,' says Aylo, 'and you shall hear it all by-and-by; only let us stop the propagation of this foolish story.'

The Ras in the instant sent for us. He was naked, sitting on a stool, and a slave swathing up his lame leg with a broad belt or bandage. I asked him, calmly and pleasantly, if I could be of any service to him? He looked at me with a grin, the most ghastly I ever saw, as half displeased. 'What,' says he, 'are you all mad? Aylo, what is the matter between him and that miscreant Guebra Mascal?'—'Why,' said I, 'I am come to tell you that myself; why do you ask Ayto Aylo? Guebra Mascal got drunk, was insolent, and struck me. I was sober and beat him, as you will see by his face; and I have not come to you to say I am sorry that I lifted my hand against your nephew; but he was in the wrong, and drunk; and I thought it was better to chastise him on the spot, than trust him to you, who perhaps might take the affair to heart; for we all know your justice, and that being your relation is no excuse when you judge between man and man.' 'I order you, Aylo,' says Michael, 'as you esteem my friendship to tell me the truth, really as it was, and without disguise or concealment.'

Aylo began accordingly to relate the whole history, when a servant called me out to Ozoro Esther. I found with her another nephew of the Ras, a much better man, called Welleta Selasse, who came from Kefla Yasous, and Guebra Mascal himself, desiring I would forgive and intercede for him, for it was a drunken quarrel without malice. Ozoro Esther had told him part. 'Come in with me,' said I, 'and you shall see I never will leave the Ras till he forgive him.' 'Let him punish him,' says Welleta Selasse; 'he is a bad man, but don't let the Ras either kill or maim him.' 'Come,' said I, 'let us go to the Ras, and he shall neither kill, maim, nor punish him if I can help it. It is my first request; if he refuses me, I will return to Jidda; come and hear.'

Aylo had urged the thing home to the Ras in the proper light—that of my safety. 'You are a wise man,' says Michael, now perfectly cool, as soon as he saw me and Welleta Selasse. 'It is a man like you that goes far in safety, which is the end we all aim at. I feel the affront offered you more than you do, but will not have the punishment attributed to you; this affair shall turn to your honour and security, and in that light only I can pass over his insolence.—Welleta Selasse' says he, falling into a violent passion in an instant, 'what sort of behaviour is this my men have adopted with strangers; and my stranger, too, and in the king's palace, and the king's servant? What! am I dead? or become incapable of governing longer?' Welleta Selasse bowed, but was afraid to speak, and indeed the Ras looked like a fiend.

'Come,' says the Ras, 'let me see your head.' I shewed him where the blood was already hardened, and said it was a very slight cut. 'A cut,' continued Michael, 'over that part, with one of our knives, is mortal.' 'You see, Sir,' said I, 'I have not even clipt the hair about the wound; it is nothing. Now give me your promise you will set Guebra Mascal at liberty; and not only that, but you are not to reproach him with the affair further than that he was drunk, not a crime in this country.' 'No, truly,' says he, 'it is not, but that is, because it is very rare that people fight with knives when they are drunk. I scarce ever heard of it, even in the camp.' 'I fancy,' said I, endeavouring to give a light turn to the conversation, 'they have not often wherewithal to get drunk in your camp.' 'Not this last year,' says he, laughing, 'there were no houses in the country.' 'But let me only merit,' said I, 'Welleta Selasse's friendship, by making him the messenger of good news to Guebra Mascal, that he is at liberty, and you have forgiven him.' 'At liberty!' says he, 'where is he?' 'In your house,' said I, 'somewhere, in irons.' 'That is Esther's intelligence,' continued the Ras; 'these women tell you all their secrets, but when I remember your behaviour to them, I do not wonder at it; and that consideration likewise obliges me to grant what you ask. Go, Welleta Selasse, and free that dog from his collar, and direct him to go to Welleta Michael, who will give him his orders to levy the meery in Woggora; let him not see my face till he returns.'

Ozoro Esther gave us breakfast, to which several of the Greeks came. After which I went to Koscam, where I heard a thousand curses upon Guebra Mascal. The whole affair was now made up, and the king was acquainted with the issue of it. I stood in my place, where he shewed me very great marks of favour; he was grave, however, and sorrowful, as if mortified with what had happened. The king ordered me to stay and dine at the palace, and he would send me my dinner. I there saw the sons of Kasmati Eshte, Aylo and Engedan, and two Welleta Selasses; one the son of Tecla Mariam, the other the son of a great nobleman in Gojam, all young men, with whom I lived ever after in perfect familiarity and friendship. The two last were my brethren Baalomaal, or gentleman of the king's bed-chamber.

They all seemed to have taken my cause to heart more than I wished them to do, for fear it should be productive of some new quarrel. For my own part, I never was so dejected in my life. The troublesome prospect before me presented itself day and night. . . .

I began, however, to look upon every thing now as full of difficulty and danger; and from this constant fretting and despondency, I found my health much impaired, and that I was upon the point of becoming seriously ill. There was one thing that contributed in some measure to dissipate these melancholy thoughts, which was, that all Gondar was in one scene of festivity. Ozoro Ayabdar, daughter of the late Welled Hawaryat, by Ozoro Altash, Ozoro Esther's sister, and the Iteghe's youngest daughter, consequently grand-daughter to Michael, was married to Powussen, now governor of Begemder. The King gave her large districts of land in that province, and Ras Michael a large portion of gold, muskets, cattle and horses. All the town, that wished to be well looked upon by either party, brought something considerable as a present. The Ras, Ozoro Esther, and Ozoro Altash, entertained all Gondar. A vast number of cattle was slaughtered every day, and the whole town looked like one great market; the common people, in every street, appearing loaded with pieces of raw beef, while drink circulated in the same proportion. The Ras insisted upon my dining with him every day, when he was sure to give me a headache with the quantity of mead, or hydromel, he forced me to swallow, a liquor that never agreed with me from the first day to the last.

After dinner we slipt away to parties of ladies, where anarchy prevailed as completely as at the house of the Ras. All the married women ate, drank and smoaked, like the men; and it is impossible to convey to the reader any idea of this bacchanalian scene in terms of common decency. I found it necessary to quit this riot for a short time, and get leave to breathe the fresh air of the country, at such a distance as that, once a day, or once in two days, I might be at the palace, and avoid the constant succession of those violent scenes of debauchery, of which no European can form any idea, and which it was impossible to escape, even at Koscam.

Although the king's favour, the protection of the Ras, and my obliging, attentive and lowly behaviour to every body, had made me as popular as I could wish at Gondar, and among the Tigrans fully as much as those of Amhara, yet it was easy to perceive, that the cause of my quarrel with Guebra Mascal was not yet forgot.

One day, when I was standing by the king in the palace, he asked, in discourse, 'Whether I, too, was not drunk in the quarrel with Guebra Mascal, before we came to blows?' and, upon my saying that I was perfectly sober, both before and after, because Anthule's red wine was finished, and I never willingly drank hydromel, or mead, he asked me with a degree of keenness, 'Did you then soberly say to Guebra Mascal, that an end of a tallow candle, in a gun in your hand, would do more execution than an iron bullet in his?'—'Certainly, Sir, I did so.'—'And why did you say this?' says the king dryly enough, and in a manner I had not before observed. 'Because,' replied I, 'it was truth, and a proper reproof to a vain man, who, whatever eminence he might have obtained in a country like this, has not knowledge enough to entitle him to the trust of cleaning a gun in mine.' 'O, ho!' continued the king; 'as for his knowledge, I am not speaking of that, but about his gun. You will not persuade me, that, with a tallow candle, you can kill a man or a horse?'—'Pardon me, Sir,' said I, bowing very respectfully, 'I will attempt to persuade you of nothing but what you please to be convinced of: Guebra Mascal is my equal, no more; you are my master, and, while I am at your court, under your protection, you are in place of my sovereign; it would be great presumption in me to argue with you, or lead to a conversation against an opinion that you profess you are already fixed in.'—'No, no,' says he, with an air of great kindness, 'by no means; I was only afraid you would expose yourself before bad people; what you say to me is nothing.'—'And what I say to you, Sir, has always been as scrupulously true, as if I had been speaking to the king, my native sovereign and master. Whether I can kill a man with a candle, or not, is an experiment that should not be made. Tell me, however, what I shall do before you, that you may deem an equivalent? Will piercing the table, upon which your dinner is served (it was of sycamore, about three quarters of an inch thick), at the length of this room, be deemed a sufficient proof of what I advance?'

'Ah, Yagoube, Yagoube,' says the king, 'take care what you say. That is indeed more than Guebra Mascal will do at that distance; but take great care; you don't know these people; they will lie themselves all day; nay, their whole life is one lie; but of you they expect better, or would be glad to find worse; take care.' Ayto Engedan, who was then present, said, 'I am sure if Yagoube says he can do it, he will do it, but how, I don't know. Can you shoot through my shield with a tallow candle?'—'To you, Ayto Engedan,' said I, 'I can speak freely; I could shoot through your shield if it was the strongest in the army, and kill the strongest man in the army that held it before him. When will you see this tried?'—'Why now,' says the king; 'there is *nobody here*.'—'The sooner the better,' said I; 'I would not wish to remain for a moment longer under so disagreeable an imputation as that of lying, an infamous one in *my* country, whatever it may be in this. Let me send for my gun; the king will look out at the window.'—'*Nobody*,' says he, 'knows any thing of it; *nobody will come*.'

The king appeared to be very anxious, and I saw plainly, incredulous. The gun was brought; Engedan's shield was produced, which was of a strong buffalo's hide. I said to him, 'This is a weak one, give me one stronger.' He shook his head, and said, 'Ah, Yagoube, you'll find it strong enough; Engedan's shield is known to be no toy.' Tecla Mariam brought such a shield, and the Billetana Gueta Tecla another, both of which were most excellent in their kind. I loaded the gun before them, first with powder, then upon it slid down one half of what we call a farthing candle; and, having beat off the handles of three shields, I put them close in contact with each other, and set them all three against a post.

'Now, Engedan,' said I, 'when you please say—Fire! but mind you have taken leave of your good shield for ever.' The word was given and the gun fired. It struck the three shields, neither in the most difficult nor the easiest part for perforation, something less than half-way between the rim and the boss. The candle went through the three shields with such violence, that it dashed itself to a thousand pieces against a stone wall behind it. I turned to Engedan, saying very lowly, gravely, and without exultation or triumph, on the contrary with absolute indifference, 'Did not I tell you your shield was naught?' A great shout of applause followed from about a thousand people that were gathered together. The three shields were carried to the king, who exclaimed in great transport, 'I did not believe it before I saw it, and I can scarcely believe it now I have seen it! Where is Guebra Mascal's confidence now? But what do either he or we know? We know nothing.' I thought he looked abashed.

'Ayto Engedan,' said I, 'we must have a touch at that table. It was said, the piercing that was more than Guebra Mascal could do. We have one half of the candle left still; it is the thinnest, weakest half, and I shall put the wick foremost, because the cotton is softest.' The table being now properly placed, to Engedan's utmost astonishment, the candle, with the wick foremost, went through the table, as the other had gone through the three shields. 'By St. Michael!' says Engedan, 'Yagoube, hereafter say to me you can raise my father Eshte from the grave, and I will believe you.' Some priests who were there, though surprised at first, seemed afterwards to treat it rather lightly, because they thought it below their dignity to be surprised at any thing. They said it was done by writing (mucktoub), by which they meant magic. Every body embraced that opinion, as an evident and rational one, and so the wonder with them ceased. But it was not so with the king: it made the most favourable and lasting impression upon his mind; nor did I ever after see, in his countenance, any marks either of doubt or diffidence, but always, on the contrary, the most decisive proofs of friendship, confidence, and attention, and the most implicit belief of every thing I advanced upon any subject from my own knowledge.

The experiment was twice tried afterwards, in presence of Ras Michael. But he would not risk his good shields, and always produced the table, saying 'Engedan and these foolish boys were rightly served; they thought Yagoube was a liar like themselves, and they lost their shields, but I believed him, and gave him my table for curiosity only, and so I saved mine.'

Travels to discover the source of the Nile,
2nd edition, vol. IV, pp. 413–32

After many adventures and campaigns with the Ras and the King, during which he developed his friendship with Ozoro Esther, Bruce at last obtained permission to attempt the accomplishment of his one great object, the discovery of the source of the Nile. This was, of course, the Blue Nile, as the extent of the White Nile was then unknown. The King actually endowed him with the lordship of Gheesh, where the springs rose. He was unable to approach the place, however, except by favour of Fasil, the Galla chief who dominated the region. In spite of intrigues against the expedition by Abba Salama, Bruce won Fasil over by his feats of horsemanship and the chief gave him his own horse to drive before him, saddled and bridled, as a surety of his favour and protection. To reach Gheesh Bruce had to go through the country of the wild Agow people and he was therefore provided with an Agow, Woldo, as his guide and seven Galla chiefs. Strates, one of the Greeks resident in Ethiopia, also accompanied him. The narrative opens when the party came within sight of their goal.

2. FINDING THE SOURCE OF THE BLUE NILE

At three quarters after one we arrived at the top of the mountain, whence we had a distinct view of all the remaining territory of Sacala, the mountain of Geesh, and church of St Michael Gheesh, about a mile and a half distant from St Michael Sacala, where we then were. We saw, immediately below us, the Nile itself, strangely diminished in size, and now only a brook that had scarcely water to turn a mill. I could not satiate myself with the sight, revolving in my mind all those classical prophecies that had given the Nile up to perpetual obscurity and concealment. . . .

I was awakened out of this delightful reverie by an alarm that we had lost Woldo our guide. Though I long had expected something from his behaviour, I did not think, for his own sake, it could be his intention to leave us. The servants could not agree when they last saw him: Strates and Aylo's servant were in the wood shooting, and we found by the gun that they were not far from us; I was therefore in hopes that Woldo, though not at all fond of fire-arms, might be in their company; but it was with great dissatisfaction I saw them appear without him. They said, that, about an hour before, they had seen some extraordinary large, rough apes, or monkeys, several of which were walking upright, and all without tails; that they had gone after them through the wood till they could scarce get out again; but they did not remember to have seen Woldo at parting. Various conjectures immediately followed; some thought he had resolved to betray and rob us; some conceived it was an instruction of Fasil's to him, in order to our being treacherously murdered; some again supposed he was slain by the wild beasts, especially those apes or baboons, whose voracity, size and fierce appearance were exceedingly magnified, especially by Strates, who had not the least doubt, if Woldo met them, but that he would be so entirely devoured, that we might seek in vain without discovering even a fragment of him. For my part, I began to think that he had been really ill when he first complained, and that the sickness might have overcome him upon the road; and this, too, was the opinion of Ayto Aylo's servant, who said, however, with a significant look, that he could not be far off; we therefore sent him, and one of the men that drove the mules, back to seek after him; and they had not gone but a few hundred yards when they found him coming, but so decrepid, and so very ill, that he said he could go no farther than the church, where he was positively resolved to take up his abode that night. I felt his pulse, examined every part about him, and saw, I thought evidently, that nothing ailed him. Without losing my temper, however, I told him firmly, that I perceived he was an impostor, that he should consider that I was a physician, as he knew I cured his master's first friend, Welleta Yasous; that the feeling of his hand told me as plain as his tongue could have done, that nothing ailed him; that it told me likewise that he had in heart some prank to play, which would turn out very much to his disadvantage. He seemed dismayed after this, said little, and only desired us to halt for a few minutes, and he should be better; 'for,' says he, 'it requires strength in us all to pass another great hill before we arrive at Geesh.'

'Look you,' said I, 'lying is to no purpose; I know where Geesh is as well as you do, and that we have no more mountains or bad places to pass through; therefore, if you choose to stay behind, you may; but tomorrow I shall inform Welleta Yasous at Bure of your behaviour.' I said this with the most determined air possible, and left them, walking as hard as I could down to the ford of the Nile. Woldo remained above with the servants, who were loading their mules; he seemed to be perfectly cured of his lameness, and was in close conversation with Ayto

Aylo's servant for about ten minutes, which I did not choose to interrupt, as I saw that man was already in possession of part of Woldo's secret. This being over they all came down to me, as I was sketching a branch of a yellow rose-tree, a number of which hang over the ford.

The whole company passed without disturbing me; and Woldo, seeming to walk as fast as ever, ascended a gentle rising hill, near the top of which is St. Michael Geesh. The Nile here is not four yards over, and above four inches deep where we crossed; it was indeed become a very trifling brook, but ran swiftly over a bottom of small stones, with hard black rock appearing amongst them: it is at this place very easy to pass, and very limpid, but, a little lower, full of inconsiderable falls; the ground rises gently from the river to the southward, full of small hills and eminences, which you ascend and descend almost imperceptibly. The whole company had halted on the north side of St. Michael's church, and there I reached them, without affecting any hurry.

It was about four o'clock in the afternoon, but the day had been very hot for some hours, and they were sitting in the shade of a grove of magnificent cedars, intermixed with some very large and beautiful cusso trees, all in flower; the men were lying on the grass, and the beasts fed, with their burdens on their backs in most luxuriant herbage. I called for my herbary, to lay the rose-branch I had in my hand smoothly, that it might dry without spoiling the shape; having only drawn its general form, the pistil and stamina, the finer parts of which (though very necessary in classing the plant) crumble and fall off, or take different forms in drying, and therefore should always be secured by drawing while green. I just said indifferently to Woldo in passing, that I was glad to see him recovered; that he would presently be well, and should fear nothing. He then got up, and desired to speak with me alone, taking Aylo's servant along with him. 'Now,' said I, very calmly, 'I know by your face you are going to tell me a lie. I do swear to you solemnly, you never, by that means, will obtain anything from me, no not so much as a good word; truth and good behaviour will get you everything; what appears a great matter in your sight, is not perhaps of such value in mine: but nothing except the truth and good behaviour will answer to you; now I know for a certainty you are no more sick than I am.' 'Sir,' said he, with a very confident look, 'you are right; I did counterfeit; I neither have been, nor am I at present, any way out of order; but I thought it best to tell you so, not to be obliged to discover another reason, that has much more weight with me, why I cannot go to Geesh, and much less show myself at the sources of the Nile, which I confess are not much beyond it, though I declare to you there is still a *hill* between you and those sources.' 'And pray,' said I calmly, 'what is this mighty reason? have you had a dream, or a vision in that trance you fell into when you lagged behind, below the church of St Michael Sacala?'

'No,' says he, 'it is neither trance, nor dream, nor devil either; I wish it were no worse; but you know as well as I, that my master Fasil defeated the Agows at the battle of Banja. I was there with my master, and killed several men, among whom some were of the Agows of this village Geesh; and you know the usage of this country; when a man, in these circumstances, falls into their hands, his blood must pay for their blood.'

I burst into a violent fit of laughter which very much disconcerted him. 'There,' said I, 'did not I say to you it was a lie you was going to tell me? do not think I disbelieve or dispute with you the vanity of having killed men; many men were slain at that battle; somebody must, and you may have been the person who slew them; but do you think that I can believe that Fasil, so deep in that account of blood, could rule the Agows in the manner he does, if he could not put a servant of his in safety among them, twenty miles from his residence? do you think I can believe this?' 'Come, come,' said Aylo's servant to Woldo, 'did you not hear the truth and good behaviour will get you everything you ask? Sir,' continues he, 'I see this affair vexes you, and what this foolish man wants will neither make you richer nor poorer; he has taken a great fancy for that crimson silk-sash which you wear about your middle. I told him to stay till you sent back to Gondar, but he says he is to go no farther than to the house of Shalaka Welled Amlac in Maitsha, and does not return to Gondar; I told him to stay till you had put your mind at ease, by seeing the fountains of the Nile which you were so anxious about. He said, after that had happened, he was sure you would not give it him, for you seemed to think little of the cataract at Goutto, and of all the rivers and churches which he had shown you; except the head of the Nile shall be finer than all these, when, in reality, it will be just like another river, you will then be dissatisfied, and not give him the sash.'

I thought there was something very natural in these suspicions of Woldo; besides, he said he was certain that, if ever the sash came into the sight of Welled Amlac, by some means or other he would get it into his hands. This rational discourse had pacified me a little; the sash was a handsome one; but it must have been fine indeed to have stood for a minute between me and the accomplishment of my wishes. I laid my hand then upon the pistols that stuck in my girdle, and drew them out to give them to one of my suite, when Woldo, who apprehended it was for another purpose, ran some paces back, and hid himself behind Aylo's servant. We were all diverted at this fright, but none so much as Strates, who thought himself revenged for the alarm he had given him, by falling through the roof of the house at Goutto. After having taken off my sash, 'Here is your sash, Woldo,' said I, 'but mark what I have said, and now most seriously repeat to you, truth and good behaviour will get anything from me; but if, in the course of this journey, you play one trick more, though ever so trifling I will bring such a vengeance upon your head, that you shall not be able to find a place to hide it in, when not the sash only will be taken from you, but your skin also will follow it: remember what happened to the Seis at Bamba.'

He took the sash, but seemed terrified at the threat, and began to make apologies. 'Come, come,' said I, 'we understand each other; no more words; it is now late; lose no more time, but carry me to Geesh, and the head of the Nile, directly, without preamble, and show me the hill that separates me from it.' He then carried me round to the south side of the church, out of the grove of trees that surrounded it. 'This is the hill,' says he, looking archly, 'that, when you was on the other side of it, was between you and the fountains of the Nile; there is no other. Look at that hillock of green sod in the middle of that watery spot; it is in that the two fountains of the Nile are to be found: Geesh is on the face of the rock where yon green trees are. If you go the length of the fountains, pull off your shoes, as you did the other day, for these people are all Pagans, worse than those that were at the ford; and they believe in nothing that you believe, but only in this river, to which they pray every day, as if it were God; but this perhaps you may do likewise.' Half undressed as I was by loss of my sash, and throwing my shoes off, I ran down the hill, towards the little island of green sods, which was about two hundred yards distant; the whole side of the hill was thick grown over with flowers, the large bulbous roots of which appearing above the surface of the ground, and their skins coming off on treading upon them, occasioned me two very severe falls before I reached the brink of the marsh; I after this came to the island of green turf, which was in form of an altar, apparently the work of art, and I stood in rapture over the principal fountain which rises in the middle of it.

It is easier to guess than to describe the situation of my mind at that moment—standing in that spot which had baffled the genius, industry and inquiry of both ancients and moderns, for the course of near three thousand years. Kings had attempted this discovery at the head of armies and each expedition was distinguished from the last, only by the difference of the numbers which had perished, and agreed alone in the disappointment which had uniformly and without exception, followed them all. Fame, riches and honour, had been held out for a series of ages to every individual of those myriads these princes commanded, without having produced one man capable of gratifying the curiosity of his sovereign, or wiping off this stain upon the enterprise and abilities of mankind, or adding this desideratum for the encouragement of geography. Though a mere private Briton, I triumphed here, in my own mind, over kings and their armies; and every comparison was leading nearer and nearer to presumption, when the place itself where I stood, the object of my vain-glory, suggested what depressed my short-lived triumph. I was but a few minutes arrived at the sources of the Nile, through numberless dangers and sufferings, the least of which would have overwhelmed me, but for the continual goodness and protection of Providence; I was, however, but then half through my journey, and all those dangers which I had already passed, awaited me again on my return. I found a despondency gaining ground fast upon me, and blasting the crown of laurels I had too rashly woven for myself. I resolved, therefore, to divert, till I could, on more solid reflection, overcome its progress.

I saw Strates expecting me on the side of the hill. 'Strates,' said I, 'faithful squire! come and triumph with your Don Quixote, at the island Barataria, where we have most wisely and fortunately brought ourselves! come and triumph with me over all the kings of the earth, all their armies, all their philosophers, and all their heroes!' 'Sir,' says Strates, 'I do not understand a word of what you say, and as little what you mean: you very well know I am no scholar. But you had much better leave that bog; come into the house and look after Woldo; I fear he has something further to seek than your sash, for he has been talking with the old devil-worshipper ever since we arrived.' 'Did they speak secretly together,' said I. 'Yes, sir, they did, I assure you.' 'And in whispers, Strates!' 'Every syllable; but for that,' replied he, 'they need not have been at the pains; they understand one another I suppose, and the devil, their master, understands them both; but as for me, I comprehend their discourse no more than if it was Greek, as they say. Greek!' says he, 'I am an ass; I should know well enough what they said if they spoke Greek.' 'Come,' said I, 'take a draught of this excellent water, and drink with me a health to his majesty King George III and a long line of princes.' I had in my hand a large cup made of cocoanut shell, which I procured in Arabia, and which was brim-full. He drank to the king speedily and cheerfully, with the addition of, 'Confusion to his enemies,' and tossed up his cap with a loud huzza. 'Now, friend,' said I, 'here is to a more humble, but still a sacred name, here is to—Maria!' He asked if that was the Virgin Mary? I answered, 'In faith, I believe so, Strates.' He did not speak, but only gave a humph of disapprobation.

The day had been very hot, and the altercation I had with Woldo had occasioned me to speak so much, that my thirst, without any help from curiosity, led me to these frequent libations at this long-sought-for spring, the most ancient of all altars. 'Strates,' said I, 'here is to our happy return. Come, friend, you are yet two toasts behind me; can you ever be satiated with this excellent water?' 'Look you, sir,' says he very gravely, 'as for King George, I drank to him with all my heart, to his children, to his brothers and sisters, God bless them all! Amen;—but as for the Virgin Mary, as I am no Papist, I beg to be excused from drinking healths which my church does not drink. As for our happy return, God knows, there is no one wishes it more sincerely than I do, for I have been long weary of this beggarly country. But you must forgive me if I refuse to drink any more water. They say these savages pray over that hole every morning to the devil, and I am afraid I feel his horns in my belly already, from the great draught of that hellish water I drank first.' It was, indeed, as cold water as ever I tasted. 'Come, come,' said I, 'don't be peevish, I have but one toast more to drink.' 'Peevish or not peevish,' replied Strates, 'a drop of it never again shall cross my throat: there is no humour in this, no joke, show us something pleasant as you used to do; but there is no jest in meddling with devil-worshippers, witchcraft, and inchantments to bring some disease upon one's self here, so far from home in the fields. No, no; as many toasts in wine as you please, or better in brandy, but no more water for Strates. I am sure I have done myself harm already with these follies—God forgive me!' 'Then,' said I, 'I will drink it alone, and you are henceforward unworthy of the name of Greek; you do not even deserve that of a Christian.' Holding the full cup then to my head 'Here is to Catharine, empress of all the Russias, and success to her heroes at Paros; and hear my prediction from this altar to-day; Ages shall not pass, before this ground, whereon I now stand, shall become a flourishing part of her dominions.'

He leaped on this a yard from the ground. 'If the old gentleman has whispered you this,' says he, 'out of the well, he has not kept you long waiting; tell truth and shame the devil, is indeed the proverb, but truth is truth, wherever it comes from, give me the cup; I will drink that health though I should die.' He then held out both his hands. 'Strates,' said I, 'be in no such haste; remember the water is inchanted by devil-worshippers: there is no jesting with these, and you are far from home, and in the fields, you may catch some disease, especially if you drink the Virgin Mary; God forgive you. Remember the horn the first draught produced; they may with this come entirely through and through.' 'The cup, the cup,' says he 'and fill it full; I defy the devil and trust in St. George and the dragon. Here is to Catharine, empress of all the Russias; confusion to her enemies, and damnation to all at Paros.' 'Well, friend,' said I 'youwas long in resolving, but you have done it at last to some purpose; I am sure I did not drink damnation to all at Paros.' 'Ah!' says he, 'but I did and will do it again—Damnation to all at Paros, and Cyprus, and Rhodes, Crete, and Mytilene into the bargain: Here it goes with all my heart. Amen, so be it.' 'And who do you think,' said I, 'are at Paros?' 'Pray, who should be there,' says he, 'but Turks and devils, the worst race of monsters and oppressors in the Levant. I have been at Paros myself; was you ever there?' 'Whether I was ever there or not, is no matter,' said I; 'the empress's fleet, and an army of Russians, are now possibly there; and here you, without provocation, have drank damnation to the Russian fleet and army, who have come so far from home, and are at this moment sword in hand, to restore you to your liberty, and the free exercise of your religion; did not I tell you, you was no Greek, and scarcely deserved the name of Christian?' 'No, no sir,' cries Strates, 'for God's sake do not say so; I would rather die. I did not understand you about Paros; there was no malice in my heart against the Russians. God will bless them and my folly can do them no harm—Huzza! Catharine and victory!' whilst he tossed his cap into the air.

A number of the Agows had appeared upon the hill, just before the valley, in silent wonder what Strates and I were doing at the altar. Two or three only had come down to the edge of the swamp, had seen the grimaces and action of Strates, and heard him huzza; on which they had asked Woldo, as he entered into the village, what was the meaning of all this? Woldo told them, that the man was out of his senses, and had been bit by a mad dog; which reconciled them immediately to us. They, moreover, said he would be infallibly cured by the Nile; but the custom, after meeting with such a misfortune, was to drink the water in the morning fasting. I was very well pleased both with this turn Woldo gave the action, and the remedy we stumbled upon by mere accident which discovered a connection, believed to subsist at this day, between this river and its ancient governor the dog star.

. . . . . .

The night of the 4th, that very night of my arrival, melancholy reflections upon my present state, the doubtfulness of my return in safety, were I permitted to make the attempt, and the fears that even this would be refused, according to the rule observed in Abyssinia with all travellers who have once entered the kingdom; the consciousness of the pain that I was then occasioning to many worthy individuals, expecting daily that information concerning my situation which it was not in my power to give them; some other thoughts, perhaps, still nearer the heart than those, crowded upon my mind, and forbade all approach of sleep.

I was at that very moment, in possession of what had, for many years, been the principal object of my ambition and wishes: indifference, which, from the usual infirmity of human nature, follows, at least for a time, complete enjoyment, had taken place of it. The marsh, and the fountains, upon comparison with the rise of many of our rivers, became now a trifling object in my sight. I remember that magnificent scene in my own native country, where the Tweed, Clyde, and Annan rise, in one hill; three rivers, as I now thought, not inferior to the Nile in beauty, preferable to it in the cultivation of those countries through which they flow; superior, vastly superior to it in the virtues and qualities of the inhabitants, and in the beauty of its flocks crowding its pastures in peace, without fear of violence from man or beast. I had seen the rise of the Rhine and Rhone, and the more magnificent sources of the Saone;

I began, in my sorrow, to treat the inquiry about the source of the Nile as a violent effort of a distempered fancy:—

> What's Hecuba to him, or he to Hecuba,
> That he should weep for her?—

Grief or despondency, now rolling upon me like a torrent; relaxed, not refreshed, by unquiet and imperfect sleep, I started from my bed in the utmost agony; I went to the door of my tent; everything was still; the Nile at whose head I stood, was not capable either to promote or to interrupt my slumbers, but the coolness and serenity of the night braced my nerves, and chased away those phantoms that, while in bed, had oppressed and tormented me.

It was true, that numerous dangers, hardships, and sorrows, had beset me through this half of my excursion; but it was still as true that another Guide, more powerful than my own courage, health or understanding, if any of these can be called man's own, had uniformly protected me in all that tedious half; I found my confidence not abated, that still the same Guide was able to conduct me to my now wished for home: I immediately resumed my former fortitude considering the Nile indeed as no more than rising from springs, as all other rivers do, but widely different in this, that it was the palm for three thousand years held out to all the nations in the world as a *detur dignissimo*, which, in my cool hours, I had thought was worth the attempting at the risk of my life which I had long resolved to lose, or lay this discovery, a trophy in which I could have no competitor, for the honour of my country, at the feet of my sovereign, whose servant I was.

Travels to discover the source of the Nile,
2nd edition, vol. v, pp. 262–74, 309–11

Bruce returned from this expedition to join the king as he was marching upon Gondar, intent to revenge himself upon those who had supported an attempt to oust Ras Michael and to set up a rival king.

3. PUNISHMENT FOR REBELLION

As for me, the king's behaviour shewed me plainly all was not right, and an accident in the way confirmed it. He had desired me to ride before him, and shew him the horse I had got from Fasil, which was then in great beauty and order, and which I had kept purposely for him. It happened that, crossing the deep bed of a brook, a plant of the kantuffa hung across it. I had upon my shoulders a white goat-skin, of which it did not take hold; but the king, who was dressed in the habit of peace, his long hair floating all around his face, wrapt up in his mantle, or thin cotton cloak, so that nothing but his eyes could be seen, was paying more attention to the horse than to the branch of kantuffa beside him; it took the first hold of his hair, and the fold of the cloak that covered his head, then spread itself over his whole shoulder in such a manner, that, notwithstanding all the help that could be given him, and that I had, at first seeing it, cut the principal bough asunder with my knife, no remedy remained but he must throw off the upper garment, and appear in the under one, or waistcoat, with his head and face bare before all the spectators.

This is accounted great disgrace to a king, who always appears covered in public. However, he did not seem to be ruffled, nor was there any thing particular in his countenance more than before, but with great composure, and in rather a low voice, he called twice, 'Who is the Shum of this district?' Unhappily he was not far off. A thin old man of sixty, and his son about thirty, came trotting, as their custom is, naked to their girdle, and stood before the king, who was, by this time, quite cloathed again. What had struck the old man's fancy, I know not, but he passed my horse laughing, and seemingly wonderfully content with himself. I could not help considering him as a type of mankind in general, never more confident and careless than when on the brink of destruction. The king asked if he was Shum of that place? He answered in the affirmative, and added, which was not asked of him, that the other was his son.

There is always near the king, when he marches, an officer called Kanitz Kitzera, the executioner of the camp; he has upon the tore of his saddle a quantity of thongs made of bull hide, rolled up very artificially; this is called the tarade. The king made a sign with his head, and another with his hand, without speaking; and two loops of the tarade were instantly thrown round the Shum and his son's neck, and they were both hoisted upon the same tree, the tarade cut and the end made fast to a branch. They were both left hanging, but I thought so aukwardly, that they would not die for some minutes, and might surely have been saved had any one dared to cut them down; but fear had fallen upon every person who had not attended the king to Tigre.

This cruel beginning seemed to me an omen that violent resolutions had been taken, the execution of which was immediately to follow; for though the king had certainly a delight in the shedding of human blood in the field, yet till that time I never saw him order an execution by the hands of the hangman; on the contrary, I have often seen him shudder and express disgust, lowly and in half words, at such executions ordered every day by Ras Michael. In this instance he seemed to have lost that feeling; and rode on, sometimes conversing about Fasil's horse, or other indifferent subjects, to those who were around him, without once reflecting upon the horrid execution he had then so recently occasioned.

In the evening of the 23d, when encamped upon Mogetch, came Sanuda, the person who had made Socinios King, and who had been Ras under him; he was received with great marks of favour, in reward of the treacherous part he had acted. He brought with him prisoners, Guebra Denghel, the Ras's son-in-law, one of the best and most amiable men in Abyssinia, but who had unfortunately embraced the wrong side of the question; and with him Sebaat Laab and Kefla Mariam, both men of great families in Tigre. These were, one after the other, thrown violently on their faces before the king. I was exceedingly distressed for Guebra Denghel; he prayed the king, with the greatest earnestness, to order him to be put to death before the door of his tent, and not delivered to his cruel father-in-law. To this the king made no answer nor did he shew any signs of pity, but waved his hand, as a sign to carry them to Ras Michael, where they were put in custody and loaded with irons.

About two hours later came Ayto Aylo, son of Kasmati Eshte, whom the king had named governor of Begemder; he brought with him Chremation, brother to Socinios, and Abba Salama the Acab Saat, who had excommunicated his father, and been instrumental in his murder by Fasil. I had a great curiosity to see how they would treat the Acab Saat; for my head was full of what I had read in the European books, of exemption that churchmen had in this country from the jurisdiction of the civil power.

Aylo had made his legs to be tied under the mule's belly, his hands behind his back, and a rope made fast to them, which a man held in his hand on one side, while another led the halter of the mule on the other, both of them with lances in their hands. Chremation had his hands bound, but his legs were not tied, nor was there any rope made fast to his hands by which he was held. While they were untying Abba Salama, I went into the presence-chamber, and stood behind the king's chair. Very soon after, Aylo's men brought in their prisoners, and, as is usual, threw them down violently with their faces to the ground; their hands being bound behind them, they had a very rude fall upon their faces.

The Acab Saat rose in a violent passion; he struggled to get loose his hands, that he might be free to use the act of denouncing excommunication, which is by lifting the right hand, and extending the fore-finger; finding that impossible, he cried out, 'Unloose my hands, or you are all excommunicated.' It was with difficulty he could be prevailed upon to hear the king, who with great composure, or rather indifference said to him, 'You are the first ecclesiastical officer in my household, you are the third in the whole kingdom; but I have not yet learned you ever had power to curse your sovereign, or exhort his subjects to murder him.

You are to be tried for this crime by the judges to-morrow, so prepare to shew in your defence, upon what precepts of Christ, or his apostles, or upon what part of the general councils, you found your title to do this.'

'Let my hands be unloosed,' cried Salama violently; 'I am a priest, a servant of God; and they have power, says David, to put kings in chains, and nobles in irons And did not Samuel hew king Agag to pieces before the Lord? I excommunicate you, Tecla Haimanout.' And he was going on, when Tecla Mariam, son of the king's secretary, a young man, struck the Acab Saat so violently on the face, that it made his mouth gush out with blood, saying, at the same time, 'What! suffer this in the king's presence?' Upon which both Chremation and the Acab Saat were hurried out of the tent without being suffered to say more; indeed the blow seemed to have so much disconcerted Abba Salama, that it deprived him for a time of the power of speaking.

In Abyssinia it is death to strike, or lift the hand to strike, before the king; but in this case the provocation was so great, so sudden, and unexpected, and the youth's worth and the insolence of the offender so apparent to every body, that a slight reproof was ordered to be given to Tecla Mariam (by his father only); but he lost no favour for what he had done, either with the King, Michael, or the people. . . .

There was at Gondar a sort of mummers, being a mixture of buffoons and ballad-singers, and posture-masters. These people, upon all public occasions, run about the streets; and on private ones, such as marriages, come to the court-yards before the houses, where they dance, and sing songs of their own composing in honour of the day, and perform all sorts of antics; many a time, on his return from the field with victory, they had met Ras Michael, and received his bounty for singing his praises, and welcoming him upon his return home. The day the Abuna excommunicated the king, this set of vagrants made part of the solemnity; they abused, ridiculed and traduced Michael in lampoons and scurrilous rhymes, calling him crooked, lame, old, and impotent, and several other opprobrious names, which did not affect him nearly so much as the ridicule of his person: upon many occasions after, they repeated this, and particularly in a song they ridiculed the horse of Sire, who had run away at the battle of Limjour, where Michael cried out, 'Send these horse to the mill.' It happened that these wretches, men and women, to the number of about thirty and upwards, were then, with very different songs, celebrating Ras Michael's return to Gondar. The King and Ras, after the proclamation, had just turned to the right to Aylo Meidan, below the palace, a large field where the troops exercise. Confu and the king's household troops were before, and about 200 of the Sire horse were behind; on a signal made by the Ras, these horse turned short and fell upon the singers, and cut them all to pieces. In less than two minutes they were all laid dead upon the field, excepting one young man, who, mortally wounded, had just strength enough to arrive within twenty yards of the king's horse, and there fell dead without speaking a word.

All the people present, most of them veteran soldiers, and consequently inured to blood, appeared shocked and disgusted at this wanton piece of cruelty. For my part, a kind of faintishness, or feebleness, had taken possession of my heart, ever since the execution of the two men on our march, about the kantuffa; and this second act of cruelty occasioned such a horror, joined with an absence of mind, that I found myself unable to give an immediate answer, though the king had spoken twice to me.

It was about nine o'clock in the morning when we entered Gondar; every person we met on the street wore the countenance of a condemned malefactor; the Ras went immediately to the palace with the king, who retired, as usual, to a kind of cage or lattice-window, where he always sits unseen when in council. We were then in the council-chamber, and four of the judges seated; none of the governors of provinces were present but Ras Michael, and Kasmati Tesfos of Sire. Abba Salama was brought to the foot of the table without irons, at perfect liberty. The accuser for the king (it is a post in this country in no great estimation) began the charge against him with great force and eloquence. He stated, one by one, the crimes committed by him at different periods; the sum of which amounted to prove Salama to be the greatest monster upon earth; among these were various kinds of murder, especially by poison; incest, with every degree collateral and descendant. He concluded this black, horrid list, with the charge of high treason, or cursing the king, and absolving his subjects from their allegiance, which he stated as the greatest crime human nature was capable of, as involving in its consequences, all sorts of other crimes. Abba Salama, though he seemed under very great impatience, did not often interrupt him, further than, 'You lie,' and, 'It is a lie,' which he repeated at every new charge. His accuser had not said one word of the murder of Joas, but passed it over without the smallest allusion to it.

In this, however, Abba Salama did not follow his example. Being desired to answer in his own defence, he entered upon it with great dignity, and an air of superiority, very different from his behaviour in the king's tent the day before: he laughed, and made extremely light of the charges on the article of women, which he neither confessed nor denied; but said these might be crimes among the Franks (looking at me) or other Christians, but not the Christians of that country, who lived under a double dispensation, the law of Moses and the law of Christ; he said the Abyssinians were *Beni Israel*, as indeed they call themselves, that is, children of Israel; and that, in every age, the patriarchs had acted as he did, and were not less beloved of God. He went roundly into the murder of Joas, and of his two brothers, Adigo and Aylo, on the mountain of Wechne, and charged Michael directly with it, as also with the poisoning the late Hatze Hannes, father of the present king.

The Ras seemed to avoid hearing, sometimes by speaking to people standing behind him, sometimes by reading a paper; in particular, he asked me, standing directly behind his chair, in a low voice, 'What is the punishment in your country for such a crime?' It was his custom to speak to me in his own language of Tigre, and one of his greatest pastimes to laugh at my faulty expression. He spoke this to me in Amharic, so I knew he wanted my answer should be understood: I therefore said, in the same low tone of voice he had spoke to me, 'High treason is punished with death in all the countries I have ever known.'—This I owed to Abba Salama, and it was not long before I had my return.

Abba Salama next went into the murder of Kasmati Eshte, which he confessed he was the promoter of. He said the Iteghe, with her brothers and Ayto Aylo, had all turned Franks, so had Gusho of Amhara; and that, in order to make the country Catholic, they had sent for priests, who lived with them in confidence, as that Frank did, pointing to me: that it was against the law of the country that I should be suffered here; that I was accursed, and should be stoned as an enemy to the Virgin Mary. There the Ras interrupted him, by saying, 'Confine yourself to your own defence; clear yourself first, and then accuse any one you please: it is the king's intention to put the law in execution against all offenders, and it is only as believing you the greatest, that he has begun with you.'

This calmness of the Ras seemed to disconcert the Acab Saat; he lost all method; he warned the Ras, that it was owing to his excommunicating Kasmati Eshte that room was made for him to come to Gondar, without that event, this king would never have been upon the throne; so that he had still done them as much good by his excommunications as he had done them harm. He told the Ras, and the judges, that they were all doubly under a curse, if they offered either to pull out his eyes, or cut out his tongue; and prayed them, bursting into tears, not so much as to think of either, if it was only for old fellowship, or friendship, which had long subsisted between them.

There is an officer, named Kal Hatze, who stands always upon steps at the side of the lattice-window, where there is a hole covered in the inside with a curtain of green taffeta; behind this curtain the king sits, and through this hole he sends what he has to say to the Board, who rise, and receive the messenger standing. He had not interfered till now, when the officer said, addressing himself to Abba Salama, 'The king requires of you to answer directly, why you persuaded the Abuna to excommunicate him? The Abuna is a slave of the Turks, and has no king; you are born under a monarchy; why did you, who are his inferior in office, take upon you to advise him at all? or why, after having presumed to advise him, did you advise him wrong, and abuse his ignorance in these matters?' This question, which was a home one, made him lose all his temper; he cursed the Abuna, called him Mahometan, Pagan, Frank, and Infidel; and was going on in this wild manner, when Tecla Haimanout, the eldest of the judges, got up, and addressing himself to the Ras, 'It is no part of my duty to hear all this railing; he has not so much as offered one fact material to his exculpation.'

The king's secretary sent up to the window the substance of his defence, the criminal was carried at some distance to the other end of the room, and the judges deliberated whilst the king was reading. Very few words were said among the rest; the Ras was all the time speaking to other people. After he had ended this, he called upon the youngest judge to give his opinion; and he gave it, 'He is guilty, and should die;' the same said all the officers, and after them the judges; and the same said Kasmati Tesfos after them. When it came to Ras Michael to give his vote, he affected moderation; he said, 'That he was accused for being his enemy and accomplice; in either case, it is not fair that he should judge him.' No superior officer being present, the last voice remained with the king, who sent Kal Hatze to the Board with his sentence; 'He is guilty, and *shall* die *the death*.—The hangman *shall* hang him upon a tree *to-day*.' The unfortunate Acab Saat was immediately hurried away by the guards to the place of execution, which is a large tree before the king's gate; where uttering, to the very last moment, curses against the King, the Ras, and the Abuna, he suffered the death he very richly deserved, being hanged in the very vestments in which he used to sit before the king, without one ornament of his civil or sacerdotal preeminence having been taken from him before the execution. In going to the tree, he said he had 400 cows, which he bequeathed to some priests to say prayers for his soul; but the Ras ordered them to be brought to Gondar, and distributed among his soldiers.

I have entered into a longer detail of this trial, at the whole of which I assisted, the rather that I might ask this question of those that maintain the absolute independence of the Abyssinian priesthood, 'Whether, if the many instances already mentioned have not had the effect, this one does not fully convince them, that all ecclesiastical persons are subject to the secular power in Abyssinia, as much as they are in Britain, or any European state whatever?'

Chremation, Socinios's brother, was next called; he seemed half dead with fear; he only denied having any concern in his brother being elected king. He said he had no post, and in this he spoke the truth, but confessed that he had been sent by Abba Salama to bring the Itchegue and the Abuna [administrative and spiritual heads of the Church] to meet him the day of excommunication at Dippabye. It was further unluckily proved against him, that he was present with his brother at plundering the houses in the night-time when the man was killed; and upon this he was sentenced to be immediately hanged. The court then broke up, and went to breakfast. All this had passed in less than two hours; it was not quite eleven o'clock when all was over; but Ras Michael had sworn he would not taste bread till Abba Salama was hanged; and on such occasions he never broke his word.

Immediately after this last execution, the kettle-drums beat at the palace-gate, and the crier made this proclamation, 'That all lands and villages, which are now, or have been given to the Abuna by the king, shall revert to the king's own use, and be subject to the government, or the Cantiba of Dembea, or such officers as the king shall afterwards appoint in the provinces where they are situated.'

I went home, and my house being but a few yards from the palace, I passed the two unfortunate people hanging upon the same branch; and, full of the cruelty of the scene I had witnessed, which I knew was but a preamble to much more, I determined firmly, at all events, to quit this country.

The next morning came on the trial of the unfortunate Guebra Denghel, Sebaat Laab, and Kefla Mariam; the Ras claimed his right of trying these three at his own house, as they were all three subjects of his government of Tigre. Guebra Denghel bore his hard fortune with great unconcern, declaring, that his only reason of taking up arms against the king was, that he saw no other way of preventing Michael's tyranny and monstrous thirst of money and of power: that the Ras was really king, had subverted the constitution, annihilated all difference of rank and persons, and transferred the efficient parts of government into the hands of his own creatures. He wished the king might know this was his only motive for rebellion, and that, unless it had been to make this declaration, he would not have opened his mouth before so partial and unjust a judge as he considered Michael to be.

But Welleta Selasse, his daughter, hearing the danger her father was in, broke suddenly out of Ozoro Esther's apartment, which was contiguous; and coming into the council-room at the instant her father was condemned to die, threw herself at the Ras's feet with every mark and expression of the most extreme sorrow. I cannot, indeed, repeat what her expressions were, as I was not present, and I thank God that I was not; I believe they are ineffable by any mouth but her own; but they were perfectly unsuccessful. The old tyrant threatened her with immediate death, spurned her away with his foot, and in her hearing ordered her father to be immediately hanged. Welleta Selasse, in a fit, or faint, which resembled death, fell speechless to the ground. The father, forgetful of his own situation, flew to his daughter's assistance, and they were both dragged out at separate doors, the one to death, the other to after-sufferings, greater than death itself.

Fortune seemed to have taken delight, from very early life, constantly to traverse the greatness and happiness of this young lady. She was first destined to be married to Joas, and the affair was nearly concluded, when the fatal discovery, made at the battle of Azazo, that the king had sent his household troops privately to fight for Fasil against Michael, prevented her marriage, and occasioned his death. She was then destined to old Hatze Hannes, Tecla Haimanout's father: Michael, who found him incapable of being a king, judged him as incapable of being a husband to a woman of the youth and charms of Welleta Selasse, and therefore deprived him at once of his life, crown, and bride. She was now not seventeen, and it was designed she should be married to the present king; Providence put a stop to a union that was not agreeable to either party. She died some time after this, before the battle of Serbraxos; being strongly pressed to gratify the brutal inclinations of the Ras, her grandfather, whom when she could not resist or avoid, she took poison: others said it was given her by Ozoro Esther from jealousy; but this was certainly without foundation. I saw her in her last moments, but too late to give her any assistance; and she had told her women-servants and slaves, that she had taken arsenic, having no other way to avoid committing so monstrous a crime as incest with the murderer of her father.

The rage, that the intercession of the daughter for her father Guebra Denghel had put the Ras into, was seen in the severity of the sentence he passed upon the other two criminals; Kefla Mariam's eyes were pulled out, Sebaat Laab's eye-lids were cut off by the roots, and both of them were exposed in the market-place to the burning sun, without any covering whatever. Sebaat Laab died of a fever in a few days; Kefla Mariam lived, if not to see, at least to hear, that he was revenged, after the battle of Serbraxos, by the disgrace and captivity of Michael.

I will spare myself the disagreeable task of shocking my readers with any further account of these horried cruelties; enough has been said to give an idea of the character of these times and people. Blood continued to be spilt as water, day after day, till the Epiphany; priests, lay-men, young men and old, noble and vile, daily found their end by the knife or the cord. Fifty-seven people died publicly by the hand of the executioner in the course of a very few days; many disappeared, and were either murdered privately, or sent to prisons, no one knew where.

The bodies of those killed by the sword were hewn to pieces and scattered about the streets, being denied burial. I was miserable, and almost driven to despair, at seeing my hunting dogs, twice let loose by the carelessness of my servants, bringing into the court-yard the head and arms of slaughtered men, and which I could no way prevent but by the destruction of the dogs themselves; the quantity of carrion, and the stench of it, brought down the hyænas in hundreds from the neighbouring mountains; and, as few people in Gondar go out after it is dark, they enjoyed the streets by themselves, and seemed ready to dispute the possession of the city with the inhabitants. Often when I went home late from the palace, and it was this time the king chose chiefly for conversation, though I had but to pass the corner of the market-place before the palace, had lanthorns with me, and was surrounded with armed men, I heard them grunting by two's and three's so near me as to be afraid they would take some opportunity of seizing me by the leg; a pistol would have frightened them, and made them speedily run, and I constantly carried two loaded at my girdle; but the discharging a pistol in the night would have alarmed every one that heard it in the town, and it was not now the time to add any thing to people's fears. I at last scarce ever went out, and nothing occupied my thoughts but how to escape from this bloody country by the way of Sennaar, and how I could best exert my power and influence over Yasine at Ras el Feel to pave my way, by assisting me to pass the desert into Atbara.

The king missing me some days at the palace, and hearing I had not been at Ras Michael's, began to inquire who had been with me. Ayto Confu soon found Yasine, who informed him of the whole matter; upon this I was sent for to the palace, where I found the king, without any body but menial servants. He immediately remarked that I looked very ill; which, indeed, I felt to be the case, as I had scarcely ate or slept since I saw him last, or even for some days before. He asked me, in a condoling tone, 'What ailed me? that, besides looking sick, I seemed as if something had ruffled me, and put me out of humour.' I told him that what he observed was true: that, coming across the market-place, I had seen Za Mariam, the Ras's door-keeper, with three men bound, one of whom he fell a-hacking to pieces in my presence. Upon seeing me running across the place, stopping my nose, he called me to stay till he should come and dispatch the other two, for he wanted to speak to me, as if he had been engaged about ordinary business: that the soldiers, in consideration of his haste, immediately fell upon the other two, whose cries were still remaining in my ears: that the hyænas at night would scarcely let me pass in the streets when I returned from the palace; and the dogs fled into my house to eat pieces of human carcases at leisure.

Although his intention was to look grave, I saw it was all he could do to stifle a laugh at grievances he thought very little of. 'The men you saw with Za Mariam just now,' says he, 'are rebels, sent by Kefla Yasous for examples: he has forced a junction with Tecla and Welleta Michael in Samen, and a road is now open through Woggora, and plenty established in Gondar. The men you saw suffer were those that cut off the provisions from coming into the city; they have occasioned the death of many poor people; as for the hyæna, he never meddles with living people, he seeks carrion, and will soon clear the streets of those incumbrances that so much offend you; people say that they are the Falasha of the mountains, who take that shape of the hyæna, and come down into the town to eat Christian flesh in the night.' 'If they depend upon Christian flesh, and eat no other,' said I, 'perhaps the hyænas of Gondar will be the worst fed of any in the world.' 'True,' says he, bursting out into a loud laughter, 'that may be; few of those that die by the knife anywhere are Christians, or have any religion at all; why then should you mind what they suffer?' 'Sir,' said I, 'that is not my sentiment; if you was to order a dog to be tortured to death before me every morning, I could not bear it. The carcases of Abba Salama, Guebra Denghel, and the rest, are still hanging where they were upon the tree; you smell the stench of them at the palace-gate, and will soon, I apprehend, in the palace itself. This cannot be pleasant, and I do assure you it must be very pernicious to your health, if there was nothing else in it. At the battle of Fagitta, though you had no intention to retreat, yet you went half a day backward, to higher ground, and purer air, to avoid the stench of the field; but here in the city you heap up carrion about your houses, where is your continual residence.'

'The Ras has given orders,' says he, gravely, 'to remove all the dead bodies before the Epiphany, when we go down to keep that festival, and wash away all this pollution in the clear-running water of the Kahha: but, tell me, Yagoube, is it really possible that you can take such things as these so much to heart? You are a brave man; we all know you are, and have seen it: we have all blamed you, stranger as you are in this country, for the little care you take of yourself; and yet about these things you are as much affected as the most cowardly woman, girl, or child could be.' 'Sir,' said I, 'I do not know if I am brave or not; but if to see men tortured, or murdered, or to live among dead bodies without concern, be courage, I have it not, nor desire to have it: war is the profession of noble minds; it is a glorious one; it is the science and occupation of kings; and many wise and many humane men have dedicated their whole life to the study of it in every country; it softens men's manners, by obliging them to society, to assist, befriend, and even save one another, though at their own risk and danger. A barbarian of that profession should be pointed at. Observe Ayto Engedan (who came at that very instant into the room); there is a young man,' said I, 'who, with the bravery, has also the humanity and gentleness of my countrymen that are soldiers.'

Engedan fell on his face before the king, as is usual, while the king went on seriously—'War you want; do you, Yagoube? war you shall have; it is not far distant, and Engedan is come to tell us how near.' They went then into a considerable conversation about Gusho, Powussen, and the preparations they were making, and where they were; with which I shall not trouble the reader, as I shall have an occasion to speak of the particulars afterwards as they arise. 'I want Confu,' says the king; 'I want him to send his men of Ras el Feel to Sennaar, and to the Baharnagash, to get horses and some coats of mail. And what do you think of sending Yagoube there? he knows their manners and their language, and has friends there to whom he is intending to escape, without so much as asking my leave.' 'Pardon me, sir,' said I; 'if I have ever entertained that thought, it is proof sufficient of the extreme necessity I am under to go.' 'Sir,' says Engedan, 'I have rode in the Koccob horse; I will do so again, if Yagoube commands them, and will stay with us till we try the horse of Begemder. I have eight or ten coats of mail, which I will give your majesty: they belonged to my father Eshte, and I took them lately from that thief Abou Barea, with whom they were left at my father's death: but I will tell your majesty, I had rather fight naked, without a coat of mail, than that you should send Yagoube to Sennaar, to purchase them from thence, for he will never return.'

Ras Michael was now announced, and we made haste to get away. 'I would have Confu, Engedan, and you, come here to-morrow night,' says the king, 'as soon as it is dark; and do not you, Yagoube, for your life, speak one word of Sennaar, till you know my will upon it.' He said this in the sternest manner, and with all the dignity and majesty of a king.

We passed the Ras in the ante-chamber, attended by a great many people. We endeavoured to slide by him in the crowd, but he noticed us, and brought us before him. We both kissed his hands, and he kept hold of one of mine, while he asked Engedan, 'Is Fasil at Ibaba?' to which he was answered, 'Yes.' 'Who is with him?' says the Ras. 'Damot, Agow, and Maitsha,' answered Engedan. 'Was you there?' says the Ras. 'No,' answered Engedan; 'I am at Tshemera, with few men.' He then turned to me, and said, 'My son is ill; Ozoro Esther has just sent to me, and complains you visit her now no more. Go see the boy, and don't neglect Ozoro Esther; she is one of your best friends.'

Travels to discover the source of the Nile,
2nd edition, vol. VI, pp. 12–31

The final extract from Bruce deals with an event at court shortly before his departure and throws light upon another aspect of Ethiopian character.

4. A NASTY SOVEREIGN

Another interview, which happened at the Kahha, was much more extraordinary in itself, though of much less importance to the state. Guangoul, chief of the Galla of Angot, that is, of the eastern Galla, came to pay his respects to the king and Ras Michael: he had with him about 500 foot and 40 horse: he brought with him a number of large horns for carrying the king's wine, and some other such trifles. He was a little, thin, cross-made man, of no apparent strength or swiftness, as far as could be conjectured; his legs and thighs being thin and small for his body, and his head large; he was of a yellow, unwholesome colour, not black nor brown; he had long hair plaited and interwoven with the bowels of oxen, and so knotted and twisted together as to render it impossible to distinguish the hair from the bowels, which hung down in long strings, part before his breast and part behind his shoulder, the most extraordinary ringlets I had ever seen. He had likewise a wreath of guts hung about his neck, and several rounds of the same about his middle, which served as a girdle, below which was a short cotton cloth dipt in butter, and all his body was wet, and running down with the same; he seemed to be about fifty years of age, with a confident and insolent superiority painted in his face. In his country it seems, when he appears in state, the beast he rides upon is a cow. He was then in full dress and ceremony, and mounted upon one, not of the largest sort, but which had monstrous horns. He had no saddle on his cow. He had short drawers, that did not reach the middle of his thighs; his knees, feet, legs, and all his body were bare. He had a shield of a single hide, warped by the heat in several directions, and much in the shape of a high-crowned, large, straw-hat, with which the fashionable women in our own country sometimes disguise themselves. He carried a short lance in his right hand, with an ill-made iron head, and a shaft that seemed to be of thorn-tree, but altogether without ornament, which is seldom the case with the arms of barbarians. Whether it was necessary for the poizing himself upon the sharp ridge of the beast's back, or whether it was meant as graceful riding, I do not know, being quite unskilled in cowmanship; but he leaned exceedingly backwards, pushing his belly forwards, and holding his left arm and shield stretched out on one side of him, and his right arm and lance in the same way on the other, like wings.

The king was seated on his ivory chair, to receive him, almost in the middle of his tent; the day was very hot and an insufferable stench of carrion soon made every one in the tent sensible of the approach of this nasty sovereign, even before they saw him. The king, when he perceived him coming, was so struck with the whole figure and appearance, that he could not contain himself from an immoderate fit of laughter, which finding it impossible to stifle, he rose from his chair, and ran as hard as he could into another apartment behind the throne.

The savage got from his cow at the door of the tent with all his tripes about him; and, while we were admiring him as a monster, seeing the king's seat empty, he took it for his own, and down he sat upon the crimson silk cushion, with the butter running from every part of him. A general cry of astonishment was made by every person in the tent: he started up I believe without divining the cause, and before he had time to recollect himself, they fell all upon him, and with pushes and blows drove this greasy chieftain to the door of the tent, staring with wild amazement not knowing what was next to happen. It is high treason, and punishable by immediate death, to sit down upon the king's chair. Poor Guangoul owed his life to his ignorance. The king had beheld the scene through the curtain; if he laughed heartily at the beginning, he laughed ten times more at the catastrophe; he came out laughing, and unable to speak. The cushion was lifted and thrown away, and a yellow Indian shawl spread on the ivory stool; and ever after, when it was placed, and the king not there, the stool was turned on its face upon the carpet to prevent such like accidents. . . .

After the king returned to the palace, great diversion was made at Guangoul's appearance, in so much that Ozoro Esther, who hated the very name of Galla, and of this race in particular, insisted upon seeing a representation of it. Doho, accordingly, a dwarf belonging to Ras Michael, very ugly, with a monstrous big head, but very sharp and clever, and capable of acting his part, was brought to represent the person of Guangoul: a burnt stick and a bad shield were provided: but the difficulty remained, how to persuade Doho, the dwarf, to put on the raw guts about his neck and waist, and, above all, to plait them in the hair, which he absolutely refused, both from religious and cleanly motives; as for the butter, it was no objection, as all the Abyssinians anoint themselves with it daily, after bathing. Here we were very near at a stand, all the ladies having in vain supplicated him to suffer for their sakes a temporary pollution, with promises that oceans of rose and scented water should be poured upon him afterwards, to restore his former sweetness. Doho was a man who constantly spent his time in reading scripture, the acts of the councils, the works of St. John Chrysostom, and other such books as they have among them. He remained inflexible: at last I suggested that several hanks of cotton, dyed blue, red, and yellow, should be got from the weavers in the Mahometan town; and these oiled, greased, and knotted properly, and twisted among the hair, well anointed with butter, would give a pretty accurate resemblance of what we saw in the king's tent. All hands were immediately set to work; the cotton was provided; Ozoro Esther's servants and slaves decked Doho to the life. I spotted his face with stibium, and others anointed him with butter: an old milk-cow was found, contrary to my experience, that suffered a rider without much impatience, and in came Guangoul into a great hall in Ozoro Esther's apartment.

Never was any thing better personated, or better received; the whole hall resounded with one cry of laughter; Doho encouraged by this, and the perfect indifference and steadiness of his cow, began to act his part with great humour and confidence: he was born in the neighbourhood of these very Galla, knew their manners, and spoke their language perfectly. Amha Yasous, Confu, Aylo, brother to Engedan, with some servants of the king, acted the part that we did in the tent the day of the audience, that is, stood on each side of the king's chair: the cow was brought into the middle of the room, and Guangoul descended with his lance and shield in great state; a cushion was not spared, nor did Doho spare the cushion: the butter shewed very distinctly where he had been sitting: we all fell upon him and belaboured him heartily, and chased him to the door. His speedy retreat was not counterfeited. Ozoro Altash, Esther's sister, and a number of the ladies were present. Ozoro Esther declared she would send for the Ras, he having been in great good humour since the arrival of Amha Yasous. I had not seen him since the recovery of his son, and happened to be at the door next him; he took me by the hand and said, 'Welleta Hawaryat (that was the name of his son) is well, you are very kind.'

Michael was esteemed the best orator in his country, and spoke his own language, Tigréan, with the utmost purity and elegance; yet in common conversation he was very sententious, two or three words at a time, but never obscure; this he had contracted by a long practice of commanding armies, where he saw as instantly and clearly, as he spoke shortly and distinctly. He bowed very civilly to the ladies, and pointed to me to sit down on the seat by him. Amha Yasous was standing before him; I hastened to sit down on the carpet at his feet, and he seemed to recollect himself, and place Amha Yasous beside him: it was easy to perceive by his look, that he gave me credit for my behaviour. When they were all seated, 'Well,' says he, in great good humour, 'what now, what is the matter? what can I do for you, Yagoube? are the women in your country as idle and foolish as these? has Ozoro Esther chosen a wife for you? she shall give you your dinner: I will give her a portion; and, as you are a horseman, the king, with Amha Yasous's leave,' said he, bowing, 'shall give you the command of the Shoa horse; I have seen them; the men, I think, are almost as white as yourself.' Amha Yasous bowed in return, and said, 'Sir, if the king bestows them so worthily, I promise to bring another thousand, as good as these, to join them after the rains, before next Epiphany.'—'And I,' says Ozoro Esther, 'for my part, I have long had a wife for him. But this is not the present business; we know your time is precious; Guangoul is without, and desires an audience of you.'—'Poh!' says the Ras, 'Guangoul is gone to Gusho, at Minziro, and there is like to be a pretty story: here are accounts from Tigre, that he has committed great barbarities in his journey, laid waste some villages, killed the people, for not furnishing him with provisions: here in Belessen he also burnt a church and a village belonging to the Iteghe, and killed many poor people; I do not know what he means; I hope they will keep him where he is, and not send him home again through Tigre.'

A communication of this kind, very uncommon from the Ras, occasioned a serious appearance in the whole company; but he had no sooner done with speaking, than in comes Doho upon his cow; neither man nor woman that had yet seen him ever laughed so heartily as the old Ras; he humoured the thing entirely; welcomed Doho in Galla language, and saw the whole farce, finished by his flight to the door, with the utmost good humour.

Travels to discover the source of the Nile,
2nd edition, vol. VI, pp. 43–9

Shortly after this the civil wars broke out with renewed fierceness. After pitched battles, in which Bruce took part, Ras Michael's enemies, the lords of rival provinces, took him prisoner and the king passed under their control. Bruce at last obtained permission to leave the country, after living there for three years. Taking a valuable collection of Amharic documents, he went out westwards towards the Atbara and Sennar, breaking his journey to stay with Ozoro Esther, now in semi-exile at Tcherkin. Meeting her there with her son and some of his other friends was, he says, 'one of the happiest moments of my life'. Here he was enthusiastically received and enjoyed some exciting hunting of buffalo, elephant and rhinoceros, of which last animal there is a pleasing illustration in his book. His journey back to Egypt was slow and dangerous; he was detained by the king of Sennar, and he had finally to cross the great desert between Shendi and Aswan.

Upon his return to England in 1774 he received no other official recognition than an interview with King George III. There was widespread refusal to believe many of his stories, especially his account of the eating of raw flesh. Much mortified, he returned to Kinnaird, his estate in Scotland, now enriched by the discovery of coal. It was twelve years before he could be persuaded to write up his travels, which were published with magnificent illustrations in five volumes in 1790. He met his death in 1794 through falling downstairs in the haste with which he ran to the staircase to show a lady to her carriage.

II

MUNGO PARK

1771–1806

Mungo Park was born near Selkirk, the son of a farmer. Having qualified as a doctor at Edinburgh University, he entered the East India Company's service as a ship's surgeon. In 1792-3 he made the voyage to Sumatra and back as medical officer on the Worcester. *On his return he was invited by the African Association (see p. 25) to undertake a journey in search of the Niger: he accepted the offer at once and sailed from Portsmouth in May 1795, arriving at Pisania on the Gambia in July. After a five months' stay here he set out for the interior accompanied by one negro servant, Johnson, a boy, two asses, and an unlucky horse. He was robbed of his goods by extortionate negro kings, and—much worse—captured and held prisoner for nearly three months by a Moorish chief named Ali at his camp at Benowm. (Park uses the term 'Moors' indiscriminately for all non-negro Moslems, except the partly Moslem Fulani, whom he calls 'Foulahs'.) This detention he always spoke of with horror: 'never did any period of my life', he wrote, 'pass away so heavily; from sunrise to sunset was I obliged to suffer with an unruffled countenance, the insults of the rudest savages on earth'. He escaped from it on 27th June, but he was only able to travel slowly on account of the condition of his horse, 'which the Moors had reduced to a perfect Rosinante'.*

5. ESCAPE FROM THE MOORS

On the afternoon of the 1st of July, as I was tending my horse in the fields, Ali's chief slave and four Moors arrived at Queira, and took up their lodging at the Dooty's [headman's] house. My interpreter, Johnson, who suspected the nature of this visit, sent two boys to overhear their conversation; from which he learnt that they were sent to convey me back to Bubaker. The same evening, two of the Moors came privately to look at my horse, and one of them proposed taking it to the Dooty's

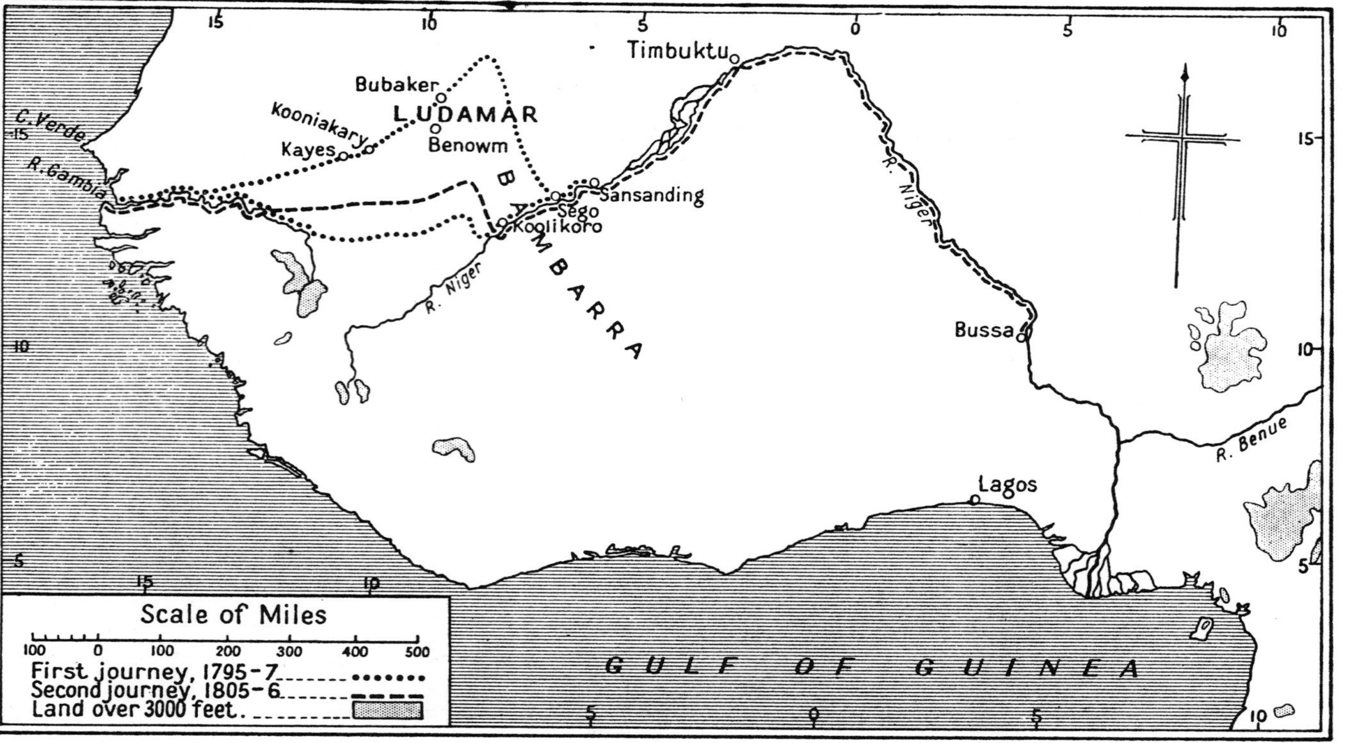

2. THE TRAVELS OF PARK, 1795–7 and 1805–6

hut, but the other observed that such a precaution was unnecessary, as I could never escape upon such an animal. They then inquired where I slept, and returned to their companions.

All this was like a stroke of thunder to me, for I dreaded nothing so much as confinement again among the Moors; from whose barbarity I had nothing but death to expect. I therefore determined to set off immediately for Bambarra; a measure which I thought offered almost the only chance of saving my life, and gaining the object of my mission. I communicated the design to Johnson, who, altho' he applauded my resolution, was so far from shewing any inclination to accompany me, that he solemnly protested, he would rather forfeit his wages than go any farther. He told me that Daman had agreed to give him half the price of a slave for his service, to assist in conducting a coffle [caravan] of slaves to Gambia, and that he was determined to embrace the opportunity of returning to his wife and family.

Having no hopes therefore of persuading him to accompany me, I resolved to proceed by myself. About midnight I got my clothes in readiness, which consisted of two shirts, two pair of trowsers, two pocket handkerchiefs, an upper and under waistcoat, a hat, and a pair of half boots; these, with a cloak, constituted my whole wardrobe. And I had not one single bead, nor any other article of value in my possession, to purchase victuals for myself, or corn for my horse.

About daybreak, Johnson, who had been listening to the Moors all night, came and whispered to me that they were asleep. The awful crisis was now arrived, when I was again either to taste the blessing of freedom, or languish out my days in captivity. A cold sweat moistened my forehead, as I thought on the dreadful alternative, and reflected that, one way or the other, my fate must be decided in the course of the ensuing day. But to deliberate was to lose the only chance of escaping. So, taking up my bundle, I stepped gently over the Negroes, who were sleeping in the open air, and having mounted my horse, I bade Johnson farewell, desiring him to take particular care of the papers I had entrusted him with, and inform my friends in Gambia that he had left me in good health, on my way to Bambarra.

I proceeded with great caution; surveying each bush, and frequently listening and looking behind me for the Moorish horsemen, until I was about a mile from the town, when I was surprised to find myself in the neighbourhood of a Korree [watering-place for cattle], belonging to the Moors. The shepherds followed me for about a mile, hooting and throwing stones after me; and when I was out of their reach, and had begun to indulge the pleasing hopes of escaping, I was again greatly alarmed to hear somebody holla behind me; and looking back, I saw three Moors on horseback, coming after me at full speed; whooping and brandishing their double-barrelled guns. I knew it was in vain, to think of escaping, and therefore turned back and met them: when two of them caught hold of my bridle, one on each side, and the third, presenting his musket told me I must go back to Ali. When the human mind has for some time been fluctuating between hope and despair, tortured with anxiety, and hurried from one extreme to another, it affords a sort of gloomy relief to know the worst that can possibly happen: such was my situation. An indifference about life, and all its enjoyments, had completely benumbed my faculties, and I rode back with the Moors with apparent unconcern. But a change took place much sooner than I had any reason to expect. In passing through some thick bushes, one of the Moors ordered me to untie my bundle, and shew them the contents. Having examined the different articles, they found nothing worth taking except my cloak, which they considered as a very valuable acquisition, and one of them pulling it from me, wrapped it about himself. This cloak had been of great use to me; it served to cover me from the rains in the day, and to protect me from the musketoes in the night; I therefore earnestly begged him to return it, and followed him some little way to obtain it; but without paying any attention to my request, he and one of his companions rode off with their prize. When I attempted to follow them, the third, who had remained with me, struck my horse over the head, and presenting his musket, told me I should proceed no further. I now perceived that these men had not been sent by any authority to apprehend me, but had pursued me solely in the view to rob and plunder me. Turning my horse's head therefore once more towards the east, and observing the Moor follow the track of his confederates, I congratulated myself on having escaped with my life, though in great distress, from such a horde of barbarians.

I was no sooner out of sight of the Moor, than I struck into the woods, to prevent being pursued, and kept pushing on, with all possible speed, until I found myself near some high rocks, which I remembered to have seen in my former route from Queira to Deena; and directing my course a little to the northward, I fortunately fell in with the path.

It is impossible to describe the joy that arose in my mind, when I looked around and concluded that I was out of danger. I felt like one recovered from sickness; I breathed freer; I found unusual lightness in my limbs; even the Desert looked pleasant; and I dreaded nothing so much as falling in with some wandering parties of Moors, who might convey me back to the land of thieves and murderers, from which I had just escaped.

I soon became sensible, however, that my situation was very deplorable; for I had no means of procuring food, nor prospect of finding water. About ten o'clock, perceiving a herd of goats feeding close to the road, I took a circuitous route to avoid being seen and continued travelling through the Wilderness, directing my course, by compass, nearly east-south-east, in order to reach, as soon as possible, some town or village of the kingdom of Bambarra.

A little after noon, when the burning heat of the sun was reflected with double violence from the hot sand, and the distant ridges of the hills, seen through the ascending vapour, seemed to wave and fluctuate like the unsettled sea, I became faint with thirst, and climbed a tree in hopes of seeing distant smoke, or some other appearance of a human habitation; but in vain: nothing appeared all around but thick underwood, and hillocks of white sand.

About four o'clock, I came suddenly upon a large herd of goats, and pulling my horse into a bush, I watched to observe if the keepers were Moors or Negroes. In a little time I perceived two Moorish boys, and with some difficulty persuaded them to approach me. They informed me that the herd belonged to Ali, and that they were going to Deena, where the water was more plentiful, and where they intended to stay, until the rain had filled the pools in the Desert. They shewed me their empty water-skins, and told me that they had seen no water in the woods. This account afforded me but little consolation; however, it was in vain to repine, and I pushed on as fast as possible, in hopes of reaching some watering-place in the course of the night. My thirst was by this time become insufferable; my mouth was parched and inflamed; a sudden dimness would frequently come over my eyes, with other symptoms of fainting; and my horse being very much fatigued, I began seriously to apprehend that I should perish of thirst. To relieve the burning pain in my mouth and throat, I chewed the leaves of different shrubs, but found them all bitter, and of no service to me.

A little before sunset, having reached the top of a gentle rising, I climbed a high tree, from the topmost branches of which I cast a melancholy look over the barren Wilderness, but without discovering the most distant trace of a human dwelling. The same dismal uniformity of shrubs and sand every where presented itself, and the horizon was as level and uninterrupted as that of the sea.

Descending from the tree, I found my horse devouring the stubble and brushwood with great avidity; and as I was now too faint to attempt walking, and my horse too much fatigued to carry me, I thought it but an act of humanity, and perhaps the last I should ever have it in my power to perform, to take off his bridle and let him shift for himself; in doing which I was suddenly affected with sickness and giddiness; and falling upon the sand, felt as if the hour of death was fast approaching. 'Here then, thought I, after a short but ineffectual struggle, terminate all my hopes of being useful in my day and generation: here must the short span of my life come to an end.'—I cast (as I believed) a last look on the surrounding scene, and whilst I reflected on the awful change that was about to take place, this world with its enjoyments seemed to vanish from my recollection. Nature, however, at length resumed its functions; and on recovering my senses, I found myself stretched upon the sand, with the bridle still in my hand, and the sun just sinking behind the trees. I now summoned all my resolution, and determined to make another effort to prolong my existence. And as the evening was somewhat cool, I resolved to travel as far as my limbs would carry me, in hopes of reaching (my only resource) a watering-place. With this view, I put the bridle on my horse, and driving him before me, went slowly along for about an hour, when I perceived some lightning from the north-east; a most delightful sight; for it promised rain. The darkness and lightning increased very rapidly; and in less than an hour I heard the wind roaring among the bushes. I had already opened my mouth to receive the refreshing drops which I expected; but I was instantly covered with a cloud of sand, driven with such force by the wind as to give a very disagreeable sensation to my face and arms; and I was obliged to mount my horse, and stop under a bush, to prevent being suffocated. The sand continued to fly in amazing quantities for near an hour, after which I again set forward, and travelled with difficulty, until ten o'clock. About this time I was agreeably surprised by some very vivid flashes of lightning, followed by a few heavy drops of rain. In a little time the sand ceased to fly, and I alighted, and spread out all my clean clothes to collect the rain, which at length I saw would certainly fall. For more than an hour it rained plentifully, and I quenched my thirst by wringing and sucking my clothes.

There being no moon, it was remarkably dark, so that I was obliged to lead my horse, and direct my way by the compass, which the lightning enabled me to observe. In this manner I travelled, with tolerable expedition, until past midnight; when, the lightning becoming more distant, I was under the necessity of groping along, to the no small danger of my hands and eyes. About two o'clock my horse started at something, and looking round, I was not a little surprised to see a light at a short distance among the trees, and supposing it to be a town, I groped along the sand in hopes of finding corn-stalks, cotton, or other appearances of cultivation, but found none. As I approached, I perceived a number of other lights in different places, and began to suspect that I had fallen upon a party of Moors. However, in my present situation, I was resolved to see who they were, if I could do it with safety. I accordingly led my horse cautiously towards the light, and heard by the lowing of the cattle, and the clamorous tongues of the herdsmen, that it was a watering-place, and most likely belonged to the Moors. Delightful as the sound of the human voice was to me, I resolved once more to strike into the woods, and rather run the risk of perishing of hunger, than trust myself again in their hands; but being still thirsty, and dreading the approach of the burning day, I thought it prudent to search for the wells, which I expected to find at no great distance. In this pursuit, I inadvertently approached so near to one of the tents, as to be perceived by a woman, who immediately screamed out. Two people came running to her assistance from some of the neighbouring tents, and passed so very near to me, that I thought I was discovered; and hastened again into the woods.

About a mile from this place, I heard a loud and confused noise somewhere to the right of my course, and in a short time was happy to find it was the croaking of frogs, which was heavenly music to my ears. I followed the sound, and at daybreak arrived at some shallow muddy pools, so full of frogs, that it was difficult to discern the water. The noise they made frightened my horse, and I was obliged to keep them quiet, by beating the water with a branch until he had drank. Having here quenched my thirst, I ascended a tree, and the morning being calm, I soon perceived the smoke of the watering-place which I had passed in the night; and observed another pillar of smoke east-south-east, distant 12 or 14 miles. Towards this I directed my route, and reached the cultivated ground a little before eleven o'clock; where seeing a number of Negroes at work planting corn, I inquired the name of the town; and was informed that it was a Foulah village, belonging to Ali, called Shrilla. I had now some doubts about entering it; but my horse being very much fatigued, and the day growing hot, not to mention the pangs of hunger which began to assail me, I resolved to venture; and accordingly rode up to the Dooty's house, where I was unfortunately denied admittance, and could not obtain even a handful of corn, either for myself or horse. Turning from this inhospitable door, I rode slowly out of the town, and perceiving some low scattered huts without the walls, I directed my route towards them; knowing that in Africa, as well as in Europe, hospitality does not always prefer the highest dwellings. At the door of one of these huts, an old, motherly-looking woman sat, spinning cotton; I made signs to her that I was hungry, and inquired if she had any victuals with her in the hut. She immediately laid down her distaff, and desired me, in Arabic, to come in. When I had seated myself upon the floor, she set before me a dish of kouskous [boiled corn], that had been left the preceding night, of which I made a tolerable meal; and in return for this kindness, I gave her one of my pocket-handkerchiefs; begging at the same time, a little corn for my horse, which she readily brought me.

Overcome with joy at so unexpected a deliverance, I lifted up my eyes to heaven, and whilst my heart swelled with gratitude, I returned thanks to that gracious and bountiful Being, whose power had supported me under so many dangers, and had now spread for me a table in the Wilderness.

Travels in the interior districts of Africa,
1st edition, pp. 171–81

After this providential deliverance Park continued his journey to the south-east. On 11th July he joined a party of Kaartans, who were fleeing from the tyranny of the Moors. He knew that he was getting near the Niger, and that he would strike it at the great market-town of Segou, for which he was now making.

6. DISCOVERY OF THE NIGER

July 18th. We continued our journey; but, owing to a light supper the preceding night, we felt ourselves rather hungry this morn ng, and endeavoured to procure some corn at a village; but without success. The towns were now more numerous, and the land that is not employed in cultivation affords excellent pasturage for large herds of cattle; but, owing to the great concourse of people daily going to and returning from Sego, the inhabitants are less hospitable to strangers.

My horse becoming weaker and weaker every day, was now of very little service to me: I was obliged to drive him before me for the greater part of the day; and did not reach Geosorro until eight o'clock in the evening. I found my companions wrangling with the Dooty, who had absolutely refused to give or sell them any provisions; and as none of us had tasted victuals for the last twenty-four hours, we were by no means disposed to fast another day, if we could help it. But finding our entreaties without effect, and being very much fatigued, I fell asleep, from which I was awakened, about midnight, with the joyful information '*kinne-nata*' (the victuals is come). This made the remainder of the night pass away pleasantly; and at daybreak, July 19th, we resumed our journey, proposing to stop at a village called Doolinkeaboo, for the night following. My fellow-travellers, having better horses than myself, soon left me; and I was walking barefoot, driving my horse, when I was met by a coffle of slaves, about seventy in number, coming from Sego. They were tied together by their necks with thongs of a bullock's hide, twisted like a rope; seven slaves upon a thong; and a man with a musket between every seven. Many of the slaves were ill conditioned, and a great number of them women. In the rear came Sidi Mahomed's servant, whom I remembered to have seen at the camp of Benowm: he presently knew me, and told me that these slaves were going to Morocco, by the way of Ludamar, and the Great Desert.

In the afternoon, as I approached Doolinkeaboo, I met about twenty Moors on horseback, the owners of the slaves I had seen in the morning; they were well armed with muskets, and were very inquisitive concerning me, but not so rude as their countrymen generally are. From them I learned that Sidi Mahomed was not at Sego, but had gone to Cancaba for gold-dust.

When I arrived at Doolinkeaboo, I was informed that my fellow-travellers had gone on; but my horse was so much fatigued that I could not possibly proceed after them. The Dooty of the town, at my request, gave me a draught of water, which is generally looked upon as an earnest of greater hospitality; and I had no doubt of making up for the toils of the day, by a good supper and a sound sleep: unfortunately, I had neither one nor the other. The night was rainy and tempestuous, and the Dooty limited his hospitality to the draught of water.

July 20th. In the morning, I endeavoured, both by entreaties and threats, to procure some victuals from the Dooty, but in vain. I even begged some corn from one of his female slaves, as she was washing it at the well, and had the mortification to be refused. However, when the Dooty was gone to the fields, his wife sent me a handful of meal, which I mixed with water, and drank for breakfast. About eight o'clock, I departed from Doolinkeaboo, and at noon stopped a few minutes at a large Korree; where I had some milk given me by the Foulahs. And hearing that two Negroes were going from thence to Sego, I was happy to have their company, and we set out immediately. About four o'clock, we stopped at a small village, where one of the Negroes met with an acquaintance, who invited us to a sort of public entertainment, which was conducted with more than common propriety. A dish, made of sour milk and meal, called *Sinkatoo*, and beer made from their corn, was distributed with great liberality; and the women were admitted into the society; a circumstance I had never before observed in Africa. There was no compulsion; every one was at liberty to drink as he pleased: they nodded to each other when about to drink, and on setting down the calabash, commonly said *berka* (thank you). Both men and women appeared to be somewhat intoxicated, but they were far from being quarrelsome.

Departing from thence, we passed several large villages, where I was constantly taken for a Moor, and became the subject of much merriment to the Bambarrans; who, seeing me drive my horse before me, laughed heartily at my appearance.—He has been at Mecca, says one; you may see that by his clothes: another asked me if my horse was sick; a third wished to purchase it, &c.; so that I believe the very slaves were ashamed to be seen in my company. Just before it was dark, we took up our lodging for the night at a small village, where I procured some victuals for myself, and some corn for my horse, at the moderate price of a button; and was told that I should see the Niger (which the Negroes call Joliba, or *the great water*), early the next day. The lions are here very numerous; the gates are shut a little after sunset, and nobody allowed to go out. The thoughts of seeing the Niger in the morning, and the troublesome buzzing of musketoes, prevented me from shutting my eyes during the night; and I had saddled my horse, and was in readiness before daylight: but, on account of the wild beasts, we were obliged to wait until the people were stirring, and the gates opened. This happened to be a market-day at Sego, and the roads were every where filled with people, carrying different articles to sell. We passed four large villages, and at eight o'clock saw the smoke over Sego.

As we approached the town, I was fortunate enough to overtake the fugitive Kaartans, to whose kindness I had been so much indebted in my journey through Bambarra. They readily agreed to introduce me to the king; and we rode together through some marshy ground, where, as I was anxiously looking around for the river, one of them called out, *geo affilli*, (see the water); and looking forwards, I saw with infinite pleasure the great object of my mission; the long sought for, majestic Niger, glittering to the morning sun, as broad as the Thames at Westminster, and flowing slowly to the *eastward*. I hastened to the brink, and, having drank of the water, lifted up my fervent thanks in prayer, to the Great Ruler of all things, for having thus far crowned my endeavours with success.

The circumstance of the Niger's flowing towards the east, and its collateral points, did not, however, excite my surprise; for although I had left Europe in great hesitation on this subject, and rather believed that it ran in the contrary direction, I had made such frequent inquiries during my progress, concerning this river; and received from Negroes of different nations, such clear and decisive assurances that its general course was *towards the rising sun*, as scarce left any doubt on my mind; and more especially as I knew that Major Houghton had collected similar information, in the same manner.

Sego, the capital of Bambarra, at which I had now arrived, consists, properly speaking, of four distinct towns; two on the northern bank of the Niger, called Sego Korro and Sego Boo; and two on the southern bank, called Sego Soo Korro and Sego See Korro. They are all surrounded with high mud-walls; the houses are built of clay, of a square form, with flat roofs; some of them have two stories, and many of them are whitewashed. Besides these buildings, Moorish mosques are seen in every quarter; and the streets, though narrow, are broad enough for every useful purpose, in a country where wheel carriages are entirely unknown. From the best inquiries I could make, I have reason to believe that Sego contains altogether about thirty thousand inhabitants. The King of Bambarra constantly resides at Sego See Korro; he employs a great many slaves in conveying people over the river, and the money they receive (though the fare is only ten Kowrie shells for each individual) furnishes a considerable revenue to the king, in the course of a year. The canoes are of a singular construction, each of them being formed of the trunks of two large trees, rendered concave, and joined together, not side by side, but end ways; the junction being exactly across the middle of the canoe: they are therefore very long and disproportionably narrow, and have neither decks nor masts; they are, however, very roomy; for I observed in one of them four horses, and several people, crossing over the river. When we arrived at this ferry, we found a great number waiting for a passage, they looked at me with silent wonder, and I distinguished, with concern, many Moors among them. There were three different places of embarkation, and the ferrymen were very diligent and expeditious; but, from the crowd of people, I could not immediately obtain a passage; and sat down upon the bank of the river, to wait for a more favourable opportunity. The view of this extensive city; the numerous canoes upon the river; the crowded population, and the cultivated state of the surrounding country, formed altogether a prospect of civilization and magnificence, which I little expected to find in the bosom of Africa.

I waited more than two hours, without having an opportunity of crossing the river; during which time the people who had crossed, carried information to Mansong the King, that a white man was waiting for a passage, and was coming to see him. He immediately sent over one of his chief men, who informed me that the king could not possibly see me, until he knew what had brought me into his country; and that I must not presume to cross the river without the king's permission. He therefore advised me to lodge at a distant village, to which he pointed, for the night; and said that in the morning he would give me further instructions how to conduct myself. This was very discouraging. However, as there was no remedy, I set off for the village; where I found, to my great mortification, that no person would admit me into his house. I was regarded with astonishment and fear, and was obliged to sit all day without victuals, in the shade of a tree; and the night threatened to be very uncomfortable, for the wind rose, and there was great appearance of a heavy rain; and the wild beasts are so very numerous in the neighbourhood, that I should have been under the necessity of climbing up the tree, and resting amongst the branches. About sunset, however, as I was preparing to pass the night in this manner, and had turned my horse loose, that he might graze at liberty, a woman, returning from the labours of the field, stopped to observe me, and perceiving that I was weary and dejected, inquired into my situation, which I briefly explained to her; whereupon, with looks of great compassion, she took up my saddle and bridle, and told me to follow her. Having conducted me into her hut, she lighted up a lamp, spread a mat on the floor, and told me I might remain there for the night. Finding that I was very hungry, she said she would procure me something to eat. She accordingly went out, and returned in a short time with a very fine fish; which, having caused to be half broiled upon some embers, she gave me for supper. The rites of hospitality being thus performed towards a stranger in distress, my worthy benefactress (pointing to the mat, and telling me I might sleep there without apprehension) called to the female part of her family, who had stood gazing on me all the while in fixed astonishment, to resume their task of spinning cotton; in which they continued to employ themselves great part of the night. They lightened their labour by songs, one of which was composed extempore; for I was myself the subject of it. It was sung by one of the young women, the rest joining in a sort of chorus. The air was sweet and plaintive, and the words, literally translated, were these.—'The winds roared, and the rains fell.—The poor white man, faint and weary, came and sat under our tree.—He has no mother to bring him milk; no wife to grind his corn. *Chorus*: Let us pity the white man; no mother has he, &c. &c.' Trifling as this recital may appear to the reader, to a person in my situation the circumstance was affecting in the highest degree. I was oppressed by such unexpected kindness; and sleep fled from my eyes. In the morning I presented my compassionate landlady with two of the four brass buttons which remained on my waistcoat; the only recompence I could make her.

July 21st. I continued in the village all this day, in conversation with the natives, who came in crowds to see me; but was rather uneasy towards evening, to find that no message had arrived from the king; the more so, as the people began to whisper, that Mansong had received some very unfavourable accounts of me, from the Moors and Slatees [black slave-merchants] residing at Sego; who it seems were exceedingly suspicious concerning the motives of my journey. I learnt that many consultations had been held with the king, concerning my reception and disposal; and some of the villagers frankly told me, that I had many enemies, and must expect no favour.

July 22nd. About eleven o'clock, a messenger arrived from the king; but he gave me very little satisfaction. He inquired particularly if I had brought any present; and seemed much disappointed when he was told that I had been robbed of every thing by the Moors. When I proposed to go along with him, he told me to stop until the afternoon, when the king would send for me.

July 23rd. In the afternoon, another messenger arrived from Mansong, with a bag in his hands. He told me, it was the king's pleasure that I should depart forthwith from the vicinage of Sego; but that Mansong, wishing to relieve a white man in distress, had sent me five thousand Kowries,[1] to enable me to purchase provisions in the course of my

[1] Mention has already been made of these little shells, . . . which pass current as money, in many parts of the East-Indies, as well as Africa. In Bambarra, and the adjacent countries, where the necessaries of life are very cheap, one hundred of them would commonly purchase a day's provisions for myself, and corn for my horse. I reckoned about two hundred and fifty Kowries, equal to one shilling. (*Park's note.*)

journey: the messenger added, that if my intentions were really to proceed to Jenne, he had orders to accompany me as a guide to Sansanding. I was at first puzzled to account for this behaviour of the king; but, from the conversation I had with the guide, I had afterwards reason to believe, that Mansong would willingly have admitted me into his presence at Sego; but was apprehensive he might not be able to protect me, against the blind and inveterate malice of the Moorish inhabitants. His conduct, therefore, was at once prudent and liberal. The circumstances under which I made my appearance at Sego, were undoubtedly such as might create in the mind of the king, a well warranted suspicion that I wished to conceal the true object of my journey. He argued, probably, as my guide argued; who, when he was told that I had come from a great distance, and through many dangers, to behold the Joliba river, naturally inquired if there were no rivers in my own country, and whether one river was not like another. Notwithstanding this, and in spite of the jealous machinations of the Moors, this benevolent prince thought it sufficient that a white man was found in his dominions, in a condition of extreme wretchedness; and that no other plea was necessary to entitle the sufferer to his bounty.

Travels, 1st edition, pp. 191–200

Leaving Segou, Park rode along the banks of the Niger for six days, until he reached the town of Silla. Here he reluctantly decided that he must turn back. The supply of money which Mansong had so generously given him was beginning to run out; the country beyond was in the hands of fanatical Moslems: it was clearly hopeless to think of travelling further down the river. Accordingly, on 30th July he began his return journey. All went comparatively well with him until 25th August, when he was attacked by robbers and plundered of everything he possessed except a shirt, a pair of trousers, and—most fortunately—his hat, the crown of which held his memoranda. On 19th September he fell seriously ill at Kamalia, where he was treate with the greatest kindness by a negro slave-dealer named Karfa Taura. He remained at Kamalia for exactly seven months and then set off with Karfa for Pisania, which he reached on 10th June 1797: on 22nd December he arrived at Falmouth.

His welcome in England was warm, but not effusive. He set to work to write an account of his journey, which appeared as Travels in the interior districts of Africa *in 1799: it had a considerable success, reaching a fourth edition in 1800. Meanwhile Park had retired to his own country, and in 1801 he set up in practice as a doctor at Peebles. He became a friend of his neighbour Walter Scott, who wrote a moving account of his last meeting with him. He was never at ease at home: he longed to return and finish the work he had begun; and when the Colonial Secretary offered him the chance of doing so in 1804, he eagerly accepted it.*

Park's second expedition was a grander affair than his first. He sailed from Portsmouth on 30th January 1805, taking with him his brother-in-law Alexander Anderson and a schoolfellow, George Scott. At Goree they picked up Lieutenant Martyn, thirty volunteer soldiers, four carpenters and two sailors. With this large company of white men Park set out from the Gambia in May: when he reached the Niger at Bamako on 19th August all but ten of his companions were dead of disease. But he refused to turn back or to slacken his pace: he was determined to sail down the river to its mouth. On 27th September he reached Sansanding: here he remained for two months, during the course of which Anderson died. From Sansanding he wrote the last of his letters to his wife which have survived.

7. LAST LETTER TO HIS WIFE

Sansanding, 19*th November*, 1805

It grieves me to the heart to write any thing that may give you uneasiness; but such is the will of him who *doeth all things well!* Your brother Alexander, my dear friend, is no more! He died of the fever at Sansanding, on the morning of the 28th of October; for particulars I must refer you to your father.

I am afraid that, impressed with a woman's fears and the anxieties of a wife, you may be led to consider my situation as a great deal worse than it really is. It is true, my dear friends, Mr. Anderson and George Scott, have both bid adieu to the things of this world; and the greater part of the soldiers have died on the march during the rainy season; but you may believe me, I am in good health. The rains are completely over, and the healthy season has commenced, so that there is no danger of sickness: and I have still a sufficient force to protect me from any insult in sailing down the river, to the sea.

We have already embarked all our things, and shall sail the moment I have finished this letter. I do not intend to stop or land any where, till we reach the coast; which I suppose will be some time in the end of January. We shall then embark in the first vessel for England. If we have to go round by the West Indies, the voyage will occupy three months longer; so that we expect to be in England on the 1st of May. The reason of our delay since we left the coast was the rainy season, which came on us during the journey; and almost all the soldiers became affected with the fever.

I think it not unlikely but I shall be in England before you receive this.—You may be sure that I feel happy at turning my face towards home. We this morning have done with all intercourse with the natives; and the sails are now hoisting for our departure for the coast.

Journal of a mission to the interior of Africa in the year 1805, 2nd edition, pp. 81–2

On the same day Park left Sansanding, with the four Europeans who were still alive, three slaves and a guide. From this time onwards all certain knowledge of him ceases; but it seems that he and all his white companions were drowned in the Niger when their boat sank after a fight with the inhabitants of Bussa.

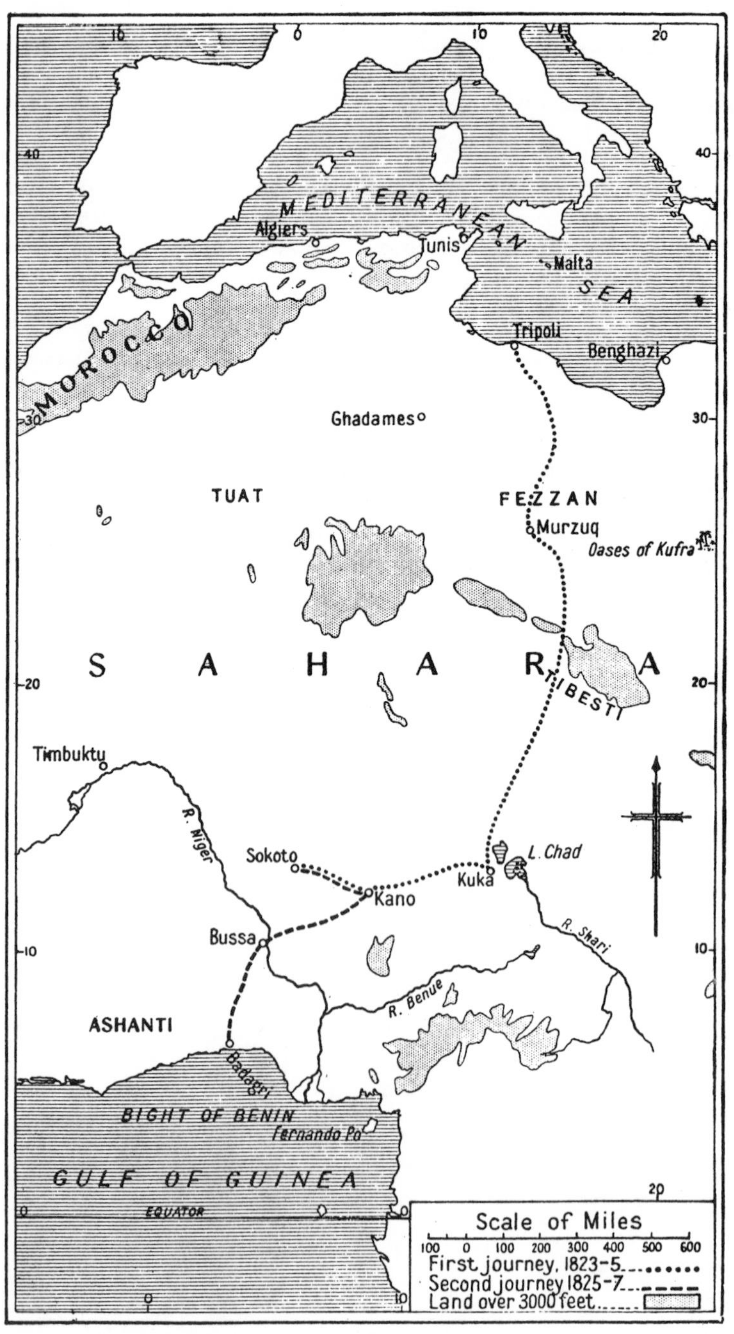

3. The Travels of Clapperton, 1822–7

III

HUGH CLAPPERTON
1788–1827

and

RICHARD LEMON LANDER
1804–1834

Clapperton, like Park, was a Lowland Scot, the son of a surgeon at Annan. After a meagre education he went to sea, first as a cabin-boy on a merchant ship and then in the navy (he was a victim of the press-gang). From 1808 to 1813 he served on the East India station: at the capture of Mauritius in 1810 he got first into the breach and himself hauled down the French flag. In 1814 he joined the British squadron on the Great Lakes of Canada: there he became romantically involved with the Hurons, and is said to have thought of marrying a Red Indian princess. In 1817 he came home on half-pay.

Three years later he met Dr. Walter Oudney, who had been invited by the British Government to undertake a mission into the interior of Africa: Clapperton volunteered to accompany him, and his offer was accepted. With them was associated Major Dixon Denham. They left Tripoli early in 1822 and made their way across the desert to Lake Chad, which they were the first Europeans to see. Here they separated, Denham going south-eastwards and finding the River Shari, Clapperton and Oudney making for the Niger through the Hausa states to the west in the company of a merchant of Fezzan named Mohamoud el Wordee. Oudney died at Murmur in January 1824, but Clapperton pushed on to Kano.

Kano was—it is still—the mercantile centre of the whole country between Lake Chad and the Niger, and at least as important as Timbuktu. Its name must continually have been mentioned to Clapperton during his journey as that of a great market, for it was the goal of the Arab caravans which travelled across the desert from Tripoli. After hearing so much of the great city for so long, it was almost inevitable that the reality should fall short of his expectation; but, as we shall see, his initial disappointment soon gave place to a deep interest in the market, which is very much the same to-day as when Clapperton wrote. There is another and fuller description of Kano, written thirty years later, in Barth's Travels and discoveries in North and Central Africa *(1857-8), vol. ii, pp. 97–147.*

8. CLAPPERTON'S ARRIVAL AT KANO

Jan. 20.—By El Wordee's advice, I prepared myself this morning for entering Kano, which was now at hand. Arrayed in naval uniform, I made myself as smart as circumstances would permit. For three miles to the north of Duakee, the country was open and well cultivated. It then became thickly covered with underwood, until we ascended a rising ground, whence we had a view of two little mounts within the walls of Kano. The soil here is a tough clay mixed with gravel, the stones of which appear to be clay iron-stone. The country was now clear of wood, except here and there a few large shady trees, resorted to as usual by the women of the country selling refreshments. The villages were numerous, and the road was thronged with people of all descriptions.

At eleven o'clock we entered Kano, the great emporium of the kingdom of Haussa, but I had no sooner passed the gates, than I felt grievously disappointed; for from the flourishing description of it given by the Arabs, I expected to see a city of surprising grandeur: I found, on the contrary, the houses nearly a quarter of a mile from the walls, and in many parts scattered into detached groups, between large stagnant pools of water. I might have spared all the pains I had taken with my toilet; for not an individual turned his head round to gaze at me, but all, intent on their own business, allowed me to pass by without notice or remark.

I went with El Wordee directly to the house of Hadje Hat Salah, to whom I had a letter of recommendation from the sheikh of Bornou. We found Hat Salah sitting under a rude porch in front of his house amid a party of Arabs, Tuaricks,[1] and people of the town. When El Wordee presented me, and told him of the sheikh's letter of recommendation, he bade me welcome, and desired me to sit down by his side. After exchanging many compliments, I inquired for the house he had hired for me, as El Wordee had sent a messenger on horseback the day before, to inform him of my approach, and to request him to have a house ready for my reception. Hat Salah now sent one of his slaves to conduct us to the house.

[1] I.e. Tuareg, known as 'the People of the Veil', a group of Hamitic tribes inhabiting the Eastern Sahara.

We had to retrace our steps more than half a mile through the market-place, which is bordered to the east and west by an extensive swamp covered with reeds and water, and frequented by wild ducks, cranes, and a filthy kind of vulture. The last is extremely useful, and by picking up offal serves as a sort of town scavenger. The house provided for me was situated at the south end of the morass, the pestilential exhalations of which, and of the pools of standing water, were increased by the sewers of the houses all opening into the street. I was fatigued and sick, and lay down on a mat that the owner of the house spread for me. I was immediately visited by all the Arab merchants who had been my fellow travellers from Kouka, and were not prevented by sickness from coming to see me. They were more like ghosts than men, as almost all strangers were at this time, suffering from intermittent fever. My house had six chambers above, extremely dark, and five rooms below, with a dismal looking entrance or lobby, a back court, draw-well and other conveniences. Little holes or windows admitted a glimmering light into the apartments. Nevertheless this was here thought a handsome mansion.

Feb. 1. 1824.—After breakfast I accompanied Hat Salah, the sheikh's agent, to the sansan [encampment], which, since it became a town, is also called Fanisoe, and presented the governor with one of the watches. He was highly pleased with it, and requested me to teach Hat Salah the use of it, that he might give lessons to the wan-bey [chief minister], who would in turn instruct him. I also showed him the sheikh's letter to his master Bello.[1] He read it, and told me I should be sent forward to Sackatoo[2] without delay in a kafila [caravan] which was then assembling.

On my return I met two governors with troops repairing to the sansan. They had each about five hundred horse and foot. The foot were armed with bows and arrows. The quiver is slung over the left shoulder, together with a small, highly ornamented leathern pouch for little necessaries, and a canteen of dried grass, so compactly plaited, that it is used for holding water. The bow unstrung is sometimes carried in the hand as a walking stick. Many carried on the head a little triangular bag, filled with bruised Guinea corn. Others wore a little conical grass cap, with a tuft of feathers. The rest of their dress consists solely of a tanned skin, strung with coarse shells, or fringed with tassels, girt round the loins, and a pair of sandals of very simple workmanship.

The cavalry were armed with shields, swords, and spears, and otherwise more sumptuously accoutred. The spear is about six feet long, the wooden shaft slender, and the point of iron. The swords are broad,

[1] The Sultan of Sokoto, who was also suzerain of the surrounding Emirates, including Kano.

[2] The accepted modern spelling of the name is 'Sokoto', but it is still pronounced, as some of the early travellers wrote it, 'Sockatoo'.

straight, and long, but require no particular description, as, by a vicissitude somewhat singular, they are in fact the very blades formerly wielded by the knights of Malta. These swords are sent from Malta to Benghazee, in the state of Tripoli, where they are exchanged for bullocks. They are afterwards carried across the desert to Bornou, thence to Haussa, and at last remounted at Kano, for the use of the inhabitants of almost all central Africa. The shields, covered with the hides of tame or wild animals, are generally plain and round. There is, however, a remarkable variety, not uncommon, of an oval shape, somewhat broader below than above, with an edging of blue cloth, forming six little lappets, one above, one below, and two on each side. In the centre of the shield there is a stripe of scarlet cloth fastened by the same studs that clinch the iron handle, and around it is scored a perfect Maltese cross. This kind of shield is borne by horsemen only; but it is found of the same shape and figure, equally among Tibboes [Tiber], Tuaricks, Felatahs,[1] and Bornouese. A cross of the same form, moulded in a sort of low relief, is not an unfrequent ornament on the clay plaster of their huts. Crosses of other forms also are sometimes cut in the doors of their houses. Several camels, loaded with quilted cotton armour, both for men and horses, were in attendance. One of the governor's slaves wore a quilted helmet of red cloth, very unwieldy, not unlike a bucket in shape, only scooped out in front for the face, and terminating on the crown in a large tin funnel, full of ostrich feathers. He was also clad in a red quilted corslet of the same cumbrous materials. The other articles of this armour are trunk hose for the rider, and a head piece, poitrel, and hausing, all quilted and arrow proof, for the horse. Armour, however, is hardly ever worn, except in actual combat, and then it must very much impede the quickness of their military evolutions. The saddles have high peaks before and behind. The stirrup irons are in the shape of a fire-shovel, turned up at the sides, and so sharp as to render spurs superfluous. This body of heavy horse protects the advance and retreat of the army, the bowmen being drawn up in the rear, and shooting from between the horsemen as occasion offers.

Feb. 10.—Kano is the capital of a province of the same name, and one of the principal towns of the kingdom of Soudan, and is situate in 12° 0′ 19″ north latitude by observation, and 9° 20′ east longitude by dead reckoning, carried on from a lunar observation at Kouka in Bornou.

Kano may contain from 30,000 to 40,000 resident inhabitants, of whom more than one half are slaves. This estimate of the population is of course conjectural, and must be received with due allowance, although I have studiously underrated my rough calculations on the subject. This

[1] I.e. the Fulani, who are to-day the ruling class in Northern Nigeria, though much mixed with the Hausa.

number is exclusive of strangers who come here in crowds during the the months from all parts of Africa, from the Mediterranean and dry Mountains of the Moon, and from Sennar and Ashantee.

The city is rendered very unhealthy by a large morass, which almost divides it into two parts, besides many pools of stagnant water, made by digging clay for building houses. The house gutters also open into the street, and frequently occasion an abominable stench. On the north side of the city are two remarkable mounts, each about 200 feet in height, lying nearly east and west from one another, and a trifling distance apart. They are formed of argillaceous iron-stone, mixed with pebbles, and a rather soft kind of marl. The city is of an irregular oval shape, about fifteen miles in circumference, and surrounded by a clay wall thirty feet high, with a dry ditch along the inside, and another on the outside. There are fifteen gates, including one ately built up. The gates are of wood, covered with sheet iron, and are regularly opened and shut at sunrise and sunset. A platform inside, with two guard-houses below it, serves to defend each entrance. Not more than one fourth of the ground within the walls is occupied by houses: the vacant space is laid out in fields and gardens. The large morass, nearly intersecting the city from east to west, and crossed by a small neck of land, on which the market is held, is overflowed in the rainy season. The water of the city being considered unwholesome, women are constantly employed hawking water about the streets, from the favourite springs in the neighbourhood. The houses are built of clay, and are mostly of a square form, in the Moorish fashion, with a central room, the roof of which is supported by the trunks of palm trees, where visitors and strangers are received. The apartments of the ground floor open into this hall of audience, and are generally used as store-rooms. A staircase leads to an open gallery overlooking the hall, and serving as a passage to the chambers of the second story, which are lighted with small windows. In a back courtyard there is a well and other conveniences. Within the enclosure in which the house stands, there are also a few round huts of clay, roofed with the stalks of Indian corn, and thatched with long grass. These are usually very neat and clean, and of a much larger size than those of Bornou. The governor's residence covers a large space, and resembles a walled village. It even contains a mosque, and several towers three or four stories high, with windows in the European style, but without glass or frame-work. It is necessary to pass through two of these towers in order to gain the suite of inner apartments occupied by the governor.

The soug, or market, is well supplied with every necessary and luxury in request among the people of the interior. It is held, as I have mentioned, on a neck of land between two swamps; and as this site is covered with water during the rainy season, the holding it here is consequently limited to the dry months, when it is numerously frequented as well by strangers as inhabitants: indeed, there is no market in Africa so well regulated. The sheikh of the soug lets the stalls at so much a month, and the rent forms a part of the revenues of the governor. The sheikh of the soug also fixes the prices of all wares, for which he is entitled to a small commission, at the rate of fifty whydah or cowries, on every sale amounting to four dollars or 8,000 cowries, according to the standard exchange between silver money and this shell currency. There is another custom regulated with equal certainty and in universal practice: the seller returns to the buyer a stated part of the price, by way of blessing, as they term it, or of luck-penny, according to our less devout phraseology. This is a discount of two per cent. on the purchase money; but, if the bargain is made in a hired house, it is the landlord who receives the luck-penny. I may here notice the great convenience of the cowrie, which no forgery can imitate; and which, by the dexterity of the natives in reckoning the largest sums, forms a ready medium of exchange in all transactions, from the lowest to the highest. Particular quarters are appropriated to distinct articles; the smaller wares being set out in booths in the middle, and cattle and bulky commodities being exposed to sale in the outskirts of the market-place: wood, dried grass, bean straw for provender, beans, Guinea corn, Indian corn, wheat, &c. are in one quarter; goats, sheep, asses, bullocks, horses, and camels, in another; earthenware and indigo in a third; vegetables and fruit of all descriptions, such as yams, sweet potatoes, water and musk melons, pappaw fruit, limes, cashew nuts, plums, mangoes, shaddocks, dates, &c. in a fourth, and so on. Wheaten flour is baked into bread of three different kinds; one like muffins, another like our twists, and the third a light puffy cake, with honey and melted butter poured over it. Rice is also made into little cakes. Beef and mutton are killed daily. Camel flesh is occasionally to be had, but is often meagre; the animal being commonly killed, as an Irish grazier might say, to save its life: it is esteemed a great delicacy, however, by the Arabs, when the carcass is fat. The native butchers are fully as knowing as our own, for they make a few slashes to show the fat, blow up meat, and sometimes even stick a little sheep's wool on a leg of goat's flesh, to make it pass with the ignorant for mutton. When a fat bull is brought to market to be killed, its horns are dyed red with henna ; drummers attend, a mob so on collects, the news of the animal's size and fatness soon spreads, and all run to buy. The colouring of the horns is effected by applying the green leaves of the henna tree, bruised into a kind of poultice. Near the shambles there is a number of cook-shops in the open air; each consisting merely of a wood fire, stuck round with wooden skewers, on which small bits of fat and lean meat, alternately mixed, and scarcely larger than a pennypiece each, are roasting. Every thing looks very clean and comfortable; and a woman does the honours of the table, with a mat dish-cover placed on her knees, from which she serves her guests, who are squatted around her. Ground gussub water is retailed at hand, to those who can afford this beverage at their repast: the price, at most, does not exceed twenty cowries, or about two farthings and 4/10 of a farthing, English money, estimating the dollar at five shillings. Those who have houses eat at home; women never resort to cook-shops, and even at home eat apart from men.

The interior of the market is filled with stalls of bamboo, laid out in regular streets; where the more costly wares are sold, and articles of dress, and other little matters of use or ornament made and repaired. Bands of musicians parade up and down to attract purchasers to particular booths. Here are displayed coarse writing paper, of French manufacture, brought from Barbary; scissors and knives, of native workmanship; crude antimony and tin, both the produce of the country; unwrought silk of a red colour, which they make into belts and slings, or weave in stripes into the finest cotton tobes; armlets and bracelets of brass; beads of glass, coral, and amber; finger rings of pewter, and a few silver trinkets, but none of gold; tobes, turkadees, and turban shawls; coarse woollen cloths of all colours; coarse calico; Moorish dresses; the cast off gaudy garbs of the Mamelukes of Barbary; pieces of Egyptian linen, checked or striped with gold; sword blades from Malta, &c. &c. The market is crowded from sunrise to sunset every day, not excepting their Sabbath, which is kept on Friday. The merchants understand the benefits of monopoly as well as any people in the world; they take good care never to overstock the market, and if any thing falls in price, it is immediately withdrawn for a few days.—The market is regulated with the greatest fairness, and the regulations are strictly and impartially enforced. If a tobe or turkadee, purchased here, is carried to Bornou or any other distant place, without being opened, and is there discovered to be of inferior quality, it is immediately sent back, as a matter of course, the name of the *dylala*, or broker, being written inside every parcel. In this case the *dylala* must find out the seller, who, by the laws of Kano, is forthwith obliged to refund the purchase money.

The slave market is held in two long sheds, one for males, the other for females, where they are seated in rows, and carefully decked out for the exhibition; the owner, or one of his trusty slaves, sitting near them. Young or old, plump or withered, beautiful or ugly, are sold without distinction; but, in other respects, the buyer inspects them with the utmost attention, and somewhat in the same manner as a volunteer seaman is examined by a surgeon on entering the navy: he looks at the tongue, teeth, eyes, and limbs, and endeavours to detect rupture by a forced cough. If they are afterwards found to be faulty or unsound, or even without any specific objection, they may be returned within three days. When taken home, they are stripped of their finery, which is sent back to their former owner. Slavery is here so common, or the mind of slaves is so constituted, that they always appeared much happier than their masters; the women, especially, singing with the greatest glee all the time they are at work. People become slaves by birth or by capture in war. The Felatahs frequently manumit slaves at the death of their master, or on the occasion of some religious festival. The letter of manumission must be signed before the cadi [a Moslem judge], and attested by two witnesses; and the mark of a cross is used by the illiterate among them, just as with us. The male slaves are employed in the various trades of building, working in iron, weaving, making shoes or clothes, and in traffic; the female slaves in spinning, baking, and selling water in the streets. Of the various people who frequent Kano, the *Nyffuans* [people of Nupe] are most celebrated for their industry; as soon as they arrive, they go to market and buy cotton for their women to spin, who, if not employed in this way, make *billam* for sale, which is a kind of flummery made of flour and tamarinds. The very slaves of this people are in great request, being invariably excellent tradesmen; and when once obtained, are never sold again out of the country.

I bought,for three Spanish dollars, an English green cotton umbrella, an article I little expected to meet with, yet by no means uncommon: my Moorish servants, in their figurative language, were wont to give it the name of 'the cloud'. I found, on inquiry, that these umbrellas are brought from the shores of the Mediterranean, by the way of Ghadamis.

Denham, Clapperton and Oudney, *Narrative of travels and discoveries in Northern and Central Africa*, 1st edition, Clapperton's narrative, pp. 39–55

While he was at Kano, Clapperton saw a boxing match, of which he gives a lively account.

9. BOXING MATCH AT KANO

Having heard a great deal of the boxers of Haussa, I was anxious to witness their performance. Accordingly I sent one of my servants last night to offer 2000 whydah for a pugilistic exhibition in the morning. As the death of one of the combatants is almost certain before the battle is over, I expressly prohibited all fighting in earnest; for it would have been disgraceful, both to myself and my country, to hire men to kill one another for the gratification of idle curiosity. About half an hour after the massi dubu[1] were gone, the boxers arrived, attended by two drums,

[1] Some jugglers who had performed before Clapperton in the morning.

and the whole body of butchers, who here compose 'the fancy.' A ring was soon formed, by the master of the ceremonies throwing dust on the spectators to make them stand back. The drummers entered the ring, and began to drum lustily. One of the boxers followed, quite naked, except a skin round the middle. He placed himself in an attitude as if to oppose an antagonist, and wrought his muscles into action, seemingly to find out that every sinew was in full force for the approaching combat; then coming from time to time to the side of the ring, and presenting his right arm to the bystanders, he said, 'I am a hyena;' 'I am a lion;' 'I am able to kill all that oppose me.' The spectators, to whom he presented himself, laid their hands on his shoulder, repeating, 'The blessing of God be upon thee;' 'Thou art a hyena;' 'Thou art a lion.' He then abandoned the ring to another, who showed off in the same manner. The right hand and arm of the pugilists were now bound with narrow country cloth, beginning with a fold round the middle finger, when, the hand being first clinched with the thumb between the fore and mid fingers, the cloth was passed in many turns round the fist, the wrist, and the fore arm. After about twenty had separately gone through their attitudes of defiance, and appeals to the bystanders, they were next brought forward by pairs. If they happened to be friends, they laid their left breasts together twice, and exclaimed, 'We are lions;' 'We are friends.' One then left the ring, and another was brought forward. If the two did not recognise one another as friends, the set-to immediately commenced. On taking their stations, the two pugilists first stood at some distance parrying with the left hand open, and, whenever opportunity offered, striking with the right. They generally aimed at the pit of the stomach, and under the ribs. Whenever they closed, one seized the other's head under his arm, and beat it with his fist, at the same time striking with his knee between his antagonist's thighs. In this position, with the head *in chancery*, they are said sometimes to attempt to gouge or scoop out one of the eyes. When they break loose, they never fail to give a swinging blow with the heel under the ribs, or sometimes under the left ear. It is these blows which are so often fatal. The combatants were repeatedly separated by my orders, as they were beginning to lose their temper. When this spectacle was heard of, girls left their pitchers at the wells, the market people threw down their baskets, and all ran to see the fight. The whole square before my house was crowded to excess. After six pairs had gone through several rounds, I ordered them, to their great satisfaction, the promised reward, and the multitude quietly dispersed.

Denham, Clapperton and Oudney, *Narrative of travels and di coveries in Northern and Central Africa*, 1st edition, Clapperton's narrative, pp. 57–9

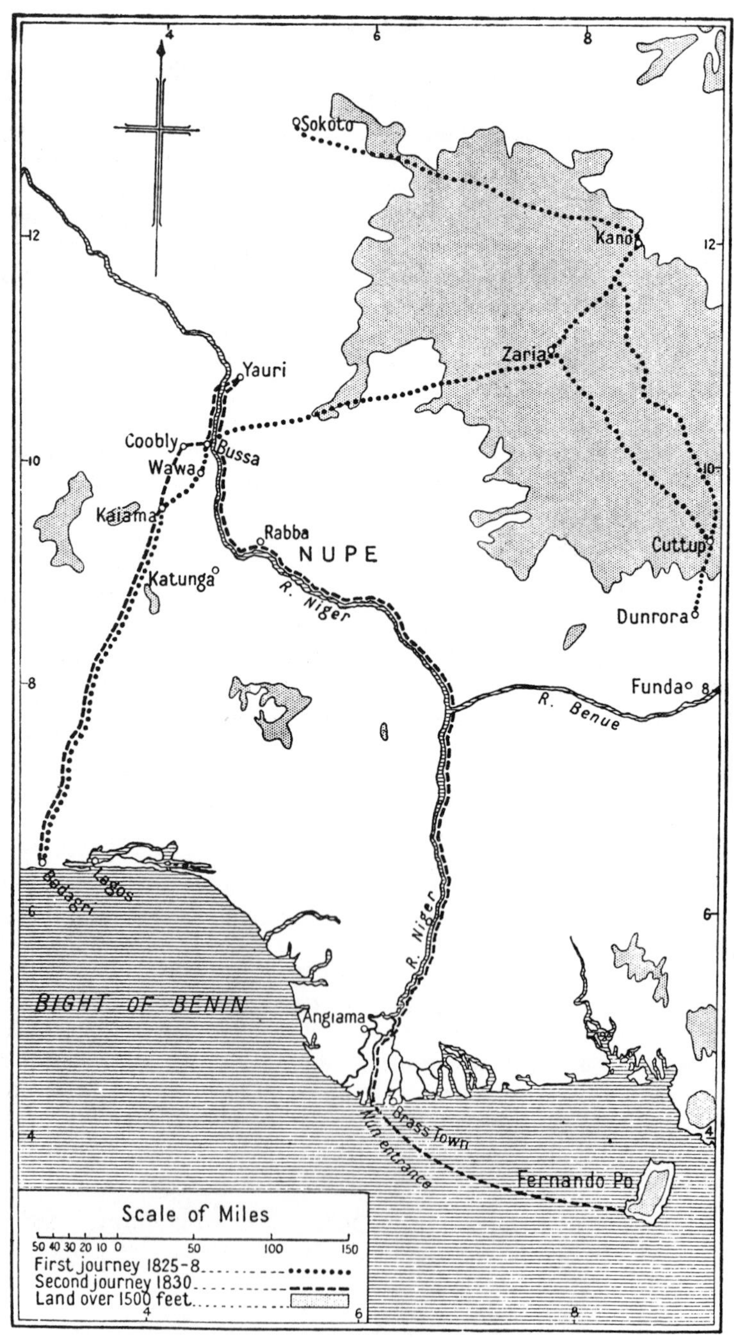

4. The Travels of Lander, 1825–34

Leaving Kano, Clapperton went on to Sokoto. Sultan Bello received him kindly but refused to let him pursue his journey to the Niger, although in fact the river lies only 150 miles away. So he was obliged to return eastwards: he met Denham at Kuka, and together they went back to Tripoli. They reached England on 1st June 1825.

Clapperton was immediately invited by the Secretary for War and the Colonies, Lord Bathurst (who was a good friend to the cause of African exploration), to lead another expedition into the interior, by a different route, northwards from the Bight of Benin, and to open up relations with Bello, who wished to conclude a treaty with England. Before the year was out Clapperton arrived at Badagri with four English companions, one of whom was his twenty-one year old servant Richard Lander.

RICHARD LEMON LANDER
1804–1834

Lander was a Cornishman, born at Truro (where his father kept an inn) in 1804. His education had been a little better than Clapperton's, but it had come to an end when he was thirteen. Since then he had led a roving life as a servant with various masters, visiting the West Indies, several parts of Europe, and South Africa. Soon after his return from the last of these journeys he offered his services to Clapperton, which were accepted. It is clear that he was romantically fired with the idea of African exploration: 'there was a charm in the very sound of Africa,' he afterwards wrote, 'that always made my heart flutter on hearing it mentioned'.

Almost as soon as they left the coast on this journey inland two of their English companions died, while the third had determined to follow another route through Dahomey, so that Clapperton and Lander had to travel on by themselves. They made first for Bussa, the town on the Niger at which Park was supposed to have met his death. Their journey was easy and not unduly slow until they reached Wawa, where they were delayed by the following adventures from 21st March to 5th April.

10. THE WIDOW ZUMA

Whilst we remained in the city of Wow Wow, we were visited almost every day by a widow lady, of Arab extraction, named *Zuma* (*Honey* in

English), between thirty and forty years of age, who, if one might be allowed to judge from the remaining charms which were still visible in her countenance, had been really beautiful in her younger years. This individual was vastly rich, being the acknowledged mistress of a thousand slaves; and from her excessive plumpness, and extraordinary size, was the exact counterpart of our bulky friend Ebo, the fat eunuch of Katunga. Zuma's affection for my master and myself was unbounded, and as it led to an adventure perhaps never equalled in novelty by any incident that has occurred to Europeans in the bosom of Africa, I hope I may be forgiven in attempting to trace its causes and effects, without which my narrative would be incomplete; for they are so intimately connected with each other, that it would be impossible to disunite them.

In order to give a clearer idea of the story, it will be necessary to remark, that Zuma was married in early life to one of the principal inhabitants of Wow Wow; but her spouse dying shortly after she had given birth to a son, she was left immensely rich, and lived in almost regal splendour in the native town of her deceased husband. Nature had endowed Zuma with an active, restless, and ambitious mind; insomuch that not long after she had become a widow, and before the regular term of mourning had expired, her weeds were thrown aside, and she aspired to the government of Wow Wow, by attempting to depose her sovereign. But Mohammed, although an imbecile and superstitious prince, could

'Bear, like a Turk, no rival near his throne!'

and was roused into action at the threatening aspect his too powerful subject had assumed. Instantly arming his vassals, he made a sudden and unexpected attack on the slaves of the rebellious lady, who for want of an efficient leader were put completely to the rout, though without bloodshed, and Zuma herself taken prisoner. Whether it was owing to the profound veneration in which that elegant lady's charms were held by the monarch, to the natural mildness of his disposition, or to the fear of stirring up the people against him, I could not learn; but certain it is that Zuma was pardoned, and set at liberty, after a confinement of only one or two days; and though she had repeated her treasonable attempt several times, even up to the period of our visiting the city, the same amiable forbearance had been extended to her.

It was the misfortune of the far-famed Zuma to fancy herself, for no reason in the world, to be extremely fair, and although she had certainly passed the 'Age of the Passions,' she took it into her head to fall desperately in love with me, whose complexion, she affirmed, rivalled her own in whiteness! The frequency of her visitations to our house nourished the tender feeling, which was encouraged by Captain Clapperton, who relished a joke with all his heart, and did his utmost to inflame the lady's passion, by passing a thousand unmeaning compliments on the regularity of my features, and the handsomeness of my person. 'See what beautiful eyes he has,' observed the Captain; 'if you were to search from Badagry to Wow Wow, you would not find such eyes.' For my own part I was but a novice in the art of courtship, and imagining it to be altogether in jest, took little pains to spoil the fun by shrinking from it. Besides, Zuma had behaved remarkably well to us in sending, repeatedly, presents of provisions, together with every luxury with which she was acquainted, and I was rather glad than otherwise to have her for our guest,

——'For the heart must
Leap kindly back to kindness;'

and neither of us wished to offend a lady of her consequence by being morose and unsociable in manners, or by repelling her advances with ridicule and contempt.

For an hour together the widow would gaze intently on me, while the most amorous glances shot from her large, full, and certainly beautiful eyes, which confused and disconcerted me not a little, even though I was surrounded by strangers and in the heart of Africa; for I had been a wanderer from my childhood, and had had but few opportunities of mingling in the delightful company of the gentler sex in my own country, and consequently was excessively bashful on coming in contact with ladies, whether in the country of the Hottentots, or the birth-place of the widow Zuma.

As for my master, he was sensibly delighted with these interviews, and with his arms folded on his breast, while thick volumes of tobacco-smoke rolled from his pipe, he with the most impenetrable gravity enjoyed the scene, and looked as happy and as much at home as if he had been seated by his friends in his native Scotland. After the widow's departure, it was his usual custom, tapping me on the shoulder, to ask how I felt my heart, and observe what a boast I could make, on our return to England, of so magnificent a conquest.

All this I took in good part for some days; but things beginning, at length, to wear a more serious aspect than I had at first anticipated, I was resolved to bring this whimsical courtship to a conclusion as speedily as possible. I was the more inclined to do so, because I did not wish to wound the feelings of even a *black* lady (for black she most certainly was, although not quite so deep a sable as the aborigines), by trifling with them; nor did I forget the exclamation of the frog in the fable:—'It may be sport to you, but it is death to us!'

Independently of the delicate state of my health, which incapacitated me from carrying on so curious an amour with the spirit and gallantry it required, I was positively afraid that, from the warmth and energy of Zuma's embraces, I should actually be pressed to death between her monstrous arms! I was but a youth, and my short residence in the country had certainly impaired a constitution originally robust and vigorous; by reason of which I was sadly apprehensive that one of her Brobdingnagian hugs would send me into the other world with very little ceremony. These reflexions I had seriously revolved in my mind; and on her next visit I candidly told the widow by signs, words, and gestures, that I could not love her; but she either did not or would not understand me. I remarked that I should never choose a *black* wife: she pointed to her face, and said she was a *white* woman. I then observed that it would be impossible for me to exist in her country, the heat being insupportable. Her reply was disinterested and tender:—'Then I will quit it, and follow you to whichever part of the world you may be inclined to lead me to.' Thus beset on all sides, I hardly knew what to say next; but after a short pause, summing up all my resolution, I gave my greasy inamorata a flat refusal to see her again in the light of a lover, as it was out of her power to awaken in my breast a corresponding sensation to that which reigned in her own! and saying this I instantly left the apartment; whilst Zuma, poor lady,

——'Rais'd a sigh so piteous and profound,
As it did seem to shatter all her bulk,
And end her being!'

I was surprised, however, to find that my cruelty had produced no visible effect on the widow, and that her *heart* was big in proportion to the largeness of her *body*; for I discovered that she could love *two* individuals at the same time with as much ardour and sincerity as *one* only. Seeing all hopes of success effectually shut out on my side, she had the good sense to discontinue her solicitations (although she continued her kindness), and looked as tenderly on me as ever; and applied herself strenuously to be on a more affectionate and friendly footing with Captain Clapperton, whose favourable notice she strove to attract by all the fascinating allurements she was mistress of; and actually went so far as to bribe Pasko, our Houssa interpreter, in order that he might use his *powerful* influence to bring the matter between my master and herself to an amicable adjustment. The old libertine accepted the present with rapture, which made the third or fourth spouse he had had since leaving Badagry, but he was prudent enough to retain his counsel within his own bosom.

A white husband and happiness were synonymous terms with the gentle and delicate Zuma, and she grasped at even the shadow of it with an eagerness and determination that caused her to overstep the boundaries of that amiable modesty which is so pleasing and peculiar a characteristic of her sex, whereby she did more towards injuring her own cause than coyness or reserve would have done. The Captain carried on the innocent game for some time, for we were greatly in want of something to enliven us; and so romantic an adventure as this, in such a place, and under such circumstances, caused us very many hours of diversion, and was an amusing subject of conversation even up to the period of my master's last illness at Soccatoo.

Poor widow Zuma! I almost fancy I see her now, waddling into our house, a moving world of flesh, 'puffing and blowing like a blacksmith's bellows,' and the very pink and essence of African fashion. Her hair used to be carefully dyed with indigo, and of a rich and vivid blue; her feet and hands stained with hennah and an extract of the goora-nut, produced alternate streaks of red and yellow; and her teeth were also tinged with a delicate crimson stain. In the adornment of her person, likewise, the buxom widow evinced considerable taste. Her bared neck and bosom were ornamented with coral and gold beads, which, contrasted with the dingy colour of her skin, occasioned a truly captivating effect! while a dress of striped silk, hanging in graceful folds from the waist to the ancles, set off her *fairy form* to the best possible advantage! Thus beautified, the accomplished Zuma used to sit cross-legged on our mat, and chewing the goora-nut, or a little tobacco-snuff, she was without exception the most ravishing object that came across our path in all our wanderings!

One day she invited my master to visit her at her own house, where she took the opportunity of displaying to him her wealth and grandeur, the number of her slaves, and her princely domestic establishment, all of which the tempter assured him he should share with her if he would consent to be her husband. No encouragement whatever was given to the lady; but when Capt. Clapperton left the town for Boussa a short time afterwards, Madam Zuma, dressed in her gaudiest attire, followed when he had got about six miles on his journey, having called before she set out to see me. On this occasion she wore a mantle of silk and gold, and loose trowsers of scarlet silk, with red morocco boots; her blue head was enveloped in the ample folds of a white turban, and she rode astride on the back of a noble horse, which came prancing before the door of our hut, decorated with a number of brass plates and bells, as well as a profusion of charms or amulets enclosed in green, red, and yellow leather. Her saddle-cloth was of scarlet, and the appearance of both widow and horse was singularly imposing. In her train were many spearmen on horseback, and bowmen on foot, with a band of musicians furnished with drums, fiddles, guitars, and flutes, who continued playing till their mistress was fairly out of the town. The widow briefly told me of her intention to accompany Capt. Clapperton to Kano, &c. &c. which éclaircissement startled me for an instant; but, putting on my most serious look, I wished her a pleasant journey, and hoped I should overtake her myself in a day or two. Zuma then took her leave, and the whole cavalcade was quickly out of sight.

I was absolutely longing to learn the issue of this strange elopement of Zuma's; and was engaged in making preparations previously to my departure for Coulfo, in Nyffe [Nupe], when a message from the king forbidding my departure from Wow Wow, diverted me from my intention, and overturned all my plans. I had an interview with the irritated Mohammed the same day, and another on the following one; but my efforts to induce him to change his resolution were abortive. He turned a deaf ear to all my eloquence, and would not suffer me to quit the town for any consideration; 'For,' said the king, 'your countryman has eloped with the captious Zuma, who will raise up enemies, and make war upon me, if she be not speedily checked; and the better way to accomplish this is to detain you here with the baggage, which will bring back the "great white man," and the widow will not be able to remain behind long after.'

In order to secure me the more effectually, our house was guarded by a dozen soldiers, who had received strict injunctions not to let me escape on any account. I contrived, however, to elude the vigilance of my keepers, and, taking with me a boy only twelve years of age, who had assisted me in making my escape, I hastily mounted my Yariba pony, and was on the road to Boussa in an instant.

At sunset I crossed the Menai, a branch of the Quorra [Niger], leading to the island; and after landing shortly entered the city. As soon as I was recognized as one of the strangers, a good house was immediately prepared for my reception, and I was presently honored with a visit from the king and queen, who informed me that my master had left Boussa, and that, if I were to travel all night, it would be impossible to overtake him before the next morning; they would therefore insist upon my remaining and sleeping in the city. My royal visitors staid with me a considerable time, and the queen gave directions about my supper, and even assisted to prepare it with her own hands.

A multitude of the usual questions were put to me by their majesties, which, on account of my almost total ignorance of the language in which they were uttered, I was not very well qualified to answer; but, notwithstanding this inconvenience, we succeeded in making ourselves pretty well understood; and from the excessive kindness, and watchful anxiety to anticipate my wants, it was evident that I was a great favourite with them.

The queen had certainly not much of the widow Zuma about her, either in appearance or manners; being delicate in person, and possessing a native delicacy and gracefulness of mien that could not fail to please. The features of the royal couple bore a closer resemblance to the European than the negro cast, and might be styled handsome, even in England; besides which an ineffable sweetness shone upon the countenance of Medaki, the queen, and there was an agreeableness in the innocent freedom of her deportment that captivated me at first sight. A tear of pity trembled in the expressive eye of Medaki, when, observing my emaciated looks, and surveying me from head to foot, she enquired if I had a mother in my own country; and when I answered that I had not, she said, 'Poor white man! then who have you at home to talk about you, and make fetishes for your preservation whilst you remain away?' I was certainly not prepared to meet with such extraordinary kindness at Boussa; and it shows the great revolution that has taken place in the opinions of the people since Mr. Park's appearance in the interior.

I had been extremely unwell before leaving Wow Wow; and my rapid journey on the back of a lean horse, without saddle or bridle, had nowise improved my health; fatigue also had rendered me so sleepy that after supper I could with difficulty keep my eyes open, and my answers to the queries of the royal pair were given at random. It was in vain that I bit my tongue and lips, and used every other means I could devise in order to arouse myself from the stupid state I was in; the inclination to slumber overcame them all, and at last I fell fast asleep. On awakening in the night I found myself alone, with a solitary lamp burning in my apartment; and was informed, an hour or two afterwards that their majesties, as soon as they saw me fairly insensible, had left me in the care of two slaves, and returned to their own abode, after expressly desiring them to make no noise that might awaken me. Next morning I went to the king to apologize for my unintentional breach of etiquette; and shaking hands with the royal couple, who wished me every happiness, I returned to Wow Wow (whither I had learnt Captain Clapperton had also gone back), in company of two armed men, who had been furnished as a protection against highway robbers, with which the road was declared to be infested. On my arrival in the city, I found that my master had entered it but a few minutes before, but had not seen the fat widow during his absence.

A short time only had elapsed before we resolved to go to the king; and being ushered into an apartment, found the important personage yawning from the effects of his afternoon's nap. The Captain was the fittest person in the world to deal with the African rulers. The first thing he did was to shake hands affectionately and heartily with the sullen Mohammed, covering his face at the same time with smiles and looks of joy on seeing him again; but the king accepted the compliment with just so good a grace as a growling mastiff would receive the caresses of a person against whom he bears a grudge; neither willing to bite the hand that pats its big head, nor wishing to be altogether on a friendly footing with its suspected friend. 'What pleasure it gives me to see you again,' said my master; 'I have not beheld so handsome a face as yours since leaving the city. I suppose you did not think it safe to send my baggage after me; and am therefore come to fetch it myself. I have seen the king of Boussa, who, with the Medaki, gave so very favorable an account of you, that really I am filled with admiration for your talents and virtues; and am sure there cannot be your equal in the whole country.' All this the great man listened to with a deal of attention, and one could perceive plainly enough that the sternness of his features gradually gave place to a softer and kindlier expression; indeed, from the commencement of the above well-timed encomium, a smile overspread his sable countenance which promised the most flattering results. His majesty then, with the utmost dignity, detailed his reasons for the line of conduct he had been obliged to adopt, in consequence of his belief that the Captain and the rebellious Zuma had entered into a conspiracy to usurp his authority; that when their treasonable object should be accomplished, he would be put out of the way, in order that my master might take the reins of government into his own hands. He added that the widow had been guilty of similar unlawful practices before, but had failed in her attempts; and that notwithstanding the lenity with which she had been treated, her thoughts were perpetually employed in devising means for the execution of her ambitious designs; and she had moreover threatened him unceasingly with raising an army to overcome and destroy him. As this was spoken with an air of great solemnity, and towards the latter part of it with emotion, which was plainly evinced by his tears, my master thought proper to disclaim, with correspondent energy and seriousness, the imputations on his own character, by professing himself a total stranger to the widow's movements from the time of his departure from Wow Wow; and as for deposing so powerful a prince as Mohammed, and taking Zuma to wife, such things were altogether beyond his ambition; and he ridiculed the very idea of it. He therefore hoped that the king would no longer refuse his permission for the party under his (Captain Clapperton's) command, to go on immediately, as he had bargained with the chief of the Houssa caravan to convey the goods to Kano, and he was impatiently waiting his arrival at the ferry. The old gentleman, however, was not quite so easily prevailed upon as we had anticipated; and in all probability was smitten with the widow's charms himself; for he declared with firmness, that until the absent lady returned, both my master and myself must abandon all thoughts of proceeding on our journey, or of again leaving Wow Wow. Further cajolery, we knew, would have been superfluous, so we were obliged to make a virtue of necessity, and wait patiently the re-appearance of our affectionate friend, the amiable Zuma. To our infinite joy that circumstance took place on the 5th of April, the day after our conference with the prince; the widow had not been able to meet with the object of her tender solicitude, and hearing that he had re-visited Wow Wow, agreeably to the prediction of Mohammed, returned to that town in much the same order as she had quitted it about a week before, without discovering the slightest symptoms either of disappointment of the ill-success of her jaunt, or fear for having so egregiously offended her sovereign.

Like most of her sex, however, Zuma knew perfectly well how to adapt her conduct to circumstances, and was, moreover, complete mistress of the art of dissimulation and deceit; for no sooner had she entered her own habitation, than her splendid habiliments were instantly thrown aside, and a dress of common country cloth substituted in their stead. Thus meanly attired, she paid her respects to Mohammed in our presence, and saluted him by falling on her knees, with her elbows to the earth, while, supporting her head on the palms of her hands, she shed a whole river of tears. Surely

> 'Heav'n gave to woman the peculiar grace,
> To spin, to weep, and cully human race.'

The great man looked sternly on her at first; but whose heart could be proof against *so much* loveliness in distress, and in that humiliating posture? Anger forsook his brow, as the prince of Wow Wow requested the repentant woman to rise; and simply upbraiding her for disregarding his authority and threatening to subvert his government, he shook hands, and desired her to go her way, but be more cautious of offending him in future. The widow accordingly left the house, and shaking the dust from her feet in token of bravado, cast a 'longing, lingering look behind;'—and we saw no more of the generous, the affectionate, but above all the enormous widow Zuma!

This singular adventure, though it caused us to laugh heartily, had been of a much more serious nature than we could have foreseen, and had given us much unnecessary trouble, as well as occasioned some days' delay; but when it was thus satisfactorily terminated, we resolved to be more guarded in encouraging, even in jest, the advances of the African belles, as our lives might thereby be endangered, by exciting the prejudices of the people against us. The widow being returned, and having promised to abide in peace, his majesty of Wow Wow offered no further impediment to our departure, and we quitted his capital on the following day.

Records of Captain Clapperton's last expedition,
vol. I, pp. 150–171

After leaving Wawa they crossed the Niger by a ferry below Bussa and made their way north-eastwards to Kano, where they arrived on 20th July. Both the travellers suffered continually from fever on the way, and at Kano Lander had a bad attack of dysentery. Clapperton had decided to go on to Sokoto by himself in order to see Bello. He travelled light, intending to return to Kano to pick up Lander and the heavy baggage and then to explore the country to the east. But on his way he learnt that Bello was away from Sokoto at the time, engaged in a campaign against Bornu. He did not reach the Sultan's camp until 15th October, when he found him completely preoccupied with the war and little interested in entering into relations with so remote and shadowy a Power as England. But Clapperton had set his heart on securing the treaty: his failure to do so preyed on his mind; and when Lander, who had meanwhile determined to follow his master from Kano, arrived on 23rd December, he found him dispirited and ill. Together they continued in the neighbourhood of Sokoto, dancing attendance on Bello. The way in which they kept up their spirits during this time is well illustrated at the beginning of the next extract.

11. THE DEATH OF CLAPPERTON

Before retiring to rest of an evening, cigars we had brought from England with us were generally produced; and we inhaled their grateful fragrance oftentimes for an hour or two. This was the only luxury left us; our tea and sugar had been consumed long before, and we fared in every respect like the Falatahs [Fulani] themselves. Squatted on mats in our huts, we spent the lingering hours in reading aloud, or chatting of our respective homes, and reciting village anecdotes; and it is really incredible to believe to what a ridiculous consequence the most trivial incident in the world was magnified in these our solitary conversations; and how often we laughed at jests which had been laughed at a thousand times before. But this can only be felt in an equal degree by persons similarly circumstanced with ourselves; every other avenue to enjoyment had been effectually blocked up; nor could we derive any pleasure from the society of the treacherous Arab or interested Falatah.

Sometimes, although neither of us was gifted with a voice of much power or compass, we attempted to sing a few English or Scotch tunes; and sometimes I played others on my bugle-horn. How often have the pleasing strains of 'Sweet, sweet Home,' resounded through the melancholy streets of Soccatoo? How often have its inhabitants listened with breathless attention to the music of the white-faced strangers? and observed to each other, as they went away, 'Surely those Christians are sending a blessing to their country and friends!' Any thing that reminded my master of his native Scotland was always heard with interest and emotion. The little poem, 'My native Highland home,' I have sung scores of times to him, as he has sat with his arms folded on his breast opposite to me in our dwelling; and notwithstanding his masculine understanding, and boasted strength of nerve, the Captain used to be somewhat moved on listening to the lines:

'Then gang wi' me to Scotland dear,
We ne'er again will roam;
And with thy smile, so bonny, cheer
My native Highland home!

For blithsome is the breath of day,
And sweet's the bonny broom,
And pure the dimpling rills that play
Around my Highland home.'

Thus our lonely evenings were spent; and when the time, the place, and the thousand other circumstances, are considered, the puerility of our amusements may surely be pardoned us. Such entertainments could not fail of awakening melancholy but pleasing associations within us; and to picture to our imaginations when in the bosom of Africa, and surrounded by wretches who sought our destruction, our own free and happy country, its heathy hills and flowery fields, and contrast them with the withering aspect of existing scenes, afforded us many an hour of delight and sorrow, gladness and gloom—although filling us with hopes that proved delusive, and expectations that we found, by fatal experience, to be in the highest degree visionary;—for, like the beautiful apple said to grow on the borders of the Red Sea, our hopes wore a fair and promising outside, but produced only bitter ashes.

For two months our manner of living and occupation were nearly unvaried. The Sheikh of Bornou had entered Houssa, during this period, with a multitude of men, and was reported to have laid siege to Kano, after the fall of which city he was to march to Soccatoo. This news terrified the inhabitants of the latter place to so great a degree, that every individual of consequence in it fled to the more secure and remote town of Magaria; and we were obliged to follow their example; but, events not turning out agreeably to anticipation, we returned to Soccatoo a week or fortnight afterwards.

On the 12th of March all thoughts of further enjoyment ceased, through the sudden illness of my dear kind master, who was attacked with dysentery on that day. He had been almost insensibly declining for a week or two previously, but without the slightest symptoms of this frightful malady. From the moment he was first taken ill, Captain Clapperton perspired freely, large drops of sweat continually rolling over every part of his body, which weakened him exceedingly; and, being unable to obtain any one, even of our own servants, to assist, I was obliged to wash the clothes, kindle and keep in the fire, and prepare the victuals with my own hands. Owing to the intense heat, my master was frequently fanned for hours together: indeed, all my leisure moments were devoted to this tedious occupation; and I have often held the fan till, from excessive weakness, it has fallen from my grasp.

Finding that, from increasing debility, I was unable to pay that unremitting attention to the numerous wants of the invalid which his melancholy state so peculiarly demanded, I sent to mallam Mudey on the 15th, entreating him to lend me a female slave to perform the operation of fanning. On her arrival the girl began her work with alacrity and cheerfulness; but soon becoming weary of her task, ran away, and never returned to our hut. I was therefore obliged to resume it myself; and, regardless of personal inconvenience and fatigue, strained every nerve, in order to alleviate, as much as possible, the sufferings occasioned by this painful disorder. My master daily grew weaker, and suffered severely from the intolerable heat of the atmosphere, the thermometer being, in the coolest place, 107 at twelve at noon, and 109 at three in the afternoon.

At his own suggestion I made a couch for him outside our dwelling, in the shade, and placed a mat for myself by its side. For five successive days I took him in my arms from his bed to the couch outside, and back again at sunset, after which he was too much debilitated to encounter even so trifling an exertion. He expressed a wish to write once, and but once, during his illness, but before paper and ink could be handed to him, he had fallen back on his bed, completely exhausted by his ineffectual attempt to sit up.

Fancying by certain suspicious symptoms, that my sick master had inadvertently taken poison, I asked him one day whether he thought that in any of his visits to the Arabs or Tuaricks in the city, any venomous ingredient had been secretly put into the camel's milk they had given him to drink, of which he was particularly fond. He replied, 'No, my dear boy, no such thing has been done, I assure you. Do you remember,' he continued, 'that when on a shooting expedition in Magaria, in the early part of February, after walking the whole of the day, exposed to the scorching rays of the sun, I was fatigued, and for some time lay under the branches of a tree? The soil on that occasion was soft and wet, and from that hour to the present I have not been free from cold. This has brought on my present disorder, from which, I believe, I shall never recover.'

For twenty days the Captain remained in a low and distressed state, and during that period was gradually but perceptibly declining; his body, from being strong and vigorous, having become exceedingly weak and emaciated, and, indeed, little better than a skeleton. There could not be a more truly pitiable object in the universe than was my poor dear master, at this time. His days were sorrowfully and ignobly wasting in vexatious indolence; he himself languishing under the influence of a dreadful disease, in a barbarous region, far, very far removed from his tenderest connections, and beloved country; the hope of life quenched in his bosom; the great undertaking, on which his whole soul was bent, unaccomplished; the active powers of his mind consumed away; and his body so torn and racked with pain, that he could move neither head, hand, nor foot without suppressed groans of anguish; while the fire and energy that used to kindle in his eye had passed away, and given place to a glossy appearance—a dull saddening expression of approaching dissolution.

In those dismal moments, Capt. Clapperton derived considerable consolation from the exercise of religious duties; and, being unable himself to hold a book in his hand, I used to read aloud to him daily and hourly some portions of the Sacred Scriptures. At times a gleam of hope, which the impressive and appropriate language of the Psalmist is so admirably calculated to excite, would pierce the thick curtain of melancholy that enveloped us; but, like the sun smiling through the dense clouds of a winter's day, it shone but faintly; and left us in a state of gloomier darkness than before.

Abderachman, an Arab from Fezzan, intruded himself one day into our hut, and wished to read some Mohammedan prayers to my master, but was instantly desired to leave the apartment, with a request that he would never enter it again. This individual was the only stranger that visited him during his sickness.

The Captain's sleep was uniformly short and disturbed, and troubled with frightful dreams, in which he often reproached the Arabs with emphasis and bitterness; but being myself almost a stranger to the language (Arabic) I could not distinctly understand the tenor of his remarks.

The unceasing agitation of mind, and exertion of body, which I had myself undergone in my unremitting duties, (never having in a single instance slept out of my clothes,) weakened me greatly; and a fever having come on me not long before my master's death, hung upon me for fifteen days, and brought me to the very verge of the grave. Almost at the commencement of this illness, there being no other person to assist me in the manner I could wish, I obtained permission to take Pasko again into our service. As soon as he entered the hut, the repentant old man fell upon his knees before the couch of his sick master, and intreated so piteously to be forgiven for the offences of which he had been guilty, that he was desired to rise, with a promise to overlook all that had passed, if his after-conduct should correspond with his apparent penitence.

By this means, the washing and all the drudgery were taken from my shoulders, which enabled me to devote my whole time and attention to my affectionate master's person; and, indeed, all my energies were required to bear me up under the pressure that almost bowed me to the dust. I fanned the invalid nearly the whole of the day, and this seemed to cool the burning heat of his body, of which he repeatedly complained. Almost the whole of his conversation reverted to his country and friends, although I never heard him regret his having left them; and he was patient and resigned to the last, a murmur of disappointment never escaping his lips.

On the first of April the patient became considerably worse; and, although evidently in want of repose, the virulence of his complaint prevented him from enjoying any refreshing slumbers. On the 9th, Maddie, a native of Bornou whom my master had retained in his service, brought him about twelve ounces of green bark, from the [shea] butter-tree, recommended to him by an Arab in the city; and assured us that it would produce the most beneficial effects. Notwithstanding all my remonstrances, a decoction of it was ordered to be prepared immediately, the too-confiding invalid remarking that no one would injure him. Accordingly, Maddie himself boiled two basons full, the whole of which stuff was swallowed in less than an hour.

On the following day he was greatly altered for the worse, as I had foretold he would be, and expressed regret for not having followed my advice. About twelve o'clock at noon, calling me to his bed-side, he said,

'Richard! I shall shortly be no more; I feel myself dying.' Almost choked with grief, I replied,

'God forbid! my dear master; you will live many years to come.'

'Do not be so much affected, my dear boy, I intreat you,' rejoined he; 'you distress me by your emotion; it is the will of the Almighty; and therefore cannot be helped. Take care of my journal and papers after my decease; and when you arrive in London, go immediately to my agents, and send for my uncle, who will accompany you to the Colonial office, and see you deposit them with the Secretary. After my body is laid in the earth, apply to Bello, and borrow money to purchase camels and provisions for crossing the desert to Fezzan in the train of the Arab merchants. On your arrival at Mourzouk, should your money be expended, send a messenger to Mr. Warrington, our Consul for Tripoli, and wait till he returns with a remittance. On your reaching the latter place, that gentleman will further advance you what money you may require, and send you to England the first opportunity. Do not lumber yourself with my books, but leave them behind, as well as my barometer and sticks, and indeed every heavy or cumbersome article you can conveniently part with; you may give them to mallam Mudey, who will preserve them. Remark whatever towns or villages you may pass through, and put on paper any thing remarkable that the chiefs of the different places may say to you.'

I said, as well as my agitation would permit me, 'If it be the will of God to take you, Sir, you may confidently rely, as far as circumstances will permit me, on my faithfully performing all that you have desired; but I hope and believe that the Almighty will yet spare you to see your home and country again.'

'I thought at one time,' continued he, 'that that would be the case, but I dare not entertain such hopes now; death is on me, and I shall not be long for this world; God's will be done.' He then took my hand betwixt his, and looking me full in the face, while a tear glistened in his eye, said in a tremulous, melancholy tone:

'My dear Richard, if you had not been with me I should have died long ago. I can only thank you with my latest breath for your devotedness and attachment to me; and if I could live to return to England with you, you should be placed beyond the reach of want; the Almighty, however, will reward you.'

This pathetic conversation, which occupied almost two hours, greatly exhausted my master, and he fainted several times whilst speaking. The same evening he fell into a slumber, from which he awoke in much perturbation, and said that he had heard with peculiar distinctness the tolling of an English funeral bell; but I entreated him to be composed, observing that sick people frequently fancy things which in reality can have no existence. He shook his head, but said nothing.

About six o'clock on the morning of the 11th April, on my asking him how he did, my master replied in a cheerful tone, that he felt much better; and requested to be shaved. He had not sufficient strength to lift his head from the pillow; and after finishing one side of the face I was obliged myself to turn his head in order to get at the other. As soon as he was shaved, he desired me to fetch him a looking-glass which hung on the opposite side of the hut; and on seeing the reflection of his face in it, observed that he looked quite as ill in Bornou on his former journey, and that as he had borne his disorder for so long a time, there was some possibility of his yet recovering. On the following day he still fancied himself to be convalescent, in which belief I myself agreed, as he was enabled to partake of a little hashed guinea fowl in the course of the afternoon, which he had not done before during the whole of his confinement, having derived his sole sustenance from a little fowl soup and milk and water.

These flattering anticipations, however, speedily vanished, for on the morning of the 13th, being awake, I was greatly alarmed on hearing a peculiar rattling noise issuing from my master's throat, and his breathing at the same time was loud and difficult. At that moment, on his calling out 'Richard!' in a low, hurried, and singular tone, I was instantly at his side, and was astonished beyond measure on beholding him sitting upright in his bed (not having been able for a long time previously to move a limb), and staring wildly around. Observing him ineffectually struggling to raise himself on his feet, I clasped him in my arms, and whilst I thus held him, could feel his heart palpitating violently. His throes became every moment less vehement, and at last they entirely ceased, insomuch that thinking he had fallen into a slumber, or was overpowered by faintings I placed his head gently on my left shoulder, gazing for an instant on his pale and altered features; some indistinct expressions quivered on his lips, and whilst he vainly strove to give them utterance, his heart ceased to vibrate, and his eyes closed for ever!

I held the lifeless body in my arms for a short period, overwhelmed with grief; nor could I bring myself to believe that the soul which had animated it with being, a few moments before, had actually quitted it.

I then unclasped my arms, and held the hand of my dear master in mine; but it was cold and dead, and instead of returning the warmth with which I used to press it, imparted some of its own unearthly chillness to my frame, and fell heavily from my grasp. O God! what was my distress in that agonizing moment? Shedding floods of tears, I flung myself along the bed of death, and prayed that Heaven would in mercy take my life!

The violence of my grief having subsided, Pasko and Mudey, whom my exclamations had brought into the apartment, fetched me water, with which I washed the corpse, and with their assistance, carried it outside the hut, laid it on a clean mat, and wrapped it in a sheet and blanket. After leaving it in this state nearly two hours, I put a large neat mat over the whole, and sent a messenger to make Bello acquainted with the mournful event, as well as to obtain his permission to have the body buried after the manner of my own country; and also to learn in what particular place the Sultan would wish to have it interred. The man soon returned with a favourable answer to the former part of my request, and about twelve o'clock on the morning of the same day, a person came into the hut, accompanied by four slaves, to dig the grave; and wished me to follow him with the corpse. Accordingly, saddling my camel, the body was placed on the animal's back, and throwing a British flag over it, I requested the men to proceed. Having passed through the dismal streets of Soccatoo, we travelled almost unobservedly, at a solemn pace, and halted near Jungavie, a small village, built on a rising ground about five miles south-east of the city. The body was then taken from the camel's back, and placed in a shed, whilst the slaves were employed in digging the grave. Their task being speedily accomplished, the corpse was borne to the brink of the pit, and I planted the flag close to it; then, uncovering my head, and opening a prayer-book, amidst showers of tears, I read the impressive funeral service of the Church of England over the remains of my valued master—the English flag waving slowly over them at the same moment. Not a single soul listened to this peculiarly distressing ceremony; for the slaves were quarrelling with each other the whole of the time it lasted.

This being done, the flag was taken away, and the body slowly lowered into the earth; and I wept bitterly as I gazed, for a last time, on all that remained of my intrepid and beloved master. The grave was quickly closed, and I returned to the village, about thirty yards to the eastward of it, and giving the most respectable inhabitants of both sexes a few trifling presents, entreated them to let no one disturb the ashes of the dead; and also offered them a sum of money to erect a shed over the spot, which having accepted, they promised to do.

Thus perished, and thus was buried, Captain Hugh Clapperton in the prime of life, and in the strength and vigour of his manhood. No one could be better qualified than he by a fearless, indomitable spirit, and utter contempt of danger and death, to undertake and carry into execution an enterprise of so great importance and difficulty, as the one with which he was entrusted. He had studied the African character in all its phases—in its moral, social, and external form; and like Alcibiades accommodated himself with equal ease to good as well [as] to bad fortune—to prosperity, as well as to adversity. He was never highly elated at the prospect of accomplishing his darling wishes—the great object of his ambition—nor deeply depressed when environed by danger, care, disappointment, and bodily suffering, which hanging heavily upon him forbade him to indulge in hopeful anticipations. The negro loved him, because he admired the simplicity of his manners, and mingled with pleasure in his favourite dance; the Arab hated him, because he was overawed by his commanding appearance, and because the keen penetrating glance of the British Captain detected his guilty thoughts, and made him quail with apprehension and fear.

Captain Clapperton's stature was tall; his disposition was warm and benevolent; his temper mild, even, and cheerful; while his ingenuous, manly countenance pourtrayed the generous emotions that reigned in his breast. In fine, he united the figure and determination of a man, with the gentleness and simplicity of a child; and, if I mistake not, he will live in the memory of many thousands of Africans, until they cease to breathe, as something more than mortal; nor have I the least doubt that the period of his visiting their country will be regarded by some as a new era, from which all events of consequence, that affect them, will hereafter be dated.

The grave was dug on a naked piece of ground, with no remarkable object near it to invite attention;—no mournful cypress or yew weeps over the lonely spot—no sculptured marble shines above all that remains of heroic enterprize and daring adventure! But the sleeper needs no funereal emblem to perpetuate his name and actions, having erected for himself a nobler and far more imperishable mausoleum in the breasts of his countrymen and the civilized world, than all the artists in the universe could rear over his ashes.

Returning, after the funeral, disconsolate and oppressed, to my solitary habitation, I leaned my head on my hands, and could not help being deeply affected with my lonesome and dangerous situation. A hundred and fifteen days' journey from the sea-coast; surrounded by a selfish and barbarous race of strangers;—my only friend and protector and last hope, mouldering in his grave, and myself suffering dreadfully from fever: I felt as if I stood alone in the world, and wished, ardently wished, I had been enjoying the same deep, undisturbed, cold sleep as my master, and in the same grave. All the trying evils I had encountered —all the afflictions I had endured—all the bereavements I had experienced, never affected me half so much as the bitter reflections of that distressing period. After a sleepless night, I went alone to the grave, and found that nothing had been done to it, nor did there seem to be the least inclination on the part of the inhabitants of the village to redeem their pledge. Knowing it would be useless to remonstrate with such wretches, I hired two slaves in Soccatoo the next day, who went to work immediately, and the shed over the grave was finished on the 15th.

Records of Captain Clapperton's last expedition,
vol. II, pp. 63–81

Lander's business was now to return to England with his master's papers. As we have seen, Clapperton advised him to travel back across the Sahara, following the route he had himself taken in 1822–4. But Lander saw a rich prize in view in another direction. Why should he not make for Funda, which he had often heard spoken of at Sokoto as a town on the Niger, and thence trace the course of the river down to its mouth?[1] *Having made up his mind to do this, he travelled back to Kano and then struck out southwards. But when he reached Dunrora, twelve days' journey from Funda, he was overtaken by some horsemen of the King of Zaria who peremptorily ordered him to accompany them back to their master. With this demand he had of course to comply. He was thus compelled to give up for the time being his hopes of solving the Niger question, and made his way back to Badagri by the same route he had taken with Clapperton on the outward journey. He reached Portsmouth on 30th April 1828.*

[1] In fact, as he subsequently discovered, Funda was on the Benue, three days' march from its junction with the Niger. It was destroyed by the Fulani in 1853.

After delivering up his master's papers, he set to work to write a short account of his adventures, which was published in 1829 with Clapperton's Narrative of a second expedition into the interior of Africa. *The following year there appeared his more finished version of the whole story,* Records of Captain Clapperton's last expedition.

Lander must have been a man of very striking personality, for though he was only twenty-five years old, and a servant at that, he prevailed upon Lord Bathurst to send him out again to Africa for the purpose of tracing the Niger from Bussa to its mouth, and he obtained leave to take with him his younger brother John. They left England on 9th January 1830 and Badagri on 31st March. Following the old route, they reached Kaiama on 28th May. Here, on 2nd June, they saw a horse race in celebration of a Moslem festival known as 'Bebun Salah', or 'Great Prayer Day'.

12. HORSE RACE AT KAIAMA

In the afternoon, all the inhabitants of the town, and many from the little villages in its neighbourhood, assembled to witness the horse-racing, which takes place always on the anniversary of the 'Bebun Salah,' and to which every one had been looking forward with impatience. Previous to its commencement, the king, with his principal attendants, rode slowly round the town, more for the purpose of receiving the admiration and plaudits of his people than to observe where distress more particularly prevailed, which was his avowed intention. A hint from the chief induced us to attend the course with our pistols, to salute him as he rode by; and as we felt a strong inclination to witness the amusements of the day, we were there rather sooner than was necessary, which afforded us, however, a fairer opportunity of observing the various groups of people which were flocking to the scene of amusement.

The race-course was bounded on the north by low granite hills; on the south by a forest; and on the east and west by tall shady trees, among which were habitations of the people. Under the shadow of these magnificent trees the spectators were assembled, and testified their happiness by their noisy mirth and animated gestures. When we arrived, the king had not made his appearance on the course; but his absence was fully compensated by the pleasure we derived from watching the anxious and animated countenances of the multitude, and in passing our opinions on the taste of the women in the choice and adjustment of their fanciful and many-coloured dresses. The chief's wives and younger children sat near us in a group by themselves; and were distinguished from their companions by their superior dress. Manchester cloths of inferior quality, but of the most showy patterns, and dresses made of common English bed-furniture, were fastened round the waist of several sooty maidens, who, for the sake of fluttering a short hour in the gaze of their countrymen, had sacrificed in clothes the earnings of a twelvemonth's labour. All the women had ornamented their necks with strings of beads, and their wrists with bracelets of various patterns, some made of glass beads, some of brass, others of copper; and some again of a mixture of both metals: their ancles also were adorned with different sorts of rings, of neat workmanship.

The distant sound of drums gave notice of the king's approach, and every eye was immediately directed to the quarter from whence he was expected. The cavalcade shortly appeared, and four horsemen first drew up in front of the chief's house, which was near the centre of the course, and close to the spot where his wives and children and ourselves were sitting. Several men bearing on their heads an immense quantity of arrows in huge quivers of leopard's skin came next, followed by two persons who, by their extraordinary antics and gestures, we concluded to be buffoons. These two last were employed in throwing sticks into the air as they went on, and adroitly catching them in falling, besides performing many whimsical and ridiculous feats. Behind these, and immediately preceding the king, a group of little boys, nearly naked, came dancing merrily along, flourishing cows' tails over their heads in all directions. The king rode onwards, followed by a number of fine-looking men, on handsome steeds; and the motley cavalcade all drew up in front of his house, where they awaited his further orders without dismounting. This we thought was the proper time to give the first salute, so we accordingly fired three rounds; and our example was immediately followed by two soldiers, with muskets which were made at least a century and a half ago.

Preparations in the mean time had been going on for the race, and the horses with their riders made their appearance. The men were dressed in caps and loose tobes and trowsers of every colour; boots of red morocco leather, and turbans of white and blue cotton. The horses were gaily caparisoned; strings of little brass bells covered their heads; their breasts were ornamented with bright red cloth and tassels of silk and cotton; a large quilted pad of neat embroidered patchwork was placed under the saddle of each; and little charms, inclosed in red and yellow cloth, were attached to the bridle with bits of tinsel. The Arab saddle and stirrup were in common use; and the whole group presented an imposing appearance.

The signal for starting was made, and the impatient animals sprung forward and set off at a full gallop. The riders brandished their spears, the little boys flourished their cows' tails, the buffoons performed their antics, muskets were discharged, and the chief himself, mounted on the finest horse on the ground, watched the progress of the race, while tears of delight were starting from his eyes. The sun shone gloriously on the tobes of green, white, yellow, blue, and crimson, as they fluttered in the breeze; and with the fanciful caps, the glittering spears, the jingling of the horses' bells, the animated looks and warlike bearing of their riders, presented one of the most extraordinary and pleasing sights that we have ever witnessed. The race was well contested, and terminated only by the horses being fatigued and out of breath; but though every one was emulous to outstrip his companion, honour and fame were the only reward of the competitors.

A few naked boys, on ponies without saddles, then rode over the course, after which the second and last heat commenced. This was not by any means so good as the first, owing to the greater anxiety which the horsemen evinced to display their skill in the use of the spear and the management of their animals. The king maintained his seat on horseback during these amusements, without even once dismounting to converse with his wives and children who were sitting on the ground on each side of him. His dress was showy rather than rich, consisting of a red cap, enveloped in the large folds of a white muslin turban; two under tobes of blue and scarlet cloth, and an outer one of white muslin, red trowsers, and boots of scarlet and yellow leather. His horse seemed distressed by the weight of his rider, and the various ornaments and trappings with which his head, breast, and body, were bedecked. The chief's eldest and youngest sons were near his women and other children, mounted on two noble looking horses. The eldest of these youths was about eleven years of age. The youngest being not more than three, was held on the back of his animal by a male attendant, as he was unable to sit upright in the saddle without this assistance. The child's dress was ill suited to his age. He wore on his head a tight cap of Manchester cotton, but it overhung the upper part of his face, and together with its ends, which flapped over each cheek, hid nearly the whole of his countenance from view; his tobe and trowsers were made exactly in the same fashion as those of a man, and two large belts of blue cotton, which crossed each other, confined the tobe to his body. The little legs of the child were swallowed up in clumsy yellow boots, big enough for his father; and though he was rather pretty, his whimsical dress gave him altogether so odd an appearance, that he might have been taken for any thing but what he really was. A few of the women on the ground by the side of the king wore large white dresses, which covered their persons like a winding-sheet. Young virgins, according to custom, appeared in a state of nudity; many of them had wild flowers stuck behind their ears, and strings of beads, &c, round their loins; but want of clothing did not seem to damp their pleasure in the entertainment for they appeared to enter into it with as much zest as any of their companions. Of the different coloured tobes worn by the men, none looked so well as those of a deep crimson colour on some of the horsemen; but the clean white tobes of the Mohammedan priests, of whom not less than a hundred were present on the occasion, were extremely neat and becoming. The sport terminated without the slightest accident, and the king's dismounting was a signal for the people to disperse.

Journal of an expedition to explore the course and termination of the Niger, 1st edition, vol. I, pp. 240–6

Three days later they left Kaiama, and passing through Wawa, where Richard Lander renewed acquaintance with the Widow Zuma, they arrived at Bussa on 17th June. Bussa remained their headquarters, from which they made visits to Yauri and Wawa, until 20th September. The king and queen behaved as kindly to them as they had to Richard Lander and Clapperton in 1826. While they were there, another Moslem festival occurred, during which the king made a remarkable speech.

13. THE KING OF BUSSA

Wednesday, September 1st.—Day was drawing to a close, and evening fast approaching, when the king came out of his residence to show himself to his people. He was attended by a number of his head men, with whom he perambulated the town; and afterwards proceeded outside the gates o offer up a short prayer with them to the gods of his religion, for he is still a pagan, as all his fathers were, though he employs Mahomedan priests to pray for his welfare, and intercede with their prophet in his behalf, agreeably to their form of worship. Several musicians were in attendance with drums, fifes, and long Arab trumpets of brass; these men preceded their sovereign, and played lustily on their instruments all the while he was returning to his house. He shortly came out again, and rode slowly up the race-course, attended by people of both sexes, most uncouthly dressed, singing and dancing before him, and followed by a party of well-dressed men mounted on mettlesome horses, and equipped as if for war. On our saluting him, the monarch stopped and sent us a goora-nut, which, on such an occasion as this, is considered as a mark of great condescension, and a sign of peculiar favour; and he stayed opposite us at least ten minutes, to give us a fair opportunity of admiring his grandeur, and diverting ourselves by the frolicsome gambols of his attendants. Smiling at our wonderment, and gratified with the respect we paid him by discharging our pistols close to his person, he nodded and passed on. The king was mounted on a fine handsome grey horse, sumptuously caparisoned; while he himself is a noble and commanding figure on horseback, and was dressed extremely well, in a red cap and large turban of the same colour, a silk damask tobe of green and crimson, made full and flowing, red cloth trousers and Arab boots. Groups of well-dressed individuals were seated under every tree with spears, quivers of arrows, long bows, and ornamented cows' tails. These latter were flourished about as the people sang; their owners threw them high into the air, and danced at the same time in the most extraordinary manner, and flung their limbs about as though they had been actuated by a supernatural power. Every one was exhilarated and in motion,—both horseman and footman, woman and child. The musicians also, not satisfied by making the whole of Boossa echo with the most grating and outrageous sounds conceivable, both sung, or rather screamed and danced, twisting their mouths, with their exertions, into all manner of wry and comical shapes. The spectacle altogether was odd and grotesque beyond description, and such an one could never enter into the dreams or waking visions of an European. Guns were fired by the king's followers, and other obstreporous and astounding noises were made by the people. Never did we see the king in a happier mood; his satisfaction seemed to be quite complete. He smiled graciously on all around him; and bestowed many an arch and significant look upon us, as if he would have said, 'Can *your* sovereign boast so splendid a retinue as mine, or display so much regal splendour?'

The ceremony was long and fatiguing; and though the king was screened from the sun's rays by two large ponderous umbrellas, and though two men were standing by, constantly fanning him, yet perspiration stood in large drops upon his forehead, and he appeared nearly exhausted. After our curiosity had been amply gratified, the king rode away, preceded by his singing and dancing women, his musicians, his bowmen, and his spearmen, with all their noise and clamour. . . . The king is a graceful rider, and displayed his horsemanship to much advantage by galloping up and down the course; and, owing to his advantageous stature, his appearance was very becoming. The sun was then setting, and as soon as he had disappeared, the amusements ceased. The people, both strangers and inhabitants, were then collected together before the king's house, for the purpose of hearing an oration from their monarch; for, in pursuance of an ancient and established practice, the king of Boossa annually harangues his people on the celebration of this festival. The sovereign is at least a head taller than any of his subjects, so that he was a remarkable and conspicuous object to every one of his audience. If such a comparison may be ventured on, the commencement of his speech was in its nature not much unlike that delivered on the opening of parliament by his Majesty of England. The king of Boossa began by assuring his people of the internal tranquillity of the empire, and of the friendly disposition of foreign powers towards him. He then exhorted his hearers to attend to the cultivation of the soil, to work diligently, and live temperately; and concluded with an injunction for them all to be abstemious in the use of beer. He declared that too much indulgence in it was the source of much evil and wretchedness, and the cause of most of the quarrels and disturbances that had taken place in the city. 'Go; retire to rest soberly and cheerfully,' said the king, 'and do as I have requested you, when you will be an example to your neighbours, and win the good opinion and applause of mankind.' The king's speech lasted for three-quarters of an hour. He spoke vehemently and with much eloquence; his language was forcible and impressive, and his action appropriate and commanding; and he dismissed the assembly with a graceful and noble air. Instead of a sceptre the monarch flourished the tuft of a lion's tail.

Journal of an expedition to explore the course and termination of the Niger, 1st edition, vol. II, pp. 162–167

Leaving Bussa in a canoe, they paddled down the river rapidly and almost without incident until they reached a village named Bocqua, just below the confluence of the Niger and the Benue.

14. AN ATTACK AVERTED

At 10 a.m., we passed a huge and naked white rock, in the form of a perfect dome, arising from the centre of the river. It was about twenty feet high, and covered with an immense quantity of white birds, in consequence of which we named it the Bird Rock: it is about three or four miles distant from Bocqua, on the same side of the river. It is safest to pass it on the south-east side, on which side is also the proper channel of the river, about three miles in width. We passed it on the western side, and were very nearly lost in a whirlpool. It was with the utmost difficulty we preserved the canoe from being carried away, and dashed against the rocks. Fortunately, I saw the danger at first, and finding we could not get clear of it, my brother and I took a paddle, and animating our men, we exerted all our strength, and succeeded in preventing her from turning round. The distance of this rock from the nearest bank is about a quarter of a mile, and the current was running with a velocity of six miles an hour, according to our estimation. Had our canoe become unmanageable, we should inevitably have perished. Shortly after, seeing a convenient place for landing, the men being languid and weary with hunger and exertion, we halted on the right bank of the river, which we imagined was most convenient for our purpose. The course of the river this morning was south-south-west, and its width varied as usual from two to six miles. The angry and scowling appearance of the firmament forewarned us of a heavy shower, or something worse, which induced us hastily to erect an awning of mats under a palm-tree's shade. As soon as we had leisure to look around us, though no habitation could anywhere be seen, yet it was evident the spot had been visited, and that very recently, by numbers of people. We discovered the remains of several extinct fires, with broken calabashes and pieces of earthen vessels, which were scattered around; and our men likewise picked up a quantity of cocoa-nut shells, and three or four staves of a powder-barrel. These discoveries, trifling as they were, filled us with pleasant and hopeful sensations; and we felt assured, from the circumstance of a barrel of powder having found its way hither, that the natives in the neighbourhood maintained some kind of intercourse with Europeans from the sea.

The spot, for a hundred yards, was cleared of grass, underwood, and vegetation of all kinds; and, on a further observation, we came to the conclusion that a market or fair was periodically held thereon. Very shortly afterwards, as three of our men were straggling about in the bush, searching for firewood, a village suddenly opened before them: this did not excite their astonishment, and they entered one of the huts which was nearest them to procure a little fire. However it happened to contain only women; but these were terrified beyond measure at the sudden and abrupt entrance of strange-looking men, whose language they did not know, and whose business they could not understand, and they all ran out in a fright into the woods, to warn their male relatives of them, who were labouring at their usual occupation of husbandry. Meanwhile our men had very composedly taken some burning embers from the fire, and returned to us in a few minutes, with the brief allusion to the circumstance of having discovered a village. They told us also that they had seen cultivated land, and that these women had run away from them as soon as they saw them. This we thought lightly of; but rejoiced that they had seen the village, and immediately sent Pascoe, Abraham, and Jowdie, in company, to obtain some fire, and to purchase a few yams for us. In about ten minutes after, they returned in haste, telling us that they had been to the village, and had asked for some fire, but that the people did not understand them, and instead of attending to their wishes, they looked terrified, and had suddenly disappeared. In consequence of their threatening attitudes, our people had left the village, and rejoined us with all the haste they could. We did not, however, think that they would attack us, and we proceeded to make our fires and then laid ourselves down.

Totally unconscious of danger, we were reclining on our mats,—for we, too, like our people, we e wearied with toil, and overcome with drowsiness,—when in about twenty minutes after our men had returned, one of them shouted, with a loud voice, 'War is coming! Oh war is coming!' and ran towards us with a scream of horror, telling us that the natives were hastening to attack us. We started up at this unusual exclamation, and, looking about us, we beheld a large party of men, almost naked, running in a very irregular manner, and with uncouth gestures, towards our little encampment. They were all variously armed with muskets, bows and arrows, knives, cutlasses, barbs, long spears, and other instruments of destruction; and, as we gazed upon this band of wild men, with their ferocious looks and hostile appearance, which was not a little heightened on observing the weapons in their hands, we felt a very uneasy kind of sensation, and wished ourselves safe out of their hands. To persons peaceably inclined, like ourselves, and who had done them no harm, we could look on their preparations with calmness; but as it is impossible to foresee to what extremities such encounters might lead, we waited the result with the most painful anxiety.

Our party was much scattered, but fortunately we could see them coming to us at some distance, and we had time to collect our men. We resolved, however, to prevent bloodshed if possible,—our numbers were too few to leave us a chance of escaping by any other way. The natives were approaching us fast, and had by this time arrived almost close to our palm tree. Not a moment was to be lost. We desired Pascoe and all our people to follow behind us at a short distance wi h the loaded muskets and pistols; and we enjoined them strictly not to fire, unless they first fired at us. One of the natives, who proved to be the chief, we perceived a little in advance of his companions; and, throwing down our pistols, which we had snatched up in the first moment of surprise, my brother and I walked very composedly, and unarmed, towards him. As we approached him, we made all the signs and motions we cou'd with our arms, to deter him and his people from firing on us. His quiver was dangling at his side, his bow was bent, and an arrow which was pointed at our breasts, already trembled on the string, when we were within a few yards of his person. This was a highly critical moment—the next might be our last. But the hand of Providence averted the blow; for just as the chief was about to pull the fatal cord, a man hat was nearest him rushed forward, and stayed his arm. At that instant we stood before him, and immediately held forth our hands; all of them trembled like aspen leaves; the chief looked up full in our faces, kneeling on the ground—

light seemed to flash from his dark, rolling eyes—his body was convulsed all over, as though he were enduring the utmost torture, and with a timorous, yet undefinable, expression of countenance, in which all the passions of our nature were strangely blended, he drooped his head, eagerly grasped our proffered hands, and burst into tears. This was a sign of friendship—harmony followed, and war and bloodshed were thought of no more. Peace and friendship now reigned among us; and the first thing that we did was to lift the old chief from the ground, and to convey him to our encampment. The behaviour of our men afforded us no little amusement, now that the danger was past. We had now had a fair trial of their courage, and should know who to trust on a future occasion. Pascoe was firm to his post, and stood still with his musket pointed at the chief's breast during the whole time. He is a brave fellow, and said to us as we passed him to our encampment with the old man, 'If the *black* rascals had fired at either of you, I should have brought the old chief down like a guinea-fowl.' It was impossible to avoid smiling at the fellow's honesty, although we were on the best of terms with the old chief,—and we have little doubt that he would have been as good as his word. As for our two brave fellows, Sam and Antonio, they took to their heels, and scampered off as fast as they could directly they saw the natives approaching us over the long grass, nor did they make their appearance again until the chief and all his people were sitting round us; and even when they did return, they were so frightened, they could not speak for some time.

All the armed villagers had now gathered round their leader, and anxiously watched his looks and gestures. The result of the meeting delighted them—every eye sparkled with pleasure—they uttered a shout of joy—they thrust their bloodless arrows into their quivers—they ran about us though they were possessed of evil spirits—they twanged their bowstrings, fired off their muskets, shook their spears, clattered their quivers, danced, put their bodies into all manner of ridiculous positions, laughed, cried, and sung in rapid succession—they were like a troop of maniacs. Never was spectacle more wild and terrific. When this sally of passion to which they had worked themselves had subsided into calmer and more reasonable behaviour, we presented each of the war-men with a quantity of needles, as a further token of our friendly intentions. The chief sat himself down on the turf, with one of us on each side of him, while the men were leaning on their weapons on his right and left. At first no one could understand us; but an old man made his appearance shortly after, who understood the Haussa language. Him the chief employed as an interpreter, and every one listened with anxiety to the following explanation which he gave us:—

'A few minutes after you first landed, one of my people came to me and said, that a number of strange people had arrived at the market-place. I sent him back again to get as near to you as he could, to hear what you intended doing. He soon after returned to me, and said that you spoke in a language which he could not understand. Not doubting that it was your intention to attack my village at night, and carry off my people, I desired them to get ready to fight. We were all prepared and eager to kill you, and came down breathing vengeance and slaughter, supposing that you were my enemies, and had landed from the opposite side of the river. But when you came to meet us unarmed, and we saw your white faces, we were all so frightened that we could not pull our bows, nor move hand or foot; and when you drew near me, and extended your hands towards me, I felt my heart faint within me and believed that you were "*Children of Heaven*" and had dropped from the skies ' Such was the effect we had produced on him; and under this impression he knew not what he did. 'And now,' said he, 'white men, all I want is your forgiveness.' 'That you shall have most heartily,' we said, as we shook hands with the old chief, and having taken care to assure him we had not come from so good a place as he had imagined, we congratulated ourselves, as well as him, that this affair had ended so happily. For our own parts, we had reason to feel the most unspeakable pleasure at its favourable termination; and we offered up internally to our merciful Creator, a prayer of thanksgiving and praise, for his providential interference in our behalf; for the Almighty had indeed, to use the words of the Psalmist of Israel, 'delivered our soul from death, and our feet from falling; and preserved us from any terror by night, and from the arrow that flieth by day; from the pestilence that walketh in darkness; and from the sickness that destroyeth at noon-day.' We were grateful to find that our blood had not been shed, and that we had been prevented from spilling the blood of others, which we imagined we should have been constrained to do from irremediable necessity. Our guns were all double-loaded with balls and slugs, our men were ready to present them, and a single arrow from a bow would have been the signal for immediate destruction. It was a narrow escape; and God grant we may never be so near a cruel death again. It was happy for us that our white faces and calm behaviour produced the effect it did on these people —in another minute our bodies would have been as full of arrows as a porcupine's is full of quills.

Journal of an expedition to explore the course and termination of the Niger, vol. III, pp. 71–80

The suspiciousness and hostility of the natives increased as they neared the sea: once they were actually attacked, but they escaped with little damage. At length on 15th November they reached Brass

Town: after some disagreeable difficulties with the captain of an English merchant ship, they sailed out of the delta by the Nun mouth and across to Fernando Po, which they reached on 1st December. They returned to England by way of Brazil, arriving in July 1831. Richard was awarded the first Gold Medal of the Royal Geographical Society (founded in the year of his return); and together the brothers wrote an account of their journey which appeared in three charming little volumes in 1832.[1]

Richard was not to remain long in England. Early in 1832 he agreed to join, in the capacity of guide, a commercial expedition to the Niger organized by Macgregor Laird, a member of the famous family of Birkenhead shipbuilders. It proved an unfortunate venture from the beginning. The voyage out (in the brig and two steamships with which the expedition was provided) was slow; disease began to attack the white men as soon as they arrived in the delta; the steamers were not a success on the river; the native chiefs were naturally hostile to what they considered as an attempt at competing with their trade. This was the reason for an attack made on Lander and his men at Angiama on 20th January 1834: Lander was wounded, but managed to retire to Fernando Po, where he died at the beginning of February—'a victim', as one of his companions wrote, 'to his too great confidence in the natives'.

Lander's books reveal his character and personality very clearly. By temperament he was gay and light-hearted, though subject to passing fits of melancholy; his gentleness and good temper never failed; his humour, if it occasionally degenerates into a rather dated facetiousness, is most refreshing. Above all, his books give a haunting impression of his youth—he was not quite thirty when he died.

[1] The preface explains that, although the book is written as if it were the work of one man, and Richard always appears in it as 'I', the first two volumes are taken from the journal of John Lander (who had some literary pretensions) and the last from Richard's. Thus of our three extracts from it, the first two are from John's part of the work. But this matters little, since the whole book was edited by a third hand and its style agrees closely with that of *Records of Captain Clapperton's last expedition*, which was entirely written by Richard.

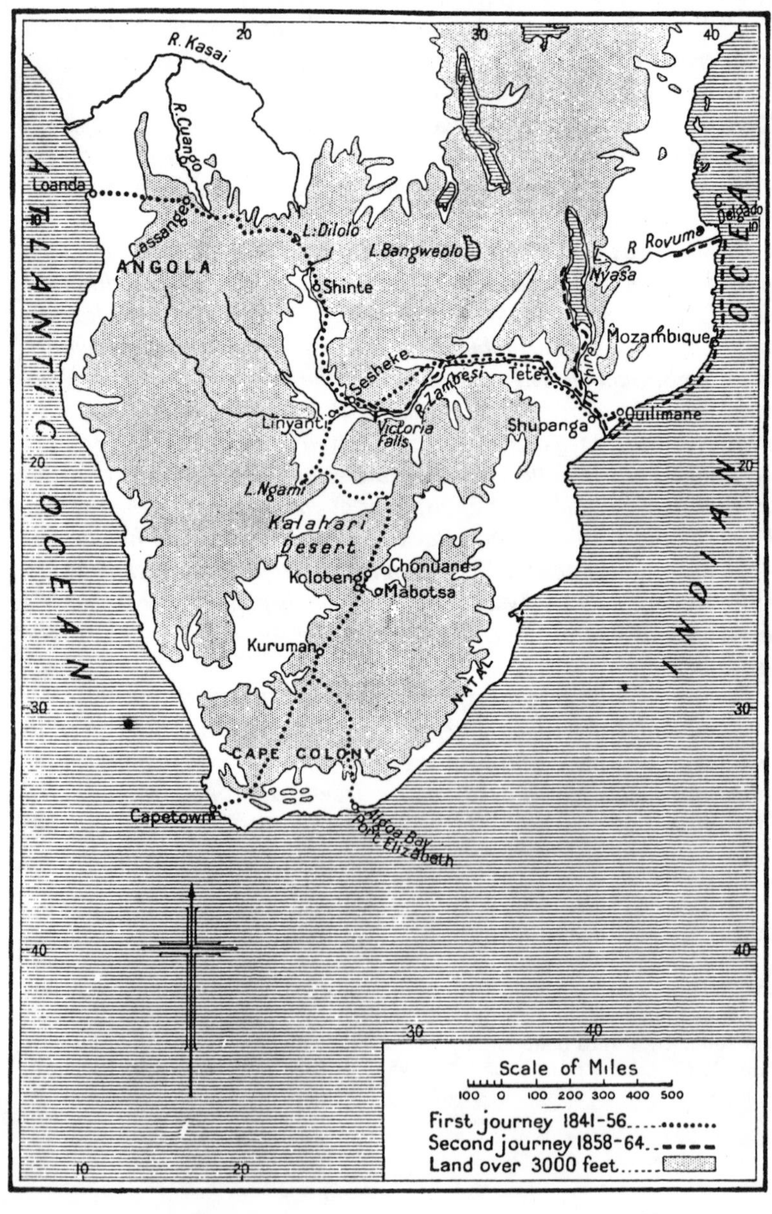

5. The Travels of Livingstone, 1841–64

IV

DAVID LIVINGSTONE

1813–1873

The story of Livingstone's life before he went out to Africa can be told in a few words. His father was a tea-merchant in a very small way: he was born at Blantyre near Glasgow. At the age of ten he went into a cotton mill, where he remained until 1836: then, fired by the idea of becoming a medical missionary in China, he entered Glasgow University, where he qualified as a doctor in 1840. Meanwhile, he had offered his services to the directors of the London Missionary Society, who accepted them after he had gone through a period of probation. The Opium War making it impossible for him to go to China as he intended, Robert Moffat (whom he met in London and who afterwards became his father-in-law) succeeded in persuading him to turn his thoughts to Africa. In December 1840 he sailed for Capetown.

He made his way up to Kuruman in Bechuanaland, Moffat's headquarters. From here he was instructed by the London Missionary Society to prospect northwards, and in 1843, after prospecting the country in several considerable journeys, he established a new base for himself.

15. ENCOUNTER WITH A LION

Returning towards Kuruman, I selected the beautiful valley of Mabotsa (lat. 25° 14′ south, long. 26° 30′ ?) as the site of a missionary station; and thither I removed in 1843. Here an occurrence took place concerning which I have frequently been questioned in England, and which, but for the importunities of friends, I meant to have kept in store to tell my children when in my dotage. The Bakatla of the village Mabotsa were much troubled by lions, which leaped into the cattle-pens by night, and destroyed their cows. They even attacked the herds in open day. This was so unusual an occurrence that the people believed that they were bewitched—'given,' as they said, 'into the power of the ions by a neighbouring tribe.' They went once to attack the animals, but, being rather a cowardly people compared to Bechuanas in general on such occasions, they returned without killing any.

It is well known that if one in a troop of lions is killed the others take the hint and leave that part of the country. So the next time the herds were attacked, I went with the people, in order to encourage them to rid themselves of the annoyance by destroying one of the marauders. We found the lions on a small hill about a quarter of a mile in length, and covered with trees. A circle of men was formed round it, and they gradually closed up, ascending pretty near to each other. Being down below on the plain with a native schoolmaster, named Mebalwe, a most excellent man, I saw one of the lions sitting on a piece of rock within the now closed circle of men. Mebalwe fired at him before I could, and the ball struck the rock on which the animal was sitting. He bit at the spot struck, as a dog does at a stick or stone thrown at him; then leaping away, broke through the opening circle and escaped unhurt. The men were afraid to attack him, perhaps on account of their belief in witchcraft. When the circle was re-formed, we saw two other lions in it; but we were afraid to fire lest we should strike the men, and they allowed the beasts to burst through also. If the Bakatla had acted according to the custom of the country, they would have speared the lions in their attempt to get out. Seeing we could not get them to kill one of the lions, we bent our footsteps towards the village; in going round the end of the hill, however, I saw one of the beasts sitting on a piece of rock as before, but this time he had a little bush in front. Being about thirty yards off, I took a good aim at his body through the bush, and fired both barrels into it. The men then called out, 'He is shot, he is shot!' Others cried, 'He has been shot by another man too; let us go to him!' I did not see any one else shoot at him, but I saw the lion's tail erected in anger behind the bush, and, turning to the people, said, 'Stop a little till I load again.' When in the act of ramming down the bullets I heard a shout. Starting, and looking half round, I saw the lion just in the act of springing upon me. I was upon a little height; he caught my shoulder as he sprang, and we both came to the ground below together. Growling horribly close to my ear, he shook me as a terrier dog does a rat. The shock produced a stupor similar to that which seems to be felt by a mouse after the first shake of the cat. It caused a sort of dreaminess, in which there was no sense of pain nor feeling of terror, though quite conscious of all that was happening. It was like what patients partially under the influence of chloroform describe, who see all the operation, but feel not the knife. This singular condition was not the result of any mental process. The shake annihilated fear, and allowed no sense of horror in looking round at the beast. This peculiar state is probably produced in all animals killed by the carnivora; and if so, is a merciful provision by our benevolent Creator for lessening the pain of death. Turning round to relieve myself of the weight, as he had one paw on the back of my head, I saw his eyes directed to Mebalwe, who was trying to shoot him at a distance of ten or fifteen yards. His gun, a flint one, missed fire in both barrels; the lion immediately left me, and, attacking Mebalwe, bit his thigh. Another man, whose life I had saved before, after he had been tossed by a buffalo, attempted to spear the lion while he was biting Mebalwe. He left Mebalwe and caught this man by the shoulder, but at that moment the bullets he had received took effect, and he fell down dead. The whole was the work of a few moments, and must have been his paroxysm of dying rage. In order to take out the charm from him, the Bakatla on the following day made a huge bonfire over the carcase, which was declared to be that of the largest lion they had ever seen. Besides crunching the bone into splinters, he left eleven teeth wounds in the upper part of my arm.

A wound from this animal's tooth resembles a gun-shot wound; it is generally followed by a great deal of sloughing and discharge, and pains are felt in the part periodically ever afterwards. I had on a tartan jacket on the occasion, and I believed that it wiped off all the virus from the teeth that pierced the flesh, for my two companions in this affray have both suffered from the peculiar pains, while I have escaped with only the inconvenience of a false joint in my limb. The man whose shoulder was wounded showed me his wound actually burst forth afresh in the same month of the following year. This curious point deserves the attention of inquirers.

Missionary travels, 1st edition, pp. 11–13

Livingstone remained at Mabotsa until 1846. He was tireless in trying to explain the doctrines of Christianity to the Bakwain tribe among whom he lived, and to Sechele their chief. His methods of argument, and the sort of acute criticism he had to meet, are well illustrated in a conversation with a Bakwain rain-doctor which he set down with striking fairness and detachment.

16. ARGUMENT WITH A RAIN-DOCTOR

The natives, finding it irksome to sit and wait helplessly until God gives them rain from heaven, entertain the more comfortable idea that they can help themselves by a variety of preparations, such as charcoal made of burned bats, inspissated renal deposit of the mountain coney (*Hyrax capensis*) (which by the way is used in the form of pills as a good anti-spasmodic, under the name of 'stone-sweat'), the internal parts of different animals—as jackals' livers, baboons' and lions' hearts, and hairy calculi from the bowels of old cows—serpents' skins and vertebræ, and every kind of tuber, bulb, root, and plant to be found in the country. Although you disbelieve their efficacy in charming the clouds to pour out their refreshing treasures, yet, conscious that civility is useful everywhere, you kindly state that you think they are mistaken as to their power; the rain-doctor selects a particular bulbous root, pounds it, and administers a cold infusion to a sheep, which in five minutes afterwards expires in convulsions. Part of the same bulb is converted into smoke, and ascends towards the sky; rain follows in a day or two. The inference is obvious. Were we as much harassed by droughts, the logic would be irresistible in England in 1857.

As the Bakwains believed that there must be some connection between the presence of 'God's Word' in their town and these successive and distressing droughts, they looked with no good will at the church-bell, but still they invariably treated us with kindness and respect. I am not aware of ever having had an enemy in the tribe. The only avowed cause of dislike was expressed by a very influential and sensible man, the uncle of Sechele. 'We like you as well as if you had been born among us; you are the only white man we can become familiar with; but we wish you to give up that everlasting preaching and praying; we cannot become familiar with that at all. You see we never get rain, while those tribes who never pray as we do obtain abundance.' This was a fact; and we often saw it raining on the hills, ten miles off, while it would not look at us 'even with one eye.' If the Prince of the power of the air had no hand in scorching us up, I fear I often gave him the credit of doing so.

As for the rain-makers, they carried the sympathies of the people along with them, and not without reason. With the following arguments they were all acquainted, and in order to understand their force we must place ourselves in their position, and believe, as they do, that all medicines act by a mysterious charm. The term for cure may be translated 'charm'.

Medical Doctor.—Hail, friend! How very many medicines you have about you this morning! Why, you have every medicine in the country here.

Rain-Doctor.—Very true, my friend; and I ought; for the whole country needs the rain which I am making.

M.D.—So you really believe that you can command the clouds? I think that can be done by God alone.

R.D.—We both believe the very same thing. It is God that makes the rain, but I pray to him by means of these medicines, and, the rain coming, of course it is then mine. It was I who made it for the Bakwains for many years, when they were at Shokuane; through my wisdom, too, their women became fat and shining. Ask them; they will tell you the same as I do.

M.D.—But we are distinctly told in the parting words of our Saviour that we can pray to God acceptably in His name alone, and not by means of medicines.

R.D.—Truly! but God told *us* differently. He made black men first, and did not love us, as he did the white men. He made you beautiful, and gave you clothing, and guns, and gunpowder, and horses, and waggons, and many other things about which we know nothing. But toward us he had no heart. He gave us nothing, except the assegai, and cattle, and rain-making; and he did not give us hearts like yours. We never love each other. Other tribes place medicines about our country to prevent the rain, so that we may be dispersed by hunger, and go to them, and augment their power. We must dissolve their charms by our medicines. God has given us one little thing, which you know nothing of. He has given us the knowledge of certain medicines by which we can make rain. *We* do not despise those things which you possess, though we are ignorant of them. We don't understand your book, but we don't despise it. *You* ought not to despise our little knowledge, though you are ignorant of it.

M.D.—I don't despise what I am ignorant of; I only think you are mistaken in saying that you have medicines which can influence the rain at all.

R.D.—That's just the way people speak when they talk on a subject of which they have no knowledge. When we first opened our eyes, we found our forefathers making rain, and we follow in their footsteps. You, who send to Kuruman for corn, and irrigate your garden, may do without rain; *we* cannot manage in that way. If we had no rain, the cattle would have no pasture, the cows give no milk, our children become lean and die, our wives run away to other tribes who do make rain, and have corn, and the whole tribe become dispersed and lost; our fire would go out.

M.D.—I quite agree with you as to the value of the rain; but you cannot charm the clouds by medicines. You wait till you see the clouds come, then you use your medicines, and take the credit which belongs to God only.

R.D.—I use my medicines, and you employ yours; we are both doctors, and doctors are not deceivers. You give a patient medicine. Sometimes God is pleased to heal him by means of your medicine: sometimes not—he dies. When he is cured, you take the credit of what God does. I do the same. Sometimes God grants us rain, sometimes not. When he does, we take the credit of the charm. When a patient dies, you don't give up trust in your medicine, neither do I when rain fails. If you wish me to leave off my medicines, why continue your own?

M.D.—I give medicines to living creatures within my reach, and can see the effects though no cure follows; you pretend to charm the clouds, which are so far above us that your medicines never reach them. The clouds usually lie in one direction, and your smoke goes in another. God alone can command the clouds. Only try and wait patiently; God will give us rain without your medicines.

R.D.—Mahala-ma-kapa-a-a!! Well, I always thought white men were wise till this morning. Who ever thought of making trial of starvation? Is death pleasant then?

M.D.—Could you make it rain on one spot and not on another?

R.D.—I wouldn't think of trying. I like to see the whole country green, and all the people glad; the women clapping their hands and giving me their ornaments for thankfulness, and lullilooing for joy.

M.D.—I think you deceive both them and yourself.

R.D.—Well, then, there is a pair of us (meaning both are rogues).

The above is only a specimen of their way of reasoning, in which, when the language is well understood, they are perceived to be remarkably acute. These arguments are generally known, and I never succeeded in convincing a single individual of their fallacy, though I tried to do so in every way I could think of. Their faith in medicines as charms is unbounded. The general effect of argument is to produce the impression that you are not anxious for rain at all; and it is very undesirable to allow the idea to spread that you do not take a generous interest in their welfare. An angry opponent of rain-making in a tribe would be looked upon as were some Greek merchants in England during the Russian war.[1]

Missionary travels, 1st edition, pp. 22–25

On leaving Mabotsa, Livingstone gradually worked his way northwards, establishing himself successively at Chonuane and Kolobeng. In 1849 he determined to cross the Kalahari Desert and find Lake Ngami, which he knew lay beyond it. With three English friends (one of them W. C. Oswell), he made the journey in exactly two months: they discovered the lake on 1st August, afterwards returning to Kolobeng. He crossed the desert again in each of the two following years, accompanied by his wife and family, and in June 1851 reached the Zambesi at Sesheke: it was on this journey that he came into contact with the slave trade for the first time.

He now determined to travel on still further north into the heart of Africa, and in order to be able to do this more easily sent his family home to England, travelling down to the Cape with them. From here he made his way back to Linyanti, the capital of the Makololo people,

[1] I.e. the Crimean War, which had only just ended when Livingstone wrote.

where he arrived in May 1853. Their chief Sekeletu welcomed him kindly and lent him twenty-seven porters, without demanding any payment. With them, and with a very small outfit of goods, he left Linyanti on 11th November, travelling up the valley of the Zambesi, striking out past Lake Dilolo and crossing the River Kasai (one of the great tributaries of the Congo) into the territory of the Kioko. Here he met with vexatious demands for tolls: a little further on, in the Chiboque country, he began to hear of slave-traders and—significant conjunction—encountered real hostility from the inhabitants. He then went north and west until he came to a spot above the valley of the Coango which made him think of Langside and Mary, Queen of Scots. On the eastern bank of the river he met a half-caste Portuguese sergeant, who set him on his way to Cassange, an outpost of the colony of Angola. Here he was treated with great kindness and forwarded to Loanda, which he reached on 31st May 1854.

Livingstone stayed nearly four months at Loanda, resisting all offers of a passage to England on the grounds that he must take his faithful Makololo porters home. This he accomplished in a march lasting almost a year: the party arrived at Linyanti on 11th September 1855. Seven weeks later Livingstone set out on the third and last part of his journey, that down the Zambesi to the east coast. On 16th November he had his first sight of the Falls which he named after the Queen.

17. DISCOVERY OF THE VICTORIA FALLS

As this was the point from which we intended to strike off to the north-east, I resolved on the following day to visit the falls of Victoria, called by the natives Mosioatunya, or more anciently Shongwe. Of these we had often heard since we came into the country: indeed one of the questions asked by Sebituane [Sekeletu's father] was, 'Have you smoke that sounds in your country?' They did not go near enough to examine them, but, viewing them with awe at a distance, said, in reference to the vapour and noise, 'Mosi oa tunya' (smoke does sound there). It was previously called Shongwe, the meaning of which I could not ascertain. The word for a 'pot' resembles this, and it may mean a seething caldron; but I am not certain of it. Being persuaded that Mr. Oswell and myself were the very first Europeans who ever visited the Zambesi in the centre of the country, and that this is the connecting link between the known and unknown portions of that river, I decided to use the same liberty as the Makololo did, and gave the only English name I have affixed to any part of the country. No better proof of previous ignorance of this river could be desired, than that an untravelled gentleman, who had spent a great part of his life in the study of the geography of Africa, and knew everything written on the subject from the time of Ptolemy downwards, actually asserted in the 'Athenæum,' while I was coming up the Red Sea, that this magnificent river, the Leeambye, had 'no connection with the Zambesi, but flowed under the Kalahari Desert, and became lost;' and 'that, as all the old maps asserted, the Zambesi took its rise in the very hills to which we have now come.' This modest assertion smacks exactly as if a native of Timbuctu should declare, that the 'Thames' and the 'Pool' were different rivers, he having seen neither the one nor the other. Leeambye and Zambesi mean the very same thing, viz. the RIVER.

Sekeletu intended to accompany me, but, one canoe only having come instead of the two he had ordered, he resigned it to me. After twenty minutes' sail from Kalai, we came in sight, for the first time, of the columns of vapour, appropriately called 'smoke,' rising at a distance of five or six miles, exactly as when large tracts of grass are burned in Africa. Five columns now arose, and bending in the direction of the wind, they seemed placed against a low ridge covered with trees; the tops of the columns at this distance appeared to mingle with the clouds. They were white below, and higher up became dark, so as to simulate smoke very closely. The whole scene was extremely beautiful; the banks and islands dotted over the river are adorned with sylvan vegetation of great variety of colour and form. At the period of our visit several trees were spangled over with blossoms. Trees have each their own physiognomy. There, towering above all, stands the great burly baobab, each of whose enormous arms would form the trunk of a large tree, beside groups of graceful palms, which, with their feathery-shaped leaves depicted on the sky, lend their beauty to the scene. As a heiroglyphic they always mean 'far from home,' for one can never get over their foreign air in a picture or landscape. The silvery mohonono, which in the tropics is in form like the cedar of Lebanon, stands in pleasing contrast with the dark colour of the motsouri, whose cypress-form is dotted over at present with its pleasant scarlet fruit. Some trees resemble the great spreading oak, others assume the character of our own elms and chestnuts; but no one can imagine the beauty of the view from anything witnessed in England: It had never been seen before by European eyes; but scenes so lovely must have been gazed upon by angels in their flight. The only want felt, is that of mountains in the background. The falls are bounded on three sides by ridges 300 or 400 feet in height, which are covered with forest, with the red soil appearing among the trees. When about half a mile from the falls, I left the canoe by which we had come down thus far, and embarked in a lighter one, with men well acquainted with the rapids, who, by passing down the centre of the stream in the eddies and still places caused by many jutting rocks, brought me to an island situated in the middle of the river, and on the edge of the lip over which the water rolls. In coming hither, there was danger of being swept down by the streams which rushed along on each side of the island; but the river was now low, and we sailed where it is totally impossible to go when the water is high. But though we had reached the island, and were within a few yards of the spot, a view from which would solve the whole problem, I believe that no one could perceive where the vast body of water went; it seemed to lose itself in the earth, the opposite lip of the fissure into which it disappeared being only 80 feet distant. At least I did not comprehend it until, creeping with awe to the verge, I peered down into a large rent which had been made from bank to bank of the broad Zambesi, and saw that a stream of a thousand yards broad leaped down a hundred feet, and then became suddenly compressed into a space of fifteen or twenty yards. The entire falls are simply a crack made in a hard basaltic rock from the right to the left bank of the Zambesi, and then prolonged from the left bank away through thirty or forty miles of hills. . . . In looking down into the fissure on the right of the island, one sees nothing but a dense white cloud, which, at the time we visited the spot, had two bright rainbows on it. (The sun was on the meridian, and the declination about equal to the latitude of the place.) From this cloud rushed up a great jet of vapour exactly like steam, and it mounted 200 or 300 feet high; there condensing, it changed its hue to that of dark smoke, and came back in a constant shower, which soon wetted us to the skin. This shower falls chiefly on the opposite side of the fissure, and a few yards back from the lip there stands a straight hedge of evergreen trees, whose leaves are always wet. From their roots a number of little rills run back into the gulf; but as they flow down the steep wall there, the column of vapour, in its ascent, licks them up clean off the rock, and away they mount again. They are constantly running down, but never reach the bottom.

On the left of the island we see the water at the bottom, a white rolling mass moving away to the prolongation of the fissure, which branches off near the left bank of the river. A piece of the rock has fallen off a spot on the left of the island, and juts out from the water below, and from it, I judged the distance which the water falls to be about 100 feet. The walls of this gigantic crack are perpendicular, and composed of one homogeneous mass of rock. The edge of that side over which the water falls, is worn off two or three feet, and pieces have fallen away, so as to give it somewhat of a serrated appearance. That over which the water does not fall is quite straight, except at the left corner, where a rent appears, and a piece seems inclined to fall off. Upon the whole, it is nearly in the state in which it was left at the period of its formation. The rock is dark brown in colour, except about ten feet from the bottom, which is discoloured by the annual rise of the water to that or a greater height. On the left side of the island we have a good view of the mass of water which causes one of the columns of vapour to ascend, as it leaps quite clear of the rock, and forms a thick unbroken fleece all the way to the bottom. Its whiteness gave the idea of snow, a sight I had not seen for many a day. As it broke into (if I may use the term) pieces of water, all rushing on in the same direction, each gave off several rays of foam, exactly as bits of steel, when burnt in oxygen gas, give off rays of sparks. The snow-white sheet seemed like myriads of small comets rushing on in one direction, each of which left behind its nucleus rays of foam. I never saw the appearance referred to noticed elsewhere. It seemed to be the effect of the mass of water leaping at once clear of the rock, and but slowly breaking up into spray.

I have mentioned that we saw five columns of vapour ascending from this strange abyss. They are evidently formed by the compression suffered by the force of the water's own fall, into an unyielding wedge-shaped space. Of the five columns, two on the right, and one on the left of the island were the largest, and the streams which formed them seemed each to exceed in size the falls of the Clyde at Stonebyres, when that river is in flood. This was the period of low water in the Leeambye, but, as far as I could guess, there was a flow of five or six hundred yards of water, which, at the edge of the fall, seemed at least three feet deep. I write in the hope that others more capable of judging distances than myself will visit this scene, and I state simply the impressions made on my mind at the time. . . .

The fissure is said by the Makololo to be very much deeper farther to the eastward; there is one part at which the walls are so sloping, that people accustomed to it, can go down by descending in a sitting position. The Makololo on one occasion, pursuing some fugitive Batoka, saw them, unable to stop the impetus of their flight at the edge, literally dashed to pieces at the bottom. They beheld the stream like a 'white cord' at the bottom, and so far down (probably 300 feet) that they became giddy, and were fain to go away, holding on to the ground. . . .

At three spots near these falls, one of them the island in the middle on which we were, three Batoka chiefs offered up prayers and sacrifices to the Barimo. They chose their places of prayer within the sound of the roar of the cataract, and in sight of the bright bows in the cloud. They must have looked upon the scene with awe. Fear may have induced the selection. The river itself is, to them, mysterious. The words of the canoe-song are—

> 'The Leeambye! Nobody knows,
> Whence it comes and whither it goes.'

The play of colours of the double iris on the cloud, seen by them elsewhere only as the rainbow, may have led them to the idea that this was the abode of Deity. Some of the Makololo who went with me near to Gonye, looked upon the same sign with awe. When seen in the heavens it is named 'motse oa barimo'—the pestle of the gods. Here they could approach the emblem, and see it stand steadily above the blustering uproar below—a type of Him who sits supreme—alone unchangeable, though ruling over all changing things. But not aware of His true character, they had no admiration of the beautiful and good in their bosoms. They did not imitate His benevolence, for they were a bloody imperious crew, and Sebituane performed a noble service, in the expulsion from their fastnesses of these cruel 'Lords of the Isles'.

Having feasted my eyes long on the beautiful sight, I returned to my friends at Kalai, and, saying to Sekeletu that he had nothing else worth showing in his country, his curiosity was excited to visit it the next day. . . . Sekeletu acknowledged to feeling a little nervous at the probability of being sucked into the gulf before reaching the island. His companions amused themselves by throwing stones down, and wondered to see them diminishing in size, and even disappearing, before they reached the water at the bottom.

I had another object in view in my return to the island. I observed that it was covered with trees, the seeds of which had probably come down with the stream from the distant north, and several of which I had seen nowhere else; and every now and then the wind wafted a little of the condensed vapour over it, and kept the soil in a state of moisture, which caused a sward of grass, growing as green as on an English lawn. I selected a spot—not too near the chasm, for there the constant deposition of the moisture nourished numbers of polypi of a mushroom shape and fleshy consistence—but somewhat back, and made a little garden. I there planted about a hundred peach and apricot stones, and a quantity of coffee-seeds. I had attempted fruit-trees before, but, when left in charge of my Makololo friends, they were always allowed to wither, after having vegetated, by being forgotten. I bargained for a hedge with one of the Makololo, and if he is faithful, I have great hopes of Mosioatunya's abilities as a nurseryman. My only source of fear is the hippopotami, whose footprints I saw on the island. When the garden was prepared, I cut my initials on a tree, and the date 1855. This was the only instance in which I indulged in this piece of vanity. The garden stands in front, and were there no hippopotami, I have no doubt but this will be the parent of all the gardens, which may yet be in this new country. We then went up to Kalai again.

Missionary travels, 1st edition, pp. 518–525

On 20th November 1855 Livingstone parted from Sekeletu, who added to his former kindnesses by giving him an escort of 114 men. With them he travelled down the Zambesi and so to Quilimane on the sea, where he arrived on 22nd May 1856. He had accomplished, with slender means, one of the greatest journeys on record.

When he reached home in the following December he had a great welcome: he quickly found himself a famous man. A little news of his journey had trickled back to England in his reports to the London Missionary Society and the Royal Geographical Society—which had awarded him its Gold Medal in the previous year. But he soon became known to the public as much more than a missionary and much more than an explorer. He made use of his fame in these capacities to put across what we should now call a 'policy for Africa', to open an attack on the slave trade, some of the results of which he had seen both on the eastern borders of Angola and on the lower Zambesi. Livingstone was able—by power of mind as well as by force of character and religious conviction—to make the widest possible appeal. He was listened to by the missionary public, by philanthropists, and by geographers, of course; but also by scientists ('no explorer on record', wrote the Astronomer Royal at the Cape, 'has determined his path with the precision you have accomplished') and even by politicians as cool and wary as Palmerston and Clarendon. This true breadth of mind, together with his deep spiritual power, puts Livingstone far above all other African travellers, in a class by himself.

It is not easy to describe the strange power of Livingstone's character in a few words: there is clear proof of it in the deep impression he made upon men of all types who met him, and upon the imagination of his country. His humanity drove him to face and struggle with cruelty rather than to avoid it: his overpowering compassion for the African people, roused by the crushing miseries of the slave trade, drove him to follow a single purpose at the cost of all that most men count as happiness.

As a result of his appeals, the British Government decided to send out an elaborately equipped expedition to the Zambesi, under his command. Its task was to see how far the river was navigable to steamers, to see what opening there might be for trade with the natives, and—above all—to discover how the slave trade might best be attacked.

With the five Englishmen under his command (one of them his brother), Livingstone started in March 1858. After considerable difficulties in entering the Zambesi, the party steamed up to Tete. Their first objective was the exploration of the River Shire: it was reported to rise in a great lake to the north named Nyasa, which Livingstone at last managed to reach on 16th September 1859. After revisiting the Victoria Falls he returned to the Shire–Nyasa area, where he saw more than he ever had before of the terrible activities of the slave-traders. Undeterred by disasters (his wife died at Shupanga in 1862), by disagreements with his English colleagues, with whom he worked far less happily than with Africans, or by the evident failure of the expedition to accomplish its purposes, he worked on feverishly, trying to open up a workable route into the interior either by the Shire or the Rovuma. At length, in July 1863, he received notice of the expedition's recall: he reached England a year later.

The rest of 1864 he spent in writing, in collaboration with his brother, the Narrative of an expedition to the Zambesi and its tributaries. *At the same time, the plan of a third journey took shape in his mind: its course and ending are described in* *Section IX below*.

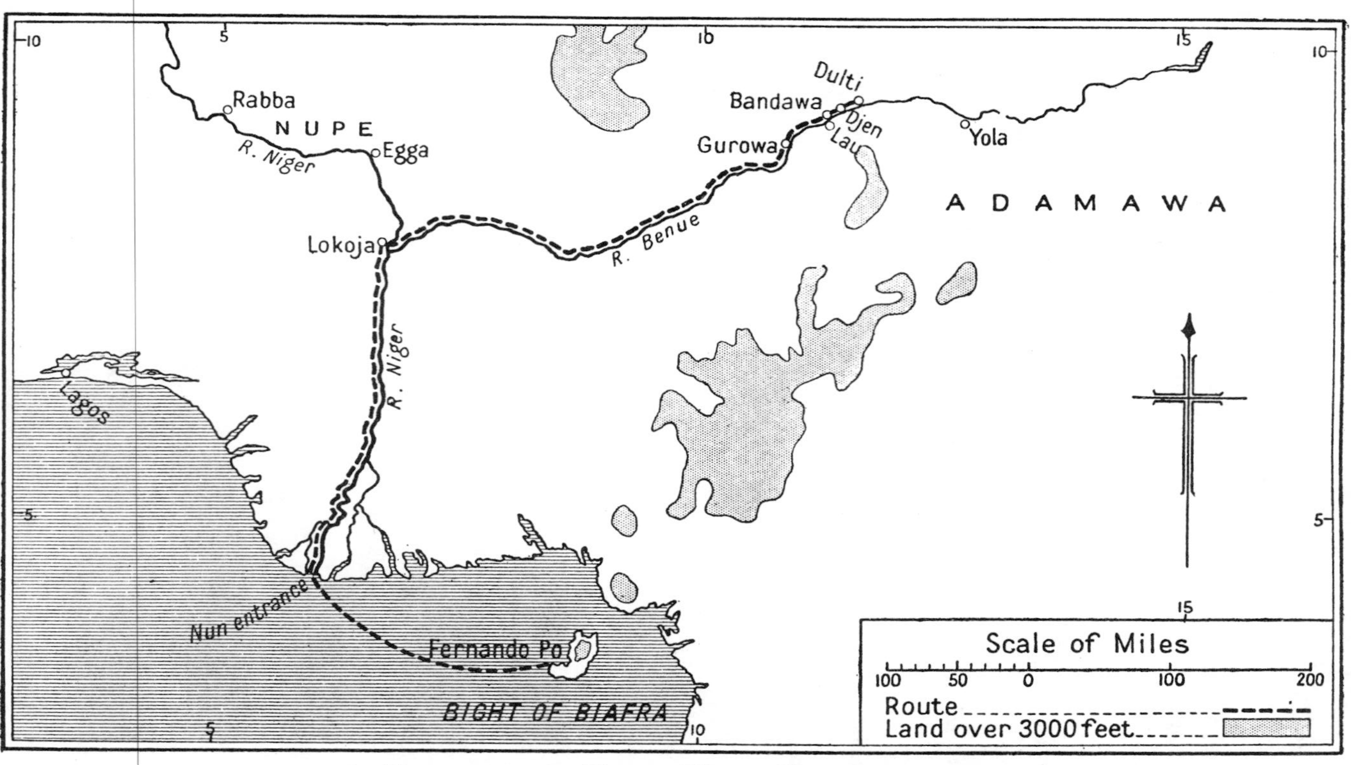

6. Route of the Third Niger Expedition, 1854

V

WILLIAM BALFOUR BAIKIE

1825–1864

Baikie was the son of a naval captain: he was born at Kirkwall in the Orkneys. After a brilliant career as a medical student at Edinburgh he became an assistant surgeon in the navy. In 1854 he was appointed surgeon and naturalist to the third Niger expedition, on the advice of Sir Roderick Murchison. The leader of the party, Captain Beecroft, died on the way out, at Fernando Po, and the command of it devolved upon Baikie. Under him the expedition was highly successful and did most valuable work, which he described himself in his Narrative of an exploring voyage (*1856*). *In 1857 he went out to Africa again as leader of the fourth Niger expedition. Soon after starting up the river its steamer was wrecked, and most of its members returned to England. Not so Baikie: he established himself at Lokoja, at the meeting of the Rivers Niger and Benue, and made it an unofficial British settlement, entering into relations with the Emir of Nupe and other local chiefs. Lokoja at once became an important commercial centre. Baikie remained there five years: for much of this time he was wholly without white companions. He collected a vast quantity of valuable information on the country, its people and their languages, most of which still remains in manuscript. In 1864 he obtained leave to return home, but he died at Sierra Leone on the way.*

He was a man of rather different type from the other great African travellers. His tastes were extremely cultivated (the catalogue of his large library, which was sold after his death, shows this very clearly): by temperament he was a calm and dispassionate scientist—an intellectual, rather than a moral or a spiritual, crusader; cool, humane, above all intelligent.

The two extracts given here are taken from his Narrative *of the expedition of 1854: they illustrate his strong nerve, his quiet sense of humour, and his scientist's curiosity. Both episodes occurred on 29th September. Leaving his little steamer the* Pleiad *further down stream, Baikie had pushed on in a canoe manned by Krumen (those invaluable sailors from the coast of Liberia), taking with him only one white companion. When they reached Dulti, the village described below (it was some 250 miles from the mouth of the Benue), they decided they must return—not because of the hostile reception they met there, but in order to rejoin the* Pleiad *and take her back to the Niger before the Benue sank too low for navigation. The hurricane described in the second extract took place on the first night of the return voyage.*

18. THE GREAT DULTI CHASE

About half-past ten we entered a creek on the north side, running nearly parallel with the river, and shortly afterwards sighted a village, at which we soon arrived. To our astonishment the first thing which brought us up was our running the bow of the gig against a hut, and on looking around we found the whole place to be flooded. We advanced right into the middle of the village, and found no resting place; right and left, before and behind, all was water. People came out of the huts to gaze at the apparition, and standing at the doors of their abodes were, without the smallest exaggeration, immersed nearly to their knees, and one child I particularly observed up to its waist. How the interiors of the huts of these amphibious creatures were constructed I cannot conjecture, but we saw dwellings from which, if inhabited, the natives must have dived like beavers to get outside. We pulled in speechless amazement through this city of waters, wondering greatly that human beings could exist under such conditions. We had heard of wild tribes living in caverns and among rocks, we had read of races in Hindustan roosting in trees, of whole families in China spending their lives on rafts and in boats in their rivers and their canals; we knew, too, of Tuariks[1] and Shanbah roaming over vast sandy deserts, and of Eskimo burrowing in snow retreats, but never had we witnessed or even dreamt of such a spectacle as that of creatures endowed like ourselves, living by choice like a colony of beavers, or after the fashion of the hippopotami and crocodiles of the neighbouring swamps.

A little distance from us we espied a large tree, round the foot of which was a patch of dry land, towards which we pulled, but grounding before reaching quite to it, Mr. May and I waded to it, instruments in hand, to take observations. We were barely allowed to conclude, when nearly the entire population of the place, half-wading, half-swimming across a small creek, came upon us, and stared at us in wild astonishment. A hurried set of sights being taken, we carried our things back into the boat, and as we wished to get another set about three quarters

[1] See p. 88 above.

of an hour after noon, we tried to amuse ourselves and to spend the intervening time as we best could. We were now able to look a little more attentively at our new friends, who in large numbers crowded round, and who, male and female, were nearly all equally destitute of a vestige of clothing. One young man understood a few words of Hausa, and by this means we learnt that this was the Dulti of which we had heard at Djin, and that the inhabitants were of the same stock as at the other villages; but they were by far more rude, more savage, and more naked than any of the other Baibai whom we had encountered. A canoe came near us, lying in the bottom of which was a curious large fish, of which I had just time to make a rough eye sketch, when I had to retreat to the boat, and Mr. May, who had been exploring in another direction, also returned. The behaviour of these wild people now attracted our notice; the men began to draw closer around us, to exhibit their arms, and to send away the women and children. Their attentions became momentarily more and more familiar, and they plainly evidenced a desire to seize and plunder our boat. A sour-looking old gentleman, who was squatting on the branch of a tree, was mentioned as their king; but if so, he made no endeavours to restrain the cupidity of his *sans-culottes*. Part of a red shirt belonging to one of our Krumen was seen peeping out from below a bag, and some advanced to lay hold of it, when suddenly my little dog, who had been lying quietly in the stern sheets, raised her head to see what was causing such a commotion. Her sudden appearance startled the Dulti warriors, who had never seen such an animal before, so they drew back to take counsel together, making signs to me to know if she could bite, to which I replied in the affirmative. Matters were beginning to look serious; our crew, as usual, were timid, and Mr. May and I had only ourselves to depend upon in the midst of three or four hundred armed savages, who were now preparing to make a rush at us. There was no help for it; we had to abandon all hopes of our remaining observations, and of so fixing an exact geographical position. As at Djin, I seized a few trinkets, and handing them hastily to those nearest to us, we shoved off while the people were examining these wondrous treasures.

Still anxious, if possible, to get some further observations not far removed from the spot where the former ones were taken, we pulled about among trees and bushes, but without any success. At length we shoved in among some long grass, hoping to find dry land, but after having proceeded until completely stopped by the thickness of the growth, we still found upwards of a fathom of water. At this moment Mr. May's ear caught a voice not far behind us; so we shoved quietly back, and found a couple of canoes trying to cut off our retreat. Seeing this we paddled vigorously back, there not being room for using our oars, and the canoes did not venture to molest us. We were quickly paddling across the flooded plain, when suddenly a train of canoes in eager pursuit issued out upon us. There were ten canoes, each containing seven or eight men, and they were sufficiently close to us to allow us to see their stores of arms. Our Kruboys worked most energetically, and we went ahead at such a rate that our pursuers had complete occupation found them in paddling, and could not use their weapons. At this moment we were about a couple of hundred yards from the river, towards which we made as straight a course as possible. Not knowing how matters might terminate, we thought it advisable to prepare for defence, so I took our revolver to load it, but now, when it was needed, the ramrod was stiff and quite immoveable. Mr. May got a little pocket-pistol ready, and we had if required a cutlass, and a ship's musket, which the Krumen, by this time in a desperate fright, wished to see prepared, as they kept calling out to us, 'Load de big gun, load de big gun.' Could an unconcerned spectator have witnessed the scene, he would have been struck with the amount of the ludicrous it contained. There were our Kruboys, all as pale as black men could be, the perspiration starting from every pore, exerting to the utmost their powerful muscles, while Mr. May and I were trying to look as unconcerned as possible, and, to lessen the indignity of our retreat, were smiling and bowing to the Dulti people, and beckoning to them to follow us. Their light canoes were very narrow, and the people were obliged to stand upright. The blades of their paddles, instead of being of the usual lozenge shape, were oblong and rectangular, and all curved in the direction of the propelling stroke. It was almost a regatta, our gig taking and keeping the lead. Ahead we saw an opening in the bush, by which we hoped to make our final retreat, but we were prepared, should the boat take the ground, to jump out at once and shove her into deep water. Fortune favoured us, we reached the doubtful spot, and with a single stroke of our paddles shot into the open river. Here we knew we were comparatively safe, as if the natives tried to molest us in the clear water, all we had to do was to give their canoes the stem and so upset them; our only fear had been that of being surrounded by them while entangled among the bushes. Our pursuers apparently guessed that we had now got the advantage, as they declined following us into the river, but turning paddled back to their watery abodes, and so ended the great Dulti chase.

Narrative of an exploring voyage up the rivers Kwora and Binue, pp. 195–200

19. HURRICANE ON THE BENUE

Although Mr. May and myself much regretted having so early reached our 'ne plus ultra,' yet our boat's crew took a very different view of the subject. Ever since we had visited Djin, they had been living in fear and trembling; and one Kruman, not content with assuring us that he was destined never again to see his wives and children, in cannibalic horror anticipated his fate and in imagination saw himself slain, cooked, and devoured. During the ascent all hands had been too closely occupied to allow of surveying, so this duty had now to be resumed, the leadsman being stationed in the bows, and Mr. May sketching in the sides of the river with their ever-varying direction, and taking outline views of the mountains. The westerly breeze blew freshly against us, and being opposed to the current caused a considerable ripple; but the stream being the stronger, we went with but little exertion on our part, at the rate of fully three knots an hour. The sun's rays falling nearly directly upon us, through a perfectly cloudless sky, were so powerfully felt, that we were obliged in self-defence to set our awning, although it somewhat impeded our progress. Just before two o'clock we reached Djin, and landing at the scattered huts to the westward of the town, got a set of sights: while thus occupied, many natives came across the swamp and gathering round, were urgent in their entreaties that we should re-visit their city, which however we respectfully declined. As they increased in numbers they showed a disposition to be again troublesome; so our operations being concluded, we gave a small present to our guide of the day previous, and took our departure. While close to a little grassy islet a few miles below this, we came upon a small herd of river horses in a sportive humour, apparently playing at bo-peep or some such analogous game. One suddenly popped up its huge head close to us, but amazed at our interruption, lost no time in again disappearing below the surface. Shortly, Mount Laird and the eastern end of Pleiad Island were made out, and passing along the northern shore of the latter, by half-past four o'clock we reached Bandawa, and by five, Lau; off both which villages we were met by numerous canoes. Below Lau we examined on the south bank what had seemed to us, during our ascent, a rocky cliff; but we now found it to consist of a bank of red clay some fifteen feet high, with a layer of vegetable mould on the top. As long as we could make out the river's sides, we continued our progress, but though now only a few miles from Gurowa, being unwilling to have a blank in our chart, we anchored for the night, although the weather looked very threatening, and distant lightning in the east presaged a storm. We made, accordingly, every preparation, having our awning ready in case of rain.

The moon set shortly after midnight, and was succeeded by intense darkness, every thing around being unnaturally still; the air was hushed, the wind no longer sighed among the branches, and nothing was heard save the rippling of the ceaseless tide. The sky became completely over-cast, one by one the stars disappeared, while numerous indications heralded an approaching tornado. A few minutes were left us to make ready to meet it, which we employed to the best advantage we could. More cable was given, all heavy weights and top-hamper were placed in the bottom of the boat, while Mr. May and I gathered our instruments and our few valuables around us, and covered ourselves as we best could with a scanty waterproof sheet we had with us, merely leaving our heads clear, so as to be able to look around. Our Krumen stripped themselves, and wrapping their blankets about them, were ready to attempt to swim for it in case of necessity. Even my little dog seemed to comprehend the coming strife of the elements, and nestled closer beside me. The rudder was shipped, and the yoke-lines laid ready to be seized at a moment's notice. By this time the eastern heavens were brightly illumined by flashes of vivid lightning, the electric clouds quickly drawing nearer and nearer to us. These flashes issued from strata higher than the pitchy tornado cloud, which, by their light, showed black as ink and rising rapidly above the horizon. Still in our immediate neighbourhood the unearthly quiet reigned, all noise, all motion being ignored, and the very atmosphere seeming a blank. In this state, however, we were not long permitted to rest; already could we distinguish the hissing of the coming whirlwind, and straining our eyes, we fancied we could discern a white line of foam stretching across the river. Presently it burst on us in full fury; the hurricane, sweeping along, enveloped our tiny craft, and large drops of rain struck fiercely against our faces as we attempted to peer into the obscure. Our only fear had been that the gale might catch us on the broadside, as, our boat being but light, it might have upset us, and left us among the crocodiles and river-horses; but, fortunately for us, it blew right a-head, and we rode easily. The rain, which threatened to be a deluge, ceased after a few minutes, and, still more to our astonishment, the wind greatly moderated, but these were succeeded by the most terrific thunderstorm I ever witnessed. Flash followed flash almost instantaneously, until at last the whole sky was lit up with one incessant glow of the most brilliant light. At last the clouds were right over head, and for upwards of an hour every part of the heavens to which we could look, had its own electric bolt. It was impossible to count such creations of the moment, but there must always have been every instant from ten to a dozen flashes, until at last we were utterly unable to distinguish each single thunder-clap, as all were mingled in one prolonged and continued peal, now for a second more faintly rolling, now again grandly swelling, and echoing in deep reverberations from the rugged sides of the mountains. Everything was plainly visible; the island near us, the banks of the river, and the more distant hills, all were distinctly seen.

Above us, around us, the forked lightning unweariedly still pursued its jagged, angular course, while one huge bolt, disdaining the tortuous path followed by its fellows, passed straight towards the earth, piercing the ground opposite to which we lay at anchor. Among the hills the storm raged still more furiously, the lightning playing unceasingly around each mountain summit, while ever and anon a bright spark would suddenly descend into some of the ravines below. Sometimes the passage of the lightning was from cloud to cloud, even at considerable distances; and then the stream of fire would spread, furcate, and divaricate, like the branch of some huge tree. These currents were of a purpler tint, and of smaller diameter, while those which descended were of a brighter red, and showed a much larger body of light. These aerial bolts were quite distinct from the ordinary discharge of two opposite clouds, and were not the mere passage of electricity from one to the other. During the occurrence of a few unusually near and vivid flashes, Mr. May and I were distinctly sensible of a feeling of warmth in our faces. At length there was a kind of lull, and the storm seemed to be decreasing, when a small whitish cloud was observed in the far east. It was a true cumulo-cirro-stratus, and must have been tremendously charged with electricity; for as it passed slowly along, we plainly saw constant powerful discharges. For some miles it continued to scatter around incessant forked bolts, but at length these became gradually fewer, and died away, while the cloud altered its shape to cirro-cumulus. A fresh breeze sprung up from the westward, and for a little time we were apprehensive of a squall up the river, which would not have been so pleasant; but fortunately this did not occur. By a little after three o'clock this magnificent storm had quite ceased, leaving no trace behind, save a distant thunder-peal, or an occasional flash of lightning among the mountains. Intense darkness prevailed; and now that the war of the elements was ended, we could hear about us the snorting of numerous hippopotami, which during the tempest had in fear been cowering among the reeds. Anxiously we waited for the morning; but it was not until half-past five that we could distinguish the river-banks; but these again visible, we weighed anchor, and resumed our voyage and our survey.

Narrative of an exploring voyage up the rivers Kwora and Binue, pp. 203–8

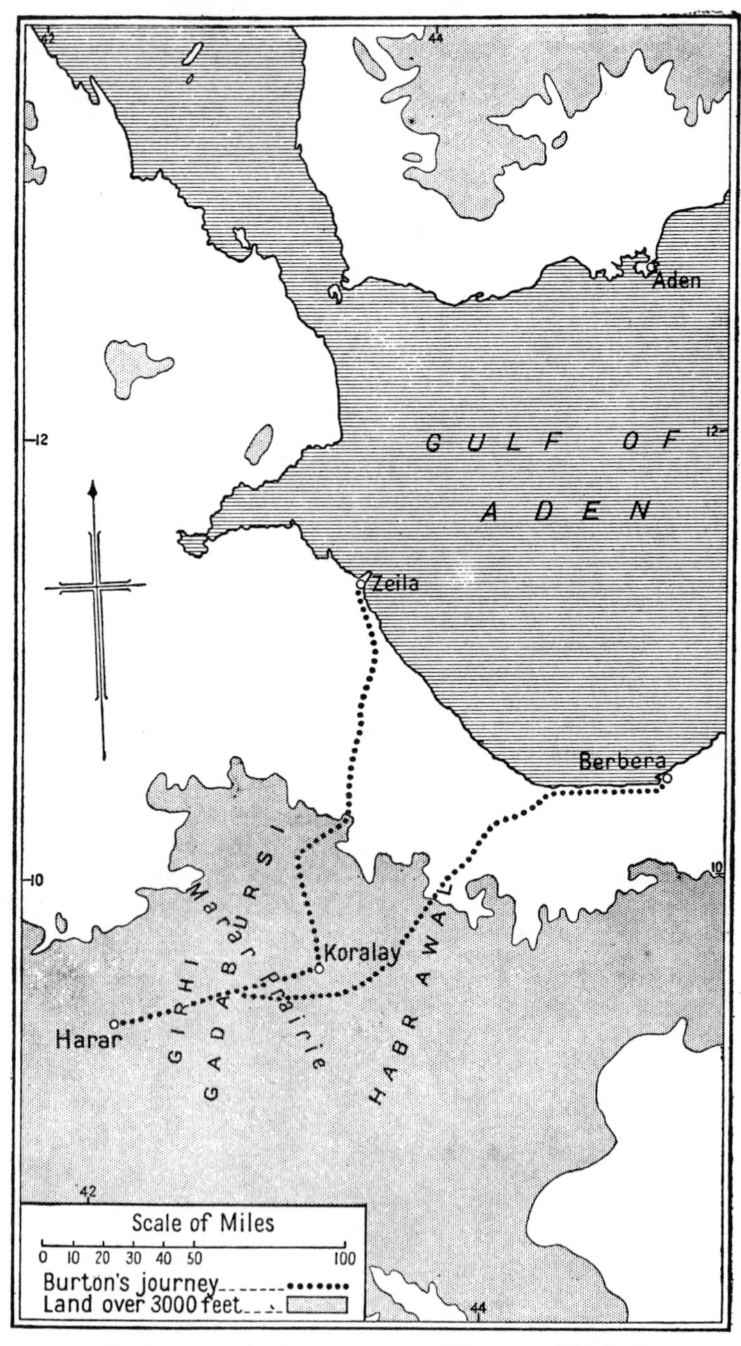

7. Burton's Journey to Harar, 1854–5

VI

SIR RICHARD FRANCIS BURTON

1821–1890

Burton was the son of a soldier. He was born upon his mother's estate near St. Albans. He had no regular education, but spent a wandering youth and was often on the continent where he became proficient both in languages and swordsmanship. After spending five terms at Oxford, where he studied Arabic, he joined the Indian army in 1842. In India he found opportunities to gratify his lust for travel in remote places and to study more languages and Eastern religions. At this time, also, he gave some offence by consorting closely with Indians and by the unfashionable frankness of his reports upon certain of their customs. This was an anticipation of the public stir he was to make in the 'eighties by his translation of the Arabian Nights *with its unexpurgated text and its uncompromising 'anthropological' notes. In 1849 he returned to England where he wrote several books upon India and its languages. In 1853 he undertook in disguise his famous and perilous journey to Mecca, and wrote three volumes upon this expedition.*

In October 1854 he arrived in Aden having obtained permission with another officer, Lieutenant Speke (see p. 181), to explore the coastland on the opposite side of the Gulf. Burton went over to Zeila, where he was hospitably received by the Shamarkay, the Governor. While the main expedition was being prepared, Burton decided to strike out alone into the unexplored country of the fanatical Moslem Somali in an attempt to reach the forbidden city of Harar, which stood between Somaliland and Abyssinia and into which no European was ever known to have entered. At Zeila he was warned that the interior was disturbed; that the direct road through the Eesa Somali was closed, and that small-pox was raging in the city. In spite of this he decided to set out, disguised as a Moslem merchant, taking a more southerly route through the country of the Gadabursi and Girhi (or Geri) Somali. He took with him two Somals who had been policemen in Aden, known as Long Guled and the Hammal, and also a Widad—which Burton translates 'hedge-priest'—a man of very doubtful character who was nicknamed 'End of Time'. He left Zeila on 27th November and the first extract describes his caravan. The opening words are explained by his having addressed his story to his friend, J. G. Lumsden.

20. EXPEDITION TO HARAR

You see, dear L., how travelling maketh man *banal.* It is the natural consequence of being forced to find, in every corner where Fate drops you for a month, a 'friend of the soul,' and a 'moon-faced beauty.' With Orientals generally, you *must* be on extreme terms, as in Hibernia, either an angel of light, or, that failing, a goblin damned. In East Africa especially, English phlegm, shyness, or pride, will bar every heart and raise every hand against you, whereas what M. Rochet calls 'a certain *rondeur* of manner' is a specific for winning affection. You should walk up to your man, clasp his fist, pat his back, speak some unintelligible words to him,—if, as is the plan of prudence, you ignore the language,—laugh a loud guffaw, sit by his side, and begin pipes and coffee. He then proceeds to utilize you, to beg in one country for your interest, and in another for your tobacco. You gently but decidedly thrust that subject out of the way, and choose what is most interesting to yourself. As might be expected, he will at times revert to his own concerns; your superior obstinacy will oppose effectual passive resistance to all such efforts; by degrees the episodes diminish in frequency and duration; at last they cease altogether. The man is now your own.

You will bear in mind, if you please, that I am a Moslem merchant, a character not to be confounded with the notable individuals seen on 'Change. Mercator in the East is a compound of tradesman, divine, and T.G. Usually of gentle birth, he is everywhere welcomed and respected; and he bears in his mind and manner that, if Allah please, he may become prime minister a month after he has sold you a yard of cloth. Commerce appears to be an accident, not an essential, with him; yet he is by no means deficient in acumen. He is a grave and reverend signior, with rosary in hand and Koran on lip, is generally a pilgrim, talks at dreary length about Holy Places, writes a pretty hand, has read and can recite much poetry, is master of his religion, demeans himself with respectability, is perfect in all points of ceremony and politeness, and feels equally at home whether sultan or slave sit upon his counter. He has a wife and children in his own country, where he intends to spend the remnant of his days; but 'the world is uncertain'—'Fate descends, and man's eye seeth it not'—'the earth is a charnel house': briefly, his many wise old saws give him a kind of theoretical consciousness that his bones may moulder in other places but his father-land.

To describe my little caravan. Foremost struts Raghe, our Eesa guide, in all the bravery of Abbanship. He is bareheaded and clothed in Tobe [cloth] and slippers: a long, heavy, horn-hilted dagger is strapped round his waist, outside his dress; in his right hand he grasps a ponderous wire-bound spear which he uses as a staff, and the left forearm supports a round targe of battered hide. Being a man of education, he bears on one shoulder a Musalla or prayer carpet of tanned leather, the article used throughout the Somali country; slung over the other is a Wesi or wicker bottle containing water for religious ablution. He is accompanied by some men who carry a little stock of town goods and drive a camel colt, which by the by they manage to lose before midnight.

My other attendants must now be introduced to you, as they are to be for the next two months companions of our journey. First in the list are Samaweda Yusuf, and Aybla Farih, buxom dames about thirty years old, who presently secured the classical nicknames of Shehrazade and Deenarzade. They look each like three average women rolled into one, and emphatically belong to that race for which the article of feminine attire, called, I believe, 'a bussle' would be quite superfluous. Wonderful, truly, is their endurance of fatigue! During the march they carry pipe and tobacco, lead and flog the camels, adjust the burdens, and will never be induced to ride, in sickness or in health. At the halt they unload the cattle, dispose the parcels in a semicircle, pitch over them the Gurgi or mat tent, cook our food, boil tea and coffee, and make themselves generally useful. They bivouack outside our abode, modesty not permitting the sexes to mingle, and in the severest cold wear no clothing but a head fillet and an old Tobe. They have curious soft voices, which contrast agreeably with the harsh organs of the males. At first they were ashamed to see me; but that feeling soon wore off, and presently they enlivened the way with pleasantries far more naïve than refined. To relieve their greatest fatigue, nothing seems necessary but the 'Jogsi:' they lie at full length, prone, stand upon each other's backs trampling and kneading with the toes, and rise like giants much refreshed. Always attendant upon these dames is Yusuf, a Zayla lad who, being one-eyed, was pitilessly named by my companions the 'Kalendar'; he prays frequently, is strict in his morals, and has conceived, like Mrs. Brownrigg, so exalted an idea of discipline, that, but for our influence, he certainly would have beaten the two female 'prentices to death. They hate him therefore, and he knows it.

Immediately behind Raghe and his party walk Shehrazade and Deenarzade, the former leading the head camel, the latter using my chibouque stick as a staff. She has been at Aden, and sorely suspects me; her little black eyes never meet mine: and frequently, with affected confusion, she turns her sable cheek the clean contrary way. Strung together by their tails, and soundly beaten when disposed to lag, the five camels pace steadily along under their burdens,—bales of Wilyati or American sheetings, Duwwarah or Cutch canvass, with indigo-dyed stuff slung along the animals' sides, and neatly sewn up in a case of matting to keep off dust and rain,—a cow's hide, which serves as a couch, covering the whole. They carry a load of 'Mushakkar' (bad Mocha dates) for the Somal, with a parcel of better quality for ourselves, and a half hundred-weight of coarse Surat tobacco; besides which we have a box of beads, and another of trinkets, mosaic-gold earrings, necklaces, watches and similar nick-nacks. Our private provisions are represented by about 300 lbs. of rice,—here the traveller's staff of life,—a large pot of 'Kawurmeh' [dried meat], dates, salt, clarified butter, tea, coffee, sugar, a box of biscuits in case of famine, 'Halwa' or Arab sweetmeats to be used when driving hard bargains, and a little turmeric for seasoning. A simple batterie de cuisine, and sundry skins full of potable water, dangle from chance rope-ends; and last, but not the least important, is a heavy box of ammunition sufficient for a three month's sporting tour. In the rear of the caravan trudges a Bedouin woman driving a donkey,—the proper 'tail' in these regions, where camels start if followed by a horse or mule. An ill-fated sheep, a parting present from the Hajj, races and frisks about the Cafilah [caravan]. It became so tame, that the Somal received an order not to 'cut' it; one day, however, I found myself dining, and that pet lamb was the menu.

By the side of the camels ride my three attendants, the pink of Somali fashion. Their frizzled wigs are radiant with grease; their Tobes are splendidly white, with borders dazzlingly red; their new shields are covered with canvass cloth; and their two spears, poised over the right shoulder, are freshly scraped, oiled, blackened and polished. They have added my spare rifle, and guns to the camel-load; such weapons are well enough at Aden, in Somali-land men would deride the outlandish tool! I told them that in my country women use bows and arrows, moreover that lancers are generally considered a corps of non-combatants; in vain! they adhered as strongly—so mighty a thing is prejudice—to their partiality for bows, arrows, and lances. Their horsemanship is peculiar, they balance themselves upon little Abyssinian saddles, extending the leg and raising the heel in the Louis Quinze style of equitation, and the stirrup is an iron ring admitting only the big toe. I follow them mounting a fine white mule, which, with its gaudily *galonné* Arab pad and wrapper cloth, has a certain dignity of look; a double-barrelled gun lies across my lap; and a rude pair of holsters, the work of Hasan Turki, contains my Colt's six-shooters.

Marching in this order, which was to serve as a model, we travelled due south along the coast, over a hard, stoneless, and alluvial plain, here dry, there muddy (where the tide reaches) across boggy creeks, broad water-courses, and warty flats of black mould powdered with nitrous salt, and bristling with the salsolaceous vegetation familiar to the Arab voyager. . . .

My arms were peeled even in the month of December; and my companions, panting with the heat, like the Atlantes of Herodotus, poured forth reproaches upon the rising sun. The townspeople, when forced to hurry across it in the hotter season, cover themselves during the day with Tobes wetted every half hour in sea water; yet they are sometimes killed by the fatal thirst which the Simun engenders. Even the Bedouins are now longing for rain; a few weeks' drought destroys half their herds.

After a month's riding across the maritime plain and plateau of Somaliland, Burton found himself leaving the end of the true arid Somali country and approaching a transitional belt between '*the desert and the sown*' *that lay between the Somali hills and those of Harar.*

Early on the 23rd December assembled the Caravan, which we were destined to escort across the Marar Prairie. Upon this neutral ground the Eesa, Berteri, and Habr Awal [three Somali tribes] meet to rob and plunder unhappy travellers. The Somal shuddered at the sight of a wayfarer, who rushed into our encampment *in cuerpo*, having barely run away with his life. Not that our caravan carried much to lose,—a few hides and pots of clarified butter, to be exchanged for the Holcus grain of the Girhi cultivators,—still the smallest contributions are thankfully received by these plunderers. Our material consisted of four or five half-starved camels, about fifty donkeys with ears cropped as a mark, and their eternal accompaniments in Somali-land, old women. The latter seemed to be selected for age, hideousness, and strength: all day they bore their babes smothered in hides upon their backs, and they carried heavy burdens apparently without fatigue. Amongst them was a Bedouin widow, known by her 'Wer,' a strip of the inner bark of a tree tied round the greasy fillet. We were accompanied by three Widads, provided with all the instruments of their craft, and uncommonly tiresome companions. They recited Koran *à tort et à travers*: at every moment they proposed Fatihahs [texts from the first chapter of the Koran], the name of Allah was perpetually upon their lips, and they discussed questions of divinity, like Gil Blas and his friends, with a violence bordering upon frenzy. One of them was celebrated for his skill in the 'Fal', or Omens: he was constantly consulted by my companions, and informed them that we had nought to fear except from wild beasts. The prediction was a good hit: I must own, however, that it was not communicated to me before fulfilment. . . .

Towards evening, as the setting sun sank slowly behind the distant western hills, the colour of the Prairie changed from glaring yellow to a golden hue, mantled with a purple flush inexpressibly lovely. The animals of the waste began to appear. Shy lynxes and jackals, fattened by many sheep's tails, warned my companions that fierce beasts were nigh, ominous anecdotes were whispered, and I was told that a caravan had lately lost nine asses by lions. As night came on, the Bedouin Kafilah, being lightly loaded, preceded us, and our tired camels lagged far behind. We were riding in rear to prevent straggling, when suddenly my mule, the hindermost, pricked his ears uneasily, and attempted to turn his head. Looking backwards, I distinguished the form of a large animal following us with quick and stealthy strides. My companions would not fire, thinking it was a man: at last a rifle-ball, pinging through the air—the moon was too young for correct shooting—put to flight a huge lion. The terror excited by this sort of an adventure was comical to look upon: the valiant Beuh, who, according to himself, had made his *preuves* in a score of foughten fields, threw his arms in the air, wildly shouting 'Libah! Libah! !—the lion! the lion! !'—and nothing else was talked of that evening.

The ghostly western hills seemed to recede as we advanced over the endless rolling plain. Presently the ground became broken and stony, the mules stumbled in deep holes, and the camels could scarcely crawl along. As we advanced, our Widads, who, poor devils! had been 'roasted' by the women all day on account of their poverty, began to recite the Koran with might, in gratitude for having escaped many perils. Night deepening, our attention was rivetted by a strange spectacle; a broad sheet of bright blaze, reminding me of Hanno's fiery river, swept apparently down a hill, and, according to my companions threatened the whole prairie. These accidents are common: a huntsman burns a tree for honey, or cooks his food in the dry grass, the wind rises and the flames spread far and wide. On this occasion no accident occurred; the hills, however, smoked like a Solfatara for two days. . . .

After another delay, and a second vain message to the Gerad Adan [head of a tribe of agricultural Somali, the Girhi], about noon appeared that dignitary's sixth wife, sister to the valiant Beuh. Her arrival disconcerted my companions, who were too proud to be protected by a woman. 'Dahabo,' however, relieved their anxiety by informing us that the Gerad had sent his eldest son Sherwa, as escort. This princess was a gipsy-looking dame, coarsely dressed, about thirty years old, with a gay leer, a jaunty demeanour, and the reputation of being 'fast'; she showed little shamefacedness when I saluted her, and received with noisy joy the appropriate present of a new and handsome Tobe. About 4 p.m. returned our second messenger, bearing with him a reproving message from the Gerad, for not visiting him without delay; in token of sincerity he forwarded his baton, a knobstick about two feet long, painted in rings of Cutch colours, red, black, and yellow alternately, and garnished on the summit with a ball of similar material.

At dawn on the 26th December, mounted upon a little pony, came Sherwa, heir presumptive to the Gerad Adan's knobstick. His father had sent him to us three days before but he feared the Gudabirsi as much as the Gudabirsi feared him, and he probably hung about our camp till certain that it was safe to enter. We received him politely, and he in acknowledgment positively declared that Beuh should not return before eating honey in his cottage. Our Abban's [protector's] heroism now became infectious. Even the End of Time, whose hot valour had long since fallen below zero, was inspired by the occasion, and recited, as usual with him in places and at times of extreme safety, the Arabs' warrior lines—

'I have crossed the steed since my eyes saw light,
I have fronted death till he feared my sight,
And the cleaving of helm, and the riving of mail
Were the dreams of my youth—are my manhood's delight.'

As we had finished loading, a mule's bridle was missed. Sherwa ordered instant restitution to his father's stranger, on the ground that all the property now belonged to the Gerad; and we, by no means idle, fiercely threatened to bewitch the kraal. The article was presently found hard by, on a hedge. This was the first and last case of theft which occurred to us in the Somali country;—I have travelled through most civilised lands, and have lost more.

At 8 a.m. we marched towards the north-west, along the southern base of the Gurays hills, and soon arrived at the skirt of the prairie, where a well-trodden path warned us that we were about to quit the desert. After advancing six miles in line we turned to the right, and recited a Fatihah over the heap of rough stones, where, shadowed by venerable trees, lie the remains of the great Shaykh Abd el Malik. A little beyond this spot rises suddenly from the plain a mass of castellated rock, the subject of many a wild superstition. Caravans always encamp beneath it, as whoso sleeps upon the summit loses his senses to evil spirits. At some future day Harar will be destroyed, and 'Jannah Siri' will become a flourishing town. We ascended it, and found no life but hawks, coneys, an owl, and a graceful species of black eagle; there were many traces of buildings, walls, ruined houses, and wells, whilst the sides and summit were tufted with venerable sycamores. This act was an imprudence; the Bedouins at once declared that we were 'prospecting' for a fort, and the evil report preceded us to Harar.

After a mile's march from Jannah Siri, we crossed a ridge of rising ground, and suddenly, as though by magic, the scene shifted.

Before us lay a little Alp; the second step of the Ethiopian Highland. Around were high and jagged hills, their sides black with the Saj [teak] and Somali pine, and their upper brows veiled with a thin growth of cactus. Beneath was a deep valley, in the midst of which ran a serpentine of shining waters, the gladdest spectacle we had yet witnessed: further in front, masses of hill rose abruptly from shady valleys, encircled on the far horizon by a straight blue line of ground, resembling a distant sea. Behind us glared the desert: we had now reached the outskirts of civilization, where man, abandoning his flocks and herds, settles, cultivates, and attends to the comforts of life.

The fields are either terraces upon the hill slopes or the sides of valleys, divided by flowery hedges with lanes between, not unlike those of rustic England, and on a nearer approach the daisy, the thistle, and the sweet briar pleasantly affected my European eyes. The villages are no longer movable: the Kraal and wigwam are replaced by the Gambisa or bell-shaped hut of Middle Africa, circular cottages of holcus wattle, covered with coarse dab and surmounted by a stiff, conical, thatch roof, above which appears the central supporting post, crowned with a gourd or ostrich egg. Strong abbatis of thorns protect these settlements, which stud the hills in all directions: near most of them are clumps of tall trees, to the southern sides of which are hung, like birdcages, long cylinders of matting, the hives of these regions. Yellow crops of holcus rewarded the peasant's toil: in some places the long stems tied in bunches below the ears as piled muskets, stood ready for the reaper; in others, the barer ground showed that the task was done. The boys sat perched upon reed platforms in the trees, and with loud shouts drove away thieving birds, whilst their fathers cut the crop with diminutive sickles, or thrashed heaps of straw with rude flails, or winnowed grain by tossing it with a flat wooden shovel against the wind. The women husked the pineapple-formed heads in mortars composed of a hollowed trunk, smeared the threshing floor with cow-dung and water to defend it from insects, piled the holcus heads into neat yellow heaps, spanned and crossed by streaks of various colours, brick-red and brownish-purple, and stacked the Karbi or straw, which was surrounded like the grain with thorn, as a defence against the wild hog. All seemed to consider it a labour of love: the harvest-home song sounded pleasantly to our ears, and, contrasting with the silent desert, the hum of man's habitation was a music.

Descending the steep slope, we reposed, after a seven miles' march, on the banks of a bright rivulet, which bisects the Kobbo or valley: it runs, according to my guides, from the north towards Ogadayn, and the direction is significant,—about Harar I found neither hill nor stream trending from east to west. The people of the Kutti [cultivated districts] flocked out to gaze upon us; they were unarmed, and did not, like the Bedouins, receive us with cries of 'Bori' [tobacco]. During the halt we bathed in the waters, upon whose banks were a multitude of huge Mantidæ, pink and tender green. Returning to the camels, I shot a kind of crow, afterwards frequently seen. It is about three times the size of our English bird, of a bluish-black with a snow-white poll, and a beak of unnatural proportions; the quantity of lead which it carried off surprised me. A number of Widads assembled to greet us, and some Habr Awal, who were returning with a caravan, gave us the salam, and called my people cousins. 'Verily,' remarked the Hammal, 'amongst friends we cut one another's throats; amongst enemies we become sons of uncles!'

At 3 p.m. we pursued our way over rising ground, dotted with granite blocks fantastically piled, and everywhere in sight of fields and villages and flowing water. A furious wind was blowing, and the End of Time quoted the Somali proverb, 'heat hurts, but cold kills:' the camels were so fatigued, and the air became so raw, that after an hour and a half's march we planted our wigwams near a village distant about seven miles from the Gurays Hills. Till late at night we were kept awake by the crazy Widads: Ao Samattar had proposed the casuistical question, 'Is it lawful to pray upon a mountain when a plain is at hand?' Some took the *pro*, others the *contra*, and the wordy battle raged with uncommon fury.

On Wednesday morning at half-past seven we started down hill towards 'Wilensi,' a small table-mountain at the foot of which we expected to find the Gerad Adan awaiting us in one of his many houses, crossed a fertile valley, and ascended another steep slope by a bad and stony road. Passing the home of Sherwa, who vainly offered hospitality, we toiled onwards, and after a mile and a half's march, which occupied at least two hours, our wayworn beasts arrived at the Gerad's village. On inquiry, it proved that the chief, who was engaged in selecting two horses and two hundred cows, the price of blood claimed by the Amir of Harar for the murder of a citizen, had that day removed to Sagharrah, another settlement.

As we entered the long straggling village of Wilensi, our party was divided by the Gerad's two wives. The Hammal, the Kalendar, Shehrazade, and Deenarzade remained with Beuh and his sister in her Gurgi [hut], whilst Long Guled, the End of Time, and I were conducted to the cottage of the Gerad's prettiest wife, Sudiyah. She was a tall woman, with a light complexion, handsomely dressed in a large Harar Tobe, with silver earrings, and the kind of necklace called Jilbah or Kardas. The Geradah (princess) at once ordered our hides to be spread in a comfortable part of the hut, and then supplied us with food—boiled beef, pumpkin, and Jowari [grain] cakes. During the short time spent in that Gambisa, I had an opportunity, dear L., of seeing the manners and customs of the settled Somal.

The interior of the cottage is simple. Entering the door, a single plank with pins for hinges fitted into sockets above and below the lintel—in fact, as artless a contrivance as ever seen in Spain or Corsica—you find a space, divided by dwarf walls of wattle and dab into three compartments, for the men, women, and cattle. The horses and cows, tethered at night on the left of the door, fill the cottage with the wherewithal to pass many a *nuit blanche*: the wives lie on the right, near a large fireplace of stones and raised clay, and the males occupy the most comfortable part, opposite to and farthest from the entrance. The thatched ceiling shines jetty with smoke, which when intolerable is allowed to escape by a diminutive window: this seldom happens, for smoke, like grease and dirt, keeping man warm, is enjoyed by savages. Equally simple is the furniture: the stem of a tree, with branches hacked into pegs, supports the shields, the assegais are planted against the wall, and divers bits of wood, projecting from the sides and the central roof-tree of the cottage, are hung with clothes and other articles that attract white ants. Gourds smoked inside, and coffee cups of coarse black Harar pottery, with deep wooden platters, and prettily carved spoons of the same material, compose the household supellex. The inmates are the Geradah and her baby, Siddik a Galla serf, the slave girls and sundry Somal: thus we hear at all times three languages spoken within the walls.

Long before dawn the goodwife rises, wakens her handmaidens, lights the fire, and prepares for the Afur or morning meal. The quern is here unknown. A flat, smooth, oval slab, weighing about fifteen pounds, and a stone roller six inches in diameter, worked with both hands, and the weight of the body kneeling ungracefully upon it on 'all fours,' are used to triturate the holcus grain. At times water must be sprinkled over the meal, until a finely powdered paste is ready for the oven: thus several hours' labour is required to prepare a few pounds of bread. About 6 a.m. there appears a substantial breakfast of roast beef and mutton, with scones of Jowari grain, the whole drenched in broth. Of the men few perform any ablutions, but all use the tooth stick before sitting down to eat. After the meal some squat in the sun, others transact business, and drive their cattle to the bush till 11 a.m., the dinner hour. There is no variety in the repasts, which are always flesh and holcus: these people despise fowls, and consider vegetables food for cattle. During the day there is no privacy; men, women, and children enter in crowds, and will not be driven away by the Geradah, who inquires screamingly if they come to stare at a baboon. My kettle especially excites their surprise; some opine that it is an ostrich, others, a serpent: Sudiyah, however, soon discovered its use, and begged irresistibly for the unique article. Throughout the day her slave girls are busied in grinding, cooking, and quarrelling with dissonant voices: the men have little occupation beyond chewing tobacco, chatting, and having their wigs frizzled by a professional coiffeur. In the evening the horses and cattle return home to be milked and stabled: this operation concluded, all apply themselves to supper with a will. They sleep but little, and sit deep into the night trimming the fire, and conversing merrily over their cups of Farshu or millet beer. I tried this mixture several times, and found it detestable: the taste is sour, and it flies directly to the head, in consequence of being mixed with some poisonous bark. It is served up in gourd bottles upon a basket of holcus heads, and strained through a pledget of cotton, fixed across the narrow mouth, into cups of the same primitive material: the drinkers sit around their liquor, and their hilarity argues its intoxicating properties. In the morning they arise with headaches and heavy eyes; but these symptoms, which we, an industrious race, deprecate, are not disliked by the Somal—they promote sleep and give something to occupy the vacant mind.

. . . . . .

On the morning after my arrival at Sagharrah I felt too ill to rise, and was treated with unaffected kindness by all the establishment. The Gerad sent to Harar for millet beer, Ao Samattar went to the gardens in search of Kat [a stimulating vegetable drug], the sons Yusuf Dera and a dwarf insisted upon firing me with such ardour that no refusal could avail: and Khayrah the wife, with her daughters, two tall dark, smiling, and well-favoured girls of thirteen and fifteen, sacrificed a sheep as my Fida, or Expiatory offering. Even the Galla Christians, who flocked to see the stranger, wept for the evil fate which had brought him so far from his fatherland, to die under a tree. Nothing, indeed, would have been easier than such operation: all required was the turning face to the wall, for four or five days. But to expire of an ignoble colic!—the thing was not to be thought of, and a firm resolution to live on sometimes, methinks, effects its object.

On the 1st January, 1855, feeling stronger, I clothed myself in my Arab best, and asked a palaver with the Gerad. We retired to a safe place behind the village, where I read with pomposity the Haji Sharmarkay's letter. The chief appeared much pleased by our having preferred his country to that of the Eesa: he at once opened the subject of the new fort, and informed me that I was the builder, as his eldest daughter had just dreamed that the stranger would settle in the land. Having discussed the project to the Gerad's satisfaction, we brought out the guns and shot a few birds for the benefit of the vulgar. Whilst engaged in this occupation appeared a party of five strangers, and three mules with ornamented Morocco saddles, bridles, bells, and brass neck ornaments, after the fashion of Harar. Two of these men, Haji Umar and Nur Ambar, were citizens: the others, Ali Hasan, Husayn Araleh, and Haji Mohammed, were Somal of the Habr Awal tribe, high in the Amir's confidence. They had been sent to settle with Adan the weighty matter of Blood-money. After sitting with us almost half-an-hour, during which they exchanged grave salutations with my attendants, inspected our asses with portentous countenances, and asked me a few questions concerning my business in those parts, they went privily to the Gerad, told him that the Arab was not one who bought and sold, that he had no design but to spy out the wealth of the land, and that the whole party should be sent prisoners in their hands to Harar. The chief curtly replied that we were his friends, and bade them 'throw far those words.' Disappointed in their designs, they started late in the afternoon, driving off their 200 cows, and falsely promising to present our salams to the Amir.

It became evident that some decided step must be taken. The Gerad confessed fear of his Harari kinsman, and owned that he had lost all his villages in the immediate neighbourhood of the city. I asked him point-blank to escort us: he as frankly replied that it was impossible. The request was lowered—we begged him to accompany us as far as the frontier: he professed inability to do so, but promised to send his eldest son, Sherwa.

Nothing then remained, dear L., but *payer d'audace*, and, throwing all forethought to the dogs, to rely upon what has made many a small man great, the good star. I addressed my companions in a set speech, advising a mount without delay. They suggested a letter to the Amir, requesting permission to enter his city: this device was rejected for two reasons. In the first place, had a refusal been returned, our journey was cut short, and our labours stultified. Secondly, the End of Time had whispered that my two companions were plotting to prevent the letter reaching its destination. He had charged his own sin upon their shoulders: the Hammal and Long Guled were incapable of such treachery. But our hedge-priest was thoroughly terrified; 'a coward body after a',' his face brightened when ordered to remain with the Gerad at Sagharrah, and though openly taunted with poltroonery, he had not the decency to object. My companions were then informed that hitherto our acts had been those of old women, not soldiers, and that something savouring of manliness must be done before we could return. They saw my determination to start alone, if necessary, and to do them justice, they at once arose. This was the more courageous in them, as alarmists had done their worst: but a day before, some travelling Somali had advised them, as they valued dear life, not to accompany that Turk to Harar. Once in the saddle, they shook off sad thoughts, declaring that if they were slain, I should pay their blood-money, and if they escaped, that their reward was in my hands. When in some danger, the Hammal especially behaved with a sturdiness which produced the most beneficial results. Yet they

RHINOCEROS
From Bruce's *Travels*

MUNGO PARK
From Park's *Travels*

Park on His Journey
From Park's *Travels*

HUGH CLAPPERTON
From Clapperton's *Journal of a Second Expedition*

Horseman of the Western Sudan
From the *Narrative* of Denham, Clapperton and Oudney

MUSICIANS OF THE WESTERN SUDAN
From the *Narrative* of Denham, Clapperton and Oudney

ENCOUNTER WITH A LION
From Livingstone's *Missionary Travels*

King Mtesa's Levee
From Speke's *Journal*

King Mtesa Reviews His Troops
From Speke's *Journal*

THE RIPON FALLS
From Speke's *Journal*

THE LAST CHARGE
From Baker's *Albert N'Yanza*

THE SLAVERS REVENGING THEIR LOSSES
From Livingstone's *Last Journals*

The Manyuema Massacre
From Livingstone's *Last Journals*

‘Dr. Livingstone, I Presume?’
From Stanley’s *How I Found Livingstone*

Livingstone Crossing a River
From Livingstone's *Last Journals*

20th April 1873 = S. service
cross. over sponge the Moenda
for food & to be near the
headmen of these parts
Muanzabamba - I am
excessively weak =
vil on the Moenda sponge 7 A.M.

25.88 } 66°
26.12 } clouds
25.70 } high

cross Lokulu in a canoe
R. is about 30 yds broad
very deep and flowing
in marshes - 2 knots
from SSE to NNW
into Lake

21st tried to ride but was
forced to lie down and
they carried me back to
vil. exhausted

22nd carried in Kitanda
over Buga S W 2¼

23rd do 1½
24th do 1
25th do 1
26th do 2½

---

to Kalunganjovu's
total 33° = 8¼

27th knocked up quite
and remain = recover
sent to buy milch
goats. We are on the
banks of R Molilamo

THE LAST ENTRIES IN LIVINGSTONE'S JOURNAL
From Livingstone's *Last Journals*

were true Easterns. Wearied by delay at Harar, I employed myself in meditating flight; they drily declared that after-wit serves no good purpose: whilst I considered the possibility of escape, they looked only at the prospect of being dragged back with pinioned arms by the Amir's guard. Such is generally the effect of the vulgar Moslems' blind fatalism.

I then wrote an English letter from the Political Agent at Aden to the Amir of Harar, proposing to deliver it in person, and throw off my disguise. Two reasons influenced me in adopting this 'neck or nothing' plan. All the races amongst whom my travels lay, hold him nidering who hides his origin in places of danger; and secondly, my white face had converted me into a Turk, a nation more hated and suspected than any Europeans, without our *prestige*. Before leaving Sagharrah, I entrusted to the End of Time a few lines addressed to Lieut. Herne at Berberah, directing him how to act in case of necessity. Our baggage was again decimated: the greater part was left with Adan, and an ass carried only what was absolutely necessary—a change of clothes, a book or two, a few biscuits, ammunition, and a little tobacco. My Girhi escort consisted of Sherwa, the Bedouin Abtidon, and Mad Said mounted on the End of Time's mule.

At 10 a.m. on the 2nd January all the villagers assembled and recited the Fatihah, consoling us with the information that we were dead men. By the worst of foot-paths we ascended the rough and stony hill behind Sagharrah, through bush and burn and over ridges of rock. At the summit was a village, where Sherwa halted, declaring that he dared not advance: a swordsman, however, was sent on to guard us through the Galla Pass. After an hour's ride we reached the foot of a tall Table-mountain called Kondura, where our road, a goat-path rough with rocks or fallen trees, and here and there arched over with giant creepers, was reduced to a narrow ledge, with a forest above and a forest below. I could not but admire the beauty of this Valombrosa, which reminded me of scenes whilome enjoyed in fair Touraine. High up on our left rose the perpendicular walls of the misty hill, fringed with tufted pine, and on the right, the shrub-clad folds fell into a deep valley. The cool wind whistled and sunbeams like golden shafts darted through tall shady trees—

> Bearded with moss, and in garments green—

the ground was clothed with dank grass, and around the trunks grew thistles, daisies, and blue flowers which at a distance might well pass for violets.

Presently we were summarily stopped by half-a-dozen Gallas attending upon one Rabah, the Chief who owns the Pass. This is the African style of toll-taking: the 'pike' appears in the form of a plump of spearmen, and the gate is a pair of lances thrown across the road. Not without trouble, for they feared to depart from the *mos majorum*, we persuaded them that the ass carried no merchandise. Then, rounding Kondura's northern flank, we entered the Amir's territory: about thirty miles distant, and separated by a series of blue valleys, lay a dark speck upon a tawny sheet of stubble—Harar.

Having paused for a moment to savour success, we began the descent. The ground was a slippery black soil—mist ever settles upon Kondura—and frequent springs oozing from the rock formed beds of black mire. A few huge Birbisa trees, the remnant of a forest still thick around the mountain's neck, marked out the road: they were branchy from stem to stern, and many had a girth of from twenty to twenty-five feet.

After an hour's ride amongst thistles, whose flowers of a bright red-like worsted were not less than a child's head, we watered our mules at a rill below the slope. Then remounting, we urged over hill and dale, where Galla peasants were threshing and storing their grain with loud songs of joy: they were easily distinguished by their African features, mere caricatures of the Somal, whose type has been Arabised by repeated immigrations from Yemen and Hadramaut. Late in the afternoon, having gained ten miles in a straight direction, we passed through a hedge of plantains, defending the windward side of Gafra, a village of Midgans who collect the Gerad Adan's grain. They shouted delight on recognizing their old friend, Mad Said, led us to an empty Gambisa, swept and cleaned it, lighted a fire, turned our mules into a field to graze, and went forth to seek food. Their hospitable thoughts, however, were marred by the two citizens of Harar, who privately threatened them with the Amir's wrath if they dared to feed that Turk. . . .

About noon we crossed the Erar River. The bed is about one hundred yards broad, and a thin sheet of clear, cool, and sweet water covered with crystal the greater part of the sand. According to my guides, its course, like that of the hills, is southerly towards the Webbe of Ogadayn: none, however, could satisfy my curiosity concerning the course of the only perennial stream which exists between Harar and the coast.

In the lower valley, a mass of waving holcus, we met a multitude of Galla peasants coming from the city market with new potlids and the empty gourds which had contained their butter, ghee, and milk: all wondered aloud at the Turk, concerning whom they had heard many horrors. As we commenced another ascent appeared a Harar Grandee mounted upon a handsomely caparisoned mule and attended by seven servants who carried gourds and skins of grain. He was a pale-faced senior with a white beard, dressed in a fine Tobe and a snowy turban with scarlet edges: he carried no shield, but an Abyssinian broadsword was slung over his left shoulder. We exchanged courteous salutations, and as I was thirsty he ordered a footman to fill a cup with water. . . .

At 2 p.m. we fell into a narrow fenced lane and halted for a few minutes near a spreading tree, under which sat women selling ghee and unspun cotton. About two miles on the crest of a hill stood the city,—the end of my present travel,—a long sombre line strikingly contrasting with the whitewashed towns of the East. The spectacle, materially speaking, was a disappointment: nothing conspicuous appeared but two grey minarets of rude shape: many would have grudged exposing three lives to win so paltry a prize. But of all that have attempted, none ever succeeded in entering that pile of stones: the thoroughbred traveller, dear L., will understand my exultation, although my two companions exchanged glances of wonder.

Spurring our mules we advanced at a long trot, when Mad Said stopped us to recite a Fatihah in honour of Ao Umar Siyad and Ao Rahmah, two great saints who repose under a clump of trees near the road. The soil on both sides of the path is rich and red: masses of plantains, limes, and pomegranates denote the gardens, which are defended by a bleached cow's skull, stuck upon a short stick, and between them are plantations of coffee, bastard saffron, and the graceful Kat. About half a mile eastward of the town appears a burn called Jalah or the Coffee Water: the crowd crossing it did not prevent my companions bathing, and whilst they donned clean Tobes I retired to the wayside, and sketched the town.

These operations over, we resumed our way up a rough *tranchée* ridged with stone and hedged with tall cactus. This ascends to an open plain. On the right lie the holcus fields, which reach to the town wall: the left is a heap of rude cemetery, and in front are the dark defences of Harar, with groups of citizens loitering about the large gateway, and sitting in chat near the ruined tomb of Ao Abdal. We arrived at 3 p.m. after riding about five hours, which were required to accomplish twenty miles in a straight direction.

Advancing to the gate, Mad Said accosted a warder, known by his long wand of office, and sent our salams to the Amir, saying that we came from Aden, and requested the honor of audience. Whilst he sped upon his errand, we sat at the foot of a round bastion, and were scrutinised, derided, and catechised by the curious of both sexes, especially by that conventionally termed the fair. . . .

After waiting half-an-hour at the gate, we were told by the returned warder to pass the threshold, and, remounting, guided our mules along the main street, a narrow up-hill lane, with rocks cropping out from a surface more irregular than a Perote pavement. Long Guled had given his animal into the hands of our two Bedouins: they did not appear till after our audience, when they informed us that the people at the entrance had advised them to escape with the beasts, an evil fate having been prepared for the proprietors.

Arrived within a hundred yards of the gate of holcus-stalks, which opens into the courtyard of this African St. James, our guide, a blear-eyed, surly-faced, angry-voiced fellow, made signs—none of us understanding his Harari—to dismount. We did so. He then began to trot, and roared out apparently that we must do the same. We looked at one another, the Hammal swore that he would perish foully rather than obey, and—conceive, dear L., the idea of a petticoated pilgrim venerable as to beard and turban breaking into a long 'double!'—I expressed much the same sentiment. Leading our mules leisurely, in spite of the guide's wrath, we entered the gate, strode down the yard, and were placed under a tree in its left corner, close to a low building of rough stone, which the clanking of frequent fetters argued to be a state-prison.

This part of the court was crowded with Gallas, some lounging about, others squatting in the shade under the palace walls. The chiefs were known by their zinc armlets, composed of thin spiral circlets, closely joined, and extending in mass from the wrist almost to the elbow: all appeared to enjoy peculiar privileges—they carried their long spears, wore their sandals, and walked leisurely about the royal precincts. A delay of half-an-hour, during which state-affairs were being transacted within, gave me time to inspect a place of which so many and such differ ent accounts are current. The palace itself is, as Clapperton describes the Fellatah Sultan's state-hall, a mere shed, a long, single-storied, windowless barn of rough stone and reddish clay, with no other insignia but a thin coat of whitewash over the door. This is the royal and vizierial distinction at Harar, where no lesser man may stucco the walls of his house. The courtyard was about eighty yards long by thirty in breadth, irregularly shaped, and surrounded by low buildings: in the centre, opposite the outer entrance, was a circle of masonry, against which were propped divers doors.

Presently the blear-eyed guide with the angry voice returned from within, released us from the importunities of certain forward and inquisitive youth, and motioned us to doff our slippers at a stone step, or rather line, about twelve feet distant from the palace-wall. We grumbled that we were not entering a mosque, but in vain. Then ensued a long dispute, in tongues mutually unintelligible, about giving up our weapons: by dint of obstinacy we retained our daggers and my revolver. The guide raised a door curtain, suggested a bow, and I stood in the presence of the dreaded chief.

The Amir, or, as he styles himself, the Sultan Ahmad bin Sultan Abubakr, sat in a dark room with whitewashed walls, to which hung—significant decorations—rusty matchlocks and polished fetters. His appearance was that of a little Indian Rajah, an etiolated youth twenty-four or twenty-five years old, plain and thin-bearded, with a yellow complexion, wrinkled brows and protruding eyes. His dress was a flowing robe of crimson cloth edged with snowy fur, and a narrow white turban tightly twisted round a tall conical cap of red velvet, like the old Turkish headgear of our painters. His throne was a common Indian Kursi, or raised cot, about five feet long, with back and sides supported by a dwarf railing: being an invalid he rested his elbow upon a pillow, under which appeared the hilt of a Cutch sabre. Ranged in double line, perpendicular to the Amir, stood the 'court', his cousins and nearest relations, with right arms bared after fashion of Abyssinia.

I entered the room with a loud 'Peace be upon ye!' to which H.H. replying graciously, and extending a hand, bony and yellow as a kite's claw, snapped his thumb and middle finger. Two chamberlains stepping forward held my forearms, and assisted me to bend low over the fingers, which however I did not kiss, being naturally averse to performing that operation upon any but a woman's hand. My two servants then took their turn: in this case, after the back was saluted, the palm was presented for a repetition. These preliminaries concluded, we were led to and seated upon a mat in front of the Amir, who directed towards us a frowning brow and an inquisitive eye.

Some inquiries were made about the chief's health: he shook his head captiously, and inquired our errand. I drew from my pocket my own letter: it was carried by a chamberlain, with hands veiled in his Tobe, to the Amir, who after a brief glance laid it upon the couch, and demanded further explanation. I then represented in Arabic that we had come from Aden, bearing the compliments of our Daulah or governor, and that we had entered Harar to see the light of H.H.'s countenance: this information concluded with a little speech, describing the changes of Political Agents in Arabia, and alluding to the friendship formerly existing between the English and the deceased chief Abubakr.

The Amir smiled graciously.

This smile I must own, dear L., was a relief. We had been prepared for the worst, and the aspect of affairs in the palace was by no means reassuring.

Whispering to his Treasurer, a little ugly man with a badly shaven head, coarse features, pug nose, angry eyes, and stubby beard, the Amir made a sign for us to retire. The *baise main* was repeated, and we backed out of the audience-shed in high favour. According to grandiloquent Bruce, 'the Court of London and that of Abyssinia are, in their principles, one:' the loiterers in the Harar palace yard, who had before regarded us with cut-throat looks, now smiled as though they loved us. Marshalled by the guard, we issued from the precincts, and after walking a hundred yards entered the Amir's second palace, which we were told to consider our home. There we found the Bedouins, who, scarcely believing that we had escaped alive, grinned in the joy of their hearts, and we were at once provided from the chief's kitchen with a dish of

Shabta, holcus cakes soaked in sour milk, and thickly powdered with red pepper, the salt of this inland region. . . .

Returning we inquired anxiously of the treasurer about my servants' arms which had not been returned, and were assured that they had been placed in the safest of store-houses, the palace. I then sent a common six-barrelled revolver as a present to the Amir, explaining its use to the bearer, and we prepared to make ourselves as comfortable as possible. The interior of our new house was a clean room, with plain walls, and a floor of tamped earth; opposite the entrance were two broad steps of masonry, raised about two feet, and a yard above the ground, and covered with hard matting. I contrived to make upon the higher ledge a bed with the cushions which my companions used as shabracques, and, after seeing the mules fed and tethered, lay down to rest, worn out by fatigue and profoundly impressed with the *poésie* of our position. I was under the roof of a bigoted prince whose least word was death; amongst a people who detest foreigners; the only European that had ever passed over their inhospitable threshold, and the fated instrument of their future downfall.

. . . . . .

The ancient capital of Hadiyah shares with Zebid, in Yemen, the reputation of being an Alma Mater, and inundates the surrounding districts with poor scholars and crazy 'Widads.' Where knowledge leads to nothing, says philosophic Volney, nothing is done to acquire it, and the mind remains in a state of barbarism. There are no establishments for learning, no endowments, as generally in the East, and apparently no encouragement to students: books also are rare and costly. None but the religious sciences are cultivated. The chief Ulema [learned men] are the Kabir Khalil, the Kabir Yunis, and the Shaykh Jami: the two former scarcely ever quit their houses, devoting all their time to study and tuition: the latter is a Somali who takes an active part in politics. . . .

Harar has not only its own tongue, unintelligible to any save the citizens; even its little population of about 8000 souls is a distinct race. The Somal say of the city that it is a Paradise inhabited by asses: certainly the exterior of the people is highly unprepossessing. Amongst the men, I did not see a handsome face: their features are coarse and debauched; many of them squint, others have lost an eye by smallpox, and they are disfigured by scrofula and other diseases: the bad expression of their countenances justifies the proverb, 'Hard as the heart of Harar.' Generally the complexion is a yellowish brown, the beard short, stubby and untractable as the hair, and the hands and wrists, feet and ancles, are large and ill-made. The stature is moderate-sized, some of the elders show the 'pudding sides' and the pulpy stomachs of Banyans, whilst others are lank and bony as Arabs or Jews. Their voices are loud and rude. The dress is a mixture of Arab and Abyssinian. They shave the head, and clip the mustachios and imperial close, like the Shafei of Yemen. Many are bareheaded, some wear a cap, generally the embroidered Indian work, or the common cotton Takiyah of Egypt: a few affect white turbans of the fine Harar work, loosely twisted over the ears. The body-garment is the Tobe, worn flowing as in the Somali country or girt with the dagger-strap round the waist: the richer classes bind under it a Futah or loin-cloth and the dignitaries have wide Arab drawers of white calico. Coarse leathern sandals, a rosary and a tooth-stick rendered perpetually necessary by the habit of chewing tobacco complete the costume: and arms being forbidden in the streets, the citizens carry wands five or six feet long.

The women, who, owing probably to the number of female slaves, are much the more numerous, appear beautiful by contrast with their lords. They have small heads, regular profiles, straight noses, large eyes, mouths approaching the Caucasian type, and light yellow complexions. . . .

Silver ornaments are worn only by persons of rank. The ear is decorated with Somali rings or red coral beads, the neck with necklaces of the same material, and the fore-arms with six or seven of the broad circles of buffalo and other dark horns prepared in Western India. Finally, stars are tattooed upon the bosom, the eyebrows are lengthened with dyes, the eyes fringed with Kohl, and the hands and feet stained with henna.

The female voice is harsh and screaming, especially when heard after the delicate organs of the Somal. The fair sex is occupied at home spinning cotton thread for weaving Tobes, sashes, and turbans; carrying their progeny perched upon their backs, they bring water from the wells in large gourds borne on the head; work in the gardens, and—the men considering, like the Abyssinians, such work a disgrace—sit and sell in the long street which here represents the Eastern bazaar. Chewing tobacco enables them to pass much of their time, and the rich diligently anoint themselves with ghee [butter], whilst the poorer classes use remnants of fat from the lamps. Their freedom of manners renders a public flogging occasionally indispensable. Before the operation begins, a few gourds full of cold water are poured over their heads and shoulders, after which a single-thonged whip is applied with vigour.

Both sexes are celebrated for laxity of morals. High and low indulge freely in intoxicating drinks, beer, and mead. The Amir has established strict patrols, who unmercifully bastinado those caught in the streets after a certain hour. They are extremely bigoted, especially against Christians, the effect of their Abyssinian wars, and are fond of 'Jihading' with the Gallas, over whom they boast many a victory. I have seen a letter addressed by the late Amir to the Hajj Sharmarkay, in which he boasts of having slain a thousand infidels, and, by way of bathos, begs for a few pounds of English gunpowder. The Harari hold foreigners in especial hate and contempt, and divide them into two orders, Arabs and Somal. The latter, though nearly one-third of the population, or 2500 souls, are, to use their own phrase, cheap as dust: their natural timidity is increased by the show of pomp and power, whilst the word 'prison' gives them the horrors.

. . . . . .

After a day's repose, we were summoned by the Treasurer, early in the forenoon, to wait upon the Gerad Mohammed. Sword in hand, and followed by the Hammal and Long Guled, I walked to the 'palace,' and entering a little ground-floor-room on the right of and close to the audience-hall, found the minister sitting upon a large dais covered with Persian carpets. He was surrounded by six of his brother Gerads or councillors, two of them in turbans, the rest with bare and shaven heads: their Tobes, as is customary on such occasions of ceremony, were allowed to fall beneath the waist. The lower part of the hovel was covered with dependents, amongst whom my Somal took their seats: it seemed to be customs' time, for names were being registered, and money changed hands. The Grandees were eating Kat, or as it is here called 'Jat.' One of the party prepared for the Prime Minister the tenderest twigs of the tree, plucking off the points of even the softest leaves. Another pounded the plant with a little water in a wooden mortar: of this paste, called 'El Madkuk,' a bit was handed to each person, who, rolling it into a ball, dropped it into his mouth. All at times, as is the custom, drank cold water from a smoked gourd, and seemed to dwell upon the sweet and pleasant draught. I could not but remark the fine flavour of the plant after the coarser quality grown in Yemen. Europeans perceive but little effect from it—friend S. and I once tried in vain a strong infusion—the Arabs, however, unaccustomed to stimulants and narcotics, declare that, like opium eaters, they cannot live without the excitement. It seems to produce in them a manner of dreamy enjoyment, which, exaggerated by time and distance, may have given rise to that splendid myth the Lotos, and the Lotophagi. It is held by the Ulema here as in Arabia, 'Akl el Salikin,' or the Food of the Pious, and literati remark that it has the singular properties of enlivening the imagination, clearing the ideas, cheering the heart, diminishing sleep, and taking the place of food. The people of Harar eat it every day from 9 a.m. till near noon, when they dine and afterwards indulge in something stronger—millet-beer and mead.

The Gerad, after polite inquiries, seated me by his right hand upon the Dais, where I ate Kat and fingered my rosary, whilst he transacted the business of the day. Then one of the elders took from a little recess in the wall a large book, and uncovering it, began to recite a long Dua or Blessing upon the Prophet: at the end of each period all present intoned the response, 'Allah bless our Lord Mohammed with his Progeny and his Companions, one and all!' This exercise lasting half-an-hour afforded me the opportunity—much desired—of making an impression. The reader, misled by a marginal reference, happened to say, 'angels, Men, and Genii': the Gerad took the book and found written, 'Men, Angels, and Genii.' Opinions were divided as to the order of beings, when I explained that human nature, which amongst Moslems is *not* a little lower than the angelic, ranked highest, because of it were created prophets, apostles, and saints, whereas the other is but a 'Wasitah' or connection between the Creator and his creatures. My theology won general approbation and a few kinder glances from the elders.

Prayer concluded, a chamberlain whispered the Gerad, who arose, deposited his black coral rosary, took up an inkstand, donned a white 'Badan' or sleeveless Arab cloak over his cotton shirt, shuffled off the Dais into his slippers, and disappeared. Presently we were summoned to an interview with the Amir: this time I was allowed to approach the outer door with covered feet. Entering ceremoniously as before, I was motioned by the Prince to sit near the Gerad, who occupied a Persian rug on the ground to the right of the throne: my two attendants squatted upon the humbler mats in front and at a greater distance. After sundry inquiries about the changes that had taken place at Aden, the letter was suddenly produced by the Amir, who looked upon it suspiciously and bade me explain its contents. I was then asked by the Gerad whether it was my intention to buy and sell at Harar: the reply was, 'We are no buyers nor sellers; we have become your guests to pay our respects to the Amir—whom may Allah preserve!—and that the friendship between the two powers may endure.' This appearing satisfactory, I added, in lively remembrance of the proverbial delays of Africa, where two or three months may elapse before a letter is answered or a verbal message delivered, that perhaps the Prince would be pleased to dismiss us soon, as the air of Harar was too dry for me, and my attendants were in danger of the smallpox, then raging in the town. The Amir, who was chary of words, bent towards the Gerad, who briefly ejaculated, 'The reply will be vouchsafed:' with this unsatisfactory answer the interview ended.

Shortly after arrival, I sent my Salam to one of the Ulema, Shaykh Jami of the Berteri Somal: he accepted the excuse of ill-health, and at once came to see me. This personage appeared in the form of a little black man aged about forty, deeply pitted by smallpox, with a protruding brow, a tufty beard and rather delicate features: his hands and feet were remarkably small. Married to a descendant of the Sherif Yunis, he had acquired great reputation as an Alim of Savan, a peace-policy-man, and an ardent Moslem. Though an imperfect Arabic scholar, he proved remarkably well read in the religious sciences, and even the Meccans had, it was said, paid him the respect of kissing his hand during his pilgrimage. In his second character, his success was not remarkable, the principal results being a spear-thrust in the head, and being generally told to read his books and leave men alone. Yet he is always doing good 'lillah,' that is to say, gratis and for Allah's sake: his pugnacity and bluntness—the prerogatives of the 'peaceful'—gave him some authority over the Amir, and he has often been employed on political missions amongst the different chiefs. Nor has his ardour for propagandism been thoroughly gratified. He commenced his travels with an intention of winning the crown of glory without delay, by murdering the British Resident at Aden: struck, however, with the order and justice of our rule, he changed his intentions and offered El Islam to the officer, who received it so urbanely, that the simple Eastern repenting having intended to cut the Kafir's throat, began to pray fervently for his conversion. Since that time he has made it a point of duty to attempt every infidel: I never heard, however, that he succeeded with a soul.

The Shaykh's first visit did not end well. He informed me that the old Usmanlis conquered Stamboul in the days of Umar. I imprudently objected to the date, and he revenged himself for the injury done to his fame by the favourite ecclesiastical process of privily damning me for a heretic, and a worse than heathen. Moreover he had sent me a kind of ritual which I had perused in an hour and returned to him: this prepossessed the Shaykh strongly against me, lightly 'skimming' books being a form of idleness as yet unknown to the ponderous East.

Our days at Harar were monotonous enough. In the morning we looked to the mules, drove out the cats—as great a nuisance here as at Aden—and ate for breakfast lumps of boiled beef with peppered holcus-scones. We were kindly looked upon by one Sultan, a sick and decrepit Eunuch, who having served five Amirs, was allowed to remain in the palace. To appearance he was mad: he wore upon his poll a motley scratch wig, half white and half black, like Day and Night in masquerades. But his conduct was sane. At dawn he sent us bad plantains, wheaten crusts, and cups of unpalatable coffee-tea, and, assisted by a crone more decrepit than himself, prepared for me his water-pipe, a gourd fitted with two reeds and a tile of baked clay by way of bowl; now he 'knagged' at the slave-girls, who were slow to work, then burst into a fury because some visitor ate Kat without offering it to him, or crossed the royal threshold in sandal or slipper. The other inmates of the house were Galla slave-girls, a great nuisance, especially one Berille, an unlovely maid, whose shrill voice and shameless manners were a sad scandal to pilgrims and pious Moslems. . . .

Our fate was probably decided by the arrival of a youth of the Ayyal

Gedid clan, who reported that three brothers had landed in the Somali country, that two of them were anxiously awaiting at Berberah the return of the third from Harar, and that, though dressed like Moslems, they were really Englishmen in government employ. Visions of cutting off caravans began to assume a hard and palpable form: the Habr Awal ceased intriguing and the Gerad Mohammed resolved to adopt the *suaviter in modo* whilst dealing with his dangerous guest.

Some days after his first visit, the Shaykh Jami, sending for the Hammal, informed him of an intended trip from Harar: my follower suggested that we might well escort him. The good Shaykh at once offered to apply for leave from the Gerad Mohammed; not, however, finding the minister at home, he asked us to meet him at the palace on the morrow, about the time of Kat-eating.

We had so often been disappointed in our hopes of a final 'lay-public,' that on this occasion much was not expected However, about 6 a.m., we were all summoned, and entering the Gerad's levee-room were, as usual, courteously received. I had distinguished his complaint—chronic bronchitis—and resolving to make a final impression, related to him all its symptoms, and promised, on reaching Aden, to send the different remedies employed by ourselves. He clung to the hope of escaping his sufferings, whilst the attendant courtiers looked on approvingly, and begged me to lose no time. Presently the Gerad was sent for by the Amir, and after a few minutes I followed him, on this occasion, alone. Ensued a long conversation about the state of Aden, of Zayla, of Berberah, and of Stamboul. The chief put a variety of questions about Arabia, and every object there: the answer was that the necessity of commerce confined us to the gloomy rock. He used some obliging expressions about desiring our friendship, and having considerable respect for a people who built, he understood, large ships. I took the opportunity of praising Harar in cautious phrase, and especially of regretting that its coffee was not better known amongst the Franks. The small wizen-faced man smiled, as Moslems say, the smile of Umar [who smiled only once]: seeing his brow relax for the first time, I told him that being now restored to health, we requested his commands for Aden. He signified consent with a nod, and the Gerad, with many compliments, gave me a letter addressed to the Political Resident, and requested me to take charge of a mule as a present. I then arose, recited a short prayer, the gist of which was that the Amir's days and reign might be long in the land, and that the faces of his foes might be blackened here and hereafter, bent over his hand and retired. Returning to the Gerad's levee-hut, I saw by the countenances of my two attendants that they were not a little anxious about the interview, and comforted them with the whispered word 'Achha'—'all right!'

Presently appeared the Gerad, accompanied by two men, who brought my servants' arms, and the revolver which I had sent to the prince. This was a *contretemps*. It was clearly impossible to take back the present, besides which, I suspected some finesse to discover my feelings towards him: the other course would ensure delay. I told the Gerad that the weapon was intended especially to preserve the Amir's life, and for further effect, snapped caps in rapid succession to the infinite terror of the august company. The minister returned to his master, and soon brought back the information that after a day or two another mule should be given to me. With suitable acknowledgments we arose, blessed the Gerad, bade adieu to the assembly, and departed joyful, the Hammal in his glee speaking broken English, even in the Amir's courtyard.

Returning home, we found the good Shaykh Jami, to whom we communicated the news with many thanks for his friendly aid. I did my best to smooth his temper about Turkish history, and succeeded. Becoming communicative, he informed me that the original object of his visit was the offer of good offices, he having been informed that in the town was a man who brought down the birds from heaven, and the citizens having been thrown into great excitement by the probable intentions of such a personage. Whilst he sat with us, Kabir Khalil, one of the principal Ulema, and one Hajj Abdullah, a Shaykh of distinguished fame who had been dreaming dreams in our favour, sent their salams. This is one of the many occasions in which, during a long residence in the East, I have had reason to be grateful to the learned, whose influence over the people when unbiassed by bigotry is decidedly for good. That evening there was great joy amongst the Somal, who had been alarmed for the safety of my companions: they brought them presents of Harari Tobes, and a feast of fowls, limes, and wheaten bread for the stranger.

On the 11th of January I was sent for by the Gerad and received the second mule. At noon we were visited by the Shaykh Jami, who, after a long discourse upon the subject of Sufiism,[1] invited me to inspect his books. When midday prayer was concluded we walked to his house, which occupies the very centre of the city: in its courtyard is 'Gay Humburti,' the historic rock upon which Saint Nur held converse with the Prophet Khizr. The Shaykh, after seating us in a room about ten feet square, and lined with scholars and dusty tomes, began reading out a treatise upon the genealogies of the Grand Masters, and showed me in half-a-dozen tracts the tenets of the different schools. The only valuable MS. in the place was a fine old copy of the Koran; the Kamus and the Sihah were there, but by no means remarkable for beauty or correctness. Books at Harar are mostly antiques, copyists being exceedingly rare, and the square massive character is more like Cufic with diacritical points, than the graceful modern Naskhi. I could not, however, but admire the bindings: no Eastern country save Persia surpasses

[1] The Eastern parent of Freemasonry. (*Burton's note.*)

them in strength and appearance. After some desultory conversation the Shaykh ushered us into an inner room, or rather a dark closet partitioned off from the study, and ranged us around the usual dish of boiled beef, holcus bread, and red pepper. After returning to the study we sat for a few minutes—Easterns rarely remain long after dinner—and took leave, saying that we must call upon the Gerad Mohammed. . . .

Our intention was to mount early on Friday morning. When we awoke, however, a mule had strayed and was not brought back for some hours. Before noon Shaykh Jami called upon us, informed us that he would travel on the most auspicious day—Monday—and exhorted us to patience, deprecating departure upon Friday, the Sabbath. Then he arose to take leave, blessed us at some length, prayed that we might be borne upon the wings of safety, again advised Monday, and promised at all events to meet us at Wilensi.

I fear that the Shaykh's counsel was on this occasion likely to be disregarded. We had been absent from our goods and chattels a whole fortnight: the people of Harar are famously fickle; we knew not what the morrow might bring forth from the Amir's mind—in fact, all these African cities are prisons on a large scale, into which you enter by your own will, and, as the significant proverb says, you leave by another's. However, when the mosque prayers ended, a heavy shower and the stormy aspect of the sky preached patience more effectually than did the divine: we carefully tethered our mules, and unwillingly deferred our departure till next morning.

First footsteps in East Africa, 1st edition, pp. 130–140, 247–266, 280–303, 323–330, 346–363

Burton returned safely to Berbera, but as a result—according to Speke—of the delay and suspicion caused by his journey to Harar, the main expedition had hardly started before it was attacked by the Somali. A spear pierced Burton's face from cheek to cheek, Speke was more seriously wounded, as he was tortured by his captors and speared in eleven places, while a third member, Stroyan, was killed.

Both men recovered from their wounds, and upon his return to England Burton gained the support of the Royal Geographical Society, and also a government grant, for an attempt to penetrate the heart of equatorial Africa from Zanzibar in order to clear up the mystery of the reported great lake or lakes. Upon this important journey he took Speke as his second in command.

After some preliminary travelling on the coast to find the best route they struck inland along the Arab slavers' line from Bagamoyo to Kazeh or Tabora, the great inland centre of the slave-trade. They were accompanied by Bombay, a Swahili who spoke Hindustani. At Tabora they met the Arab who had been the first to reach Uganda a few years before, and were told that there were three great lakes. They then pushed on westwards with increasing difficulty. They met with opposition from the tribes, while Burton was constantly prostrated with fever and Speke almost blind with ophthalmia. To judge by Burton's references—and lack of references—to Speke at this moment of their great achievement in African discovery, the rift which was to embitter their future lives had already opened between them. The extract which follows is Burton's account of the discovery of the first of the great African lakes.

21. DISCOVERY OF LAKE TANGANYIKA

The 10th February saw us crossing the normal sequence of jungly and stony 'neat's-tongues,' divided by deep and grassy swamps, which, stagnant in the dry weather, drain after rains the northern country to the Malagarazi River. We passed over by a felled tree-trunk an unfordable rivulet, hemmed in by a dense and fetid thicket; and the asses summarily pitched down the muddy bank into the water, swam across and wriggled up the slimy off-side like cats. Thence a foul swamp of black mire led to the Ruguvu or Luguvu River, the western boundary of Uvinza and the eastern frontier of Ukaranga. This stream, which can be forded during the dry season, had spread out after the rains over its borders of grassy plain; we were delayed till the next morning in a miserable camping ground, a mud-bank thinly veiled with vegetation, in order to bridge it with branching trees. An unusual downfall during the night might have caused serious consequences;—provisions had now disappeared, moreover the porters considered the place dangerous.

The 10th February began with the passage of the Ruguvu River, where again our goods and chattels were fated to be thoroughly sopped. I obtained a few corn-cobs from a passing caravan of Wanyamwezi, and charged them with meat and messages for the party left behind. A desert march, similar to the stage last travelled, led us to the Unguwwe or Uvungwe River, a shallow, muddy stream, girt in as usual by dense vegetation; and we found a fine large kraal on its left bank. After a cold and rainy night, we resumed our march by fording the Unguwwe. Then came the weary toil of fighting through tiger and spear-grass, with reeds, rushes, a variety of ferns, before unseen, and other lush and lusty growths, clothing a succession of rolling hills, monotonous swellings, where the descent was ever a reflection of the ascent. The paths were broken, slippery, and pitted with deep holes; along their sides, where the ground lay exposed to view, a conglomerate of ferruginous red clay—suggesting a resemblance to the superficies of Londa, as described by Dr. Livingstone—took the place of the granites and sandstones of the eastern countries, and the sinking of the land towards the Lake became palpable. In the jungle were extensive clumps of bamboo and rattan; the former small, the latter of poor quality; the bauhinia, or black-wood, and the salsaparilla vine abounded; wild grapes of diminutive size, and of the austerest flavour, appeared for the first time upon the sunny hill-sides which Bacchus ever loves, and in the lower swamps plantains grew almost wild. In parts the surface was broken into small deep hollows, from which sprang pyramidal masses of the hugest trees. Though no sign of man here met the eye, scattered fields and plantations showed that villages must be somewhere near. Sweet water was found in narrow courses of black mud, which sorely tried the sinews of laden man and beast. Long after noon, we saw the caravan halted by fatigue upon a slope beyond a weary swamp: a violent storm was brewing, and whilst half the sky was purple black with nimbus, the sun shone stingingly through the clear portion of the empyrean. But these small troubles were lightly borne; already in the far distance appeared walls of sky-blue cliff with gilded summits, which were as a beacon to the distressed mariner.

On the 13th February we resumed our travel through screens of lofty grass, which thinned out into a straggling forest. After about an hour's march, as we entered a small savannah, I saw the Fundi before alluded to running forward and changing the direction of the caravan. Without supposing that he had taken upon himself this responsibility, I followed him. Presently he breasted a steep and stony hill, sparsely clad with thorny trees: it was the death of my companion's riding-ass. Arrived with toil,—for our fagged beasts now refused to proceed,—we halted for a few minutes upon the summit. 'What is that streak of light which lies below?' I inquired of Seedy Bombay. 'I am of opinion,' quoth Bombay, 'that that is *the* water.' I gazed in dismay; the remains of my blindness, the veil of trees, and a broad ray of sunshine illuminating but one reach of the Lake, had shrunk its fair proportions. Somewhat prematurely I began to lament my folly in having risked life and lost health for so poor a prize, to curse Arab exaggeration, and to propose an immediate return, with the view of exploring the Nyanza, or Northern Lake. Advancing, however, a few yards, the whole scene suddenly burst upon my view, filling me with admiration, wonder, and delight. . . .

Nothing, in sooth, could be more picturesque than this first view of the Tanganyika Lake, as it lay in the lap of the mountains, basking in the gorgeous tropical sunshine. Below and beyond a short foreground of rugged and precipitous hill-fold, down which the foot-path zigzags painfully, a narrow strip of emerald green, never sere and marvellously fertile, shelves towards a ribbon of glistening yellow sand, here bordered by sedgy rushes, there cleanly and clearly cut by the breaking wavelets. Further in front stretch the waters, an expanse of the lightest and softest blue, in breadth varying from thirty to thirty-five miles, and sprinkled by the crisp east-wind with tiny crescents of snowy foam. The background in front is a high and broken wall of steel-coloured mountain, here flecked and capped with pearly mist, there standing sharply pencilled against the azure air; its yawning chasms, marked by a deeper plum-colour, fall towards dwarf hills of mound-like proportions, which apparently dip their feet in the wave. To the south, and opposite the long low point, behind which the Malagarazi River discharges the red loam suspended in its violent stream, lie the bluff headlands and capes of Uguhha, and, as the eye dilates, it falls upon a cluster of outlying islets, speckling a sea-horizon. Villages, cultivated lands, the frequent canoes of the fishermen on the waters, and on a nearer approach the murmurs of the waves breaking upon the shore, give a something of variety, of movement, of life to the landscape, which, like all the fairest prospects in these regions, wants but a little of the neatness and finish of Art,—mosques and kiosks, palaces and villas, gardens and orchards—contrasting with the profuse lavishness and magnificence of nature, and diversifying the unbroken *coup d'œil* of excessive vegetation, to rival, if not to excel, the most admired scenery of the classic regions. The riant shores of this vast crevasse appeared doubly beautiful to me after the silent and spectral mangrove-creeks on the East-African seaboard, and the melancholy, monotonous experience of desert and jungle scenery, tawny rock and sun-parched plain or rank herbage and flats of black mire. Truly it was a revel for soul and sight! Forgetting toils, dangers, and the doubtfulness of return, I felt willing to endure double what I had endured; and all the party seemed to join with me in joy. My purblind companion found nothing to grumble at except the 'mist and glare before his eyes.' Said bin Salim looked exulting,—*he* had procured for me this pleasure,—the monoculous Jemadar grinned his congratulations, and even the surly Baloch made civil salams.

The lake regions of Central Africa, vol. II, pp. 40–44

Speke's temporary blindness upon this occasion led him to describe this incident in his journal in the following words: 'From the summit of the Eastern horn the lovely Tanganyika Lake could be seen in all its glory by everybody but myself.'

After a hurried exploration of part of the lake, they returned to Tabora to recuperate. From this point they describe events in somewhat different terms. Speke writes as though, owing to Burton being quite 'done up', he took the initiative in pressing to be allowed to go on alone to look for the lake which the Arabs reported in the north. Burton writes of Speke as 'being a fit person to be detached upon this duty', all the more as his presence was 'by no means desirable at Kazeh. To associate at the same time with Arabs and Anglo-Indians who are ready to take offence when it is least intended, who expect servility as their due and whose morgue of colour induces them to treat all skins a shade darker than their own as "niggers", is even more difficult than to avoid rupture when placed between two friends who have quarrelled with each other'.

Speke therefore struck out to the north without Burton. On 30th July 1858 he saw the waters of the southernmost creek of Africa's greatest lake. By little more than intuition and reliance upon Arab information he decided that this lake—to which, following the example set by Livingstone, he gave the somewhat unimaginative name Victoria—must be the source of the Nile, though he could have no conception then of its shape or its immensity. He returned to find Burton inclined to give little welcome or even credence to his news.

22. EXPLORERS DIFFER

At length my companion had been successful, his 'flying trip' had led him to the northern water, and he had found its dimensions surpassing our most sanguine expectations. We had scarcely, however, breakfasted, before he announced to me the startling fact that he had discovered the sources of the White Nile. It was an inspiration perhaps: the moment he sighted the Nyanza, he felt at once no doubt but that the 'Lake at his feet gave birth to the interesting river which had been the subject of so much speculation, and the object of so many explorers.' The fortunate discoverer's conviction was strong, his reasons were weak—were of the category alluded to by the damsel Luceter, when justifying her penchant in favour of 'the lovely gentleman' Sir Proteus:—

> 'I have no other but a woman's reason,
> I think him so because I think him so';

and probably his sources of the Nile grew in his mind as his Mountains of the Moon had grown under his hand. . . .

What tended at the time to make me the more sceptical was the substantial incorrectness of the geographical and other details brought back by my companion. This was natural enough. Bombay, after misunderstanding his master's ill-expressed Hindostani, probably mistranslated the words into Kiswahili to some travelled African, who in turn passed on the question in a wilder dialect to the barbarian or barbarians under examination. During such a journey to and fro words must be liable to severe accidents. . . . And what knowledge of Asiatic customs can be expected from the writer of these lines? 'The Arabs at Unyanyembe had advised my donning their habit for the trip in order to attract less attention, a vain precaution, which I believe they suggested more to gratify their own vanity *in seeing an Englishman lower himself to their position*, than for any benefit I might receive by doing so.' (Blackwood, loco cit). This galamatias of the Arabs!—the haughtiest and the most clannish of all Oriental peoples.

But difference of opinion was allowed to alter companionship. After a few days it became evident to me that not a word could be uttered upon the subject of the Lake, the Nile, and his *trouvaille* generally without offence. By a tacit agreement it was, therefore, avoided, and I should never have resumed it had my companion not stultified the results of the expedition by putting forth a claim which no geographer can admit and which is at the same time so weak and flimsy that no geographer has yet taken the trouble to contradict it.

The lake regions of Central Africa,
vol. II, pp. 204–209

The two men travelled back together on very unhappy terms, which were not improved by Burton having to nurse his companion in a state of delirium. Speke now revealed all the grievances he had accumulated against Burton since a moment during the Somali attack upon them outside Berbera, when Speke believed an exclamation by Burton to have reflected upon his courage.

Their future controversy will, however, be more suitably included in the notes upon Speke in the next section. It remains here to summarize the rest of Burton's life, crowded as it was with his travels and with writing the seventy books and other publications which resulted from them. In 1861 he married, without her parents' consent, Isabel Arundel. She had since girlhood been in love with a man whose reputation, virile personality and bronzed and scarred face had appealed to her strong sense of romance. He travelled in North

America and was a consul in West Africa, Brazil, Damascus and Trieste. Always regarded as a difficult, and, from some aspects, a dangerous man, he had to wait until 1886 for official recognition, in the form of knighthood, which he had so long desired. At the same time came the fortune which he owed to the literary and pornographic success of his Arabian Nights. *After his death his wife published an expurgated edition of this book and erected over him a monument in the form of a stone tent.*

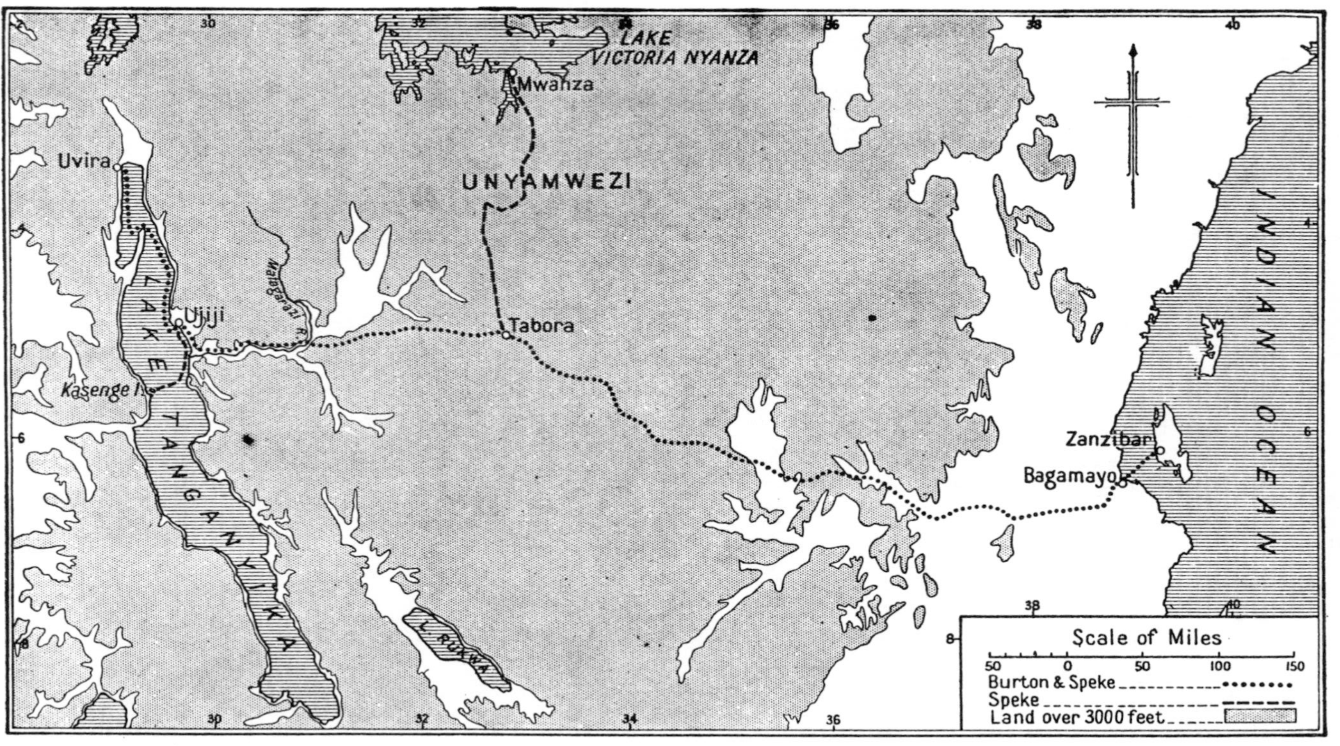

8. The Travels of Burton and Speke, 1857–9

VII

JOHN HANNING SPEKE

1827–1864

Speke's home was Ilminster in Somerset, and his parents both came from the landed gentry. He disliked school but developed early a love of natural history and of wandering in the countryside. At seventeen he obtained a commission in the Indian army and saw much fighting with it, spending his leaves exploring and shooting big game. Soon after he reached the age of twenty he began to dream of exploring Africa and finding the Equatorial Nile. In 1854 he obtained permission to traverse Somaliland in company with Burton. The disastrous end of that attempt has been described in the section upon Burton, and also the expedition of 1856–9 when Lakes Tanganyika and Victoria were discovered.

After Speke and Burton, now on bad terms, returned in 1859 to the coast, Burton fell ill again and Speke went on ahead to England to claim the main credit for the discoveries and to obtain funds from the Royal Geographical Society to finance a new expedition—from which Burton was to be excluded—in order to verify the relationship of Lake Victoria to the White Nile.

Upon this new expedition Speke took with him a more congenial companion than Burton, the resolute but gentle James Grant. He had an escort of freed slaves (Wanguana) and Baluchi soldiers from the Sultan of Zanzibar with Mabruki and Bombay, who had been with him before when he found the two great lakes, as headmen. In Unyamwezi the Arab traders helped the travellers and gave them information of the country west and north of Lake Victoria. But here their serious troubles began with fever and fatigue, wars between Arabs and natives and the extortions of chiefs, among them Suwarora of Usui. At last, however, the travellers reached the relatively important kingdoms of the Lake region, where the pastoral Hima people had established their rule over the agricultural negroid tribes. They received a great welcome at the court of the king of Karagwe, the intelligent and courteous Rumanika, who is described in the first extract from

Speke's book, while the second gives his visit to the neighbouring kingdom of Uganda.

23. THE EVER-SMILING KING

To do royal honours to the king of this charming land I ordered my men to put down their loads and fire a volley. This was no sooner done than as we went to the palace gate, we received an invitation to come in at once, for the king wished to see us before attending to anything else. Now, leaving our traps outside, both Grant and myself, attended by Bombay and a few of the seniors of my *Wanguana*, entered the vestibule, and walking through extensive enclosures studded with huts of kingly dimensions, were escorted to a pent-roofed baraza, which the Arabs had built as a sort of government office, where the king might conduct his state affairs.

Here, as we entered, we saw sitting cross-legged on the ground Rumanika the king, and his brother Nnanaji, both of them men of noble appearance and size. The king was plainly dressed in an Arab's black choga, and wore, for ornament, dress stockings of rich-coloured beads, and neatly-worked wristlets of copper. Nnanaji, being a doctor of very high pretensions, in addition to a check cloth wrapped round him, was covered with charms. At their sides lay huge pipes of black clay. In their rear, squatting quiet as mice, were all the king's sons, some six or seven lads, who wore leather middle-coverings, and little dream-charms tied under their chins. The first greetings of the king, delivered in good Kisuahili, were warm and affecting, and in an instant we both felt and saw we were in the company of men who were as unlike as they could be to the common order of the natives of the surrounding districts. They had fine oval faces, large eyes, and high noses, denoting the best blood of Abyssinia. Having shaken hands in true English style, which is the peculiar custom of the men of this country, the ever-smiling Rumanika begged us to be seated on the ground opposite to him, and at once wished to know what we thought of Karague, for it had struck him his mountains were the finest in the world; and the lake, too, did we not admire it? Then laughing, he inquired—for he knew all the story—what we thought of Suwarora, and the reception we had met with in Usui. When this was explained to him, I showed him that it was for the interest of his own kingdom to keep a check on Suwarora, whose exorbitant taxations prevented the Arabs from coming to see him and bringing things from all parts of the world. He made inquiries for the purpose of knowing how we found our way all over the world; for on the former expedition a letter had come to him for Musa, who no sooner read it than he said I had called him and he must leave, as I was bound for Ujiji.

This of course led to a long story, describing the world, the proportions of land and water, and the power of ships, which conveyed even elephants and rhinoceros—in fact, all the animals in the world—to fill our menageries at home,—&c. &c.; as well as the strange announcement that we lived to the northward, and had only come this way because his friend Musa had assured me without doubt that he would give us the road on through Uganda. Time flew like magic, the king's mind was so quick and inquiring; but as the day was wasting away, he generously gave us our option to choose a place for our residence in or out of his palace, and allowed us time to select one. We found the view overlooking the lake to be so charming, that we preferred camping outside, and set our men at once to work cutting sticks and long grass to erect themselves sheds.

One of the young princes—for the king ordered them all to be constantly in attendance on us—happening to see me sit on an iron chair, rushed back to his father and told him about it. This set all the royals in the palace in a state of high wonder, and ended by my getting a summons to show off the white man sitting on his throne; for of course I could only be, as all of them called me, a king of great dignity, to indulge in such state. Rather reluctantly I did as I was bid, and allowed myself once more to be dragged into court. Rumanika, as gentle as ever, then burst into a fresh fit of merriment, and after making sundry enlightened remarks of inquiry, which of course were responded to with the greatest satisfaction, finished off by saying, with a very expressive shake of the head, 'Oh, these Wazungu, these Wazungu! (white men) they know and do everything.'

. . . . . .

A long theological and historical discussion ensued, which so pleased the king, that he said he would be delighted if I would take two of his sons to England, that they might bring him a knowledge of everything. Then turning again to the old point, his utter amazement that we should spend so much property in travelling, he wished to know what we did it for; when men had such means they would surely sit down and enjoy it. 'Oh no,' was the reply; 'we have had our fill of the luxuries of life; eating, drinking, or sleeping have no charms for us now; we are above trade, therefore require no profits, and seek for enjoyment the run of the world. To observe and admire the beauties of creation are worth much more than beads to us. But what led us this way we have told you before: it was to see your majesty in particular, and the great kings of Africa—and at the same time to open another road to the north, whereby the best manufactures of Europe would find their way to Karague, and you would get so many more guests.' In the highest good humour the king said 'As you have come to see me and see sights, I will order some boats and show you over the lake, with musicians to play before you, or anything else that you like.' Then, after looking over our pictures with intensest delight, and admiring our beds, boxes, and outfit in general, he left for the day.

In the afternoon, as I had heard from Musa that the wives of the king and princes were fattened to such an extent that they could not stand upright, I paid my respects to Wazezeru, the king's eldest brother—who, having been born before his father ascended his throne, did not come in the line of succession—with the hope of being able to see for myself the truth of the story. There was no mistake about it. On entering the hut I found the old man and his chief wife sitting side by side on a bench of earth strewed over with grass, and partitioned like stalls for sleeping apartments, whilst in front of them were placed numerous wooden pots of milk, and hanging from the poles that supported the beehive-shaped hut, a large collection of bows six feet in length, whilst below them were tied an even larger collection of spears, intermixed with a goodly assortment of heavy-headed assagais. I was struck with no small surprise at the way he received me, as well as with the extraordinary dimensions, yet pleasing beauty, of the immoderately fat fair one his wife. She could not rise; and so large were her arms that, between the joints, the flesh hung down like large loose-stuffed puddings. Then in came their children, all models of the Abyssinian type of beauty, and as polite in their manners as thorough-bred gentlemen. They had heard of my picture-books from the king and all wished to see them; which they no sooner did, to their infinite delight, especially when they recognized any of the animals, than the subject was turned by my inquiring what they did with so many milk-pots. This was easily explained by Wazezeru himself, who, pointing to his wife said, 'This is all the product of those pots: from early youth upwards, we keep those pots to their mouths, as it is the fashion at court to have very fat wives.'

27th.—Ever anxious to push on with the journey, as I felt every day's delay only tended to diminish my means—that is my beads and copper wire—I instructed Bombay to take the under-mentioned articles to Rumanika as a small sample of the products of my country;[1] to say I felt quite ashamed of their being so few and so poor, but I hoped he would forgive my shortcomings, as he knew I had been so often robbed on the way to him; and I trusted, in recollection of Musa, he would give me leave to go on to Uganda, for every day's delay was consuming my supplies. Nnanaji, however, it was said, should get something; so, in

[1] *Rumanika's present.* One block-tin box, one Raglan coat, five yards scarlet broadcloth, two coils copper wire, a hundred large blue-egg beads, five bundles best variegated beads, three bundles minute beads—pink, blue and white. (*Speke's note.*)

addition to the king's present I apportioned one out for him, and Bombay took both up to the palace. Everybody, I was pleased to hear, was surprised with both the quantity and the quality of what I had been able to find them; for, after the plundering in Ugogo, the immense consumption caused by long delays on the road, the fearful prices I had had to pay for my porters' wages, the enormous taxes I had been forced to give both in Msalala and Uzinza, besides the constant thievings in camp, all of which was made public by the constantly-recurring tales of my men, nobody thought I had got anything left.

Rumanika, above all, was as delighted as if he had come in for a fortune, and sent to say the Raglan coat was a marvel, and the scarlet broadcloth the finest thing he had ever seen. Nobody but Musa had ever given him such beautiful beads before, and none ever gave with such free liberality. Whatever I wanted I should have in return for it, as it was evident to him I had really done him a great honour in visiting him. Neither his father nor any of his forefathers had had such a great favour shown them. He was alarmed, he confessed, when he heard we were coming to visit him, thinking we might prove some fearful monsters that were not quite human, but now he was delighted beyond all measure with what he saw of us. A messenger should be sent at once to the king of Uganda to inform him of our intention to visit him with his own favourable report of us. This was necessary according to the etiquette of the country. Without such a recommendation our progress would be stopped by the people, whilst with one word from him all would go straight; for was he not the gatekeeper, enjoying the full confidence of Uganda? A month, however, must elapse, as the distance to the palace of Uganda was great; but, in the mean time, he would give me leave to go about in his country to do and see what I liked, Nnanaji and his sons escorting me everywhere. Moreover, when the time came for my going on to Uganda, if I had not enough presents to give the king, he would fill up the complement from his own stores, and either go with me himself or send Nnanaji to conduct me as far as the boundary of Uganda, in order that Rogero might not molest us on the way.

. . . . . .

31*st*.—Ever proud of his history since I had traced his descent from Abyssinia and King David whose hair was as straight as my own, Rumanika dwelt on my theological disclosures with the greatest delight, and wished to know what difference existed between the Arabs and ourselves; to which Baraka replied, as the best means of making him understand, that whilst the Arabs had only one Book, we had two; to which I added, Yes that is true in a sense; but the real merits lie in the fact that we have got the better *book*, as may be inferred from the obvious fact that we are more prosperous, and their superiors in all things, as I would prove to him if he would allow me to take one of his sons home to learn that *book*; for then he would find his tribe, after a while, better off than the Arabs are. Much delighted, he said he would be very glad to give me two boys for that purpose.

Then, changing the subject, I pressed Rumanika, as he said he had no idea of a God or future state, to tell me what advantage he expected from sacrificing a cow yearly at his father's grave. He laughingly replied that he did not know, but he hoped he might be favoured with better crops if he did so. He also placed pombe and grain, he said, for the same reason, before a large stone on the hill-side, although it could not eat, or make any use of it; but the coast-men were of the same belief as himself, and so were all the natives. No one in Africa, as far as he knew, doubted the power of magic and spells; and if a fox barked when he was leading an army to battle, he would retire at once, knowing that this prognosticated evil. There were many other animals, and lucky and unlucky birds, which all believed in.

I then told him it was fortunate he had no disbelievers like us to contend with in battle, for we, instead of trusting to luck and such omens, put our faith only in skill and pluck which Baraka elucidated from his military experience in the wars in British India. Lastly, I explained to him how England formerly was as unenlightened as Africa, and believing in the same sort of superstitions, and the inhabitants were all as naked as his skin-wearing Wanyambo; but now, since they had grown wiser, and saw through such impostures, they were the greatest men in the world. He said, for the future, he would disregard what the Arabs said, and trust to my doctrines, for without doubt he had never seen such a wise man as myself; and the Arabs themselves confirmed this when they told him that all their beads and cloths came from the land of the Wazungu or white men. . . .

7th.—Our spirits were now further raised by the arrival of a semi-Hindu-Suahili, named Juma, who had just returned from a visit to the king of Uganda, bringing back with him a large present of ivory and slaves; for he said he had heard from the king of our intention to visit him, and that he had despatched officers to call us immediately. This intelligence delighted Rumanika as much as it did us, and he no sooner heard it than he said, with ecstasies, 'I will open Africa, since the white men desire it; for did not Dagara command us to show deference to strangers?' Then, turning to me, he added, 'My only regret is, you will not take something as a return for the great expenses you have been put to in coming to visit me.' The expense was admitted, for I had now been obliged to purchase from the Arabs upwards of £400 worth of beads, to keep such a store in reserve for my return from Uganda as would enable me to push on to Gondokoro. . . .

8th to 10th.—At last we heard the familiar sound of the Uganda drum.

Maula, a royal officer, with a large escort of smartly-dressed men, women and boys, leading their dogs and playing their reeds, announced to our straining ears the welcome intelligence that their king had sent them to call us. N'yamgundu, who had seen us in Usui, had marched on to inform the king of our advance and desire to see him; and he, intensely delighted at the prospect of having white men for his guests, desired no time should be lost in our coming on. Maula told us that his officers had orders to supply us with everything we wanted whilst passing through his country, and that there would be nothing to pay.

One thing only now embarrassed me—Grant was worse, without hope of recovery for at least one or two months. This large body of Waganda could not be kept waiting. To get on as fast as possible was the only chance of ever bringing the journey to a successful issue; so, unable to help myself, with great remorse at another separation, on the following day I consigned my companion, with several Wanguana, to the care of my friend Rumanika. . . .

This business concluded in camp, I started my men and went to the palace to bid adieu to Rumanika, who appointed Rozaro, one of his officers, to accompany me wherever I went in Uganda, and to bring me back safely again. At Rumanika's request I then gave Mtesa's pages some ammunition to hurry on with to the great king of Uganda, as his majesty had ordered them to bring him, as quickly as possible, some strengthening powder, and also some powder for his gun. Then, finally, to Maula, also under Rumanika's instructions, I gave two copper wires and five bundles of beads; and when all was completed, set out on the march, perfectly sure in my mind that before very long I should settle the great Nile problem for ever; and, with this consciousness, only hoping that Grant would be able to join me before I should have to return again, for it was never supposed for a moment that it was possible I ever could go north from Uganda. Rumanika was the most resolute in this belief, as the kings of Uganda, ever since that country was detached from Unyoro, had been making constant raids, seizing cattle and slaves from the surrounding countries.

Journal of the discovery of the source of the Nile, 1st edition, pp. 202–205, 208–211, 240–242, 243–245

24. DISCOVERY OF UGANDA

[14 Feb. 1862.] Here I was also brought to a standstill, for N'yamgundu said I must wait for leave to approach the palace. He wished to have a look at the presents I had brought for Mtesa. I declined to gratify it, taking my stand on my dignity; there was no occasion for any distrust on such a trifling matter as that, for I was not a merchant who sought for gain, but had come at great expense, to see the king of this region. I begged, however, he would go as fast as possible to announce my arrival, explain my motive for coming here, and ask for an early interview, as I had left my brother Grant behind at Karague, and found my position, for want of a friend to talk to, almost intolerable. It was not the custom of my country for great men to consort with servants, and until I saw him, and made friends, I should not be happy. I had a great deal to tell him about as he was the father of the Nile, which river drained the N'yanza down to my country to the northward. With this message N'yamgundu hurried off as fast as possible. . . .

[16 Feb.] I then very much wished to go and see the escape of the Mwerango river, as I still felt a little sceptical as to its origin, whether or not it came off those smaller lakes I had seen on the road the day before I crossed the river; but no one would listen to my project. They all said I must have the king's sanction first, else people, from not knowing my object, would accuse me of practising witchcraft and would tell their king so. They still all maintained that the river did come out of the lake, and said, if I liked to ask the king's leave to visit the spot, then they would go and show it me. I gave way, thinking it prudent to do so, but resolved in my mind I would get Grant to see it in boats on his voyage from Karague. There were no guinea-fowls to be found here, nor a fowl, in any of the huts, so I requested Rozaro to hurry off to Mtesa, and ask him to send me something to eat. He simply laughed at my request, and said I did not know what I was doing. It would be as much as my life was worth to go one yard in advance of this until the king's leave was obtained. I said, rather than be starved to death in this ignominious manner, I would return to Karague; to which he replied, laughing, 'Whose leave have you got to do that? Do you suppose you can do as you like in this country?'

[17 Feb.] Next day, in the evening, N'yamgundu returned full of smirks and smiles, dropped on his knees at my feet and, in company with his 'children', set to n'yanzigging, according to the form of that state ceremonial already described (a form of giving thanks to great men). In his excitement he was hardly able to say all he had to communicate. Bit by bit, however, I learned that he first went to the palace, and, finding the king had gone off yachting to the Murchison Creek, he followed him there. The king for a long while would not believe his tale that I had come, but being assured he danced with delight, swore he would not taste food until he had seen me. 'Oh,' he said, over and over again and again, according to my informer, 'can this be true? Can the white man have come all this way to see me? What a strong man he must be too, to come so quickly! Here are seven cows, four of them milch ones, as you say he likes milk, which you will give him; and there are three for yourself for having brought him so quickly. Now hurry off as fast as you can, and tell him I am more delighted at the prospect of seeing him than he can be to see me. There is no place here fit for his reception. I was on a pilgrimage which would have kept me here seven days longer; but as I am so impatient to see him, I will go off to my palace at once, and will send word for him to advance as soon as I arrive there.'

[18 Feb.] About noon the succeeding day, some pages ran in to say we were to come along without a moment's delay, as their king had ordered it. He would not taste food until he saw me, so that everybody might know what great respect he felt for me. In the meanwhile, however, he wished for some gunpowder. I packed the pages off as fast as I could with some, and then tried myself to follow, but my men were all either sick or out foraging, and therefore we could not get under way until the evening. . . .

[19 Feb.] One march more and we came in sight of the king's kibuga or palace, in the province of Bandawarogo, N. lat. 0° 21′ 19″, and E. long. 32° 44′ 30″. It was a magnificent sight. A whole hill was covered with gigantic huts, such as I had never seen in Africa before. I wished to go up to the palace at once, but the officers said, 'No, that would be considered indecent in Uganda; you must draw up your men, and fire your guns off, to let the king know you are here; we will then show you your residence, and to-morrow you will doubtless be sent for, as the king could not now hold a levee whilst it is raining.' I made the men fire, and then was shown into a lot of dirty huts, which they said were built expressly for all the king's visitors. The Arabs, when they came on their visits always put up here, and I must do the same. At first I stuck out on my claims as a foreign prince, whose royal blood could not stand such an indignity. The palace was my sphere, and unless I could get a hut there, I would return without seeing the king.

In a terrible fright at my blustering, N'yamgundu fell at my feet, and implored me not o be hasty. The king did not understand who I was, and could not be spoken to then. He implored me to be content with my lot for the present, after which the king, when he knew all about it, would do as I liked, he was sure, though no strangers had ever yet been allowed to reside within the royal enclosures. I gave way to this good man's appeal, and cleaned my hut by firing the ground, for, like all the huts, in this dog country, it was full of fleas. Once ensconced there, the king's pages darted in to see me, bearing a message from their master, who said he was sorry the rain prevented him from holding a levee that day, but the next he would be delighted to see me. Irungu, with all Suwarora's men, then came to a collection of huts near where I was residing, and whilst I lay in bed that night, Irungu with all his wives came in to see me and beg for beads.

[19 Feb.] To-day the king sent his pages to announce his intention of holding a levee in my honour. I prepared for my first presentation at court, attired in my best, though in it I cut a poor figure in comparison with the display of the dressy Waganda. They wore neat bark cloaks resembling the best yellow corduroy cloth, crimp and well set, as if stiffened with starch, and over that, as upper-cloaks, a patchwork of small antelope skins, which I observed were sewn together as well as any English glovers could have pieced them; whilst their head-dresses, generally, were abrus turbans, set off with highly-polished boar-tusks, stick-charms, seeds, beads, or shells; and on their necks, arms and ankles they wore other charms of wood, or small horns stuffed with magic powder, and fastened on by strings generally covered with snake-skin. N'yamgundu and Maula demanded, as their official privilege, a first peep; and this being refused, they tried to persuade me that the articles comprising the present required to be covered with chintz, for it was considered indecorous to offer anything to his majesty in a naked state. This little interruption over, the articles enumerated below[1] were conveyed to the palace in solemn procession thus:—With N'yamgundu, Maula, the pages, and myself on the flanks, the Union Jack carried by the kirangozi guide led the way followed by twelve men as a guard of honour, dressed in red flannel cloaks, and carrying their arms sloped, with fixed bayonets; whilst in their rear were the rest of my men, each carrying some article as a present.

On the march towards the palace, the admiring courtiers, wonder-struck at such an unusual display, exclaimed in raptures of astonishment, some with both hands at their mouths, and others clasping their heads with their hands 'Irungi! irungi!' which may be translated 'Beautiful! beautiful!' I thought myself everything was going on as well as could be wished; but before entering the royal enclosures, I found, to my disagreeable surprise, that the men with Suwarora's hongo or offering, which consisted of more than a hundred coils of wire, were ordered to lead the procession, and take precedence of me. There was something specially aggravating in this precedence; for it will be remembered that these very brass wires which they saw, I had myself intended for Mtesa, that they were taken from me by Suwarora as far back as Usui, and it would never do, without remonstrance, to have them boastfully paraded before my eyes in this fashion. My protests, however, had no effect upon the escorting Wakungu [nobles]. Resolving to make them catch it, I walked along as if ruminating in anger up the broad highroad into a cleared square, which divides Mtesa's domain on the south from his

[1] 1 block-tin box, 4 rich silk cloths, 1 rifle (Whitworth's), 1 gold chronometer, 1 revolver pistol, 3 rifled carbines, 3 sword bayonets, 1 box ammunition, 1 box bullets, 1 box gun-caps, 1 telescope, 1 iron chair, 10 bundles best beads, 1 set of table-knives, spoons, and forks. (*Speke's note.*)

Kamraviona's or commander-in-chief on the north, and then turned into the court. The palace or entrance quite surprised me by its extraordinary dimensions and the neatness with which it was kept. The whole brow and sides of the hill on which we stood were covered with gigantic grass huts, thatched as neatly as so many heads dressed by a London barber, and fenced all round with the tall yellow reeds of the common Uganda tiger-grass; whilst within the enclosure, the lines of huts were joined together, or partitioned off into courts, with walls of the same grass. It is here most of Mtesa's three or four hundred women are kept, the rest being quartered chiefly with his mother, known by the title of N'yamasore, or queen-dowager. They stood in little groups at the doors, looking at us, and evidently passing their own remarks, and enjoying their own jokes, on the triumphal procession. At each gate as we passed, officers on duty opened and shut it for us, jingling the big bells which are hung upon them, as they sometimes are at shop-doors to prevent a silent stealthy entrance.

The first court passed, I was even more surprised to find the unusual ceremonies that awaited me. There courtiers of high dignity stepped forward to greet me, dressed in the most scrupulously neat fashions. Men, women, bulls, dogs, and goats, were led about by strings; cocks and hens were carried in men's arms; and little pages, with rope-turbans, rushed about, conveying messages, as if their lives depended on their swiftness, everyone holding his skin-cloak tightly round him lest his naked legs might by accident be shown.

This, then, was the ante-reception court; and I might have taken possession of the hut, in which musicians were playing and singing on large nine-stringed harps, like the Nubian tambira, accompanied by harmonicons. By the chief officers in waiting, however, who thought fit to treat us like Arab merchants, I was requested to sit on the ground outside in the sun with my servants. Now, I had made up my mind never to sit upon the ground as the natives and Arabs are obliged to do, nor to make my obeisance in any other manner than is customary in England, though the Arabs had told me that from fear they had always complied with the manners of the court. I felt that if I did not stand up for my social position at once, I should be treated with contempt during the remainder of my visit, and thus lose the vantage-ground I had assumed of appearing rather as a prince than a trader, for the purpose of better gaining the confidence of the king. To avert over-hastiness, however—for my servants began to be alarmed as I demurred against doing as I was bid—I allowed five minutes to the court to give me a proper reception, saying, if it were not conceded I would then walk away.

Nothing, however, was done. My own men, knowing me, feared for me, as they did not know what a 'savage' king would do in case I carried out my threat; whilst the Waganda, lost in amazement at what seemed little less than blasphemy, stood still as posts. The affair ended by my walking straight away home, giving Bombay orders to leave the present on the ground and to follow me.

Although the king is said to be unapproachable, excepting when he chooses to attend court—a ceremony which rarely happens—intelligence of my hot wrath and hasty departure reached him in an instant. He first, it seems, thought of leaving his toilet-room to follow me, but, finding I was walking fast and had gone far, changed his mind, and sent Wakungu running after me. Poor creatures! they caught me up, fell upon their knees, and implored I would return at once, for the king had not tasted food, and would not until he saw me. I felt grieved at their touching appeals; but, as I did not understand all they said, I simply replied by patting my heart and shaking my head, walking if anything all the faster.

On my arrival at my hut, Bombay and others came in, wet through with perspiration, saying the king had heard of all my grievances. Suwarora's hongo was turned out of court, and, if I desired it, I might bring my own chair with me, for he was very anxious to show me great respect—although such a seat was exclusively the attribute of the king, no one else in Uganda daring to sit on an artificial seat.

My point was gained, so I cooled myself with coffee and a pipe, and returned rejoicing in my victory, especially over Suwarora. After returning to the second tier of huts from which I had retired, everybody appeared to be in a hurried, confused state of excitement, not knowing what to make out of so unprecedented an exhibition of temper. In the most polite manner, the officers in waiting begged me to be seated on my iron stool, which I had brought with me, whilst others hurried in to announce my arrival. But for a few minutes only I was kept in suspense, when a band of music, the musicians wearing on their backs long-haired goat-skins, passed me, dancing as they went along, like bears in a fair, and playing on reed instruments worked over with pretty beads in various patterns, from which depended leopard-cat skins—the time being regulated by the beating of long hand drums.

The mighty king was now reported to be sitting on his throne in the state hut of the third tier. I advanced, hat in hand, with my guard of honour following, formed in 'open ranks,' who in their turn were followed by the bearers carrying the present. I did not walk straight up to him as if to shake hands, but went outside the ranks of a three sided square of squatting Wakungu, all habited in skins, mostly cow-skins; some few of whom had, in addition, leopard-cat skins girt round the waist, the sign of royal blood. Here I was desired to halt and sit in the glaring sun; so I donned my hat, mounted my umbrella, a phenomenon which set them all a-wondering and laughing, ordered the guard to close ranks, and sat gazing at the novel spectacle A more theatrical sight I never saw. The king, a good-looking, well-figured, tall young man of twenty five, was sitting on a red blanket spread upon a square platform of royal grass, encased in tiger-grass reeds, scrupulously well dressed in a new mbugu [cloth made of bark]. The hair of his head was cut short, excepting on the top, where it was combed up into a high ridge, running from stem to stern like a cockscomb. On his neck was a very neat ornament—a large ring, of beautifully-worked small beads, forming elegant patterns by their various colours. On one arm was another bead ornament, prettily devised; and on the other a wooden charm, tied by a string covered with snake-skin. On every finger and every toe he had alternate brass and copper rings; and above the ankles, half-way up to the calf, a stocking of very pretty beads. Everything was light, neat and elegant in its way; not a fault could be found with the taste of his 'getting up'. For a handkerchief he held a well-folded piece of bark, and a piece of gold-embroidered silk, which he constantly employed to hide his large mouth when laughing, or to wipe it after a drink of plantain-wine, of which he took constant and copious draughts from neat little gourd-cups, administered by his ladies-in-waiting, who were at once his sisters and wives. A white dog, spear, shield and woman—the Uganda cognisance—were by his side, as also a knot of staff officers, with whom he kept up a brisk conversation on one side; and on the other was a band of Wichwezi, or lady-sorcerers, such as I have already described.

I was now asked to draw nearer within the hollow square of squatters, where leopard-skins were strewed upon the ground, and a large copper kettledrum, surmounted with brass bells on arching wires, along with two other smaller drums covered with cowrie-shells, and beads of colour worked into patterns, were placed. I now longed to open conversation, but knew not the language, and no one near me dared speak, or even lift his head from fear of being accused of eyeing the women; so the king and myself sat staring at one another for full an hour—I mute, but he pointing and remarking with those around him on the novelty of my guard and general appearance, and even requiring to see my hat lifted, the umbrellas shut and opened, and the guards face about and show off their red cloaks—for such wonders had never been seen in Uganda.

Then, finding the day waning, he sent Maula on an embassy to ask me if I had seen him; and on receiving my reply, 'Yes, for full one hour,' I was glad to find him rise, spear in hand, lead his dog, and walk unceremoniously away through the enclosure into the fourth tier of huts; for this being a pure levee day, no business was transacted.

The king's gait in retiring was intended to be very majestic, but did not succeed in conveying to me that impression. It was the traditional walk of his race, founded on the step of the lion; but the outward sweep of the legs, intended to represent the stride of the noble beast, appeared to me only to realize a very ludicrous kind of waddle, which made me ask Bombay if anything serious was the matter with the royal person.

I had now to wait for some time, almost as an act of humanity; for I was told the state secret, that the king had retired to break his fast and eat for the first time since hearing of my arrival; but the repast was no sooner over than he prepared for the second act, to show off his splendour, and I was invited in, with all my men, to the exclusion of all his own officers save my two guides. Entering as before, I found him standing on a red blanket, leaning against the right portal of the hut, talking and laughing, handkerchief in hand, to a hundred or more of his admiring wives, who, all squatting on the ground outside, in two groups, were dressed in new mbugus. My men dared not advance upright, nor look upon the women, but, stooping, with lowered heads and averted eyes, came cringing after me. Unconscious myself, I gave loud and impatient orders to my guard, rebuking them for moving like frightened geese, and, with hat in hand, stood gazing on the fair sex till directed to sit and cap.

Mtesa then inquired what messages were brought from Rumanika; to which Maula, delighted with the favour of speaking to royalty, replied by saying, Rumanika had gained intelligence of Englishmen coming up the Nile to Gani and Kidi. The king acknowledged the truthfulness of their story, saying he had heard the same himself; and both Wakungu, as is the custom in Uganda, thanked their lord in a very enthusiastic manner, kneeling on the ground—for no one can stand in the presence of his majesty—in an attitude of prayer, and throwing out their hands as they repeated the words, N'yanzig, N'yanzig, ai N'yanzig Mkahma wangi, &c. &c., for a considerable time; when thinking they had done enough of this, and heated with the exertion, they threw themselves flat upon their stomachs, and, floundering about like fish on land, repeated the same words over and over again, and rose doing the same, with their faces covered with earth; for majesty in Uganda is never satisfied till subjects have grovelled before it like the most abject worms. This conversation over, after gazing at me, and chatting with his women for a considerable time, the second scene ended. The third scene was more easily arranged, for the day was fast declining. He simply moved with his train of women to another hut, where, after seating himself upon his throne, with his women around him, he invited me to approach the nearest limits of propriety, and to sit as before. Again he asked me if I had seen him—evidently desirous of indulging in his regal pride; so I made the most of the opportunity thus afforded me of opening a conversation by telling him of those grand reports I had formerly heard about him, which induced me to come all this way to see him, and the trouble it had cost me to reach the object of my desire; at the same time taking a gold ring from off my finger, and presenting it to him, I said, 'This is a small token of friendship; if you will inspect it, it is made after the fashion of a dog-collar, and being the king of metals, gold, is in every respect appropriate to your illustrious race.'

He said, in return, 'If friendship is your desire, what would you say if I showed you a road by which you might reach your home in one month?' Now everything had to be told to Bombay, then to Nasib, my Kiganda interpreter, and then to either Maula, or N'yamgundu, before it was delivered to the king for it was considered indecorous to transmit any message to his majesty excepting through the medium of one of his officers. Hence I could not get an answer put in; for as all Waganda are rapid and impetuous in their conversation, the king probably forgetting he had put a question, hastily changed the conversation and said 'What guns have you got? Let me see the one you shoot with.' I wished still to answer the first question first, as I knew he referred to the direct line to Zanzibar across the Masai and was anxious without delay to open the subject of Petherick and Grant; but no one dared to deliver my statement. Much disappointed, I then said, 'I had brought the best shooting gun in the world—Whitworth's rifle—which I begged he would accept, with a few other trifles; and, with his permission, I would lay them upon a carpet at his feet, as is the custom of my country when visiting sultans.' He assented, sent all his women away, and had an mbugu spread for the purpose, on which Bombay, obeying my order, first spread a red blanket and then opened each article one after the other, when Nasib, according to the usage already mentioned, smoothed them down with his dirty hands, or rubbed them against his sooty face, and handed them to the king to show there was no poison or witchcraft in them. Mtesa appeared quite confused with the various wonders as he handled them, made silly remarks, and pondered over them like a perfect child, until it was quite dark. Torches were then lit, and guns, pistols, powder, boxes, tools, beads—the whole collection, in short—were tossed together topsy-turvy, bundled into mbugus, and carried away by the pages. Mtesa now said, 'It is late, and time to break up; what provision would you wish to have?' I said, 'A little of everything, but no one thing constantly.' 'And would you like to see me to-morrow?' 'Yes, every day.' 'Then you can't to-morrow for I have business; but the next day come if you like. You can now go away, and here are six pots of plantain wine for you; my men will search for food tomorrow.'

[21 Feb.] In the morning, whilst it rained, some pages drove in twenty cows and ten goats, with a polite metaphorical message from their king, to the effect that I had pleased him much, and he hoped I would accept these few 'chickens' until he could send more,—when both Maula and N'yamgundu, charmed with their success in having brought a welcome guest to Uganda, never ceased showering eulogiums on me for my fortune in having gained the countenance of their king. The rain falling was considered at court a good omen, and everybody declared the king mad with delight. Wishing to have a talk with him about Petherick and Grant, I at once started off the Wakungu to thank him for the present, and to beg pardon for my apparent rudeness of yesterday, at the same time requesting I might have an early interview with his majesty, as I had much of importance to communicate; but the solemn court formalities which these African kings affect as much as Oriental emperors, precluded my message from reaching the king. I heard, however, that he had spent the day receiving Suwarora's hongo of wire, and that the officer who brought them was made to sit in an empty court, whilst the king sat behind a screen, never deigning to show his majestic person. I was told, too, that he opened conversation by demanding to know how it happened that Suwarora became possessed of the wires, for they were made by the white men to be given to himself, and Suwarora must therefore have robbed me of them; and it was by such practices he, Mtesa, never could see any visitors. The officer's reply was, Suwarora would not show the white men any respect, because they were wizards who did not sleep in houses at night, but flew up to the tops of hills, and practised sorcery of every abominable kind. The king to this retorted, in a truly African fashion, 'That's a lie; I can see no harm in this white man; and if he had been a bad man, Rumanika would not have sent him on to me.' At night, when in bed, the king sent his pages to say, if I desired his friendship I would lend him one musket to make up six with what I had given him, for he intended visiting his relations the following morning. I sent three, feeling that nothing would be lost by being 'open-handed.'

[22 Feb.] To-day the king went the round of his relations, showing the beautiful things given him by the white man—a clear proof that he was much favoured by the 'spirits,' for neither his father nor any of his forefathers had been so recognized and distinguished by any 'sign' as a rightful inheritor to the Uganda throne: an anti-Christian interpretation of omens, as rife in these dark regions now as it was in the time of King Nebuchadnezzar. At midnight the three muskets were returned, and I was so pleased with the young king's promptitude and honesty, I begged he would accept them.

[23 Feb.] At noon Mtesa sent his pages to invite me to his palace. I went, with my guard of honour and my stool, but found I had to sit waiting in an ante-hut three hours with his commander-in-chief and other high officers before he was ready to see me. During this time Wasoga minstrels, playing on tambira, and accompanied by boys playing on a harmonicon, kept us amused; and a small page, with a large bundle of grass, came to me and said, 'The king hopes you won't be offended if required to sit on it before him; for no person in Uganda, however high in office, is ever allowed to sit upon anything raised above the ground, nor can anybody but himself sit upon such grass as this; it is all that his throne is made of. The first day he only allowed you to sit on your stool to appease your wrath.'

On consenting to do in 'Rome as the Romans do,' when my position was so handsomely acknowledged, I was called in, and found the court sitting much as it was on the first day's interview, only that the number of squatting Wakungu was much diminished; and the king, instead of wearing his ten brass and copper rings, had my gold one on his third finger. This day, however, was cut out for business, as, in addition to the assemblage of officers, there were women, cows, goats, fowls, confiscations, baskets of fish, baskets of small antelopes, porcupines, and curious rats caught by his gamekeepers, bundles of mbugu, &c. &c., made by his linen-drapers, coloured earths and sticks by his magician, all ready for presentation; but, as rain fell, the court broke up, and I had nothing for it but to walk about under my umbrella, indulging in angry reflections against the haughty king for not inviting me into his hut.

When the rain had ceased, and we were again called in, he was found sitting in state as before, but this time with the head of a black bull placed before him, one horn of which, knocked off, was placed alongside, whilst four living cows walked about the court.

I was now requested to shoot the four cows as quickly as possible; but having no bullets for my gun, I borrowed the revolving pistol I had given him, and shot all four in a second of time; but as the last one, only wounded, turned sharply upon me, I gave him the fifth and settled him. Great applause followed this *wonderful* feat, and the cows were given to my men. The king now loaded one of the carbines I had given him with his own hands, and giving it full-cock to a page, told him to go out and shoot a man in the outer court; which was no sooner accomplished than the little urchin returned to announce his success, with a look of glee such as one would see in the face of a boy who had robbed a bird's nest, caught a trout, or done any other boyish trick. The king said to him, 'And did you do it well?' 'Oh yes, capitally.' He spoke the truth, no doubt, for he dared not have trifled with the king; but the affair created hardly any interest. I never heard, and there appeared no curiosity to know, what individual human being the urchin had deprived of life.

. . . . . .

[27 Feb.] To call upon the queen-mother respectfully, as it was the opening visit, I took, besides the medicine-chest, a present of eight brass and copper wire, thirty blue-egg beads, one bundle of diminutive beads, and sixteen cubits of chintz, a small guard, and my throne of royal grass. The palace to be visited lay half a mile beyond the king's, but the highroad to it was forbidden me, as it is considered uncourteous to pass the king's gate without going in. So after winding through back-gardens, the slums of Bandowaroga, I struck upon the highroad close to her majesty's, where everything looked like the royal palace on a miniature scale. A large cleared space divided the queen's residence from her Kamraviona's. The outer enclosures and courts were fenced with tiger-grass; and the huts, though neither so numerous nor so large, were constructed after the same fashion as the king's. Guards also kept the doors, on which large bells were hung to give alarm, and officers in waiting watched the throne-rooms. All the huts were full of women, save those kept as waiting-rooms, where drums and harmonicons were placed for amusement. On first entering, I was required to sit in a waiting-hut till my arrival was announced; but that did not take long, as the queen was prepared to receive me; and being of a more affable disposition than her son, she held rather a levee of amusement than a stiff court of show. I entered the throne-hut as the gate of that court was thrown open, with my hat off, but umbrella held over my head, and walked straight towards her till ordered to sit upon my bundle of grass.

Her majesty—fat, fair, and forty-five—was sitting, plainly garbed in mbugu, upon a carpet spread upon the ground within a curtain of mbugu, her elbow resting on a pillow of the same bark material; the only ornaments on her person being an abrus necklace, and a piece of mbugu tied round her head, whilst a folding looking-glass, much the worse for wear, stood open by her side. An iron rod like a spit, with a cup on the top, charged with magic powder, and other magic wands, were placed before the entrance; and within the room, four Mabandwa sorceresses or devil-drivers, fantastically dressed, as before described, and a mass of other women, formed the company. For a short while we sat at a distance exchanging inquiring glances at one another, when the women were dismissed, and a band of music, with a court full of Wakungu, was ordered in to change the scene. I also got orders to draw near and sit fronting her within the hut. Pombe, the best in Uganda, was then drunk by the queen, and handed to me and to all the high officers about her, when she smoked her pipe, and bade me smoke mine. The musicians, dressed in long-haired Usoga goat-skins, were now ordered to strike up, which they did, with their bodies swaying or dancing like bears in a fair. Different drums were then beat, and I was asked if I could distinguish their different tones.

The queen, full of mirth, now suddenly rose, leaving me sitting, whilst she went to another hut, changed her mbugu for a deole, and came back again for us to admire her, which was no sooner done to her heart's content, than a second time, by her order, the court was cleared, and, when only three or four confidential Wakungu were left, she took up a small faggot of well-trimmed sticks, and, selecting three, told me she had three complaints. 'This stick,' she says, 'represents my stomach, which gives me much uneasiness; this second stick my liver, which causes shooting pains all over my body; and this third one my heart, for I get constant dreams at night about Sunna, my late husband, and they are not pleasant.' The dreams and sleeplessness I told her was a common widow's complaint, and could only be cured by her majesty making up her mind to marry a second time; but before I could advise for the bodily complaints, it would be necessary for me to see her tongue, feel her pulse, and perhaps, also, her sides. Hearing this, the Wakungu said, 'Oh, that can never be allowed without the sanction of the king;' but the queen, rising in her seat, expressed her scorn at the idea of taking advice from a mere stripling, and submitted herself for examination.

I then took out two pills, the powder of which was tasted by the Wakungu to prove that there was no devilry in 'the doctor,' and gave orders for them to be eaten at night, restricting her pombe and food until I saw her again. My game was now advancing, for I found through her I should get the key to an influence that might bear on the king, and was much pleased to hear her express herself delighted with me for everything I had done except stopping her grog, which, naturally enough in this great pombe-drinking country, she said would be a very trying abstinence.

The doctoring over, her majesty expressed herself ready to inspect the honorarium I had brought for her, and the articles were no sooner presented by Bombay and Nasib, with the usual formalities of stroking to insure their purity, than she, boiling with pleasure, showed them all to her officers, who declared, with a voice of most exquisite triumph, that she was indeed the most favoured of queens. Then, in excellent good taste, after saying that nobody had ever given her such treasures, she gave me in return, a beautifully-worked pombe sucking-pipe, which was acknowledged by every one to be the greatest honour she could pay me.

Not satisfied with this, she made me select, though against my desire, a number of sambo, called here gundu, rings of giraffe hair wound round with thin iron or copper wire, and worn as anklets; and crowned all with sundry pots of pombe, a cow, and a bundle of dried fish, of the description given in the woodcut, called by my men Samaki Kambari. This business over, she begged me to show her my picture-books, and was so amused with them that she ordered her sorceresses and all the other women in again to inspect them with her. Then began a warm and complimentary conversation, which ended by an inspection of my rings and all the contents of my pockets, as well as of my watch, which she called Lubari—a term equivalent to a place of worship, the object of worship itself, or the iron horn or magic pan. Still she said I had not yet satisfied her; I must return again two days hence, for she liked me much—excessively—she could not say how much; but now the day was gone, I might go. With this queer kind of adieu she rose and walked away, leaving me with my servants to carry the royal present home.

He describes another visit to the Queen.

[3 March.] I told her I had visited all the four quarters of the globe, and had seen all colours of people, but wondered where she got her pipe from, for it was much after the Rumish (Turkish) fashion, with a long stick. Greatly tickled at the flattery, she said, 'We hear men like yourself come to Amara from the other side and drive cattle away.' 'The Gallas, or Abyssinians, who are tall and fair, like Rumanika' I said, 'might do so, for they live not far off on the other side of Amara, but we never fight for such paltry objects. If cows fall into our hands when fighting we allow our soldiers to eat them, while we take the government of the country into our own hands.' She then said, 'We hear you don't like the Unyamuezi route, we will open the Ukori one for you.' 'Thank your majesty,' said I, in a figurative kind of speech to please Waganda ears; and turning the advantage of the project on her side. 'You have indeed hit the right nail on the head. I do not like the Unyamuezi route, as you may well imagine, when I tell you I have lost so much property there by mere robbery of the people and their kings. The Waganda do not see me in a true light; but if they have patience for a year or two, until the Ukori road is open, and trade between our respective countries shall commence, they will then see the fruits of my advent; so much so, that every Mganda will ray the first Uganda year dates from the arrival of the first Mzungu (white) visitor. As one coffee-seed sown brings forth fruit in plenty, so my coming here may be considered.' All appreciated this speech, saying, 'The white man, he even speaks beautifully! beautifully! beautifully! beautifully!' and, putting their hands to their mouths, they looked askance at me, nodding their admiring approval.

The queen and her ministers then plunged into pombe and became uproarious, laughing with all their might and main. Small bugu cups were not enough to keep up the excitement of the time, so a large wooden trough was placed before the queen and filled with liquor. If any was spilt, the Wakungu instantly fought over it, dabbing their noses on the ground, or grabbing it with their hands, that not one atom of the queen's favour might be lost; for everything must be adored that comes from royalty, whether by design or accident. The queen put her head to the trough and drank like a pig from it, and was followed by her ministers. The band, by order, then struck up a tune called the Milele, playing on a dozen reeds, ornamented with beads and cow-tips, and five drums of various tones and sizes, keeping time. The musicians dancing with zest, were led by four bandmasters, also dancing, but with their backs turned to the company to show off their long, shaggy, goat-skin jackets, sometimes upright, at other times bending and on their heels, like the hornpipe-dancers of western countries.

It was a merry scene, but soon became tiresome; when Bombay, by way of flattery, and wishing to see what the queen's wardrobe embraced, told her, Any woman, however ugly, would assume a goodly appearance if prettily dressed; upon which her gracious majesty immediately rose, retired to her toilet hut, and soon returned attired in a common check cloth, an abrus tiara, a bead necklace, and with a folding looking-glass, when she sat, as before, and was handed a blown-glass cup of pombe, with a cork floating on the liquor, and a napkin mbugu covering the top, by a naked virgin. For her condescension in assuming plain raiment, everybody of course, n'yanzigged. Next, she ordered her slave girls to bring a large number of sambo (anklets) and begged me to select the best, for she liked me much. In vain I tried to refuse them: she had given more than enough for a keepsake before, and I was not hungry for property; still I had to choose some, or I would give offence. She then gave me a basket of tobacco, and a nest of hen eggs for her 'son's' breakfast. When this was over, the Mukonderi, another dancing tune with instruments something like clarionets, was ordered; but it had scarcely been struck up, before a drenching rain, with strong wind, set in and spoilt the music, though not the playing—for none dared stop without an order; and the queen, instead of taking pity, laughed most boisterously over the exercise of her savage power as the unfortunate musicians were nearly beaten down by the violence of the weather.

When the rain ceased, her majesty retired a second time to her toilet-hut, and changed her dress for a puce-coloured wrapper, when I, ashamed of having robbed her of so many sambo, asked her if she would allow me to present her with a little English 'wool' to hang up instead of her mbugu curtain on cold days like this. Of course she could not decline, and a large double scarlet blanket was placed before her. 'Oh, wonder of wonders!' exclaimed all the spectators, holding their mouths in both hands at a time—such a 'pattern' had never been seen here before. It stretched across the hut, was higher than the men could reach—indeed it was a perfect marvel; and the man must be a good one who brought such a treasure as this to Uddu. 'And why not say Uganda?' I asked. 'Because all this country is called Uddu. Uganda is personified by Mtesa; and no one can say he has seen Uganda until he has been presented to the king.'

As I had them all in a good humour now, I complained I did not see enough of the Waganda—and as every one dressed so remarkably well, I could not discern the big men from the small; could she not issue some order by which they might call on me, as they did not dare do so without instruction, and then I, in turn, would call on them? Hearing this, she introduced me to her prime minister, chancellor of exchequer, women-keepers, hang-men, and cooks as the first nobles in the land, that I might recognise them again if I met them on the road. All n'yanzigged for this great condescension, and said they were delighted with their guest; then producing a strip of common joho to compare it with my blanket, they asked if I could recognise it. Of course, said I, it is made in my country, of the same material, only of coarser quality, and everything of the same sort is made in Uzungu [white man's country]. Then, indeed, said the whole company, in one voice, we do like you and your cloth too—but you most. I modestly bowed my head, and said their friendship was my chief desire.

This speech also created great hilarity; the queen and councillors all became uproarious. The queen began to sing and the councillors to join in a chorus; then all sang and all drank, and drank and sang, till, in their heated excitement, they turned the palace into a pandemonium; still there was not noise enough, so the band and drums were called again, and tomfool—for Uganda, like the old European monarchies, always keeps a jester—was made to sing in the gruff, hoarse, unnatural voice which he ever affects to maintain his character, and furnished with pombe when his throat was dry.

Now all of a sudden, as if a devil had taken possession of the company, the prime minister with all the courtiers jumped upon their legs, seized their sticks, for nobody can carry a spear when visiting, swore the queen had lost her heart to me, and running into the yard, returned, charging and jabbering at the queen; retreated and returned again, as if they were going to put an end to her for the guilt of loving me, but really to show their devotion and true love to her. The queen professed to take this ceremony with calm indifference, but her face showed that she enjoyed it. I was now getting very tired of sitting on my low stool and begged for leave to depart, but N'yamasore would not hear of it; she loved me a great deal too much to let me go away at this time of day, and forthwith ordered in more pombe. The same roystering scene was repeated; cups were too small, so the trough was employed; and the queen graced it by drinking, pig-fashion, first, and then handing it round to the company.

. . . . . .

[12 March.] Immediately after breakfast the king sent his pages in a great hurry to say he was waiting on the hill for me, and begged I would bring all my guns immediately. I prepared, thinking, naturally enough, that some buffaloes had been marked down; for the boys, as usual, were perfectly ignorant of his designs. To my surprise, however, when I mounted the hill half-way to the palace, I found the king standing, dressed in a rich filigreed waistcoat, trimmed with gold embroidery tweedling the loading-rod in his finger, and an alfia cap on his head, whilst his pages held his chair and guns, and a number of officers, with dogs and goats for offerings, squatting before him.

When I arrived, hat in hand, he smiled, examined my firearms, and proceeded for sport, leading the way to a high tree, on which some adjutant birds were nesting, and numerous vultures resting. This was the sport; Bana must shoot a nundo (adjutant) for the king's gratification. I begged him to take a shot himself, as I really could not demean myself by firing at birds sitting on a tree; but it was all of no use—no one could shoot as I could, and they must be shot. I proposed frightening them out with stones, but no stone could reach so high; so, to cut the matter short, I killed an adjutant on the nest, and, as the vultures flew away, brought one down on the wing, which fell in a garden enclosure.

The Waganda were for a minute all spell-bound with astonishment, when the king jumped frantically in the air, clapping his hands above his head, and singing out, 'Woh, woh! woh! what wonders! Oh, Bana, Bana! what miracles he performs!' [Bana=Bwana, Swahili for master]—and all the Wakungu followed in chorus 'Now load, Bana—load, and let us see you do it,' cried the excited king; but before I was half loaded he said, 'Come along, come along, and let us see the bird.' Then directing the officers which way to go—for, by the etiquette of the court of Uganda, every one must precede the king—he sent them through a court where his women, afraid of the gun, had been concealed. Here the rush onward was stopped by newly made fences, but the king roared to the officers to knock them down. This was no sooner said than done, by the attendants in a body shoving on and trampling them under, as an elephant would crush small trees to keep his course. So pushing, floundering through plantain and shrub, pell-mell one upon the other, that the king's pace might not be checked, or any one come in for a royal kick or blow, they came upon the prostrate bird. 'Woh! woh, woh!' cried the king again, 'there he is, sure enough; come here, women—come and look what wonders!' And all the women, in the highest excitement 'woh-wohed' as loud as any of the men. But that was not enough. 'Come along, Bana,' said the king, 'we must have some more sport;' and, saying this, he directed the way towards the queen's palace, the attendants leading, followed by the pages, then the king, next myself—for I never would walk before him—and finally the women, some forty or fifty, who constantly attended him.

. . . .

[24 March.] Then twenty naked virgins, the daughters of Wakungu, all smeared and shining with grease, each holding a small square of mbugu for a fig leaf, marched in a line before us, as a fresh addition to the harem, whilst the happy fathers floundered n'yanzigging on the ground, delighted to find their darlings appreciated by the king. Seeing this done in such a quiet mild way before all my men who dared not lift their heads to see it, made me burst into a roar of laughter, and the king, catching the infection from me, laughed as well: but the laughing did not end there—for the pages for once giving way to nature, kept bursting—my men chuckled in sudden gusts—while even the women, holding their mouths for fear of detection responded—and we all laughed together. Then a sedate old dame rose from the squatting mass, ordered the virgins to right-about, and marched them off, showing their still more naked reverses. I now obtained permission for the Wakungu to call upon me, and fancied I only required my interpreters to speak out like men when I had anything to say, to make my residence in Uganda both amusing and instructive; but though the king, carried off by the prevailing good humour of the scene we had both witnessed, supported me, I found that he had counter-ordered what he had said as soon as I had gone, and in fact, no Mkungu ever dared come near me.

[25 March.] To-day I visited Usungu again, and found him better. He gave pombe and plantains for my people, but would not talk to me, though I told him he had permission to call on me.

I have now been for some time within the court precincts, and have consequently had an opportunity of witnessing court customs. Among these, nearly every day since I have changed my residence, incredible as it may appear to be, I have seen one, two, or three of the wretched palacewomen led away to execution, tied by the hand, and dragged along by one of the body guard, crying out, as she went to premature death, 'Hai Minange!' (O my lord!) 'Kbakka!' (my king!) at the top of her voice, in the utmost despair and lamentation; and yet there was not a soul who dared lift hand to save any of them, though many might be heard privately commenting on their beauty. . . .

[27 March.] After breakfast I started on a visit to Congow; but finding he had gone to the king as usual, called at Masimbi's and he being absent also, I took advantage of my proximity to the queen's palace to call on her majesty. For hours I was kept waiting; firstly, because she was at breakfast; secondly, because she was 'putting on medicine;' and, thirdly, because the sun was too powerful for her complexion; when I became tired of her nonsense, and said, 'If she does not wish to see me, she had better say so at once, else I shall walk away; for the last time I came I saw her but for a minute when she rudely turned her back upon me, and left me sitting by myself.' I was told not to be in a hurry—she would see me in the evening. This promise might probably be fulfilled six blessed hours from the time when it was made; but I thought to myself, every place in Uganda is alike when there is no company at home, and so I resolved to sit the time out, like patience on a monument, hoping something funny might turn up after all.

At last her majesty stumps out, squats behind my red blanket, which is converted into a permanent screen, and says hastily, or rather testily, 'Can't Bana perceive the angry state of the weather?—clouds flying about, and the wind blowing half a gale? Whenever that is the case, I cannot venture out.' Taking her lie without an answer, I said, I had now been fifty days or so doing nothing in Uganda—not one single visitor of my own rank ever came near me, and I could not associate with people far below her condition and mine—in fact, all I had to amuse me at home now was watching a hen lay her eggs upon my spare bed. . . .

The Wakungu than changed the subject by asking, if I married a black woman, would there be any offspring, and what would be their colour? The company now became jovial when the queen improved it by making a significant gesture, and with roars of laughter asking me if I would like to be her son-in-law, for she had some beautiful daughters, either of the Wahuma or Waganda breed. Rather staggered at first by this awful proposal, I consulted Bombay what I should do with one if I got her. He, looking more to number one than my convenience, said, 'By all means accept the offer, for if *you* don't like her, *we* should, and it would be a good means of getting her out of this land of death, for all black people love Zanzibar.' The rest need not be told; as a matter of course I had to appear very much gratified, and as the bowl went round, all became uproarious. I must wait a day or two, however, that a proper selection might be made; and when the marriage came off I was to chain the fair one two or three days, until she became used to me, else, from mere fright, she might run away. . . .

. . . . . .

[30 March.] To fulfil my engagement with the queen, I walked off to her palace with stomach medicine, thinking we were now such warm friends, all pride and distant ceremonies would be dispensed with; but, on the contrary, I was kept waiting for hours till I sent in word to say, if she did not want medicine I wished to go home, for I was tired of Uganda and everything belonging to it. This message brought her to her gate, where she stood laughing till the Wahuma girls she had promised me, one of twelve and the other a little older, were brought in and made to squat in front of us. The elder, who was in the prime of youth and beauty, very large of limb, dark in colour, cried considerably; whilst the younger one, though very fair, had a snubby nose and everted lips, and laughed as if she thought the change in her destiny very good fun. I had now to make my selection, and took the smaller one, promising her to Bombay as soon as we arrived on the coast, where, he said, she would be considered a Hubshi or Abyssinian. But when the queen saw what I had done, she gave me the other as well, saying the little one was too young to go alone, and, if separated, she would take fright and run away. Then with a gracious bow I walked off with my two fine specimens of natural history, though I would rather have had princes, that I might have taken them home to be instructed in England; but the queen, as soon as we had cleared the palace, sent word to say that she must have another parting look at her son with his wives. Still laughing, she said, 'That will do; you look beautiful; now go away home,' and off we trotted, the elder sobbing bitterly, the younger laughing.

As soon as we reached home, my first enquiry was concerning their histories, of which they appeared to know but very little. The elder, whom I named Meri (plantains), was obtained by Sunna, the late king, as a wife from Nkole; and though she was a mere Kahala, or girl, when the old king died, he was so attached to her he gave her twenty cows, in order that she might fatten up on milk after her native fashion; but on Sunna's death, when the establishment of women was divided, Meri fell to N'yamasore's (the queen's) lot. The lesser one, who still retains the name of Kahala, said she was seized in Unyoro by the Waganda, who took her to N'yamasore, but what became of her father and mother she could not say.

It was now dinner time, and as the usual sweet potatoes and goat's flesh were put upon my box-table I asked them to dine with me, and we became great friends, for they were assured they would finally get good houses and gardens at Zanzibar; but nothing would induce either of them to touch food that had been cooked with butter. A dish of plantains and goat-flesh was then prepared; but though Kahala wished to eat it, Meri rejected the goat's flesh, and would not allow Kahala to taste it either; and thus began a series of domestic difficulties. On inquiring how I could best deal with my difficult charge, I was told the Wahuma pride was so great, and their tempers so strong, they were more difficult to break in than a phunda, or donkey, though, when once tamed, they became the best of wives.

On 23rd April Speke accompanied the king on a frolicsome expedition to the lake.

[26 April.] We started early in the usual manner; but after working up and down the creek, inspecting the inlets for hippopotami, and tiring from want of sport, the king changed his tactics, and, paddling and steering himself with a pair of new white paddles, finally directed the boats to an island occupied by the Mgussa, or Neptune of the N'yanza, not in person —for Mgussa is a spirit—but by his familiar or deputy, the great medium who communicates the secrets of the deep to the king of Uganda. In another sense, he might be said to be the presiding priest of the source of the mighty Nile, and as such was, of course, an interesting person for me to meet. The first operation on shore was picknicking, when many large bugus of pombe were brought for the king; next, the whole party took a walk, winding through the trees, and picking fruit, enjoying themselves amazingly, till, by some unlucky chance, one of the royal wives, a most charming creature, and truly one of the best of the lot, plucked a fruit and offered it to the king, thinking, doubtless, to please him greatly; but he, like a madman, flew into a towering passion, and said it was the first time a woman ever had the impudence to offer him anything, and ordered the pages to seize, bind, and lead her off to execution.

These words were no sooner uttered by the king than the whole bevy of pages slipped their cord turbans from their heads, and rushed like a pack of cupid beagles upon the fairy queen, who, indignant at the little urchins daring to touch her majesty, remonstrated with the king, and tried to beat them off like flies, but was soon captured, overcome, and dragged away, crying, in the names of the Kamraviona and Mzungu (myself) for help and protection; whilst Lubuga, the pet sister, and all the other women, clasped the king by his legs, and, kneeling, implored forgiveness for their sister. The more they craved for mercy, the more brutal he became, till at last he took a heavy stick and began to belabour the poor victim on the head.

Hitherto I had been extremely careful not to interfere with any of the king's acts of arbitrary cruelty knowing that such interference, at an early stage, would produce more harm than good. This last act of barbarism, however, was too much for my English blood to stand; and as I heard my name, Mzungu, imploringly pronounced, I rushed at the king, and, staying his uplifted arm, demanded from him the woman's life. Of course I ran imminent risk of losing my own in thus thwarting the capricious tyrant; but his caprice proved the friend of both. The novelty of interference even made him smile, and the woman was instantly released.

Proceeding on through the trees of this beautiful island, we next turned into the hut of the Mgussa's familiar, which at the farther end was decorated with many mystic symbols—amongst others a paddle, the badge of his high office—and for some time we sat chatting, when pombe was brought, and the spiritual medium arrived. He was dressed Wichwezi fashion, with a little white goat-skin apron, adorned with numerous charms, and used a paddle for a mace or walking-stick. He was not an old man, though he affected to be so—walking very slowly and deliberately, coughing asthmatically, glimmering with his eyes, and mumbling like a witch. With much affected difficulty he sat at the end of the hut beside the symbols alluded to, and continued his coughing full half an hour, when his wife came in in the same manner, without saying a word, and assumed the same affected style. The king jokingly looked at me and laughed, and then at these strange creatures by turn, as much as to say, 'What do you think of them?' but no voice was heard save that of the old wife, who croaked like a frog for water, and, when some was brought, croaked again because it was not the purest of the lake's produce—had the first cup changed, wetted her lips with the second, and hobbled away in the same manner as she came.

At this juncture the Mgussa's familiar motioned the Kamraviona and several officers to draw around him, when in a very low tone, he gave them all the orders of the deep, and walked away. His revelations seemed unpropitious, for we immediately repaired to our boats and returned to our quarters.

. . . . . .

[3 May.] I now received a letter from Grant to say he was coming by boat from Kitangule, and at once went to the palace to give the welcome news to the king. The road to the palace I found thronged with people; and in the square outside the entrance there squatted a multitude of attendants, headed by the king, sitting on a cloth, dressed in his national costume, with two spears and a shield by his side. On his right hand the pages sat waiting for orders, while on his left there was a small squatting cluster of women, headed by Wichwezis, or attendant sorceresses, offering pombe. In front of the king, in form of a hollow square, many ranks deep, sat the victorious officers lately returned from the war, variously dressed; the nobles distinguished by their leopard-cat skins and dirks, the commoners by coloured mbugu and cow or antelope skin cloaks; but all their faces and arms were painted, red, black, or smoke-colour. Within the square of men immediately fronting the king, the war arms of Uganda were arranged in three ranks; the great war drum, covered with a leopard skin, and standing on a large carpeting of them, was placed in advance; behind this, propped or hung on a rack of iron, were a variety of the implements of war in common use, offensive and defensive, as spears—of which two were of copper, the rest iron—and shields of wood and leather; whilst in the last row or lot were arranged systematically, with great taste and powerful effect, the supernatural arms, the god of Uganda, consisting of charms of various descriptions and in great numbers. Outside the square again, in a line with the king, were the household arms, a very handsome copper kettledrum, of French manufacture, surmounted on the outer edge with pretty little brass bells depending from swan-neck-shaped copper wire, two new spears, a painted leather shield, and magic wands of various devices, deposited on a carpet of leopard skins—the whole scene giving the effect of true barbarous royalty in its uttermost magnificence.

Approaching, as usual, to take my seat beside the king, some slight sensation was perceptible, and I was directed to sit beyond the women. The whole ceremonies of this grand assemblage were now obvious. Each regimental commandant in turn narrated the whole services of his party distinguishing those subs who executed his orders well and successfully from those who either deserted before the enemy or feared to follow up their success. The king listened attentively, making, let us suppose, very shrewd remarks concerning them; when to the worthy he awarded pombe, helped with gourd-cups from large earthen jars, which was n'yanzigged for vehemently; and to the unworthy, execution. When the fatal sentence was pronounced, a terrible bustle ensued, the convict wrestling and defying, whilst the other men seized, pulled and tore the struggling wretch from the crowd, bound him hands and head together, and led or rather tumbled him away. . . .

On 27th May Grant arrived from Karagwe. Speke constantly pressed for permission to go north through Unyoro to Gondokoro, where he hoped to meet the trader Petherick. Until 3rd July the king prevaricated.

[3 July.] The moment of triumph had come at last, and suddenly the road was granted! The king presently let us see the motive by which he had been influenced. He said he did not like having to send to Rumanika for everything: he wanted his visitors to come to him direct: moreover, Rumanika had sent him a message to the effect that we were not to be shown anything out of Uganda, and when we had done with it, were to be returned to him. Rumanika, indeed! who cared about Rumanika? Was not Mtesa the king of the country, to do as he liked? and we all laughed. Then the king, swelling with pride, asked me whom I liked best—Rumanika or himself—an awkward question, which I disposed of by saying I liked Rumanika very much because he spoke well, and was very communicative; but I also liked Mtesa, because his habits were much like my own—fond of shooting and roaming about; whilst he had learnt so many things from my teaching, I must ever feel a yearning towards him.

. . . . . .

On the way home, one of the king's favourite women overtook us, walking, with her hands clasped at the back of her head, to execution, crying 'N'yawo!' in the most pitiful manner. A man was preceding her, but did not touch her; for she loved to obey the orders of her king voluntarily, and, in consequence of previous attachment, was permitted as a mark of distinction, to walk free. Wondrous world! it was not ten minutes since we parted from the king, yet he had found time to transact this bloody piece of business.

[7 July.] Early in the morning the king bade us come to him to say farewell. Wishing to leave behind a favourable impression I instantly complied. On the breast of my coat, I suspended the necklace the queen had given me, as well as his knife, and my medals. I talked with him in as friendly and flattering a manner as I could, dwelling on his shooting, the pleasant cruising on the lake, and our sundry picnics, as well as the grand prospect there was now of opening the country to trade, by which his guns, the best in the world, would be fed with powder—and other small matters of a like nature—to which he replied with great feeling and good taste. We then all rose with an English bow, placing the hand on the heart whilst saying adieu; and there was a complete uniformity in the ceremonial, for whatever I did, Mtesa, in an instant, mimicked with the instinct of a monkey.

We had, however, scarcely quitted the palace gate before the king issued himself, with his attendants and his brothers leading, and women bringing up the rear; here K'yengo and all the Wazina joined in the procession with ourselves, they kneeling and clapping their hands after the fashion of their own country. Budja (their guide to the north) just then made me feel very anxious, by pointing out the position of Urondogani, as I thought, too far north. I called the king's attention to it, and in a moment he said he would speak to Budja in such a manner that he would leave no doubts in my mind, for he liked me much, and desired to please me in all things. As the procession now drew close to our camp and Mtesa expressed a wish to have a final look at my men, I ordered them to turn out with their arms and n'yanzig for the many favours they had received. Mtesa, much pleased, complimented them on their goodly appearance, remarking that with such a force I would have no difficulty in reaching Gani, and exhorted them to follow me through fire and water; then, exchanging adieus again, he walked ahead in gigantic strides up the hill, the pretty favourite of his harem, Lubuga—beckoning and waving with her little hands and crying 'Bana! Bana!'—trotting after him conspicuous amongst the rest, though all showed a little feeling at the severance. We saw them no more.

Journal of the discovery of the source of the Nile, 1st edition, pp. 280–316, 334–336, 357–370, 394–396, 405–406, 445–452

After leaving Uganda, Speke sent Grant on to Unyoro with the stores to make contact with its difficult monarch, Kamrasi, while he himself marched eastwards looking for the Nile. He struck it somewhat north of its egress from Lake Victoria and followed it down the left bank, seeking for the essential proof of his theory.

25. DISCOVERY OF THE SOURCE OF THE NILE

[25 July 1862.] I marched up the left bank of the Nile at a considerable distance from the water, to the Isamba Rapids, passing through rich jungle and plantain gardens. Nango, an old friend and district officer of the place, first refreshed us with a dish of plantain-squash and dried fish with pombe. He told us he is often threatened by elephants, but he sedulously keeps them off with charms; for if they ever tasted a plantain they would never leave the garden until they had cleared it out. He then took us to see the nearest falls of the Nile—extremely beautiful but very confined. The water ran deep between its banks, which were covered with fine grass, soft cloudy acacias, and festoons of lilac convolvuli; whilst here and there, where the land had slipped above the rapids, bared places of red earth could be seen, like that of Devonshire; there, too, the waters, impeded by a natural dam, looked like a huge mill-pond, sullen and dark, in which two crocodiles, laving about, were looking out for prey. From the high banks we looked down upon a line of sloping wooded islets lying across the stream, which divide its waters, and, by interrupting them, cause at once both dam and rapids. The whole was more fairylike, wild, and romantic than—I must confess that my thoughts took that shape—anything I ever saw outside of a theatre. It was exactly the sort of place, in fact, where, bridged across from one side-slip to the other, on a moonlight night, brigands would assemble to enact some dreadful tragedy. Even the Wanguana seemed spellbound at the novel beauty of the sight, and no one thought of moving till hunger warned us night was setting in, and we had better look out for lodgings.

[25 July.] Start again, and after drinking pombe with Nango, when we heard that three Wakungu had been seized at Kari, in consequence of the murder, the march was recommenced, but soon after stopped by the mischievous machinations of our guide, who pretended it was too late in the day to cross the jungles on ahead, either by the road to the source or the palace, and therefore would not move till the morning; then, leaving us, on the pretext of business, he vanished, and was never seen again. A small black fly, with thick shoulders and bullet-head, infests the place, and torments the naked arms and legs of the people with its sharp stings to an extent that must render life miserable to them.

[27 July.] After a long struggling march, plodding through huge grasses and jungle, we reached a district which I cannot otherwise describe than by calling it a 'Church Estate'. It is dedicated in some mysterious manner to Lubari (Almighty) and although the king appeared to have authority over some of the inhabitants of it, yet others had apparently a sacred character, exempting them from the civil power, and he had no right to dispose of the land itself. In this territory there are small villages only at every fifth mile, for there is no road, and the lands run high again, whilst, from want of a guide, we often lost the track. It now transpired that Budja, when he told at the palace that there was no road down the banks of the Nile, did so in consequence of his fear that if he sent my whole party here they would rob these church lands, and so bring him into a scrape with the wizards or ecclesiastical authorities. Had my party not been under control, we could not have put up here; but on my being answerable that no thefts should take place, the people kindly consented to provide us with board and lodgings, and we found them very obliging. One elderly man—half-witted—they said the king had driven his senses from him by seizing his house and family—came at once on hearing of our arrival, laughing and singing in a loose jaunty maniacal manner, carrying odd sticks, shells and a bundle of mbugu rags, which he deposited before me, dancing and singing again, then retreating and bringing some more with a few plantains from a garden, which I was to eat, as kings lived upon flesh, and 'poor Tom' wanted some, for he lived with lions and elephants in a hovel beyond the gardens, and his belly was empty. He was precisely a black specimen of the English parish idiot.

[28 July.] At last, with a good push for it, crossing hills and threading huge grasses, as well as extensive village plantations lately devastated by elephants—they had eaten all that was eatable, and what would not serve for food they had destroyed with their trunks, not one plantain or one hut being left entire—we arrived at the extreme end of the journey, the farthest point ever visited by the expedition on the same parallel of latitude as king Mtesa's palace, and just forty miles east of it.

We were well rewarded; for the 'stones,' as the Waganda call the falls, was by far the most interesting sight I had seen in Africa. Everybody ran to see them at once, though the march had been long and fatiguing, and even my sketch-block was called into play. Though beautiful, the scene was not exactly what I expected; for the broad surface of the lake was shut out from view by a spur of hill, and the falls, about 12 feet deep, and 400 to 500 feet broad, were broken by rocks. Still it was a sight that attracted one to it for hours—the roar of the waters, the thousands of passenger-fish, leaping at the falls with all their might, the Wasoga and Waganda fishermen coming out in boats and taking post on all the rocks with rod and hook, hippopotami and crocodiles lying sleepily on the water, the ferry at work above the falls, and cattle driven down to drink at the margin of the lake,—made, in all, with the pretty nature of the country—small hills, grassy-topped, with trees in the folds, and gardens on the lower slopes—as interesting a picture as one could wish to see.

The expedition had now performed its functions. I saw that old father

Nile without any doubt rises in the Victoria N'yanza, and as I had foretold, that lake is the great source of the holy river which cradled the first expounder of our religious belief. I mourned, however, when I thought how much I had lost by the delays in the journey having deprived me of the pleasure of going to look at the north-east corner of the N'yanza to see what connection there was, by the strait so often spoken of, with it and the other lake where the Waganda went to get their salt, and from which another river flowed to the north, making 'Usoga an island.' But I felt I ought to be content with what I had been spared to accomplish; for I had seen full half of the lake, and had information given me of the other half, by means of which I knew all about the lake, as far, at least, as the chief objects of geographical importance were concerned.

Journal of the discovery of the source of the Nile,
1st edition, pp. 464–467

Speke named these falls Ripon after Lord de Grey and Ripon, President of the Royal Geographical Society. He then endeavoured to follow the course of the Nile northwards. He was, however, forced away from the river by the hostility of some of the natives and was obliged to cut across to Kamrasi's. After being delayed and persecuted by this suspicious and greedy king, they moved on to the north. They were unable to keep touch with the Nile and did not find Lake Albert. Coming through the ghastly preserves of the so-called 'Turkish' slave-raiders from Egypt and the Sudan, who were spreading their depredations ever further south, they encountered Mr. Samuel Baker walking by the river at Gondokoro. Reference will be made again in the next section to their meeting.

We must briefly follow through the rest of Speke's life. Speke and Grant reached England early in 1863. Their great discoveries were acclaimed, though the Government gave Speke no reward except the right to add a hippopotamus and a crocodile to his coat-of-arms. As, however, Speke had failed to trace the course of the Nile northwards from Lake Victoria, Burton challenged his whole theory, both as to the Nile having its source in the lake and as to the size and importance of the lake itself. He even published a map in 1864 in which the lake was marked as 'supposed site' and the connection further west from Lake Tanganyika, through a speculative Lake Albert, maintained. It was decided that the bitter controversy between the two explorers should be settled by confronting them publicly at the meeting of the British Association at Bath.

Speke is said to have dreaded the ordeal though, as further exploration was to show, his theories were correct in spite of his incomplete evidence. The meeting did not, however, take place. When Burton was on the platform and the audience had been kept waiting for twenty-five minutes, news came that while Speke, who had gone out shooting that morning, had been climbing over a wall, both barrels of his shot-gun had gone off, and he had died at once. The verdict at the inquest was 'accidental death'.

VIII
SIR SAMUEL WHITE BAKER
1821–1893

Baker was born at Enfield and was the son of an English landowner, member of a Bristol family with estates and commercial connections in the West Indies. He was, for the most part, educated privately and finished his studies in Germany. In 1840 he married the daughter of a rector and shortly afterwards he was attracted by accounts of big-game shooting to visit Ceylon. His connection with the island, where he fostered an experiment in English colonization, lasted until 1855. He then returned to England where his wife died of typhus. After some rather aimless wandering and sport in the Near East in 1859 he took over the supervision of some railway construction on the Danube, during which he learned confidence in handling gangs of men. At this time he married his second wife, Fraülein von Sass.

In 1861 he decided to embark with his new wife upon exploration in Central Africa. A man of great physical strength and powerful build, the greatest big-game hunter of his age, he was naturally attracted by this adventurous enterprise. He hoped that he might meet Speke and Grant upon their way north from Lake Victoria. After a preliminary fourteen months exploring the tributaries flowing from Abyssinia into the Nile, Baker and his wife set out from Khartoum at the end of 1862. They were provided with a firman *from the viceroy of Egypt which was only of limited use among the Sudan officials, as these were mostly deep in the terrible slave trade which was being extended every year further south, and were fearful of Baker's revelations.*

Baker took three ships and 100 men up the Nile. He had considerable difficulty with both, but managed to reach Gondokoro, the Equatorial headquarters of the mixed Arab and Egyptian slave-traders (generally known as Turks), in February 1863. Here, as a result of the intrigues and opposition of the Arabs and the hostility of the ill-treated tribes in the neighbourhood, the Bakers had an uncomfortable and even dangerous time. A serious mutiny on the part of

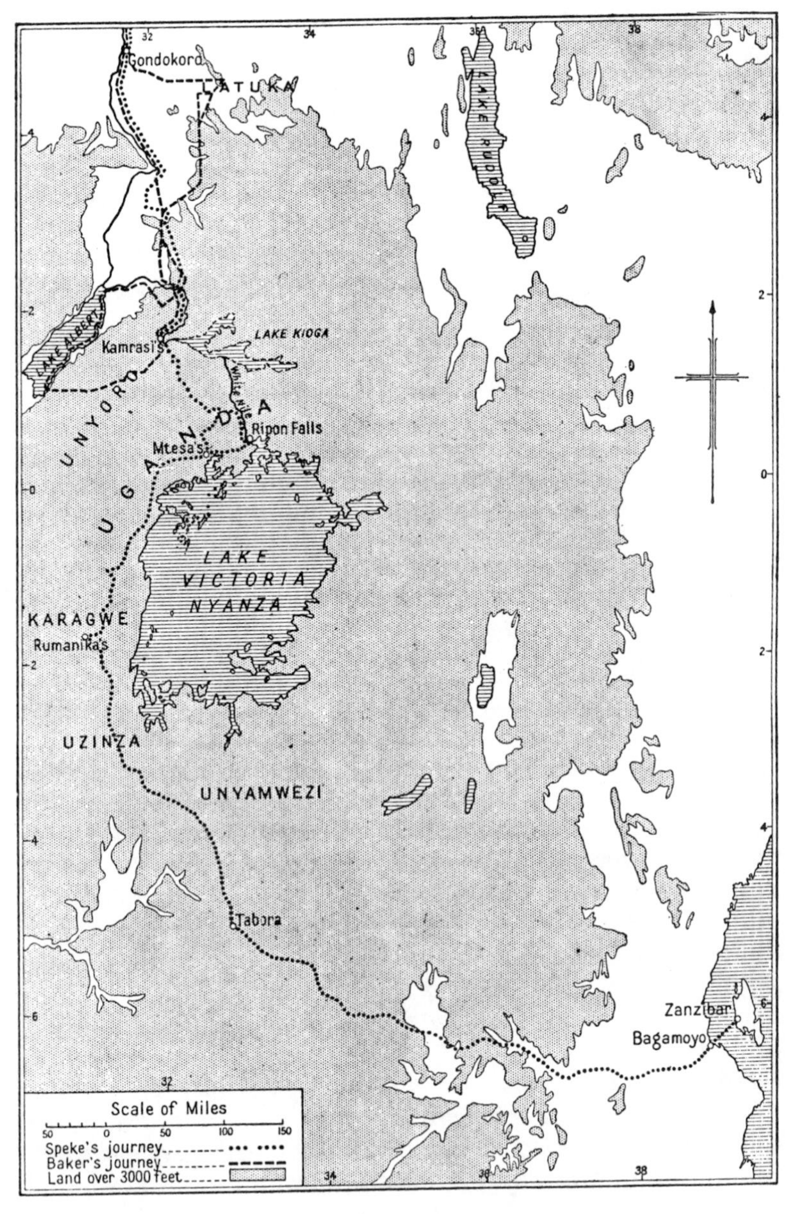

9. The Travels of Speke and Baker, 1860–5

Baker's own men was overcome as much by the outstanding courage and common sense of his wife as by his own vigorous action. The dramatic meeting with Speke and Grant followed, and he was able to replenish their stores. In spite of joy at the meeting, Baker was dashed in his hopes of carrying out his own discoveries until the liberal-minded Speke told him of rumours of the existence of a large undiscovered lake to the south-west connected with the Nile system and generously showed him his own sketch maps to help him. In March 1863 the traveller and his wife struck south upon the most perilous part of their journey. Baker was forced to seek the guidance and company of slave-traders and to endure the brutal and treacherous character of these men who plotted with his own rascally followers, and raised the hostility of the tribes which they massacred and plundered on the way. There were further mutinies and desertions; both travellers suffered from fever and sickness and all their transport animals died.

By the beginning of April they had reached the Latuka country and here Baker persuaded the chief to arrange an elephant hunt of which he gives a characteristic account.

26. ENCOUNTER WITH AN ELEPHANT

In about ten minutes we saw the Latookas hurrying towards us, and almost immediately after, I saw two enormous bull elephants with splendid tusks about a hundred yards from us, apparently the leaders of an approaching herd. The ground was exceedingly favourable, being tolerably open, and yet with sufficient bush to afford a slight cover. Presently, several elephants appeared and joined the two leaders—there was evidently a considerable number in the herd, and I was on the point of dismounting to take the first shot on foot, when the Latookas, too eager, approached the herd: their red and blue helmets at once attracted the attention of the elephants, and a tremendous rush took place, the whole herd closing together and tearing off at full speed. 'Follow me!' I hallooed to my men, and touching my horse with the spur I intended to dash into the midst of the herd. Just at that instant, in his start, my horse slipped and fell suddenly upon his side, falling upon my right leg and thus pinning me to the ground. He was not up to my weight, and releasing myself, I immediately mounted my old Abyssinian hunter, 'Tetel,' and followed the tracks of the elephants at full speed, accompanied by two of the Latookas, who ran like hounds. Galloping through the green but thornless bush, I soon came in sight of a grand bull elephant, steaming along like a locomotive engine straight before me. Digging in the spurs, I was soon within twenty yards of him; but the ground was so unfavourable, being full of buffalo holes, that I could not pass him. In about a quarter of an hour, after a careful chase over deep ruts and gullies concealed in high grass, I arrived at a level space, and shooting ahead, I gave him a shoulder shot with the Reilly No. 10 rifle. I saw the wound in a good place, but the bull rushed along all the quicker, and again we came into bad ground that made it unwise to close. However, on the first opportunity I made a dash by him, and fired my left-hand barrel at full gallop. He slackened his speed, but I could not halt to reload, lest I should lose sight of him in the high grass and bush.

Not a man was with me to hand a spare rifle. My cowardly fellows, although light-weights and well mounted, were nowhere; the natives were outrun, as of course was Richarn, who, not being a good rider, had preferred to hunt on foot. In vain I shouted for the men; and I followed the elephant with an empty rifle for about ten minutes, until he suddenly turned round, and stood facing me in an open spot in grass about nine or ten feet high. 'Tetel' was a grand horse for elephants, not having the slightest fear, and standing fire like a rock, never even starting under the discharge of the heaviest charge of powder. I now commenced reloading, when presently one of my men, Yaseen, came up upon 'Filfil.' Taking a spare gun from him, I rode rapidly past the elephant and suddenly reining up, I made a good shot exactly behind the bladebone. With a shrill scream, the elephant charged down upon me like a steam-engine. In went the spurs. 'Tetel' knew his work, and away he went over the ruts and gullies, the high dry grass whistling in my ears as we shot along at full speed, closely followed by the enraged bull for about two hundred yards.

The elephant then halted: and turning the horse's head, I again faced him and reloaded. I thought he was dying, as he stood with trunk drooping, and ears closely pressed back upon his neck. Just at this moment I heard the rush of elephants advancing through the green bush upon the rising ground above the hollow formed by the open space of high withered grass in which we were standing facing each other. My man Yaseen had bolted with his fleet horse at the first charge and was not to be seen. Presently, the rushing sound increased, and the heads of a closely packed herd of about eighteen elephants showed above the low bushes, and they broke cover, bearing down directly upon me, both I and my horse being unobserved in the high grass. I never saw a more lovely sight; they were all bulls with immense tusks. Waiting until they were within twenty yards of me, I galloped straight at them, giving a yell that turned them. Away they rushed up the hill, but at so great a pace, that upon the rutty and broken ground I could not overtake them, and they completely distanced me. Tetel, although a wonderfully steady hunter, was an uncommonly slow horse, but upon this day he appeared to be slower than usual, and I was not at the time aware that he was seriously ill. By following three elephants separated from the herd I came up to them by a short cut, and singling out a fellow with enormous tusks, I rode straight at him. Finding himself overhauled, he charged me with such quickness and followed me up so far, that it was with the greatest difficulty that I cleared him. When he turned, I at once returned to the attack; but he entered a thick thorny jungle through which no horse could follow, and I failed to obtain a shot.

I was looking for a path through which I could penetrate the bush, when I suddenly heard natives shouting in the direction where I had left the wounded bull. Galloping towards the spot, I met a few scattered natives; among others, Adda. After shouting for some time, at length Yaseen appeared upon my horse Filfil; he had fled as usual when he saw the troop of elephants advancing and no one knows how far he had ridden before he thought it safe to look behind him. With two mounted gun bearers and five others on foot I had been entirely deserted through the cowardice of my men. The elephant that I had left as dying was gone. One of the Latookas had followed upon his tracks, and we heard this fellow shooting in the distance. I soon overtook him, and he led rapidly upon the track through the thick bushes and high grass. In about a quarter of an hour we came up with the elephant; he was standing in bush, facing us at about fifty yards distance, and immediately perceiving us, he gave a saucy jerk with his head, and charged most determinedly. It was exceedingly difficult to escape, owing to the bushes which impeded the horse, while the elephant crushed them like cobwebs: however, by turning my horse sharp round a tree I managed to evade him after a chase of about a hundred and fifty yards. Disappearing in the jungle after his charge, I immediately followed him. The ground was hard, and so trodden by elephants that it was difficult to single out the track. There was no blood upon the ground, but only on the trees every now and then, where he had rubbed past them in his retreat. After nearly two hours passed in slowly following upon his path, we suddenly broke cover and saw him travelling very quietly through an extensive plain of high grass. The ground was gently inclining upwards on either side the plain, but the level was a mass of deep, hardened ruts, over which no horse could gallop. Knowing my friend's character, I rode up the rising ground to reconnoitre: I found it tolerably clear of holes, and far superior to the rutty bottom. My two mounted gun-bearers had now joined me, and far from enjoying the sport, they were almost green with fright when I ordered them to keep close to me and to advance. I wanted them to attract the elephant's attention, so as to enable me to obtain a good shoulder shot. Riding along the open plain, I at length arrived within about fifty yards of the bull when he slowly turned. Reining 'Tetel' up,

I immediately fired a steady shot at the shoulder with the Reilly No. 10:—for a moment he fell upon his knees, but, recovering with wonderful quickness, he was in full charge upon me. Fortunately I had inspected my ground previous to the attack and away I went up the inclination to my right, the spurs hard at work and the elephant screaming with rage, *gaining* on me. My horse felt as though made of wood, and clumsily rolled along in a sort of cow-gallop;—in vain I dug the spurs into his flanks, and urged him by rein and voice: not an extra stride could I get out of him, and he reeled along as though thoroughly exhausted, plunging in and out of the buffalo holes instead of jumping them. Hamed was on my horse 'Mouse,' who went three to 'Tetel's' one, and instead of endeavouring to divert the elephant's attention, he shot ahead, and thought of nothing but getting out of the way. Yaseen, on 'Filfil,' had fled in another direction, thus I had the pleasure of being hunted down upon a sick and disabled horse. I kept looking round, thinking that the elephant would give in:—we had been running for nearly half a mile, and the brute was overhauling me so fast that he was within ten or twelve yards of the horse's tail, with his trunk stretched out to catch him. Screaming like the whistle of an engine, he fortunately so frightened the horse that he went his best, although badly, and I turned him suddenly down the hill and doubled back like a hare. The elephant turned up the hill, and entering the jungle, he relinquished the chase, when another hundred yards' run would have bagged me.

In a life's experience in elephant-hunting, I never was hunted for such a distance. Great as were Tetel's good qualities for pluck and steadiness, he had exhibited such distress and want of speed, that I was sure he failed through some sudden malady. I immediately dismounted, and the horse laid down, as I thought to die.

Whistling loudly, I at length recalled Hamed, who had still continued his rapid flight without once looking back, although the elephant was out of sight. Yaseen was, of course, nowhere; but after a quarter of an hour's shouting and whistling, he reappeared, and I mounted Filfil, ordering Tetel to be led home.

The Albert N'Yanza, 1st edition, vol. I, pp. 264–272

On 10th February 1864 they reached the headquarters of Kamrasi, King of Unyoro, the most northerly of the important African sovereigns of the Lake regions, who had just given Speke and Grant a difficult time. He took advantage of their helpless condition—they had now only thirteen porters left—to extort from Baker almost everything he possessed, while Baker desperately tried to obtain his permission and help to discover the great unknown western lake. Kamrasi at length agreed to provide a guide and porters for this expedition.

27. DISCOVERY OF LAKE ALBERT

The day of starting at length arrived; the chief and guide appeared, and we were led to the Kafoor river, where canoes were in readiness to transport us to the south side. This was to our old quarters on the marsh, The direct course to the lake was west and I fully expected some deception, as it was impossible to trust Kamrasi. I complained to the guide. and insisted upon his pointing out the direction of the lake, which he did, in its real position, west; but he explained that we must follow the south bank of the Kafoor river for some days, as there was an impassable morass that precluded a direct course. This did not appear satisfactory, and the whole affair looked suspicious, as we had formerly been deceived by being led across the river in the same spot, and not allowed to return. We were now led along the banks of the Kafoor for about a mile, until we arrived at a cluster of huts: here we were to wait for Kamrasi, who had promised to take leave of us. The sun was overpowering and we dismounted from our oxen, and took shelter in a blacksmith's shed. In about an hour Kamrasi arrived, attended by a considerable number of men, and took his seat in our shed. I felt convinced that his visit was simply intended to peel the last skin from the onion. I had already given him nearly all that I had, but he hoped to extract the whole before I should depart.

He almost immediately commenced the conversation by asking for a pretty yellow muslin Turkish handkerchief fringed with silver drops that Mrs. Baker wore upon her head: one of these had already been given to him, and I explained that this was the last remaining, and that she required it. He 'must' have it. It was given. He then demanded other handkerchiefs. We had literally nothing but a few most ragged towels; he would accept no excuse, and insisted upon a portmanteau being unpacked, that he might satisfy himself by actual inspection. The luggage, all ready for the journey, had to be unstrapped and examined, and the rags were displayed in succession; but so wretched and uninviting was the exhibition of the family linen, that he simply returned them, and said 'they did not suit him.' Beads he must have or I was 'his enemy.' A selection of the best opal beads was immediately given him. I rose from the stone upon which I was sitting, and declared that we must start immediately. 'Don't be in a hurry,' he replied, 'you have plenty of time; but you have not given me that watch you promised me.' This was my only watch that he had begged for, and had been refused every day during my stay at M'rooli. So pertinacious a beggar I had never seen. I explained to him that, without the watch, my journey would be useless, but that I would give him all that I had except the watch when the exploration should be completed, as I should require nothing on my direct return to Gondokoro. At the same time, I repeated to him the arrangement for the journey that he had promised, begging him not to deceive me, as my wife and I should both die if we were compelled to remain another year in this country by losing the annual boats in Gondokoro. The understanding was this: he was to give me porters to the lake, where I was to be furnished with canoes to take me to Magungo, which was situated at the junction of the Somerset. From Magungo he told me that I should see the Nile issuing from the lake close to the spot where the Somerset entered, and that the canoes should take me down the river, and porters should carry my effects from the nearest point to Shooa and deliver me at my old station without delay. Should he be faithful to this engagement, I trusted to procure porters from Shooa, and to reach Gondokoro in time for the annual boats. I had arranged that a boat should be sent from Khartoum to await me at Gondokoro early in this year, 1864; but I felt sure that should I be long delayed, the boat would return without me, as the people would be afraid to remain alone at Gondokoro after the other boats had quitted.

In our present weak state another year of Central Africa without quinine appeared to warrant death; it was a race against time, all was untrodden ground before us, and the distance quite uncertain. I trembled for my wife, and weighed the risk of another year in this horrible country should we lose the boats. With the self-sacrificing devotion that she had shown in every trial, she implored me not to think of any risks on her account, but to push forward and discover the lake—that she had determined not to return until she herself reached the 'M'wootan N'zige.'

I now requested Kamrasi to allow us to take leave, as we had not an hour to lose. In the coolest manner he replied, 'I will send you to the lake and to Shooa, as I have promised; but, *you must leave your wife with me!*'

At that moment we were surrounded by a great number of natives, and my suspicions of treachery at having been led across the Kafoor river appeared confirmed by this insolent demand. If this were to be the end of the expedition I resolved that it should also be the end of Kamrasi, and, drawing my revolver quietly, I held it within two feet of his chest, and looking at him with undisguised contempt, I told him that if I touched the trigger, not all his men could save him: and that if he dared to repeat the insult I would shoot him on the spot. At the same time I explained to him that in my country such insolence would entail bloodshed, and that I looked upon him as an ignorant ox who knew no better, and that this excuse alone could save him. My wife, naturally indignant, had risen from her seat, and, maddened with the excitement of the moment, she made him a little speech in Arabic (not a word of which he understood), with a countenance almost as amiable as the head of Medusa. Altogether the *mise en scène* utterly astonished him; the woman Bacheeta, although savage, had appropriated the insult to her mistress, and she also fearlessly let fly at Kamrasi, translating as nearly as she could the complimentary address that 'Medusa' had just delivered.

Whether this little *coup de théâtre* had so impressed Kamrasi with British female independence that he wished to be off his bargain, I cannot say, but with an air of complete astonishment, he said, 'Don't be angry! I had no intention of offending you by asking for your wife; I will give you a wife, if you want one, and I thought you might have no objection to give me yours; it is my custom to give visitors pretty wives, and I thought you might exchange. Don't make a fuss about it; if you don't like it, there's an end of it; I will never mention it again.' This very practical apology I received very sternly, and merely insisted upon starting. He seemed rather confused at having committed himself, and to make amends he called his people and ordered them to carry our loads. His men ordered a number of women, who had assembled out of curiosity, to shoulder the luggage and carry it to the next village, where they would be relieved. I assisted my wife upon her ox, and with a very cold adieu to Kamrasi, I turned my back most gladly on M'rooli.

The country was a vast flat of grass land interspersed with small villages and patches of sweet potatoes; these were very inferior, owing to the want of drainage. For about two miles we continued on the banks of the Kafoor river; the women who carried the luggage were straggling in disorder, and my few men were much scattered in their endeavours to collect them. We approached a considerable village, but just as we were nearing it, out rushed about six hundred men with lances and shields, screaming and yelling like so many demons. For the moment, I thought it was an attack, but almost immediately I noticed that women and children were mingled with the men. My men had not taken so cool a view of the excited throng that was now approaching us at full speed, brandishing their spears and engaging with each other in mock combat. 'There's a fight!—there's a fight!' my men exclaimed; 'we are attacked! fire at them, Hawaga.' However, in a few seconds I persuaded them that it was a mere parade, and that there was no danger. With a rush, like a cloud of locusts, the natives closed around us, dancing, gesticulating, and yelling before my ox, feigning to attack us with spears and shields, then engaging in sham fights with each other, and behaving like so many madmen. A very tall chief accompanied them; and one of their men was suddenly knocked down, and attacked by the crowd with sticks and lances, and lay on the ground covered with blood: what his offence had been I did not hear. The entire crowd were most grotesquely got up, being dressed in either leopard or white monkey skins, with cows' tails strapped on behind, and antelopes' horns fitted upon their heads, while their chins were ornamented with false beards, made of the bushy ends of cows' tails sewed together. Altogether, I never saw a more unearthly set of creatures; they were perfect illustrations of my childish ideas of devils—horns, tails, and all, excepting the hoofs; they were our escort! furnished by Kamrasi to accompany us to the lake. Fortunately for all parties the Turks were not with us on that occasion, or the satanic escort would certainly have been received with a volley when they so rashly advanced to compliment us by their absurd performances.

We marched till 7 P.M. over flat, uninteresting country, and then halted at a miserable village which the people had deserted, as they expected our arrival. The following morning I found much difficulty in getting our escort together, as they had been foraging throughout the neighbourhood; these 'devil's own' were a portion of Kamrasi's troops, who considered themselves entitled to plunder *ad libitum* throughout the march; however, after some delay, they collected, and their tall chief approached me, and begged that a gun might be fired as a curiosity. The escort had crowded around us, and as the boy Saat was close to me, I ordered him to fire his gun. This was Saat's greatest delight, and bang went one barrel unexpectedly, close to the tall chief's ear. The effect was charming. The tall chief, thinking himself injured, clasped his head with both hands, and bolted through the crowd, which, struck with a sudden panic, rushed away in all directions, the 'devil's own' tumbling over each other, and utterly scattered by the second barrel which Saat exultantly fired in derision as Kamrasi's warlike regiment dissolved before a sound. I felt quite sure, that in the event of a fight, one scream from the 'baby,' with its charge of forty small bullets, would win the battle, if well delivered into a crowd of Kamrasi's troops.

That afternoon, after a march through a most beautiful forest of large mimosas in full blossom, we arrived at the morass that had necessitated this great *détour* from our direct course to the lake. It was nearly three-quarters of a mile broad, and so deep, that in many places the oxen were obliged to swim; both Mrs. Baker and I were carried across on our angareps [wicker bed-steads] by twelve men with the greatest difficulty; the guide, who waded before us to show the way, suddenly disappeared in a deep hole, and his bundle that he had carried on his head, being of light substance, was seen floating like a buoy upon the surface; after a thorough sousing, the guide reappeared, and scrambled out, and we made a circuit, the men toiling frequently up to their necks through mud and water. On arrival at the opposite side we continued through the same beautiful forest, and slept that night at a deserted village, M'Baze.

I obtained two observations; one of Capella, giving lat. 1° 24′ 47″ N., and of Canopus 1° 23′ 29″.

The next day we were much annoyed by our native escort; instead of attending to us, they employed their time capering and dancing about, screaming and gesticulating, and suddenly rushing off in advance whenever we approached a village, which they plundered before we could arrive. In this manner every place was stripped; nor could we procure anything to eat unless by purchasing it for beads from the native escort. We slept at Karche lat. 1° 19′ 31″ N.

We were both ill, but were obliged to ride through the hottest hours of the sun, as our followers were never ready to start at an early hour in the morning. The native escort were perfectly independent, and so utterly wild and savage in their manner, that they appeared more dangerous than the general inhabitants of the country. My wife was extremely anxious, since the occasion of Kamrasi's 'proposal,' as she was suspicious that so large an escort as three hundred men had been given for some treacherous purpose, and that I should perhaps be waylaid to enable them to steal her for the king. I had not the slightest fear of such an occurrence, as sentries were always on guard during the night, and I was well prepared during the day.

On the following morning we had the usual difficulty in collecting porters, those of the preceding day having absconded, and others were recruited from distant villages by the native escort, who enjoyed the excuse of hunting for porters, as it gave them an opportunity of foraging throughout the neighbourhood. During this time we had to wait until the sun was high; we thus lost the cool hours of morning and it increased our fatigue. Having at length started, we arrived in the afternoon at the Kafoor river, at a bend from the south where it was necessary to cross over in our westerly course. The stream was in the centre of a marsh, and although deep, it was so covered with thickly-matted water-grass and other aquatic plants, that a natural floating bridge was established by a carpet of weeds about two feet thick: upon this waving and unsteady surface the men ran quickly across, sinking merely to the ankles, although beneath the tough vegetation there was deep water. It was equally impossible to ride or to be carried over this treacherous surface; thus I led the way, and begged Mrs. Baker to follow me on foot as quickly as possible, precisely in my track. The river was about eighty yards wide, and I had scarcely completed a fourth of the distance and looked back to see if my wife followed close to me when I was horrified to see her standing in one spot, and sinking gradually through the weeds, while her face was distorted and perfectly purple. Almost as soon as I perceived her, she fell, as though shot dead. In an instant I was by her side; and with the assistance of eight or ten of my men, who were fortunately close to me, I dragged her like a corpse through the yielding vegetations, and up to our waists we scrambled across to the other side, just keeping her head above the water: to have carried her would have been impossible, as we should all have sunk together through the weeds. I laid her under a tree and bathed her head and face with water, as for the moment I thought she had fainted; but she lay perfectly insensible, as though dead, with teeth and hands firmly clenched and her eyes open, but fixed. It was a *coup de soleil.*

Many of the porters had gone on ahead with the baggage; and I started off a man in haste to recall an angarep upon which to carry her, and also for a bag with a change of clothes, as we had dragged her through the river. It was in vain that I rubbed her heart, and the black women rubbed her feet, to endeavour to restore animation. At length the litter came, and after changing her clothes, she was carried mournfully forward as a corpse. Constantly we had to halt and support her head as a painful rattling in the throat betokened suffocation. At length we reached a village and halted for the night.

I laid her carefully in a miserable hut, and watched beside her. I opened her clenched teeth with a small wooden wedge, and inserted a wet rag, upon which I dropped water to moisten her tongue, which was dry as fur. The unfeeling brutes that composed the native escort were yelling and dancing as though all were well, and I ordered their chief at once to return with them to Kamrasi, as I would travel with them no longer. At first they refused to return; until at length I vowed that I would fire into them should they accompany us on the following morning. Day broke, and it was a relief to have got rid of the brutal escort. They had departed, and I had now my own men, and the guides supplied by Kamrasi.

There was nothing to eat in this spot. My wife had never stirred since she fell by the *coup de soleil,* and merely respired about five times in a minute. It was impossible to remain; the people would have starved. She was laid gently upon her litter, and we started forward on our funeral course. I was ill and broken-hearted, and I followed by her side, through the long day's march over wild park-lands and streams, with thick forest and deep marshy bottoms; over undulating hills, and through valleys of tall papyrus rushes, which, as we brushed through them on our melancholy way, waved over the litter like the black plumes of a hearse. We halted at a village, and again the night was passed in watching. I was wet and coated with mud from the swampy marsh, and shivered with ague; but the cold within was greater than all. No change had taken place; she had never moved. I had plenty of fat, and I made four balls of about half a pound, each of which would burn for three hours. A piece of a broken water-jar formed a lamp, several pieces of rag serving for wicks. So in solitude the still calm night passed away as I sat by her side and watched. In the drawn and distorted features that lay before me I could hardly trace the same face that for years had been my comfort through all the difficulties and dangers of my path. Was she to die? Was so terrible a sacrifice to be the result of my selfish exile?

Again the night passed away. Once more the march. Though weak and ill, and for two nights without a moment's sleep, I felt no fatigue, but mechanically followed by the side of the litter as though in a dream. The same wild country diversified with marsh and forest. Again we halted. The night came, and I sat by her side in a miserable hut, with the feeble lamp flickering while she lay as in death. She had never moved a muscle since she fell. My people slept. I was alone, and no sound broke the stillness of the night. The ears ached at the utter silence, till the sudden wild cry of a hyena made me shudder as the horrible thought rushed through my brain, that, should she be buried in this lonely spot, the hyena would . . . disturb her rest.

The morning was not far distant; it was past four o'clock. I had passed the night in replacing wet cloths upon her head and moistening her lips, as she lay apparently lifeless on her litter. I could do nothing more; in solitude and abject misery in that dark hour, in a country of savage heathens, thousands of miles away from a Christian land, I beseeched an aid above all human, trusting alone to Him.

The morning broke; my lamp had just burned out, and cramped with the night's watching, I rose from my low seat, and seeing that she lay in the same unaltered state, I went to the door of the hut to breathe one gasp of the fresh morning air. I was watching the first red streak that heralded the rising sun, when I was startled by the words 'Thank God' faintly uttered behind me. Suddenly she had awoke from her torpor and with a heart overflowing I went to her bedside. Her eyes were full of madness! She spoke; but the brain was gone!

I will not inflict a description of the terrible trial of seven days of brain fever, with its attendant horrors. The rain poured in torrents, and day after day we were forced to travel, for want of provisions, not being able to remain in one position. Every now and then we shot a few guinea-fowl, but rarely; there was no game, although the country was most favourable. In the forest we procured wild honey, but the deserted villages contained no supplies, as we were on the frontier of Uganda, and M'tesa's people had plundered the district. For seven nights I had not slept, and although as weak as a reed, I had marched by the side of her litter. Nature could resist no longer. We reached a village one evening; she had been in violent convulsions successively—it was all but over. I laid her down on her litter within a hut; covered her with a Scotch plaid; and I fell upon my mat insensible, worn out with sorrow and fatigue. My men put a new handle to the pickaxe that evening, and sought for a dry spot to dig her grave!

The sun had risen when I woke. I had slept, and, horrified as the idea flashed upon me that she must be dead, and that I had not been with her, I started up. She lay upon her bed, pale as marble, and with that calm serenity that the features assume when the cares of life no longer act upon the mind, and the body rests in death. The dreadful thought bowed me down; but as I gazed upon her in fear, her chest gently heaved, not with the conclusive throbs of fever, but naturally. She was asleep; and when at a sudden noise she opened her eyes, they were calm and clear. She was saved! When not a ray of hope remained, God alone knows what helped us. The gratitude of that moment I will not attempt to describe.

Fortunately there were many fowls in this village; we found several nests of fresh eggs in the straw which littered the hut; these were most acceptable after our hard fare, and produced a good supply of soup.

Having rested for two days, we again moved forward, Mrs. Baker being carried on a litter. We now continued on elevated ground on the north side of a valley running from west to east, about sixteen miles broad, and exceedingly swampy. The rocks composing the ridge upon which we travelled due west were all gneiss and quartz, with occasional breaks, forming narrow valleys, all of which were swamps choked with immense papyrus rushes, that made the march very fatiguing. In one of these muddy bottoms one of my riding oxen that was ill stuck fast, and we were obliged to abandon it, intending to send a number of natives to drag it out with ropes. On arrival at a village our guide started about fifty men for this purpose, while we continued our journey.

That evening we reached a village belonging to a headman and very superior to most that we had passed on the route from M'rooli: large sugar-canes of the blue variety were growing in the fields, and I had seen coffee growing wild in the forest in the vicinity. I was sitting at the door of the hut about two hours after sunset, smoking a pipe of excellent tobacco, when I suddenly heard a great singing in chorus advancing rapidly from a distance towards the entrance of the courtyard. At first I imagined that the natives intended dancing, which was an infliction that I wished to avoid, as I was tired and feverish; but in a few minutes the boy Saat introduced a headman, who told me that the riding ox had died in the swamp where he had stuck fast in the morning and that the natives had brought his body to me. 'What!' I replied, 'brought his body, the entire ox, to me?' 'The entire ox as he died is delivered at your door,' answered the headman. 'I could not allow any of your property to be lost upon the road. Had the body of the ox not been delivered to you, we might have been suspected of having stolen it.' I went to the entrance of the courtyard and amidst a crowd of natives I found the entire ox exactly as he had died. They had carried him about eight miles on a litter, which they had constructed of two immensely long posts with cross-pieces of bamboo, upon which they had laid the body. They would not eat the flesh, and seemed quite disgusted at the idea, as they replied that 'it had died.'

It is a curious distinction of the Unyoro people, that they are peculiarly clean feeders, and will not touch either the flesh of animals that have died, neither of those that are sick; nor will they eat the crocodile. They asked for no remuneration for bringing their heavy load so great a distance; and they departed in good humour as a matter of course.

Never were such contradictory people as these creatures; they had troubled us dreadfully during the journey, as they would suddenly exclaim against the weight of their loads, and throw them down, and bolt into the high grass; yet now they had of their own free will delivered to me a whole dead ox from a distance of eight miles, precisely as though it had been an object of the greatest value.

The name of this village was Parkani. For several days past our guides had told us that we were very near to the lake, and we were now assured that we should reach it on the morrow. I had noticed a lofty range of mountains at an immense distance west, and I had imagined that the lake lay on the other side of this chain; but I was now informed that those mountains formed the western frontier of the M'wootan N'zige, and that the lake was actual y within a march of Parkani. I could not believe it possible that we were so near the object of our search. The guide Rabonga now appeared, and declared that if we started early on the following morning we should be able to wash in the lake by noon!

That night I hardly slept. For years I had striven to reach the 'sources of the Nile.' In my nightly dreams during the arduous voyage I had always failed, but after so much hard work and perseverance the cup was at my very lips, and I was to *drink* at the mysterious fountain before another sun could set—at the great reservoir of Nature that ever since creation had baffled all discovery.

I had hoped, and prayed, and striven through all kinds of difficulties, in sickness, starvation, and fatigue to reach that hidden source; and when it had appeared impossible we had both determined to die upon the road rather than return defeated. Was it possible that it was so near, and that to-morrow we could say, 'the work is accomplished?'

[14 March.] The sun had not risen when I was spurring my ox after the guide, who, having been promised a double handful of beads on arrival at the lake, had caught the enthusiasm of the moment. The day broke beautifully clear, and having crossed a deep valley between the hills, we toiled up the opposite slope. I hurried to the summit The glory of our prize burst suddenly upon me! There, like a sea of quicksilver, lay far beneath the grand expanse of water—a boundless sea horizon on the south and south-west glittering in the noon-day sun; and on the west, at fifty or sixty miles' distance, blue mountains rose from the bosom of the lake to a height of about 7,000 feet above its level.

It is impossible to describe the triumph of that moment;—here was the reward for all our labour—for the years of tenacity with which we had toiled through Africa. England had won the sources of the Nile! Long before I reached this spot, I had arranged to give three cheers with all our men in English style in honour of the discovery, but now that I looked down upon the great inland sea lying nestled in the very heart of Africa, and thought how vainly mankind had sought these sources throughout so many ages, and reflected that I had been the humble instrument permitted to unravel this portion of the great mystery when so many greater than I had failed, I felt too serious to vent my feelings in vain cheers for victory, and I sincerely thanked God for having guided and supported us through all dangers to the good end. I was about 1,500 feet above the lake, and I looked down from the steep granite cliff upon those welcome waters—upon that vast reservoir which nourished Egypt and brought fertility where all was wilderness—upon that great source so long hidden from mankind; that source of bounty and of blessings to millions of human beings; and as one of the greatest objects in nature, I determined to honour it with a great name. As an imperishable memorial of one loved and mourned by our gracious Queen and deplored by every Englishman, I called this great lake 'the Albert N'yanza.' The Victoria and the Albert lakes are the two sources of the Nile.

The Albert N'Yanza, 1st Edition, vol. II, pp. 74–96

Baker and his wife, after further dangers and privations, returned safely from this expedition. The traveller obtained full recognition and a knighthood for his discovery. He returned to the same scene in 1869, but this time with a well-equipped military expedition and holding from the Khedive of Egypt the appointment of Governor-General of the basin of the Nile. He was charged to extend the frontiers of the Egyptian Empire and to suppress the slave-trade. The brave Lady Baker again accompanied him. He met with serious difficulties and had to fight against the slave-traders, the tribes they raised against him and also against the son of Kamrasi, Kabarega, whose kingdom he nominally annexed to Egypt in 1872. In 1873 he left Equatoria. The account of this expedition is contained in another lively book, Ismailïa. *His appointment was the precedent for that of a still more distinguished foreigner, General Gordon. After a full, vigorous and successful life, he died in 1893.*

IX
DAVID LIVINGSTONE and SIR HENRY MORTON STANLEY
1841–1904

At the beginning of 1865 Livingstone received a letter from his old friend Sir Roderick Murchison, the President of the Royal Geographical Society, suggesting that he should return to Africa to solve 'a question of intense geographical interest... namely the watershed or watersheds of South Africa', and that he should make his way up to the Nile basin by way of the River Rovuma and the Great Lakes. To this proposal Livingstone agreed, while declining to go out solely as an explorer. 'What my inclination leads me to prefer', he characteristically replied, 'is to have intercourse with the people, and do what I can by talking to enlighten them on the slave-trade, and give them some idea of our religion. . . . I shall enjoy myself, and feel that I am doing my duty.' In this spirit he left England for the last time in August 1865.

Travelling out by way of India, he reached Zanzibar at the end of the following January: on 4th April 1866 he began his march inland from Mikindani Bay. On this journey he took no Europeans with him. Of his African companions, three, Chumah, Susi and Wikatani, had been rescued from slavery during the Zambesi expedition. He passed round the south end of Lake Nyasa, and then struck out north-north-west, crossing the Loangwa and making for Lake Tanganyika. Shortly before reaching the Chambezi, on 20th January 1867, there occurred the first and greatest of his disasters: one of his porters deserted with a load containing his medicine-chest. He was in a marshy and fever-laden country, in the wet season, entirely without medical supplies. 'I felt as if I had now received the sentence of death,' he wrote in his journal; and he was probably right.

On 1st April he sighted Lake Tanganyika. Delayed by much illness and by a war in the country of Itawa, he went on slowly to the north-

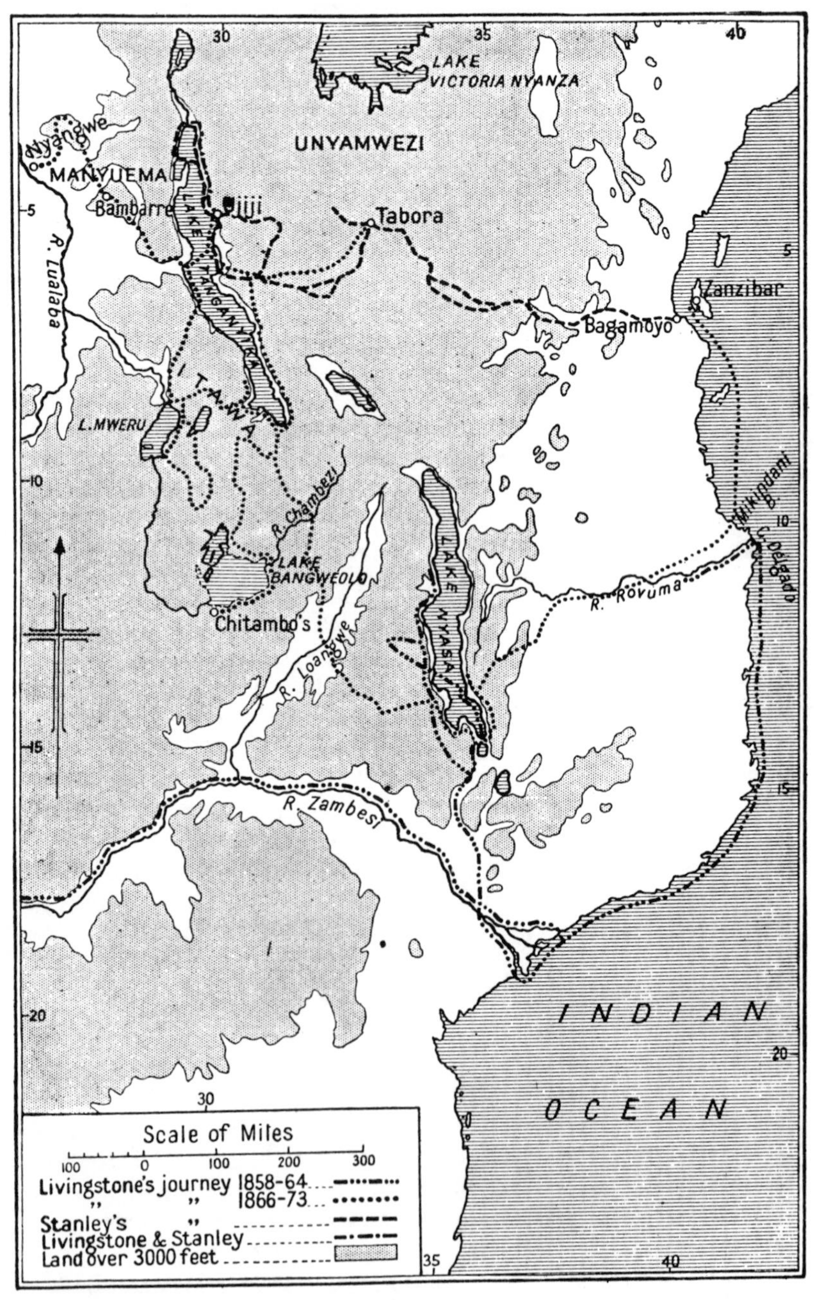

10. The Travels of Livingstone and Stanley, 1866–73

west, discovering Lake Mweru on 8th November: from here he turned south and reached Lake Bangweolo (which he was also the first European to see) on 18th July 1868. He then decided to go across to Ujiji, hoping to find there stores (above all, medicines), which he had previously ordered. But when he arrived there, on 14th March 1869, he discovered that nearly everything had been stolen.

Four months later he recrossed the lake and made for Manyuema, a country into which the slave-traders were just beginning to feel their way: he continually saw scenes such as that depicted in the illustration opposite page 234. Here he spent two years and a quarter: his main object during this time was to find the River Lualaba, which took him more than eighteen months, for he was weakened by disease and largely dependent on the whims of the Arab slavers, with whom he was often obliged to travel. He records that he read through the whole Bible four times while he was in Manyuema. To his intense disappointment, he received no answer to his repeated requests for assistance from Zanzibar. When, in February 1871, ten men did reach him, it soon appeared that they had not come to help but to hinder him by their mutinous conduct and intrigues with the Arabs. (They had in reality been sent by the Indian, or Banian, slave-dealers, who were afraid of the disclosures which he might make about their trade.) In the following month he at length reached the Lualaba at Nyangwe. Here, while he was waiting for canoes to take him down the river, he gained further experience of the slave trade.

28. MANYUEMA MASSACRE

24*th May*.—The market is a busy scene—everyone is in dead earnest—little time is lost in friendly greetings; vendors of fish run about with potsherds full of snails or small fishes or young *Clarias capensis* smoke-dried and spitted on twigs, or other relishes to exchange for cassava roots dried after being steeped about three days in water—potatoes, vegetables, or grain, bananas, flour, palm-oil, fowls, salt, pepper; each is intensely eager to barter food for relishes, and makes strong assertions as to the goodness or badness of everything: the sweat stands in beads on their faces—cocks crow briskly, even when slung over the shoulder with their heads hanging down, and pigs squeal. Iron knobs, drawn out at each end to show the goodness of the metal, are exchanged for cloth of the Muabe palm. They have a large funnel of basketwork below the vessel holding the wares, and slip the goods down if they are not to be seen. They deal fairly, and when differences arise they are easily settled by the men interfering or pointing to me; they appeal to each other, and have a strong sense of natural justice. With so much food changing hands amongst the three thousand attendants much benefit is derived; some come from twenty to twenty-five miles. The men flaunt about in gaudy-coloured lambas of many folded kilts—the women work hardest —the potters slap and ring their earthenware all round, to show that there is not a single flaw in them. I bought two finely shaped earthen bottles of porous earthenware, to hold a gallon each, for one string of beads, the women carry huge loads of them in their funnels above the baskets, strapped to the shoulders and forehead, and their hands are full besides; the roundness of the vessels is wonderful, seeing no machine is used: no slaves could be induced to carry half as much as they do willingly. It is a scene of the finest natural acting imaginable. The eagerness with which all sorts of assertions are made—the eager earnestness with which apparently all creation, above, around, and beneath, is called on to attest the truth of what they allege—and then the intense surprise and withering scorn cast on those who despise their goods: but they show no concern when the buyers turn up their noses at them. Little girls run about selling cups of water for a few small fishes to the half-exhausted wordy combatants. To me it was an amusing scene. I could not understand the words that flowed off their glib tongues, but the gestures were too expressive to need interpretation.

27th May.—Hassani told me that since he had come, no Manyuema had ever presented him with a single mouthful of food, not even a potato or banana, and he had made many presents. Going from him into the market I noticed that one man presented a few small fishes, another a sweet potato and a piece of cassava, and a third two small fishes, but the Manyuema are not a liberal people. Old men and women who remained in the half-deserted villages we passed through in coming north, often ran forth to present me with bananas, but it seemed through fear; when I sat down and ate the bananas they brought beer of bananas, and I paid for all. A stranger in the market had ten human under jaw-bones hung by a string over his shoulder: on inquiry he professed to have killed and eaten the owners, and showed with his knife how he cut up his victim. When I expressed disgust he and others laughed. I see new faces every market-day. Two nice girls were trying to sell their venture, which was roasted white ants, called 'Gumbe.'

30*th May.*—The river fell four inches during the last four days; the colour is very dark brown, and large quantities of aquatic plants and trees float down. Mologhwe, or chief Ndambo, came and mixed blood with the intensely bigoted Moslem Hassani [a slave-trader]: this is to secure the nine canoes. He next went over to have more palaver about them, and they do not hesitate to play me false by detraction. The Manyuema, too, are untruthful, but very honest; we never lose an article by them: fowls and goats are untouched, and if a fowl is lost, we know that it has been stolen by an Arab slave. When with Mohamad Bogharib [an Arab slave-trader], we had all to keep our fowls at the Manyuema villages to prevent them being stolen by our own slaves, and it is so here. Hassani denies complicity with them, but it is quite apparent that he and others encourage them in mutiny.

5th June, 1871.—The river rose again six inches and fell three. Rain nearly ceased, and large masses of fleecy clouds float down here from the north-west, with accompanying cold.

7th June.—I fear that I must march on foot, but the mud is forbidding.

11th June.—New moon last night, and I believe Dugumbe [another slave-trader] will leave Kasonga's to-day. River down three inches.

14th June.—Hassani got nine canoes, and put sixty-three persons in three: I cannot get one. Dugumbe reported near, but detained by his divination, at which he is an expert; hence his native name is 'Molembalemba'—'writer, writing.'

16th June.—The high winds and drying of soap and sugar tell that the rains are now over in this part.

18th June.—Dugumbe arrived, but passed to Moene Nyangwe's, and found that provisions were so scarce and dear there, as compared with our market, that he was fain to come back to us. He has a large party and 500 guns. He is determined to go into new fields of trade, and has all his family with him, and intends to remain six or seven years, sending regularly to Ujiji for supplies of goods.

20th June.—Two of Dugumbe's party brought presents of four large fundos of beads each. All know that my goods are unrighteously detained by Shereef and they show me kindness, which I return by some fine calico which I have. Among the first words Dugumbe said to me were, 'Why, your own slaves are your greatest enemies: I will buy you a canoe, but the Banian slaves' slanders have put all the Manyuema against you.' I knew that this was true, and that they were conscious of the sympathy of the Ujijian traders, who hate to have me here.

24th June.—Hassani's canoe party in the river were foiled by narrows, after they had gone down four days. Rocks jut out on both sides, not opposite, but alternate to each other; and the vast mass of water of the great river jammed in, rushes round one promontory on to another, and a frightful whirlpool is formed in which the first canoe went and was overturned, and five lives lost. Had I been there, mine would have been the first canoe, for the traders would have made it a point of honour to give me the precedence (although actually to make a feeler of me), while they looked on in safety. The men in charge of Hassani's canoes were so frightened by this accident that they at once resolved to return, though they had arrived in the country of the ivory: they never looked to see whether the canoes could be dragged past the narrows, as anyone else would have done. No better luck could be expected after all their fraud and duplicity in getting the canoes; no harm lay in obtaining them, but why try to prevent me getting one?

27th June.—In answer to my prayers for preservation, I was prevented going down to the narrows, formed by a dyke of mountains cutting across country, and jutting a little ajar, which makes the water in an enormous mass wheel round behind it helplessly, and if the canoes reach the rock against which the water dashes, they are almost certainly overturned. As this same dyke probably cuts across country to Lomame, my plan of going to the confluence and then up won't do, for I should have to go up rapids again. Again, I was prevented from going down Luamo, and on the north of its confluence another cataract mars navigation in the Lualaba, and my safety is thereby secured. We don't always know the dangers that we are guided past.

28th June.—The river has fallen two feet: dark brown water, and still much wreck floating down.

Eight villages are in flames, set afire to by a slave of Syde bin Habib [a slave-trader], called Manilla, who thus shows his blood friends of the Bagenya how well he can fight against the Mohombo, whose country the Bagenya want! The stragglers of this camp are over on the other side helping Manilla, and catching fugitives and goats. The Bagenya are fishermen by taste and profession, and sell the produce of their nets and weirs to those who cultivate the soil, at the different markets. Manilla's foray is for an alleged debt of three slaves, and ten villages are burned. . . .

7th July.—I was annoyed by a woman frequently beating a slave near my house, but on my reproving her she came and apologized. I told her to speak softly to her slave, as she was now the only mother the girl had; the slave came from beyond Lomame, and was evidently a lady in her own land: she calls her son Mologwe, or chief, because his father was a headman.

Dugumbe advised my explaining my plan of procedure to the slaves, and he evidently thinks that I wish to carry it towards them with a high hand. I did explain all the exploration I intended to do: for instance, the fountains of Herodotus—beyond Katanga—Katanga itself, and the underground dwellings, and then return. They made no remarks, for they are evidently pleased to have me knuckling down to them; when pressed on the point of proceeding, they say they will only go with Dugumbe's men to the Lomame, and then return. River fallen three inches since the 5th.

10th July.—Manyuema children do not creep, as European children do, on their knees, but begin by putting forward one foot and using one knee. Generally a Manyuema child uses both feet and both hands, but never both knees: one Arab child did the same; he never crept, but got up on both feet, holding on till he could walk.

New moon last night of seventh Arab month.

11*th July.*—I bought the different species of fish brought to market, in order to sketch eight of them, and compare them with those of the Nile lower down: most are the same as in Nyassa. A very active species of Glanis, of dark olive-brown, was not sketched, but a spotted one, armed with offensive spikes in the dorsal and pectoral fins, was taken. Sesamum seed is abundant just now and cakes are made of ground-nuts, as on the West Coast. Dugumbe's horde tried to deal in the market in a domineering way. 'I shall buy that,' said one. 'These are mine,' said another; 'no one must touch them but me,' but the market-women taught them that they could not monopolize, but deal fairly. They are certainly clever traders, and keep each other in countenance, they stand by each other, and will not allow overreaching, and they give food astonishingly cheap: once in the market they have no fear.

12*th and* 13*th July.*—The Banian slaves declared before Dugumbe that they would go to the River Lomame, but no further: he spoke long to them, but they will not consent to go further. When told that they would thereby lose all their pay, they replied, 'Yes, but not our lives,' and they walked off from him muttering, which is insulting to one of his rank. I then added, 'I have goods at Ujiji; I don't know how many, but they are considerable, take them all, and give me men to finish my work; if not enough, I will add to them, only do not let me be forced to return now I am so near the end of my undertaking.' He said he would make a plan in conjunction with his associates, and report to me.

14*th July.*—I am distressed and perplexed what to do so as not to be foiled, but all seems against me.

15*th July.*—The reports of guns on the other side of the Lualaba all the morning tell of the people of Dugumbe murdering those of Kimburu and others who mixed blood with Manilla. 'Manilla is a slave, and how dares he to mix blood with chiefs who ought only to make friends with free men like us'—this is their complaint. Kimburu gave Manilla three slaves, and he sacked ten villages in token of friendship; he proposed to give Dugumbe nine slaves in the same operation, but Dugumbe's people destroy his villages, and shoot and make his people captives to punish Manilla; to make an impression, in fact, in the country that they alone are to be dealt with—'make friends with us, and not with Manilla or anyone else'—such is what they insist upon.

About 1500 people came to market, though many villages of those that usually come from the other side were now in flames, and every now and then a number of shots were fired on the fugitives.

It was a hot, sultry day, and when I went into the market I saw Adie and Manilla, and three of the men who had lately come with Dugumbe.

I was surprised to see these three with their guns, and felt inclined to reprove them, as one of my men did, for bringing weapons into the market, but I attributed it to their ignorance, and, it being very hot, I was walking away to go out of the market, when I saw one of the fellows haggling about a fowl, and seizing hold of it. Before I had got thirty yards out, the discharge of two guns in the middle of the crowd told me that slaughter had begun: crowds dashed off from the place, and threw down their wares in confusion, and ran. At the same time that the three opened fire on the mass of people near the upper end of the market-place volleys were discharged from a party down near the creek on the panic-stricken women, who dashed at the canoes. These, some fifty or more, were jammed in the creek, and the men forgot their paddles in the terror that seized all. The canoes were not to be got out, for the creek was too small for so many; men and women, wounded by the balls, poured into them, and leaped and scrambled into the water, shrieking. A long line of heads in the river showed that great numbers struck out for an island a full mile off: in going towards it they had to put the left shoulder to a current of about two miles an hour; if they had struck away diagonally to the opposite bank, the current would have aided them, and, though nearly three miles off, some would have gained land: as it was, the heads above water showed the long line of those that would inevitably perish.

Shot after shot continued to be fired on the helpless and perishing. Some of the long line of heads disappeared quietly; whilst other poor creatures threw their arms high, as if appealing to the great Father above, and sank. One canoe took in as many as it could hold, and all paddled with hands and arms: three canoes, got out in haste, picked up sinking friends, till all went down together, and disappeared. One man in a long canoe, which could have held forty or fifty, had clearly lost his head; he had been out in the stream before the massacre began, and now paddled up the river nowhere, and never looked to the drowning. By-and-bye all the heads disappeared; some had turned down stream towards the bank, and escaped. Dugumbe put people into one of the deserted vessels to save those in the water, and saved twenty-one, but one woman refused to be taken on board from thinking that she was to be made a slave of; she preferred the chance of life by swimming, to the lot of a slave: the Bagenya women are expert in the water, as they are accustomed to dive for oysters, and those who went down stream may have escaped, but the Arabs themselves estimated the loss of life at between 330 and 400 souls. The shooting-party near the canoes were so reckless, they killed two of their own people; and a Banyamwezi follower, who got into a deserted canoe to plunder, fell into the water, went down, then came up again, and down to rise no more.

My first impulse was to pistol the murderers, but Dugumbe protested against my getting into a blood-feud, and I was thankful afterwards that

I took his advice. Two wretched Moslems asserted 'that the firing was done by the people of the English;' I asked one of them why he lied so, and he could utter no excuse; no other falsehood came to his aid as he stood abashed before me, and so telling him not to tell palpable falsehoods, I left him gaping.

After the terrible affair in the water, the party of Tagamoio, who was the chief perpetrator, continued to fire on the people there and fire their villages. As I write I hear the loud wails on the left bank over those who are there slain, ignorant of their many friends now in the depths of Lualaba. Oh, let Thy kingdom come! No one will ever know the exact loss on this bright sultry summer morning, it gave me the impression of being in Hell. All the slaves in the camp rushed at the fugitives on land, and plundered them: women were for hours collecting and carrying loads of what had been thrown down in terror.

Some escaped to me, and were protected: Dugumbe saved twenty-one, and of his own accord liberated them, they were brought to me, and remained over night near my house. One woman of the saved had a musket-ball through the thigh, another in the arm. I sent men with our flag to save some, for without a flag they might have been victims, for Tagamoio's people were shooting right and left like fiends. I counted twelve villages burning this morning. I asked the question of Dugumbe and others, 'Now for what is all this murder?' All blamed Manilla as its cause, and in one sense he was the cause; but it is hardly credible that they repeat it is in order to be avenged on Manilla for making friends with headmen, he being a slave. I cannot believe it fully. The wish to make an impression in the country as to the importance and greatness of the new comers was the most potent motive; but it was terrible that the murdering of so many should be contemplated at all. It made me sick at heart. Who could accompany the people of Dugumbe and Tagamoio to Lomame and be free from blood-guiltiness?

I proposed to Dugumbe to catch the murderers, and hang them up in the market-place, as our protest against the bloody deeds before the Manyuema. If, as he and others added, the massacre was committed by Manilla's people, he would have consented; but it was done by Tagamoio's people, and others of this party, headed by Dugumbe. This slaughter was peculiarly atrocious, inasmuch as we have always heard that women coming to or from market have never been known to be molested: even when two districts are engaged in actual hostilities, 'the women,' say they, 'pass among us to market unmolested,' nor has one ever been known to be plundered by the men. These Nigger Moslems are inferior to the Manyuema in justice and right. The people under Hassani began the superwickedness of capture and pillage of all indiscriminately. Dugumbe promised to send over men to order Tagamoio's men to cease firing and burning villages; they remained over among the ruins, feasting on goats and fowls all night, and next day (16th) continued their infamous work till twenty-seven villages were destroyed.

16*th July*.—I restored upwards of thirty of the rescued to their friends: Dugumbe seemed to act in good faith, and kept none of them; it was his own free will that guided him. Women are delivered to their husbands, and about thirty-three canoes left in the creek are to be kept for the owners too.

12 a.m.—Shooting still going on on the other side, and many captives caught. At 1 p.m. Tagamoio's people began to cross over in canoes, beating their drums, firing their guns, and shouting, as if to say, 'See the conquering heroes come;' they are answered by the women of Dugumbe's camp lullilooing, and friends then fire off their guns in joy. I count seventeen villages in flames, and the smoke goes straight up and forms clouds at the top of the pillar, showing great heat evolved, for the houses are full of carefully-prepared firewood. Dugumbe denies having sent Tagamoio on this foray, and Tagamoio repeats that he went to punish the friends made by Manilla, who, being a slave, had no right to make war and burn villages; that could only be done by free men. Manilla confesses to me privately that he did wrong in that, and loses all his beads and many friends in consequence.

2 p.m.—An old man, called Kabobo, came for his old wife; I asked her if this were her husband, she went to him, and put her arm lovingly around him, and said 'Yes.' I gave her five strings of beads to buy food, all her stores being destroyed with her house; she bowed down, and put her forehead to the ground as thanks, and old Kabobo did the same: the tears stood in her eyes as she went off. Tagamoio caught 17 women, and other Arabs of his party, 27; dead by gunshot, 25. The heads of two headmen were brought over to be redeemed by their friends with slaves.

3 p.m.—Many of the headmen who have been burned out by the foray came over to me, and begged me to come back with them, and appoint new localities for them to settle in again, but I told them that I was so ashamed of the company in which I found myself, that I could scarcely look the Manyuema in the face. They had believed that I wished to kill them—what did they think now? I could not remain among bloody companions, and would flee away, I said, but they begged me hard not to leave until they were again settled.

The open murder perpetrated on hundreds of unsuspecting women fills me with unspeakable horror: I cannot think of going anywhere with the Tagamoio crew; I must either go down or up Lualaba, whichever the Banian slaves choose.

4 p.m.—Dugumbe saw that by killing the market people he had committed a great error, and speedily got the chiefs who had come over to me to meet him at his house, and forthwith mix blood: they were in bad case. I could not remain to see to their protection, and Dugumbe being

the best of the whole horde, I advised them to make friends, and then appeal to him as able to restrain to some extent his infamous underlings. One chief asked to have his wife and daughter restored to him first, but generally they were cowed, and the fear of death was on them. Dugumbe said to me, 'I shall do my utmost to get all the captives, but he must make friends now, in order that the market may not be given up.' Blood was mixed, and an essential condition was, 'You must give us chitoka,' or market. He and most others saw that in theoretically punishing Manilla, they had slaughtered the very best friends that strangers had. The Banian slaves openly declare that they will go only to Lomame, and no further. Whatever the Ujijian slavers may pretend, they all hate to have me as a witness of their cold-blooded atrocities. The Banian slaves would like to go with Tagamoio, and share in his rapine and get slaves. I tried to go down Lualaba, then up it, and west, but with bloodhounds it is out of the question. I see nothing for it but to go back to Ujiji for other men, though it will throw me out of the chance of discovering the fourth great Lake in the Lualaba line of drainage, and other things of great value.

At last I said that I would start for Ujiji, in three days, on foot. I wished to speak to Tagamoio about the captive relations of the chiefs, but he always ran away when he saw me coming.

17*th July*.—All the rest of Dugumbe's party offered me a share of every kind of goods they had, and pressed me not to be ashamed to tell them what I needed. I declined everything save a little gunpowder, but they all made presents of beads, and I was glad to return equivalents in cloth. It is a sore affliction, at least forty-five days in a straight line—equal to 300 miles, or by the turnings and windings 600 English miles—and all after feeding and clothing the Banian slaves for twenty-one months! But it is for the best though; if I do not trust to the riffraff of Ujiji, I must wait for other men at least ten months there. With help from above I shall yet go through Rua, see the underground excavations first, then on to Katanga, and the four ancient fountains eight days beyond, and after that Lake Lincoln.

18*th July*.—The murderous assault on the market people felt to me like Gehenna, without the fire and brimstone; but the heat was oppressive, and the firearms pouring their iron bullets on the fugitives, was not an inapt representative of burning in the bottomless pit.

The terrible scenes of man's inhumanity to man brought on severe headache, which might have been serious had it not been relieved by a copious discharge of blood; I was laid up all yesterday afternoon, with the depression the bloodshed made,—it filled me with unspeakable horror. 'Don't go away,' say the Manyuema chiefs to me; but I cannot stay here in agony.

Last journals, vol. II, pp. 125–139

After this massacre, which deeply affected Livingstone in mind and health, he felt unable to bear any longer the company of the Arabs. His porters being quite out of hand, he set out with a few servants and carriers for Ujiji. On the way he was nearly killed in an ambush by a chief who mistook him for a slaver. His feet suffered terribly from the rocky track and he was in a sad and emaciated condition ('a mere ruckle of bones' in his own words) when he reached Ujiji. Here he found that the stores which had been sent up from the coast and upon which, after nearly six years' lonely wandering out of touch with civilization, he had been counting so much for food, medicine and clothing, had been plundered by the Arabs, in the hope that he was dead. He was thus in a state of destitution and weakness when he was found by H. M. Stanley, who must now be briefly introduced.

SIR HENRY MORTON STANLEY

1841–1904

Stanley was a Welshman, born at Denbigh: his real name was John Rowlands. He passed nine years of his childhood in the St. Asaph workhouse under a sadistic schoolmaster, from whose tyranny he ran away in 1856. Three years later he shipped as a cabin-boy for America: at New Orleans he was adopted by a kindly cotton-broker who gave him the names Henry Stanley. After fighting in the Civil War (first in one army, then in the other, then in the United States navy), he drifted into journalism. He 'covered' Napier's Abyssinian campaign of 1868 for the New York Herald *with such success that he was taken on to its permanent staff and received from it a number of similar commissions in Europe and the East.*

One of these was to 'find' Livingstone, whose movements had been a mystery to the outside world since he left for the interior of Africa in March 1866. On this mission Stanley arrived at Zanzibar at the beginning of 1871. Keeping his intention secret, he left Bagamoyo on 21st March, having engaged some of the men who had accompanied Burton and Speke including Mabruki and Bombay. (The latter ended his days in Zanzibar on a pension from the Royal Geographical

Society.) Although Stanley was able to provide himself with stores and porters upon a lavish scale which contrasted strikingly with the poverty of Livingstone's equipment, it must be admitted that this journey, the first undertaken by a European by this route since it had been discovered by Burton and Speke, was an act of enterprise and courage.

After various adventures, he reached the great inland centre of the Arab slave-traders at Tabora. Here he joined the Arabs in their campaign against Mirambo, a native war-leader who had defied them. After this he travelled forward with great care, in order to avoid Mirambo's raiding forces. This extract is taken from that point when, in great excitement, he was approaching Lake Tanganyika where he hoped to encounter Livingstone. On 9th November—Livingstone was so far out as to give the date of the meeting as 24th October—his caravan was almost in sight of the lake. On its shore at Ujiji was Livingstone, completely ignorant of its approach.

29. STANLEY FINDS LIVINGSTONE

Presently we found the smooth road, and we trod gaily with elastic steps, with limbs quickened for the march which we all knew to be drawing near its end. What cared we now for the difficulties we had encountered—for the rough and cruel forests, for the thorny thickets and hurtful grass, for the jangle of all savagedom, of which we had been the joyless audience! To-morrow! Ay, the great day draws nigh, and we may well laugh and sing while in this triumphant mood. We have been sorely tried; we have been angry with each other when vexed by troubles, but we forget all these now, and there is no face but is radiant with the happiness we have all deserved.

We made a short halt at noon, for rest and refreshment. I was shown the hills from which the Tanganika could be seen, which bounded the valley of the Liuche on the east. I could not contain myself at the sight of them. Even with this short halt I was restless and unsatisfied. We resumed the march again. I spurred my men forward with the promise that to-morrow should see their reward. Fish and beer should be given them, as much as they could eat and drink.

We were in sight of the villages of the Wakaranga; the people caught sight of us, and manifested considerable excitement. I sent men ahead to reassure them, and they came forward to greet us. This was so new and welcome to us, so different from the turbulent Wavinza and the blackmailers of Uhha, that we were melted. But we had no time to loiter by the way to indulge our joy. I was impelled onward by my almost uncontrollable feelings. I wished to resolve my doubts and fears. Was HE still there? Had HE heard of my coming? Would HE fly?

How beautiful Ukaranga appears! The green hills are crowned by clusters of straw-thatched cones. The hills rise and fall; here denuded and cultivated, there in pasturage, here timbered, yonder swarming with huts. The country has somewhat the aspect of Maryland.

We cross the Mkuti, a glorious little river! We ascend the opposite bank, and stride through the forest like men who have done a deed of which they may be proud. We have already travelled nine hours, and the sun is sinking rapidly towards the west; yet, apparently, we are not fatigued.

We reach the outskirts of Niamtaga, and we hear drums beat. The people are flying into the woods; they desert their villages, for they take us to be Ruga-Ruga—the forest thieves of Mirambo, who, after conquering the Arabs of Unyanyembe, are coming to fight the Arabs of Ujiji. Even the King flies from his village, and every man, woman, and child, terror-stricken, follows him. We enter into it and quietly take possession, and my tent is set. Finally, the word is bruited about that we are Wangwana, from Unyanyembe.

'Well, then, is Mirambo dead?' they ask.

'No,' we answer.

'Well, how did you come to Ukaranga?'

'By way of Ukonongo, Ukawendi, and Uhha.'

'Oh-hi-le!' Then they laugh heartily at their fright, and begin to make excuses. The King is introduced to me, and he says he had only gone to the woods in order to attack us again—he meant to have come back and killed us all, if we had been Ruga-Ruga. But then we know the poor King was terribly frightened, and would never have dared to return, had we been Ruga-Ruga—not he. We are not, however, in a mood to quarrel with him about an idiomatic phrase peculiar to him, but rather take him by the hand and shake it well, and say we are so very glad to see him. And he shares in our pleasure, and immediately three of the fattest sheep, pots of beer, flour, and honey are brought to us as a gift, and I make him happier still with two of the finest cloths I have in my bales; and thus a friendly pact is entered into between us.

While I write my diary of this day's proceedings, I tell Selim to lay out my new flannel suit, to oil my boots, to chalk my helmet, and fold a new puggaree around it, that I may make as presentable an appearance as possible before the white man with the grey beard, and before the Arabs of Ujiji, for the clothes I have worn through jungle and forest are in tatters. Good-night; only let one day come again, and we shall see what we shall see.

November 10th. Friday.—The 236th day from Bagamoyo, and the

51st day from Unyanyembe. General direction to Ujiji, west-by-south. Time of march, six hours.

It is a happy, glorious morning. The air is fresh and cool. The sky lovingly smiles on the earth and her children. The deep woods are crowned in bright green leafage; the water of the Mkuti, rushing under the emerald shade afforded by the bearded banks, seems to challenge us for the race to Ujiji, with its continuous brawl.

We are all outside the village cane fence, every man of us looking as spruce, as neat, and happy as when we embarked on the dhows at Zanzibar, which seems to us to have been ages ago—we have witnessed and experienced so much.

'Forward!'

'Ay Wallah, ay Wallah, bana yango!' and the light-hearted braves stride away at a rate which must soon bring us within view of Ujiji. We ascend a hill overgrown with bamboo, descend into a ravine through which dashes an impetuous little torrent, ascend another short hill, then, along a smooth footpath running across the slope of a long ridge, we push on as only eager, light-hearted men can do.

In two hours I am warned to prepare for a view of the Tanganika, for, from the top of a steep mountain the kirangozi [leader of the caravan] says I can see it. I almost vent the feelings of my heart in cries. But wait, we must behold it first. And we press forward and up the hill breathlessly, lest the grand scene hasten away. We are at last on the summit. Ah! not yet can it be seen. A little further on—just yonder, oh! there it is—a silvery gleam. I merely catch sight of it between the trees, and—but here it is at last! True—THE TANGANIKA! and there are the blue-black mountains of Ugoma and Ukaramba. An immense broad sheet, a burnished bed of silver—lucid canopy of blue above—lofty mountains are its valances, palm forests form its fringes! The Tanganika! —Hurrah! and the men respond to the exultant cry of the Anglo-Saxon with the lungs of Stentors, and the great forests and the hills seem to share in our triumph.

'Was this the place where Burton and Speke stood, Bombay, when they saw the lake first?'

'I don't remember, master; it was somewhere about here, I think.'

'Poor fellows! The one was half-paralyzed, the other half-blind,' said Sir Roderick Murchison, when he described Burton and Speke's arrival in view of the Tanganika.

And I? Well, I am so happy that, were I quite paralysed and blinded, I think that at this supreme moment I could take up my bed and walk, and all blindness would cease at once. Fortunately, however, I am quite well; I have not suffered a day's sickness since the day I left Unyanyembe. . . .

We are descending the western slope of the mountain, with the valley of the Liuche before us. Something like an hour before noon we have gained the thick matete brake, which grows on both banks of the river; we wade through the clear stream, arrive on the other side, emerge out of the brake, and the gardens of the Wajiji are around us—a perfect marvel of vegetable wealth. Details escape my hasty and partial observation. I am almost overpowered with my own emotions. I notice the graceful palms, neat plots, green with vegetable plants, and small villages surrounded with frail fences of the matete-cane.

We push on rapidly, lest the news of our coming might reach the people of Bunder Ujiji before we come in sight, and are ready for them. We halt at a little brook, then ascend the long slope of a naked ridge, the very last of the myriads we have crossed. This alone prevents us from seeing the lake in all its vastness. We arrive at the summit, travel across and arrive at its western rim, and—pause, reader—the port of Ujiji is below us, embowered in the palms, only five hundred yards from us! At this grand moment we do not think of the hundreds of miles we have marched, of the hundreds of hills that we have ascended and descended, of the many forests we have traversed, of the jungles and thickets that annoyed us, of the fervid salt plains that blistered our feet, of the hot suns that scorched us, nor of the dangers and difficulties, now happily surmounted. At last the sublime hour has arrived!—our dreams, our hopes, and anticipations are now about to be realized! Our hearts and our feelings are with our eyes, as we peer into the palms and try to make out in which hut or house lives the white man with the grey beard we heard about on the Malagarazi.

'Unfurl the flags, and load your guns!'

'Ay Wallah, ay Wallah, bana!' respond the men, eagerly.

'One, two, three,—fire!'

A volley from nearly fifty guns roars like a salute from a battery of artillery: we shall note its effect presently on the peaceful-looking village below.

'Now, kirangozi, hold the white man's flag up high, and let the Zanzibar flag bring up the rear. And you men keep close together, and keep firing until we halt in the market-place, or before the white man's house. You have said to me often that you could smell the fish of the Tanganika—I can smell the fish of the Tanganika now. There are fish and beer, and a long rest waiting for you. MARCH!'

Before we had gone a hundred yards our repeated volleys had the effect desired. We had awakened Ujiji to the knowledge that a caravan was coming, and the people were witnessed rushing up in hundreds to meet us. The mere sight of the flags informed every one immediately that we were a caravan, but the American flag borne aloft by gigantic Asmani, whose face was one vast smile on this day, rather staggered them at first. However, many of the people who now approached us remembered the flag. They had seen it float above the American Consulate, and from the mast-head of many a ship in the harbor of Zanzibar, and they were soon heard welcoming the beautiful flag with cries of 'Bindera Kisungu!'—a white man's flag! 'Bindera Merikani!'—the American flag!

Then we were surrounded by them: by Wajiji, Wanyamwezi, Wangwana, Warundi, Waguhha, Wamanyuema and Arabs, and were almost deafened with the shouts of 'Yambo, yambo, bana! Yambo, bana! Yambo, bana!' To all and each of my men the welcome was given.

We were now about three hundred yards from the village of Ujiji, and the crowds are dense about me. Suddenly I hear a voice on my right say,

'Good morning, sir!'

Startled at hearing this greeting in the midst of such a crowd of black people, I turn sharply around in search of the man, and see him at my side, with the blackest of faces, but animated and joyous—a man dressed in a long white shirt, with a turban of American sheeting around his woolly head, and I ask:

'Who the mischief are you?'

'I am Susi, the servant of Dr. Livingstone,' said he, smiling, and showing a gleaming row of teeth.

'What! Is Dr. Livingstone here?'

'Yes, sir.'

'In this village?'

'Yes, sir.'

'Are you sure?'

'Sure, sure, sir. Why, I leave him just now.'

'Good morning, sir,' said another voice.

'Hallo,' said I, 'is this another one?'

'Yes, sir.'

'Well, what is your name?'

'My name is Chumah, sir.'

'What! are you Chumah, the friend of Wekotani?'

'Yes, sir.'

'And is the Doctor well?'

'Not very well, sir.'

'Where has he been so long?'

'In Manyuema.'

'Now, you Susi, run, and tell the Doctor I am coming.'

'Yes, sir,' and off he darted like a madman.

But by this time we were within two hundred yards of the village, and the multitude was getting denser, and almost preventing our march. Flags and streamers were out; Arabs and Wangwana were pushing their way through the natives in order to greet us, for according to their account, we belonged to them. But the great wonder of all was, 'How did you come from Unyanyembe?'

Soon Susi came running back, and asked me my name; he had told the Doctor that I was coming, but the Doctor was too surprised to believe him, and, when the Doctor asked him my name, Susi was rather staggered.

But, during Susi's absence, the news had been conveyed to the Doctor that it was surely a white man that was coming, whose guns were firing and whose flag could be seen; and the great Arab magnates of Ujiji—Mohammed bin Sali, Sayd bin Majid, Abid bin Suliman, Mohammed bin Gharib, and others—had gathered together before the Doctor's house, and the Doctor had come out from his veranda to discuss the matter and await my arrival.

In the meantime, the head of the Expedition had halted, and the kirangozi was out of the ranks, holding his flag aloft, and Selim said to me, 'I see the Doctor, sir. Oh, what an old man! He has got a white beard.' And I—what would I not have given for a bit of friendly wilderness, where, unseen, I might vent my joy in some mad freak, such as idiotically biting my hand, turning a somersault, or slashing at trees, in order to allay those exciting feelings that were well-nigh uncontrollable. My heart beats fast, but I must not let my face betray my emotions, lest it shall detract from the dignity of a white man appearing under such extraordinary circumstances.

So I did that which I thought was most dignified. I pushed back the crowds, and, passing from the rear, walked down a living avenue of people, until I came in front of the semicircle of Arabs, in the front of which stood the white man with the grey beard. As I advanced slowly towards him I noticed he was pale, looked wearied, had a grey beard, wore a bluish cap with a faded gold band round it, had on a red-sleeved waistcoat, and a pair of grey tweed trousers. I would have run to him, only I was a coward in the presence of such a mob—would have embraced him, only, he being an Englishman, I did not know how he would receive me;[1] so I did what cowardice and false pride suggested was the

[1] 'This Englishman, as I afterwards found, was a military man returning to his country from India, and crossing the Desert at this part in order to go through Palestine. As for me, I had come pretty straight from England, and so here we met in the wilderness at about half-way from our respective starting-points. As we approached each other, it became with me a question whether we should speak; I thought it likely that the stranger would accost me, and in the event of his doing so, I was quite ready to be as sociable and chatty as I could be, according to my nature; but still I could not think of anything particular that I had to say to him; of course among civilized people, the not having anything to say is no excuse at all for not speaking, but I was shy, and indolent, and I felt no great wish to stop, and talk like a morning visitor, in the midst of those broad solitudes. The traveller perhaps felt as I did, for except that we lifted our hands to our caps, and waved our arms in courtesy, we passed each other as if we had passed in Bond Street.'—Kinglake's *Eothen*. (*Stanley's note.*)

best thing—walked deliberately to him, took off my hat, and said:

'Dr. Livingstone, I presume?'

'YES,' said he, with a kind smile, lifting his cap slightly.

I replace my hat on my head, and he puts on his cap, and we both grasp hands, and I then say aloud:

'I thank God, Doctor, I have been permitted to see you.'

He answered, 'I feel thankful that I am here to welcome you.'

I turn to the Arabs, take off my hat to them in response to the saluting chorus of 'Yambos' I receive, and the Doctor introduces them to me by name. Then, oblivious of the crowds, oblivious of the men who shared with me my dangers, we—Livingstone and I—turn our faces towards his tembe [hut]. He points to the veranda, or rather mud platform, under the broad overhanging eaves; he points to his own particular seat, which I see his age and experience in Africa has suggested, namely a straw mat, with a goatskin over it, and another skin nailed against the wall to protect his back from contact with the cold mud. I protest against taking this seat, which so much more befits him than me, but the Doctor will not yield: I must take it.

We are seated—the Doctor and I—with our backs to the wall. The Arabs take seats on our left. More than a thousand natives are in our front, filling the whole square densely, indulging their curiosity, and discussing the fact of two white men meeting at Ujiji—one just come from Manyuema, in the west, the other from Unyanyembe, in the east.

Conversation began. What about? I declare I have forgotten. Oh! we mutually asked questions of one another, such as:

'How did you come here?' and 'Where have you been all this long time?—the world has believed you to be dead.' Yes, that was the way it began; but whatever the Doctor informed me, and that which I communicated to him, I cannot correctly report, for I found myself gazing at him, conning the wonderful man at whose side I now sat in Central Africa. Every hair of his head and beard, every wrinkle of his face, the wanness of his features, and the slightly wearied look he wore, were all imparting intelligence to me—the knowledge I craved for so much ever since I heard the words, 'Take what you want, but find Livingstone.' What I saw was deeply interesting intelligence to me, and unvarnished truth. I was listening and reading at the same time. What did these dumb witnesses relate to me?

Oh, reader, had you been at my side on this day in Ujiji, how eloquently could be told the nature of this man's work! Had you been there but to see and hear! His lips gave me the details; lips that never lie. I cannot repeat what he said; I was too much engrossed to take my notebook out, and begin to stenograph his story. He had so much to say that he began at the end, seemingly oblivious of the fact that five or six years had to be accounted for. But his account was oozing out; it was growing fast into grand proportions—into a most marvellous history of deeds.

The Arabs rose up, with a delicacy I approved, as if they intuitively knew that we ought to be left to ourselves. I sent Bombay with them to give them the news they also wanted so much to know about the affairs at Unyanyembe. Sayd bin Majid was the father of the gallant young man whom I saw at Masange, and who fought with me at Zimbizo, and who soon afterwards was killed by Mirambo's Ruga-Ruga in the forest of Wilyankuru; and, knowing that I had been there, he earnestly desired to hear the tale of the fight; but they had all friends at Unyanyembe, and it was but natural that they should be anxious to hear of what concerned them.

After giving orders to Bombay and Asmani for the provisioning of the men of the Expedition, I called 'Kaif-Halek,' or 'How-do-ye-do,' and introduced him to Dr. Livingstone as one of the soldiers in charge of certain goods left at Unyanyembe, whom I had compelled to accompany me to Ujiji, that he might deliver in person to his master the letter-bag he had been entrusted with by Dr. Kirk [the British vice-consul at Zanzibar]. This was that famous letter-bag marked 'Nov. 1st, 1870,' which was now delivered in the Doctor's hands 365 days after it left Zanzibar! How long, I wonder, had it remained at Unyanyembe had I not been despatched into Central Africa in search of the great traveller?

The Doctor kept the letter-bag on his knee, then, presently, opened it, looked at the letters contained there, and read one or two of his children's letters, his face in the meanwhile lighting up.

He asked me to tell him the news. 'No, Doctor,' said I, 'read your letters first, which I am sure you must be impatient to read.'

'Ah,' said he, 'I have waited years for letters, and I have been taught patience. I can surely afford to wait a few hours longer. No, tell me the general news: how is the world getting along?'

'You probably know much already. Do you know that the Suez Canal is a fact—is opened, and a regular trade carried on between Europe and India through it?'

'I did not hear about the opening of it. Well, that is grand news! What else?'

Shortly I found myself enacting the part of an annual periodical to him. There was no need of exaggeration—of any penny-a-line news, or of any sensationalism. The world had witnessed and experienced much the last few years. The Pacific Railroad had been completed; Grant had been elected President of the United States; Egypt had been flooded with *savants*; the Cretan rebellion had terminated; a Spanish revolution had driven Isabella from the throne of Spain, and a Regent had been appointed; General Prim was assassinated; a Castelar had electrified Europe with his advanced ideas upon the liberty of worship; Prussia had humbled Denmark, and annexed Schleswig-Holstein, and her armies were now around Paris; the 'Man of Destiny' was a prisoner at Wilhelmshöhe; the Queen of Fashion and the Empress of the French was a fugitive; and the child born in the purple had lost for ever the Imperial crown intended for his head; the Napoleon dynasty was extinguished by the Prussians, Bismarck and Von Moltke; and France, the proud empire, was humbled to the dust.

What could a man have exaggerated of these facts? What a budget of news it was to one who had emerged from the depths of the primeval forests of Manyuema! The reflection of the dazzling light of civilization was cast on him while Livingstone was thus listening in wonder to one of the most exciting pages of history ever repeated. How the puny deeds of barbarism paled before these! Who could tell under what new phases of uneasy life Europe was laboring even then, while we, two of her lonely children, rehearsed the tale of her late woes and glories? More worthily, perhaps, had the tongue of a lyric Demodocus recounted them; but, in the absence of the poet, the newspaper correspondent performed his part as well and truthfully as he could.

Not long after the Arabs had departed, a dishful of hot hashed-meat cakes was sent to us by Sayd bin Majid, and a curried chicken was received from Mohammed bin Sali, and Moeni Kheri sent a dishful of stewed goat-meat and rice; and thus presents of food came in succession, and as fast as they were brought we set to. I had a healthy, stubborn digestion—the exercise I had taken had put it in prime order; but Livingstone—he had been complaining that he had no appetite, that his stomach refused everything but a cup of tea now and then—he ate also —ate like a vigorous, hungry man; and, as he vied with me in demolishing the pancakes, he kept repeating, 'You have brought me new life. You have brought me new life.'

'Oh, by George!' I said, 'I have forgotten something. Hasten, Selim, and bring that bottle; you know which; and bring me the silver goblets. I brought this bottle on purpose for this event, which I hoped would come to pass, though often it seemed useless to expect it.'

Selim knew where the bottle was, and he soon returned with it—a bottle of Sillery champagne; and, handing the Doctor a silver goblet brimful of the exhilarating wine, and pouring a small quantity into my own, I said,

'Dr. Livingstone, to your very good health, sir.'

'And to yours,' he responded.

And the champagne I had treasured for this happy meeting was drunk with hearty good wishes to each other.

But we kept on talking and talking, and prepared food was being brought to us all that afternoon; and we kept on eating every time it was brought, until I had eaten even to repletion and the Doctor was obliged to confess that he had eaten enough. Still, Halimah, the female cook of the Doctor's establishment, was in a state of the greatest excitement. She had been protruding her head out of the cookhouse to make sure that there were really two white men sitting down in the veranda, when there used to be only one, who would not, because he could not, eat anything; and she had been considerably exercised in her mind about this fact. She was afraid the Doctor did not properly appreciate her culinary abilities; but now she was amazed at the extraordinary quantity of food eaten, and she was in a state of delightful excitement. We could hear her tongue rolling off a tremendous volume of clatter to the wondering crowds who halted before the kitchen to hear the current of news with which she edified them. Poor, faithful soul! While we listened to the noise of her furious gossip, the Doctor related her faithful services, and the terrible anxiety she evinced when the guns first announced the arrival of another white man in Ujiji; how she had been flying about in a state of the utmost excitement, from the kitchen into his presence, and out again into the square, asking all sorts of questions; how she was in despair at the scantiness of the general larder and treasury of the strange household; how she was anxious to make up for their poverty by a grand appearance—to make up a sort of Barmecide feast to welcome the white man. 'Why,' said she, 'is he not one of us? Does he not bring plenty of cloth and beads? Talk about the Arabs! Who are they that they should be compared to white men? Arabs, indeed!'

The Doctor and I conversed upon many things, especially upon his own immediate troubles, and his disappointment, upon his arrival in Ujiji, when told that all his goods had been sold, and he was reduced to poverty. He had but twenty cloths or so left of the stock he had deposited with the man called Sherif, the half-caste drunken tailor, who was sent by the British Consul in charge of the goods. Besides which he had been suffering from an attack of dysentery, and his condition was most deplorable. He was but little improved on this day though he had eaten well, and already began to feel stronger and better.

This day, like all others, though big with happiness to me, at last was fading away. We, sitting with our faces looking to the east, as Livingstone had been sitting for days preceding my arrival, noted the dark shadows which crept up above the grove of palms beyond the village, and above the rampart of mountains which we had crossed that day, now looming through the fast approaching darkness; and we listened with our hearts full of gratitude to the great Giver of Good and Dispenser of all Happiness, to the sonorous thunder of the surf of the Tanganika, and to the chorus which the night insects sang. Hours passed, and we were still sitting there with our minds busy upon the day's remarkable events, when I remembered that the traveller had not yet read his letters.

'Doctor,' I said, 'you had better read your letters. I will not keep you up any longer.'

'Yes,' he answered, 'it is getting late; and I will go and read my friends' letters. Good-night, and God bless you.'

'Good-night, my dear Doctor; and let me hope that your news will be such as you desire.'

And now, dear reader, having related succinctly 'How I found Livingstone,' I bid you also 'Good-night.'

I woke up early next morning with a sudden start. The room was strange! It was a house, and not my tent! Ah, yes! I recollected I had discovered Livingstone, and I was in his house. I listened, that the knowledge dawning on me might be confirmed by the sound of his voice. I heard nothing but the sullen roar of the surf.

I lay quietly in bed. Bed! Yes, it was a primitive four-poster, with the leaves of the palm-tree spread upon it instead of down, and horsehair and my bearskin spread over this serving me in place of linen. I began to put myself under a rigid mental cross-examination, and to an analysation of my position.

'What was I sent for?'

'To find Livingstone.'

'Have you found him?'

'Yes, of course; am I not in his house? Whose compass is that hanging on a peg there? Whose clothes, whose boots, are those? Who reads those newspapers, those "Saturday Reviews" and numbers of "Punch" lying on the floor?'

'Well, what are you going to do now?'

'I shall tell him this morning who sent me, and what brought me here. I will then ask him to write a letter to Mr. Bennett, and to give what news he can spare. I did not come here to rob him of his news. Sufficient for me is it that I have found him. It is a complete success so far. But it will be a greater one if he gives me letters for Mr. Bennett, and an acknowledgment that he has seen me.'

'Do you think he will do so?'

'Why not? I have come here to do him a service. He has no goods. I have. He has no men with him. I have. If I do a friendly part by him, will he not do a friendly part by me? What says the poet?—

> Nor hope to find
> A friend, but who has found a friend in thee.
> All like the purchase; few the price will pay:
> And this makes friends such *wonders* here below.

I have paid the purchase, by coming so far to do him a service. But I think, from what I have seen of him last night, that he is not such a niggard and misanthrope as I was told he was by a man who said he knew him. He exhibited considerable emotion despite the monosyllabic greeting, when he shook my hand. Neither did he run away, as I was told he would; though perhaps that was because he had no time. Still, if he was a man to feel annoyance at any person coming after him, he would not have received me as he did, nor would he ask me to live with him, but he would have surlily refused to see me, and told me to mind my own business, and he would mind his. Neither does he mind my nationality; for "here," said he, "Americans and Englishmen are the same people. We speak the same language and have the same ideas." Just so, Doctor; I agree with you. Here at least, Americans and Englishmen shall be brothers, and whatever I can do for you, you may command me as freely as if I were flesh of your flesh, bone of your bone.'

I dressed myself quietly, intending to take a stroll along the Tanganika before the Doctor should rise; opened the door, which creaked horribly on its hinges, and walked out to the veranda.

'Halloa, Doctor!—you up already? I hope you have slept well?'

'Good morning, Mr. Stanley! I am glad to see you. Hope you rested well. I sat up late reading my letters. You have brought me good and bad news. But sit down.' He made a place for me by his side. 'Yes, many of my friends are dead. My eldest son has met with a sad accident—that is, my boy Tom; my second son, Oswell, is at college studying medicine, and is doing well, I am told. Agnes, my eldest daughter, has been enjoying herself in a yacht, with "Sir Paraffine" Young and his family. Sir Roderick, also, is well, and expresses a hope that he will soon see me. You have brought me quite a budget.'

The man was not an apparition, then, and yesterday's scenes were not the result of a dream! and I gazed on him intently, for thus I was assured he had not run away, which was the great fear that constantly haunted me as I was journeying to Ujiji.

'Now, Doctor,' said I, 'you are, probably, wondering why I came here?'

'It is true,' said he; 'I have been wondering. I thought you, at first, an emissary of the French Government, in the place of Lieutenant Le Saint, who died a few miles above Gondokoro. I heard you had boats, plenty of men, and stores, and I really believed you were some French officer, until I saw the American flag; and, to tell you the truth, I was rather glad it was so, because I could not have talked to him in French; and if he did not know English, we had been a pretty pair of white men in Ujiji! I did not like to ask you yesterday, because it was none of my business.'

'Well,' said I, laughing, 'for your sake I am glad that I am an American, and not a Frenchman, and that we can understand each other perfectly without an interpreter. I see that the Arabs are wondering that you, an Englishman, and I, an American, understand each other. We must take care not to tell them that the English and Americans have fought, and that there are "Alabama" claims left unsettled, and that we have such people as Fenians in America, who hate you. But seriously, Doctor—now don't be frightened when I tell you that I have come after —YOU!'

'After me?'

'Yes.'

'How?'

'Well. You have heard of the "New York Herald"?'

'Oh—who has not heard of that newspaper?'

'Sh-sh! Without his father's knowledge or consent, Mr. James Gordon Bennett, son of Mr. James Gordon Bennett, the proprietor of the "Herald," has commissioned me to find you—to get whatever news of your discoveries you like to give—and to assist you, if I can, with means.'

'Young Mr. Bennett told you to come after me, to find me out, and help me! It is no wonder, then, you praised Mr. Bennett so much last night.'

'I know him—I am proud to say—to be just what I say he is. He is an ardent, generous, and true man.'

'Well, indeed! I am very much obliged to him; and it makes me feel proud to think that you Americans think so much of me. You have just come in the proper time; for I was beginning to think that I should have to beg from the Arabs. Even they are in want of cloth, and there are but few beads in Ujiji. That fellow Sherif has robbed me of all. I wish I could embody my thanks to Mr. Bennett in suitable words; but if I fail to do so, do not, I beg of you, believe me the less grateful.'

'And now, Doctor, having disposed of this little affair, Ferajji shall bring breakfast; if you have no objection.'

'You have given me an appetite,' he said. 'Halimah is my cook, but she never can tell the difference between tea and coffee.'

Ferajji, the cook, was ready as usual with excellent tea, and a dish of smoking cakes; 'dampers', as the Doctor called them. I never did care much for this kind of a cake fried in a pan, but they were necessary to the Doctor, who had nearly lost all his teeth from the hard fare of Lunda. He had been compelled to subsist on green ears of Indian corn; there was no meat in that district; and the effort to gnaw at the corn ears had loosened all his teeth. I preferred the corn scones of Virginia, which, to my mind, were the nearest approach to palatable bread obtainable in Central Africa.

The Doctor said he had thought me a most luxurious and rich man when he saw my great bath-tub carried on the shoulders of one of my men; but he thought me still more luxurious this morning, when my knives and forks, and plates, and cups, saucers, silver spoons, and silver tea-pot were brought forth shining and bright, spread on a rich Persian carpet, and observed that I was well attended to by my yellow and ebon Mercuries.

This was the beginning of our life at Ujiji. I knew him not as a friend before my arrival. He was only an object to me—a great item for a daily newspaper, as much as other subjects in which the voracious news-loving public delight. I had gone over battlefields, witnessed revolutions, civil wars, rebellions, émeutes and massacres; stood close to the condemned murderer to record his last struggles and last sighs; but never had I been called to record anything that moved me so much as this man's woes and sufferings, his privations and disappointments, which now were poured into my ear. Verily did I begin to perceive that 'the Gods above do with just eyes survey the affairs of men.' I began to recognize the hand of an overruling and kindly Providence.

How I found Livingstone, 2nd edition, pp. 402–425

Stanley's visit, though recorded in Livingstone's journal with a reserve which contrasts with Stanley's expressive record, was very beneficial to the Doctor. Stanley's company, his stores, especially his food and his medicine, helped to restore a little the Doctor's spirits, though his constitution must have been too deeply overstrained to be radically improved by this temporary refreshment.

The two men made an expedition up Lake Tanganyika in canoes. They were attacked by tribes maddened by the injuries of the slavers, but were saved by the calm, unprovocative behaviour of Livingstone which astonished and impressed his companion, if only for the moment. They reached a point further north than that attained by Burton and Speke and they were thus able to settle a very important question about the source of the Nile by ascertaining that, contrary to Burton's opinion, the Rusizi river flowed into, not out of, the Lake.

Livingstone steadily refused all Stanley's pleas that he should return with him. He was determined to verify the connection between the 'fountains' mentioned by Herodotus, which he believed to be in the region of Lake Bangweolo, and the Nile. He thought this connection might be west of Tanganyika, possibly through the Lualaba river, and another lake to the north. Accordingly the two men travelled together to Tabora, and Stanley offered to hurry to the coast and to send back to Livingstone, who now had only Susi, Chumah, and a few other faithful servants, a band of porters to enable him to continue his exploration.

THE PARTING

At last, after four months together, all Stanley's preparations being made and all Livingstone's letters written, the time came when Stanley must set out for the coast.

30. THE PARTING

March 13*th.*—The last day of my stay with Livingstone has come and gone, and the last night we shall be together is present, and I cannot evade the morrow! I feel as though I would rebel against the fate which drives me away from him. The minutes beat fast, and grow into hours. Our door is closed, and we are both of us busy with our own thoughts. What his thoughts are I know not. Mine are sad. My days seem to have been spent in an Elysian field; otherwise, why should I so keenly regret the near approach of the parting hour? Have I not been battered by successive fevers, prostrate with agony day after day lately? Have I not raved and stormed in madness? Have I not clenched my fists in fury, and fought with the wild strength of despair, when in delirium? Yet, I regret to surrender the pleasure I have felt in this man's society, though so dearly purchased. And I cannot resist the sure advance of time, which flies this night as if it mocked me, and gloated on the misery it created! Be it so! How many times have I not suffered the pang of parting with friends! I wished to linger longer, but the inevitable would come—Fate sundered us. This is the same regretful feeling, only it is more poignant, and the farewell may be for ever! For ever? And 'For ever,' echo the reverberations of a woful whisper.

I have noted down all he has said to-night; but the reader shall not share it with me. It is mine!

I am jealous as he is himself of his Journal; and I have written in German text, and in round hand, on either side of it, on the waterproof canvas cover, 'POSITIVELY NOT TO BE OPENED;' to which he has affixed his signature. I have stenographed every word he has said to me respecting the equable distribution of certain curiosities among his friends and children, and his last wish about 'his dear old friend, Sir Roderick Murchison,' because he has been getting anxious about him ever since we received the newspapers at Uganda, when we read that the old man was suffering from a paralytic stroke. I must be sure to send him the news, as soon as I get to Aden; and I have promised that he will receive the message from me quicker than anything was ever received in Central Africa.

'To-morrow night, Doctor, you will be alone!'

'Yes; the house will look as though a death had taken place. You had better stop until the rains, which are now near, are over.'

'I would to God I could, my dear Doctor; but every day I stop here.

now that there is no necessity for me to stay longer, keeps you from your work and home.'

'I know; but consider your health—you are not fit to travel. What is it? Only a few weeks longer. You will travel to the coast just as quickly when the rains are over as you will by going now. The plains will be inundated between here and the coast.'

'You think so; but I will reach the coast in forty days; if not in forty, I will in fifty—certain. The thought that I am doing you an important service will spur me on.'

March 14*th*.—At dawn we were up, the bales and baggage were taken outside of the building, and the men prepared themselves for the first march towards home.

We had a sad breakfast together. I could not eat, my heart was too full; neither did my companion seem to have an appetite. We found something to do which kept us longer together. At 8 o'clock I was not gone, and I had thought to have been off at 5 a.m.

'Doctor,' said I, 'I will leave two men with you, who will stop to-day and to-morrow with you, for it may be that you have forgotten something in the hurry of my departure. I will halt a day at Tura, on the frontier of Unyamwezi, for your last word, and your last wish; and now we must part—there is no help for it. Good-bye.'

'Oh, I am coming with you a little way. I must see you off on the road.'

'Thank you. Now, my men, Home! Kirangozi, lift the flag, and MARCH!'

The house looked desolate—it faded from our view. Old times, and the memories of my aspirations and kindling hopes, came strong on me. The old hills round about, that I once thought tame and uninteresting, had become invested with histories and reminiscences for me. On that burzani I have sat hour after hour, dreaming, and hoping, and sighing. On that col I stood, watching the battle and the destruction of Tabora. Under that roof I have sickened and been delirious, and cried out like a child at the fate that threatened my mission. Under that banian tree lay my dead comrade—poor Shaw! I would have given a fortune to have had him by my side at this time. From that house I started on my journey to Ujiji; to it I returned as to a friend, with a newer and dearer companion; and now I leave all. Already it all appears like a strange dream.

We walked side by side; the men lifted their voices in a song. I took long looks at Livingstone, to impress his features thoroughly on my memory.

'The thing is, Doctor, so far as I can understand it, you do not intend to return home until you have satisfied yourself about the "Source of the Nile." When you have satisfied yourself, you will come home and satisfy others. Is it not so?'

'That is it, exactly. When your men come back, I shall immediately start for Ufipa; then, crossing the Rungwa River, I shall strike south, and round the extremity of the Tanganika. Then, a south-east course will take me to Chicumbi's, on the Luapula. On crossing the Luapula, I shall go direct west to the copper-mines of Katanga. Eight days south of Katanga, the natives declare the fountains to be. When I have found them, I shall return by Katanga to the underground houses of Rua. From the caverns, ten days north-east will take me to Lake Kamolondo. I shall be able to travel from the lake, in your boat, up the River Lufira, to Lake Lincoln. Then, coming down again, I can proceed north, by the Lualaba, to the fourth lake—which, I think, will explain the whole problem; and I will probably find that it is either Chowambe (Baker's lake), or Piaggia's lake.'

'And how long do you think this little journey will take you?'

'A year and a half, at the furthest, from the day I leave Unyanyembe.'

'Suppose you say two years; contingencies might arise, you know. It will be well for me to hire these new men for two years; the day of their engagement to begin from their arrival at Unyanyembe.'

'Yes, that will do excellently well.'

'Now, my dear Doctor, the best friends must part. You have come far enough; let me beg of you to turn back.'

'Well, I will say this to you: you have done what few men could do—far better than some great travellers I know. And I am grateful to you for what you have done for me. God guide you safe home and bless you, my friend.'

'And may God bring you safe back to us all, my dear friend. Farewell!'

'Farewell!'

We wrung each other's hands, and I had to tear myself away before I unmanned myself; but Susi, and Chumah, and Hamoydah—the Doctor's faithful fellows—they must all shake and kiss my hands before I could quite turn away. I betrayed myself!

'Good-bye, Doctor—dear friend!'

'Good-bye!'

'MARCH! Why do you stop? Go on! Are you not going home?' And my people were driven before me. No more weakness. I shall show them such marching as will make them remember me. In forty days I shall do what took me three months to perform before.

My friendly reader, I wrote the above extracts in my Diary on the evening of each day. I look at them now after six months have passed away; yet I am not ashamed of them; my eyes feel somewhat dimmed at the recollection of the parting. I dared not erase, nor modify what I had penned, while my feelings were strong. God grant that if ever you take to travelling in Africa you will get as noble and true a man for your companion as David Livingstone! For four months and four days I lived with him in the same house, or in the same boat, or in the same tent, and I never found a fault in him. I am a man of a quick temper, and often without sufficient cause, I dare say, have broken ties of friendship; but with Livingstone I never had cause for resentment, but each day's life with him added to my admiration for him.

How I found Livingstone, 2nd edition, pp. 622–628

Stanley's journey back to the coast was quick and uneventful. Staying at Zanzibar only to arrange for the dispatch of porters up to Ujiji, he returned to England with his news and with the letters and papers he had brought from Livingstone. Here he met with a mortifying reception; for though Livingstone's family and Granville, the Foreign Secretary, believed what he said, many people (including the President of the Royal Geographical Society) were incredulous. In due course his story came to be accepted, even by the doubters: but he never forgot their mistrust. It was another step in the process of disillusionment which had been begun by the cruelties of his childhood and which ended by making him a bitter and lonely man. Though he was one of the greatest of African travellers, he was also one of the most ruthless and brutal.

Between 1874 and 1889 he made three more journeys in Africa: the first led directly to the founding of the Congo Free State; the second was undertaken in the service of King Leopold II of the Belgians, for the purpose of establishing the Free State's government; the third, the 'Emin Pasha Relief Expedition', helped to make Uganda a British sphere of influence. From 1895 to 1900 he was a Liberal Unionist M.P.: in 1899 he was created a G.C.B. But he never quite lived down the mistrust and dislike he so often inspired: it followed him even to the grave; for Dean Robinson refused permission for him to be buried in Westminster Abbey.

Livingstone's refusal, after nearly six years of lonely wandering, to return with Stanley to health and safety must always excite wonder. It was the more astonishing in view of the severe sufferings he had endured and their effect upon his physique. He appears to have been moved by two great purposes that were closely linked in his mind, to reveal the full ravages of the Arab slave-trade and to find the ultimate sources of the Nile.

He set off from Tabora in August 1872 and after skirting the southern shore of Lake Tanganyika he struck south-west. Almost from the first he was ill with fever and dysentery and soon his caravan ran into heavy rains and country almost bare of food. He struggled on and at last reached the network of streams flowing into the marshy rim of Lake Bangweolo. It is at this point that the final extract from his journal begins. It has been given almost in full, as it did not seem possible to break it up into shorter extracts without marring the picture of the man and his task and blurring the cumulative effect of the difficulties and sufferings which led to the end.

31. THE DEATH OF LIVINGSTONE

9th February.—Slept in a most unwholesome, ruined village. Rank vegetation had run over all, and the soil smelled offensively. Crossed a sponge [a marsh], then a rivulet, and sponge running into the Miwale River, then by a rocky passage we crossed the Mofiri, or great Tinga-tinga, a water running strongly waist and breast deep, above thirty feet broad here, but very much broader below. After this we passed two more rills and the River Methonua, but we built a camp above our former one. The human ticks called 'papasi' by the Suaheli, and 'kara-patos' by the Portuguese, made even the natives call out against their numbers and ferocity.

10th February.—Back again to our old camp on the Lovu or Lofu by the bridge. We left in a drizzle, which continued from 4 a.m. to 1 p.m. We were three hours in it, and all wetted, just on reaching camp, by 200 yards of flood mid-deep; but we have food.

11th February.—Our guides took us across country, where we saw tracks of buffaloes, and in a meadow, the head of a sponge, we saw a herd of Hartebeests. A drizzly night was followed by a morning of cold wet fog, but in three hours we reached our old camp: it took us six hours to do this distance before, and five on our return. We camped on a deep bridged stream, called the Kiachibwe.

12th February.—We crossed the Kasoso, which joins the Mokisya, a river we afterwards crossed: it flows N.W., then over the Mofungwe. The same sponges everywhere.

13th February.—In four hours we came within sight of the Luena and Lake, and saw plenty of elephants and other game, but very shy. The forest trees are larger. The guides are more at a loss than we are, as they always go in canoes in the flat rivers and rivulets. Went E., then S.E. round to S.

14th February.—Public punishment to Chirango for stealing beads, fifteen cuts; diminished his load to 40 lbs., giving him blue and white beads to be strung. The water stands so high in the paths that I cannot walk dryshod, and I found in the large bougas or prairies in front, that it lay knee deep, so I sent on two men to go to the first villages of Matipa for large canoes to navigate the Lake, or give us a guide to go east to the Chambeze, to go round on foot. It was Halima who informed on Chirango, as he offered her beads for a cloth of a kind which she knew had not hitherto been taken out of the baggage. This was so far faithful in her, but she has an outrageous tongue. I remain because of an excessive hæmorrhagic discharge.

If the good Lord gives me favour, and permits me to finish my work, I shall thank and bless Him, though it has cost me untold toil, pain, and travel; this trip has made my hair all grey.

15th February, Sunday.—Service. Killed our last goat while waiting for messengers to return from Matipa's. Evening: the messenger came back, having been foiled by deep tinga-tinga and bouga. He fired his gun three times, but no answer came, so as he had slept one night away he turned, but found some men hunting, whom he brought with him. They say that Matipa is on Chirube islet, a good man too, but far off from this.

16th February.—Sent men by the hunter's canoe to Chirube, with a request to Matipa to convey us west if he has canoes, but, if not, to tell us truly, and we will go east and cross the Chambeze where it is small. Chitunkubwe's men ran away, refusing to wait till he had communicated with Matipa. Here the water stands underground about eighteen inches from the surface. The guides played us false, and this is why they escaped.

17th February.—The men will return to-morrow, but they have to go all the way out to the islet of Chirube to Matipa's.

Suffered a furious attack at midnight from the red Sirafu or Driver ants. Our cook fled first at their onset. I lighted a candle, and remembering Dr. Van der Kemp's idea that no animal will attack man unprovoked, I lay still. The first came on my foot quietly, then some began to bite between the toes, then the larger ones swarmed over the foot and bit furiously, and made the blood start out. I then went out of the tent, and my whole person was instantly covered as close as small-pox (not confluent) on a patient. Grass fires were lighted, and my men picked some off my limbs and tried to save me. After battling for an hour or two they took me into a hut not yet invaded, and I rested till they came, the pests, and routed me out there too! Then came on a steady pour of rain, which held on till noon, as if trying to make us miserable. At 9 a.m. I got back into my tent. The large Sirafu have mandibles curved like reaping-sickles, and very sharp—as fine at the point as the finest needle or a bee's sting. Their office is to remove all animal refuse, cockroaches, &c., and they took all my fat. Their appearance sets every cockroach in a flurry, and all ants, white and black, get into a panic. On man they insert the sharp curved mandibles, and then with six legs push their bodies round so as to force the points by lever power. They collect in masses in their runs and stand with mandibles extended, as if defying attack. The large ones stand thus at bay whilst the youngsters hollow out a run half an inch wide, and about an inch deep. They remained with us till late in the afternoon, and we put hot ashes on the defiant hordes. They retire to enjoy the fruits of their raid, and come out fresh another day.

18*th February.*—We wait hungry and cold for the return of the men who have gone to Matipa, and hope the good Lord will grant us influence with this man.

. . . . . .

4*th March.*—Sent canoes off to bring our men over to the island of Matipa. They brought ten, but the donkey could not come as far through the 'tinga-tinga' as they, so they took it back for fear that it should perish. I spoke to Matipa this morning to send more canoes, and he consented. We move outside, as the town swarms with mice, and is very closely built and disagreeable. I found mosquitoes in the town.

5*th March.*—Time runs on quickly. The real name of this island is Masumbo, and the position may be probably long. 31° 3′; lat. 10° 11′ S. Men not arrived yet. Matipa very slow.

6*th March.*—Building a camp outside the town for quiet and cleanliness, and no mice to run over us at night. This islet is some twenty or thirty feet above the general flat country and adjacent water.

At 3 p.m. we moved up to the highest part of the island where we can see around us and have the fresh breeze from the Lake. Rainy as we went up, as usual.

7*th March.*—We expect some men to-day. I tremble for the donkey! Camp sweet and clean, but it, too, has mosquitoes, from which a curtain protects me completely—a great luxury, but unknown to the Arabs, to whom I have spoken about it. Abed was overjoyed by one I made for him; others are used to their bites, as was the man who said that he would get used to a nail through the heel of his shoe. The men came at 3 p.m., but eight had to remain, the canoes being too small. The donkey had to be tied down, as he rolled about on his legs and would have forced his way out. He bit Mabruki Speke's lame hand, and came in stiff from lying tied all day. We had him shampooed all over, but he could not eat dura—he feels sore. Susi did well under the circumstances, and we had plenty of flour ready for all. Chanza is near Kabinga, and this last chief is coming to visit me in a day or two.

8th March.—I press Matipa to get a fleet of canoes equal to our number, but he complains of their being stolen by rebel subjects. He tells me his brother Kabinga would have been here some days ago but for having lost a son, who was killed by an elephant: he is mourning for him but will come soon. Kabinga is on the other side of the Chambeze. A party of male and female drummers and dancers is sure to turn up at every village; the first here had a leader that used such violent antics perspiration ran off his whole frame. I gave a few strings of beads, and the performance is repeated to-day by another lot, but I rebel and allow them to dance unheeded. We got a sheep for a wonder for a doti; fowls and fish alone could be bought, but Kabinga has plenty of cattle. . . .

The eight men came from Motovinza this afternoon, and now all our party is united. The donkey shows many sores inflicted by the careless people, who think that force alone can be used to inferior animals.

11th March.—Matipa says 'Wait; Kabinga is coming, and he has canoes.' Time is of no value to him. His wife is making him pombe, and will drown all his cares, but mine increase and plague me. Matipa and his wife each sent me a huge calabash of pombe; I wanted only a little to make bread with.

By putting leaven in a bottle and keeping it from one baking to another (or three days) good bread is made, and the dough being surrounded by banana leaves or maize leaves (or even forest leaves of hard texture and no taste, or simply by broad leafy grass), is preserved from burning in an iron pot. The inside of the pot is greased, then the leaves put in all round, and the dough poured in to stand and rise in the sun.

Better news comes: the son of Kabinga is to be here to-night, and we shall concoct plans together.

12th March.—The news was false, no one came from Kabinga. The men strung beads to-day, and I wrote part of my despatch for Earl Granville.

13th March.—I went to Matipa, and proposed to begin the embarkation of my men at once, as they are many, and the canoes are only sufficient to take a few at a time. He has sent off a big canoe to reap his millet, when it returns he will send us over to see for ourselves where we can go. I explained the danger of setting my men astray.

14th March.—Rains have ceased for a few days. Went down to Matipa and tried to take his likeness for the sake of the curious hat he wears.

15th March.—Finish my despatch so far.

16th March, Sunday.—Service. I spoke sharply to Matipa for his duplicity. He promises everything and does nothing: he has in fact no power over his people. Matipa says that a large canoe will come tomorrow, and next day men will go to Kabinga to reconnoitre. There may be a hitch there which he did not take into account; Kabinga's son, killed by an elephant, may have raised complications: blame may be attached to Matipa, and in their dark minds it may appear all important to settle the affair before having communication with him. Ill all day with my old complaint.

17*th March.*—The delay is most trying. So many detentions have occurred they ought to have made me of a patient spirit.

As I thought, Matipa told us to-day that it is reported he has some Arabs with him who will attack all the Lake people forthwith, and he is anxious that we shall go over to show them that we are peaceful.

18*th March.*—Sent off men to reconnoitre at Kabinga's and to make a camp there. Rain began again after nine days' dry weather, N.W. wind, but in the morning fleecy clouds came from S.E. in patches. Matipa is acting the villain, and my men are afraid of him: they are all cowards, and say that they are afraid of me, but this is only an excuse for their cowardice.

19*th March* [his birthday].—Thanks to the Almighty Preserver of men for sparing me thus far on the journey of life. Can I hope for ultimate success? So many obstacles have arisen. Let not Satan prevail over me, Oh! my good Lord Jesus.

8 a.m. Got about 20 people off to canoes. Matipa not friendly. They go over to Kabinga on S.W. side of the Chambeze, and thence we go overland. 9 a.m. Men came back and reported Matipa false again; only one canoe had come. I made a demonstration by taking quiet possession of his village and house; fired a pistol through the roof and called my men, ten being left to guard the camp; Matipa fled to another village. The people sent off at once and brought three canoes, so at 11 a.m. my men embarked quietly. They go across the Chambeze and build a camp in its left bank. All Kabinga's cattle are kept on an island called Kalilo, near the mouth of the Chambeze, and are perfectly wild: they are driven into the water like buffaloes, and pursued when one is wanted for meat. No milk is ever obtained of course.

20*th March.*—Cold N.W. weather, but the rainfall is small, as the S.E. stratum comes down below the N.W. by day. Matipa sent two large baskets of flour (cassava), a sheep, and a cock. He hoped that we should remain with him till the water of the over-flood dried, and help him to fight his enemies, but I explained our delays, and our desire to complete our work and meet Baker.

21*st March.*—Very heavy N.W. rain and thunder by night, and by morning. I gave Matipa a coil of thick brass wire, and his wife a string of large neck beads, and explained my hurry to be off. He is now all fair, and promises largely: he has been much frightened by our warlike demonstration. I am glad I had to do nothing but make a show of force.

22*nd March.*—Susi not returned from Kabinga. I hope that he is getting canoes, and men also, to transport us all at one voyage. It is flood as far as the eye can reach; flood four and six feet deep, and more, with three species of rushes, two kinds of lotus, or sacred lily, papyrus, arum, &c. One does not know where land ends, and Lake begins: the presence of land-grass proves that this is not always overflowed.

23rd March.—Men returned at noon. Kabinga is mourning for his son killed by an elephant, and keeps in seclusion. The camp is formed on the left bank of the Chambeze.

24th March.—The people took the canoes away, but in fear sent for them. I got four, and started with all our goods, first giving a present that no blame should follow me. We punted six hours to a little islet without a tree, and no sooner did we land than a pitiless pelting rain came on. We turned up a canoe to get shelter. We shall reach the Chambeze to-morrow. The wind tore the tent out of our hands, and damaged it too; the loads are all soaked, and with the cold it is bitterly uncomfortable. A man put my bed into the bilge, and never said, 'Bale out,' so I was safe for a wet night, but it turned out better than I expected. No grass, but we made a bed of the loads, and a blanket fortunately put into a bag.

25th March.—Nothing earthly will make me give up my work in despair. I encourage myself in the Lord my God, and go forward.

We got off from our miserably small islet of ten yards at 7 a.m., a grassy sea on all sides, with a few islets in the far distance. Four varieties of rushes around us, triangular and fluted, rise from eighteen inches to two feet above the water. The caterpillars seem to eat each other, and a web is made round others; the numerous spiders may have been the workmen of the nest. The wind on the rushes makes a sound like the waves of the sea. The flood extends out in slightly depressed arms of the Lake for twenty or thirty miles, and far too broad to be seen across; fish abound, and ant-hills alone lift up their heads; they have trees on them. Lukutu flows from E. to W. to the Chambeze, as does the Lubanseusi also. After another six hours' punting, over the same wearisome prairie or Bouga, we heard the merry voices of children. It was a large village, on a flat, which seems flooded at times, but much cassava is planted on mounds, made to protect the plants from the water, which stood in places in the village, but we got a dry spot for the tent. The people offered us huts. We had as usual a smart shower on the way to Kasenga, where we slept. We passed the Islet Luangwa.

26th March.—We started at 7.30, and got into a large stream out of the Chambeze, called Mabziwa. One canoe sank in it, and we lost a slave girl of Amoda. Fished up three boxes, and two guns, but the boxes being full of cartridges were much injured; we lost the donkey's saddle too. After this mishap we crossed the Lubanseusi, near its confluence with the Chambeze, 300 yards wide and three fathoms deep, and a slow current. We crossed the Chambeze. It is about 400 yards wide, with a quick clear current of two knots, and three fathoms deep, like the Lubanseusi; but that was slow in current, but clear also. There is one great lock after another, with thick mats of hedges, formed of aquatic plants between. The volume of water is enormous. We punted five hours, and then camped.

27th March.—I sent canoes and men back to Matipa's to bring all the men that remained, telling them to ship them at once on arriving, and not to make any talk about it. Kabinga keeps his distance from us, and food is scarce; at noon he sent a man to salute me in his name.

28th March.—Making a pad for a donkey, to serve instead of a saddle. Kabinga attempts to sell a sheep at an exorbitant price, and says that he is weeping over his dead child. Mabruki Speke's hut caught fire at night, and his cartridge box was burned.

29th March.—I bought a sheep for 100 strings of beads. I wished to begin the exchange by being generous, and told his messenger so; then a small quantity of maize was brought, and I grumbled at the meanness of the present: there is no use in being bashful, as they are not ashamed to grumble too. The man said that Kabinga would send more when he had collected it.

30th March, Sunday.—A lion roars mightily. The fish-hawk utters his weird voice in the morning, as if he lifted up to a friend at a great distance, in a sort of falsetto key.

5 p.m. Men returned, but the large canoe having been broken by the donkey, we have to go back and pay for it, and take away about twenty men now left. Matipa kept all the payment from his own people, and so left us in the lurch; thus another five days is lost.

31st March.—I sent the men back to Matipa's for all our party. I give two dotis to repair the canoe. Islanders are always troublesome, from a sense of security in their fastnesses. Made stirrups of thick brass wire four-fold; they promise to do well. Sent Kabinga a cloth, and a message, but he is evidently a niggard, like Matipa: we must take him as we find him, there is no use in growling. Seven of our men returned, having got a canoe from one of Matipa's men. Kabinga, it seems, was pleased with the cloth, and says that he will ask for maize from his people, and cut it for me; he has rice growing. He will send a canoe to carry me over the next river.

3rd April, 1873.—Very heavy rain last night. Six inches fell in a short time. The men at last have come from Matipa's.

4th April.—Sent over to Kabinga to buy a cow, and got a fat one for 2½ dotis, to give the party a feast ere we start. The kambari fish of the Chambeze is three feet three inches in length.

Two others, the 'polwe' and 'lopatakwao,' all go up the Chambeze to spawn when the rains begin. Casembe's people make caviare of the spawn of the 'pumbo.'

5th April.—March from Kabinga's on the Chambeze, our luggage in canoes, and men on land. We punted on flood six feet deep, with many ant-hills all about, covered with trees. Course S.S.E. for five miles, across the River Lobingela, sluggish, and about 300 yards wide.

6th April.—Leave in the same way, but men were sent from Kabinga to steal the canoes, which we paid his brother Mateysa handsomely for. A stupid drummer, beating the alarm in the distance, called us inland; we found the main body of our people had gone on, and so by this, our party got separated, and we pulled and punted six or seven hours S.W. in great difficulty, as the fishermen we saw refused to show us where the deep water lay. The whole country S. of the Lake was covered with water thickly dotted over with lotus-leaves and rushes. It has a greenish appearance, and it might be well on a map to show the spaces annually flooded by a broad wavy band, twenty, thirty, and even forty miles out from the permanent banks of the Lake: it might be coloured light green. The broad estuaries, fifty or more miles, into which the rivers form themselves, might be coloured blue, but it is quite impossible at present to tell where land ends, and Lake begins; it is all water, water everywhere, which seems to be kept from flowing quickly off by the narrow bed of the Luapula, which has perpendicular banks, worn deep down in new red sandstone. It is the Nile apparently enacting its inundations, even at its sources. The amount of water spread out over the country constantly excites my wonder; it is prodigious. Many of the ant-hills are cultivated and covered with dura, pumpkins, beans, maize, but the waters yield food plenteously in fish and lotus-roots. A species of wild rice grows, but the people neither need it nor know it. A party of fishermen fled from us, but by coaxing we got them to show us deep water. They then showed us an islet, about thirty yards square, without wood, and desired us to sleep there. We went on, and then they decamped.

Pitiless pelting showers wetted everything; but near sunset we saw two fishermen paddling quickly off from an ant-hill, where we found a hut, plenty of fish, and some firewood. There we spent the night, and watched by turns, lest thieves should come and haul away our canoes and goods. Heavy rain. One canoe sank, wetting everything in her. The leaks in her had been stopped with clay, and a man sleeping near the stern had displaced this frail caulking. We did not touch the fish, and I cannot conjecture who has inspired fear in all the inhabitants.

7th April.—Went on S.W., and saw two men, who guided us to the River Muanakazi, which forms a connecting link between the River Lotingila and the Lolotikila, about the southern borders of the flood. Men were hunting, and we passed near large herds of antelopes, which made a rushing, plunging sound as they ran and sprang away among the waters. A lion had wandered into this world of water and ant-hills, and roared night and morning, as if very much disgusted: we could sympathise with him! Near to the Muanakazi at a broad bank in shallow water near the river, we had to unload and haul. Our guides left us, well pleased with the payment we had given them. The natives beating a drum on our east made us believe them to be our party, and some thought that they heard two shots. This misled us, and we went towards the sound through papyrus, tall rushes, arums, and grass, till tired out, and took refuge on an ant-hill for the night. Lion roaring. We were lost in stiff grassy prairies, from three to four feet deep in water, for five hours. We fired a gun in the stillness of the night, but received no answer; so on the *8th* we sent a small canoe at daybreak to ask for information and guides from the village where the drums had been beaten. Two men came, and they thought likewise that our party was south-east; but in that direction the water was about fifteen inches in spots and three feet in others, which caused constant dragging of the large canoe all day, and at last we unloaded at another branch of the Muanakazi with a village of friendly people. We slept there.

All hands at the large canoe could move her only a few feet. Putting all their strength to her, she stopped at every haul with a jerk, as if in a bank of adhesive plaister. I measured the crown of a papyrus plant or palm, it was three feet across horizontally, its stalk eight feet in height. Hundreds of a large dark-grey hairy caterpillar have nearly cleared off the rushes in spots, and now live on each other. They can make only the smallest progress by swimming or rather wriggling in the water: their motion is that of a watch-spring thrown down, dilating and contracting.

9th April.—After two hours' threading the very winding, deep channel of this southern branch of the Muanakazi, we came to where our land party had crossed it and gone on to Gandochite, a chief on the Lolotikila. My men were all done up, so I hired a man to call some of his friends to take the loads; but he was stopped by his relations in the way, saying, 'You ought to have one of the traveller's own people with you.' He returned, but did not tell us plainly or truly till this morning.

10th April.—The headman of the village explained, and we sent two of our men, who had a night's rest with the turnagain fellow of yesterday. I am pale, bloodless, and weak from bleeding profusely ever since the 31st of March last: an artery gives off a copious stream, and takes away my strength. Oh, how I long to be permitted by the Over Power to finish my work.

12th April.—Cross the Muanakazi. It is about 100 or 130 yards broad, and deep. Great loss of *αἷμα* made me so weak I could hardly walk, but tottered along nearly two hours, and then lay down quite done. Cooked coffee—our last—and went on, but in an hour I was compelled to lie down. Very unwilling to be carried, but on being pressed I allowed the men to help me along by relays to Chinama, where there is much cultivation. We camped in a garden of dura.

13*th April.*—Found that we had slept on the right bank of the Lolotikila, a sluggish, marshy-looking river, very winding, but here going about south-west. The country is all so very flat that the rivers down here are of necessity tortuous. Fish and other food abundant, and the people civil and reasonable. They usually partake largely of the character of the chief, and this one, Gondochite, is polite. The sky is clearing, and the S.E. wind is the lower stratum now. It is the dry season well begun. Seventy-three inches is a higher rainfall than has been observed anywhere else, even in northern Manyuema; it was lower by inches than here far south on the watershed. In fact, this is the very heaviest rainfall known in these latitudes; between fifty and sixty is the maximum.

One sees interminable grassy prairies with lines of trees, occupying quarters of miles in breadth, and these give way to bouga or prairie again. The bouga is flooded annually, but its vegetation consists of dry land grasses. Other bouga extend out from the Lake up to forty miles, and are known by aquatic vegetation, such as lotus, papyrus, arums, rushes of different species, and many kinds of purely aquatic subaqueous plants which send up their flowers only to fructify in the sun, and then sink to ripen one bunch after another. Others, with great cabbage-looking leaves, seem to remain always at the bottom. The young of fish swarm, and bob in and out from the leaves. A species of soft moss grows on most plants, and seems to be good fodder for fishes, fitted by hooked or turned-up noses to guide it into their maws.

One species of fish has the lower jaw turned down into a hook, which enables the animal to hold its mouth close to the plant as it glides up and down, sucking in all the soft pulpy food. The superabundance of gelatinous nutriment makes these swarmers increase in bulk with extraordinary rapidity, and the food supply of the people is plenteous in consequence. The number of fish caught by weirs, baskets, and nets now, as the waters decline, is prodigious. The fish feel their element becoming insufficient for comfort, and retire from one bouga to another towards the Lake; the narrower parts are duly prepared by weirs to take advantage of their necessities; the sun heat seems to oppress them and force them to flee. With the south-east aerial current comes heat and sultriness. A blanket is scarcely needed till the early hours of the morning, and here, after the turtle doves and cocks give out their warning calls to the watchful, the fish-eagle lifts up his remarkable voice. It is pitched in a high falsetto key, very loud, and seems as if he were calling to some one in the other world. Once heard, his weird unearthly voice can never be forgotten—it sticks to one through life.

We were four hours in being ferried over the Loitikila, or Lolotikila, in four small canoes, and then two hours south-west down its left bank to another river, where our camp has been formed. I sent over a present to the headman, and a man returned with the information that he was ill at another village, but his wife would send canoes to-morrow to transport us over and set us on our way to Muanazambamba, south-west, and over Lolotikila again.

14*th April.*—At a branch of the Lolotikila.

15*th April.*—Cross Lolotikila again (where it is only fifty yards) by canoes, and went south-west an hour. I, being very weak, had to be carried part of the way. Am glad of resting; αἶμα flowed copiously last night. A woman, the wife of the chief, gave a present of a goat and maize.

16*th April.*—West south-west two and a half hours, and crossed the Lombatwa River of 100 yards in width, rush deep, and flowing fast in aquatic vegetation, papyrus, &c., into the Loitikila. In all about three hours south-west.

17*th April.*—A tremendous rain after dark burst all our now rotten tents to shreds. Went on at 6.35 a.m. for three hours, and I, who was suffering severely all night, had to rest. We got water near the surface by digging in yellow sand. Three hills now appear in the distance. Our course, S.W. three and three-quarters hours to a village on the Kazya River. A Nyassa man declared that his father had brought the heavy rain of the 16th on us. We crossed three sponges.

18*th April.*—On leaving the village on the Kazya, we forded it and found it seventy yards broad, waist to breast deep all over. A large weir spanned it, and we went on the lower side of that. Much papyrus and other aquatic plants in it. Fish are returning now with the falling waters, and are guided into the rush-cones set for them. Crossed two large sponges, and I was forced to stop at a village after travelling S.W. for two hours: very ill all night, but remembered that the bleeding and most other ailments in this land are forms of fever. Took two scruple doses of quinine, and stopped it quite.

19*th April.*—A fine bracing S.E. breeze kept me on the donkey across a broad sponge and over flats of white sandy soil and much cultivation for an hour and a half, when we stopped at a large village on the right bank of [Livingstone leaves a blank here], and men went over to the chief Muanzambamba to ask canoes to cross to-morrow. I am excessively weak, and but for the donkey could not move a hundred yards. It is not all pleasure this exploration. The Lavusi hills are a relief to the eye in this flat upland. Their forms show an igneous origin. The river Kazya comes from them and goes direct into the Lake. No observations now, owing to great weakness; I can scarcely hold the pencil, and my stick is a burden. Tent gone; the men build a good hut for me and the luggage. S.W. one and a half hour.

20*th April*, Sunday.—Service. Cross over the sponge, Moenda, for food and to be near the headman of these parts, Moanzambamba. I am excessively weak. Village on Moenda sponge, 7 a.m. Cross Lokulu in a canoe. The river is about thirty yards broad, very deep, and flowing in marshes two knots from S.S.E. to N.N.W. into Lake.

21*st.*—Tried to ride, but was forced to lie down, and they carried me back to vil. exhausted.

Last Journals, vol. II, pp. 274–303

The last entries reproduced in the facsimile require some explanation. On 21st April he was too weak to sit upon his donkey and fell to the ground. He was carried back to the village, and the next day a bed-like litter (Kitandu) was made of poles and he was taken a short distance. He was carried like this for three more days, suffering terrible pain from acute dysentery and from the movement of the litter. On the 25th, still pursuing his quest, he asked the villagers if they knew of a hill which was the source of four rivers. The facsimile shows that he was too weak to write anything but the date and the hours of travel. On 27th April comes the last entry:

'27. Knocked up quite and remain—recover sent to buy milch goats. We are on the banks of the Molilamo.'

What happened afterwards was pieced together into a story from the accounts of his servants, and published by the editor of the Last Journals, *the Rev. Horace Waller. Two days later, on the 29th, his men managed to get him across a river in a small canoe, though every movement was pain and they frequently had to put down the litter on the other side to let him lie still. They had a hut built for him in the next village. Here he lay all day in great weakness and suffering. That night the boy told off to watch saw that Livingstone was kneeling by his bed. After sleeping for some time he looked in again and saw his master in the same position. He called Susi and Chumah, and they and others of the men came into the hut. A candle was burning and by its light they saw the Doctor kneeling with his head in his hands. He was dead.*

At dawn the men met to decide what to do in their leaderless condition, separated from their base at the coast by a journey of 1,500 miles through difficult and dangerous country. Their decision was remarkable. They resolved to hold together and to carry back their master's remains and all his property, including his journals, to the coast. They buried his heart under a tree, embalmed the emaciated form and wrapped it up so as to look like one of the long bales they carried. They thus triumphed not only over physical fear but also over their superstitious dread of a dead body, an attitude which was certain to be shared by the tribes through which they must pass and which did upon at least one occasion seriously endanger them.

The journey back took them nine months and on its course some of the party died and others nearly died. They were attacked by wild animals: they were blackmailed for tolls: once they had to fight their way out from a hostile tribe. That they maintained their courage and their discipline is shown by their safe arrival at last at Tabora. Here they met Lieutenant Cameron, on his way inland to relieve Livingstone. He did everything he could to persuade the men to bury their master there, pointing out to them the great danger of the rest of the journey. They absolutely refused, and went on until they reached the coast and finally handed over their burden to the British Consul. Livingstone was buried in Westminster Abbey on 18th April 1874 and Susi, Chumah and another of his servants came to England and were present at the funeral.

LIST OF BOOKS

The following list gives the chief works relating to Africa written by the travellers who are represented in this book, together with such biographies or other sources of information about them as have been published. Only the dates of the first editions have been given; but where cheap modern reprints are available, they have been mentioned. The books which appear under the heading 'General Works' may be recommended as authoritative introductions to the subjects with which they deal: to them, and to the *Dictionary of National Biography*, we are indebted for much of the information contained in our editorial matter. As some of these works have been extensively revised since their first publication, we have cited the latest and best editions of them.

BRUCE

Travels to discover the source of the Nile (5 vols., 1790).

SEE ALSO:

A. MURRAY, *Account of the life and writings of James Bruce* (1808).

SIR F. B. HEAD, *The life of Bruce, the African traveller* (1830).

SIR R. L. PLAYFAIR, *Travels in the footsteps of Bruce* (1877). Deals with Bruce's travels in North Africa and reproduces some of his drawings.

PARK

Travels in the interior districts of Africa (1799). Reissued in 'Everyman's Library', 1907.

Journal of a mission to the interior of Africa in 1805 (1815).

SEE ALSO:

J. THOMSON, *Mungo Park and the Niger* (1890).

S. GWYNN, *Mungo Park and the Niger* (1934).

CLAPPERTON

D. DENHAM, H. CLAPPERTON and W. OUDNEY, *Travels and discoveries in Northern and Central Africa in 1822–4* (1826).

Journal of a second expedition into the interior of Africa . . . by the late Commander Clapperton, of the Royal Navy. To which is added, the journal of Richard Lander from Kano to the sea-coast (1829).

SEE ALSO:

R. LANDER, *Records of Captain Clapperton's last expedition* (2 vols., 1829).

T. NELSON, *A biographical memoir of the late Dr. W. Oudney, Captain H. Clapperton, and Major A. G. Laing* (1830).

LANDER

(For his two works published in 1829, see under Clapperton)

Journal of an expedition to explore the course and termination of the Niger (3 vols., 1832). Written in collaboration with his brother John.

SEE ALSO:

M. LAIRD and R. A. K. OLDFIELD, *Narrative of an expedition into the interior of Africa, by the River Niger* (2 vols., 1837).

W. TREGELLAS, *Cornish worthies* (1884), vol. II, pp. 199–218.

LIVINGSTONE

Missionary travels and researches in South Africa (1857).

Narrative of an expedition to the Zambesi and its tributaries (1865). Written in collaboration with his brother Charles.

The last journals of David Livingstone in Central Africa, ed. H. Waller (2 vols., 1874).

SEE ALSO:

W. G. BLAIKIE, *The personal life of David Livingstone* (1880).

R. COUPLAND, *Kirk on the Zambesi* (1928). Deals with Livingstone's second (Zambesi) expedition.

R. J. CAMPBELL, *Livingstone* (1929).

J. I. MACNAIR, *Livingstone the liberator* ('Collins Classics', 1940).

Some letters from Livingstone, 1840–1872, ed. D. Chamberlin (1940).

J. SIMMONS, *Livingstone and Africa* (1955).

F. DEBENHAM, *The Road to Ilala* (1955).

BAIKIE

Narrative of an exploring voyage up the Rivers Kwora and Binue (1856).

SEE ALSO:

S. A. CROWTHER, *Journal of an expedition up the Niger and Tshadda Rivers* (1855).

A. G. C. HASTINGS, *The voyage of the* Dayspring (1926).

BURTON

First footsteps in East Africa; or, an exploration of Harar (1856). Re-issued in 'Everyman's Library', 1910.

The lake regions of Central Africa (2 vols., 1860).

Abeokuta and the Camaroons mountains (2 vols., 1863).
Wanderings in West Africa, by a F.R.G.S. [i.e. Burton] (2 vols., 1863).
A mission to Gelele, King of Dahome (2 vols., 1864).
The Nile basin (1864).
Zanzibar; city, island, and coast (2 vols., 1872).
The lands of Cazembe. Lacerda's journey to Cazembe in 1798 (1873). Translated and annotated by Burton.
Two trips to gorilla land and the cataracts of the Congo (2 vols., 1876).
To the Gold Coast for gold (2 vols., 1883). Written in collaboration with V. L. Cameron.

SEE ALSO:

I. BURTON, *The life of Captain Sir Richd. F. Burton* (2 vols., 1893).
H. J. SCHONFIELD, *Richard Burton, explorer* (1936).
J. BURTON, *Sir Richard Burton's wife* (1942).

SPEKE

'Journal of a cruise on the Tanganyika Lake, Central Africa' and 'Captain J. H. Speke's discovery of the Victoria Nyanza Lake, the supposed source of the Nile. From his journal' in *Blackwood's Magazine*, vol. LXXXVI (1859), pp. 339–357, 391–419, 565–582.
Journal of the discovery of the source of the Nile (1863). Reissued in 'Everyman's Library', 1906.
What led to the discovery of the source of the Nile (1864).

BAKER

The Albert N'Yanza, great basin of the Nile (2 vols., 1866).
The Nile tributaries of Abyssinia (1867).
Ismailïa (2 vols., 1874).

SEE ALSO:

T. D. MURRAY and A. S. WHITE, *Sir Samuel Baker. A memoir* (1895).

STANLEY

How I found Livingstone in Central Africa (1872).
My Kalulu, prince, king, and slave; a story of Central Africa (1873).
Coomassie and Magdala: the story of two British campaigns in Africa (1874).
Through the dark continent (2 vols., 1878).
The Congo and the founding of its Free State (2 vols., 1885).
In darkest Africa, or the quest, rescue and retreat of Emin, Governor of Equatoria (2 vols., 1890).
My dark companions and their strange stories (1893).
The autobiography of Sir Henry Morton Stanley, ed. D. Stanley (1909).

SEE ALSO:

A. J. A. SYMONS, *H. M. Stanley* ('Great Lives' series, 1933).

GENERAL WORKS

J. N. L. BAKER, *A history of geographical discovery and exploration* (ed. 2, 1937).

Cambridge history of the British Empire, vol. II (1940), ch. xvii, 'The Exploration of Africa' (by E. Heawood), and ch. xviii, 'British Enterprise in Tropical Africa' (by A. P. Newton).

SIR H. H. JOHNSTON, *The Nile quest* (1903), *The opening up of Africa* ('Home University Library'), and *A history of the colonization of Africa by alien races* (ed. 2, 1913).

SIR J. S. KELTIE, *The partition of Africa* (ed. 2, 1895).

R. COUPLAND, *The British anti-slavery movement* ('Home University Library', 1933).

E. W. BOVILL, *Caravans of the old Sahara: an introduction to the history of the Western Sudan* (1933).

W. FITZGERALD, *Africa : a social, economic and political geography of its main regions* (ed. 8, 1955).

C. G. SELIGMAN, *The races of Africa* ('Home University Library' : new and revised edition, 1957).

INDEX